631

# Trollope-to-Reader

Trollopes

# Trollope-to-Reader

## A Topical Guide to Digressions in the Novels of Anthony Trollope

*Compiled by*
## MARY L. DANIELS

GREENWOOD PRESS
Westport, Connecticut • London, England

**Library of Congress Cataloging in Publication Data**

Trollope, Anthony, 1815-1882.
  Trollope-to-reader.

  Includes bibliographical references and index.
  1. Trollope, Anthony, 1815-1882—Dictionaries,
indexes, etc., 2. Digression (Rhetoric) I. Daniels,
Mary L. II. Title.
PR5686.A23 1983    823'.8    83-10873
ISBN 0-313-23877-4 (lib. bdg.)

Library of Congress Catalog Card Number 83-10873
ISBN: 0-313-23877-4

First published in 1983

Greenwood Press
A division of Congressional Information Service, Inc.
88 Post Road West, Westport, Connecticut 06881

Printed in the United States of America

10  9  8  7  6  5  4  3  2  1

To
John, Carter, Evan, and Fred

# Contents

# Acknowledgments

My heartfelt appreciation goes to the libraries at Orlando, Florida; Boothbay Harbor, Maine; Bowdoin College, Brunswick, Maine; and Seminole Community College, Sanford, Florida, for their help in locating the novels; to Theresa Roff, Bernice Waldron, and my husband for their help in the preparation of the manuscript; and to Marilyn Brownstein of Greenwood Press for her patience and understanding.

# Introduction

In the one-hundred-one years since his death, Anthony Trollope's novels have been read, ignored, revived, criticized, analyzed, serialized for radio, and televised. Writers from the times of Hawthorne and James up to the present have dissected Trollope through his themes, his plots, his characters, and have guessed about interpreting him.

That studying his forty-seven novels by these traditional methods is fruitful, no one will deny. No doubt he did have strong feelings about the materialism of London (The Way We Live Now); certainly he did not approve of obsessive jealousy (He Knew He Was Right), excessive secretiveness (Kept in the Dark), or forgery (Orley Farm). But does the theme of a particular novel truly reveal all of its author? May he not have a story to tell merely as a good story and not one on which he means to hang a philosophy? To hold otherwise would be to eliminate all the lighter romances such as The Small House at Allington, The Belton Estate, and Rachel Ray.

If themes do not lead to a perfect understanding of an author, what about plots and characters? Trollope was a good storyteller despite what he himself said of his lack of plotting ability. His books lend themselves well to the activity-oriented eye of the television camera and surely reveal some of his views of the complexity of the human condition.

Do we come closer to Trollope through his characters? Of course every analysis of his people will bring him closer to us. Yet Trollope wrote with such sympathy and understanding of the good in his villains and of the faults in his heroes that most of his characters are done in shades of grey, not black and white. His only unshaded villain is Undy Scott. But we feel more sympathy for Lady Mason even though she was a forger, for example, than we do for the rightful heir to Orley Farm. However, the study of an author through his characters always shackles the critic by forcing him to

choose a viewpoint.  Which character speaks for the writer?
I have never been entirely sure that Trollope's heart did
not lie nearer to the gay, impulsive Lady Glencora than it
did to the sober soul of honor, Plantagenet Palliser, her
husband, despite what Trollope says of him in the Autobiography (1883; London:  Oxford University Press, 1953, The
World's Classics # 239).  And among the clergy would he love
most the humble warden, Mr. Harding, the pleasant rural Mr.
Comfort, the dogged, erudite Mr. Crawley, the vulnerable
Mark Robarts, or the urbane Archdeacon Grantly, a man who
understood himself thoroughly?  Certainly the characters are
convincing enough for one to feel that they are real.  When
the dying Duke of Omnium is amused--almost kept alive--by
the stories about that scapegrace, Lizzie Eustace, and can
hardly wait for the next bit of gossip Madame Max will bring
him, I found myself equally as eager to hear and quite convinced that the Duke as well as Lizzie was a real person.
     It was this interest in the complications of these
various literary approaches to Trollope's novels as well as
the certainty that I would not be bored that saw me through
two cases of pneumonia one winter and gave my husband a
sure-fire successful trip to the library for more Trollope.
Then, while waiting for the next book, I tried to establish
the Trollopeian stance.
     He can be misleading.  For example, his novels have many
strong female characters, women who would be better fitted
for Parliament than some of the men who sat.  Lady Laura
Kennedy most surely is more capable than, say, Lord Fawn.
But Lady Laura does not wish to be in Parliament.  And
little Mary Lovelace, though she may disclaim all desire to
support the "Disabilities," manages her husband much more
cleverly than he does her.
     So the plots and characters might lead us to think one
way about Trollope's women while his comments and asides
uniformly make the neck hairs bristle on the napes of
today's women, liberated or otherwise.  Thus the digressions
by the author seem to me to be enlightening.
     The Victorian author had this one advantage not usual
with the modern writer.  A style no longer popular allowed
the earlier novelist to digress, to comment, to expound his
own views.  The plot often stops, the characters freeze, and
the author speaks directly to the reader.  This he usually
does in explanation of some action by or to a character.
For instance, we feel the humiliation of Sir Thomas when he
is treated by his inferiors "with patronising good nature,
listening with an air of half-attention to what he said, and
then not taking the slightest heed of a word of it.  Who
does not know this transparent pretence of courtesies, which
of all discourtesies is the most offensive?" (italics mine).
In just such manner does Trollope bring us close to his
people.  We feel with and for them through our own experi-
ences.  In his digressions, Trollope took full advantage of
this discursive style.  He digresses frequently, sometimes
at length, sometimes in short comments, and all too often in
asides buried within a sentence yet capable of being mined.

These digressions are pure Trollope--at least of that moment --undiluted by plot, character, theme, or modern exegesis. By studying these digressions alone, we should be able to trace any changes in Trollope's thinking without reference to what we think he meant or to what a particular character said or did.

During the period in which he wrote, the franchise had been extended, married women's property rights had been revised, and government policies on agriculture and empire had caused many changes in England.  Did Trollope change too?  Did his later writings reflect such new conditions?   Some critics claim that he grew more somber as he aged.   If he did, do his digressions change markedly?

Far from agreeing with those critics who see a progression toward somberness I can cite among the later novels Ayala's Angel, one of his lightest and most romantic books, Mr. Scarborough's Family, a nineteenth century scam worthy of today's con man, or the touching An Old Man's Love.   On the other hand, there is the grim beginning of his writing career with novels of the Irish famine.  Of such various viewpoints are critical literary books made.  Even Trollope himself never understood why others didn't share his enthusiasm for what he thought was the fun in The Struggles of Brown, Jones, and Robinson.

In refuting the critics of the ageing Trollope, I have used the traditional method of examining theme and plot. But one can also look at the digressions, which are here presented chronologically by topics, and add a dimension to the usual approach.

More to the point of this volume, however, is the pleasure one derives from reading Trollope's comments.  His range is vast; his views are Victorian, often universally applicable yet sometimes surprisingly modern.   Criticized for having little humor, Trollope can come out with a comment such as this one about "the figure of William Pitt, who looks as though he had just entered the church for the first time in his life and was anything but pleased at finding himself there" (The Warden, London:   Oxford University Press, 1968, The World's Classics # 217 p. 202).

Humor, wisdom, and a true reflection of the society of the last half of the nineteenth century--all these are revealed in the little essays of Anthony Trollope.

This volume, then, contains the Trollope digressions in all forty-seven novels.   The subject matter is arranged alphabetically by topics.  Within each topic the digressions are arranged chronologically by date of the completion of the work, not by publication.  Generally the categories are determined by nouns and subdivided by adjectives:  MEN; MEN, OLD; MEN, YOUNG.  Occasionally the adjective predominates as in the case of IRISH AGENTS; IRISH BISHOPS; IRISH CHILDREN because the importance of the quotation rests on the adjective.  With few exceptions the spelling and punctuation, both sometimes erratic, are Trollope's own.  Brackets are used to explain obscurities.  When possible, I have used Trollope's words within the brackets; otherwise the emendations are mine. Of necessity there has been some pruning. Following the topical digressions, there is an index to those digressions referring to specific people and places in the novels.

Immediately following this introduction and preceding the text is an alphabetical list of the novels and the editions consulted by the compiler. A code is used to represent the books in the citations. There is also a list of the novels in chronological order by date of completion. Each quotation in the text is followed first by the code for the novel, then the page number in Arabic numerals, the chapter in Roman, and finally the volume, if any, in Roman. For example, under the heading of "ABUSE," the entry "PF 73, XLVII, II" indicates Phineas Finn, page 73, Chapter XLVII, Volume II. The same system is used in the index to proper names. The book ends with bibliographical notes on a few basic sources other than the novels.

It is in good Trollopeian tradition thus to gather material from literature. Anthony's father labored for years over an Encyclopedia Ecclesiastica which would "describe all the ecclesiastical terms, including denominations of every fraternity of monks and every convent of nuns, with all their orders and subdivisions" (Autobiography, p. 12). And Anthony himself in the penultimate paragraph of his Autobiography says, "If I live a few years longer, I shall, I think, leave in my copies of these [our old English] dramatists, down to the time of James I, written criticisms on every play. No one who has not looked closely into it knows how many there are."

I wasn't aware of how many digressions there were in the Trollope novels, either, until this present volume was begun. And even now each re-reading of a novel turns up another one or two.

Chronologically, Trollope's first digression, from The Macdermots of Ballycloran is WALKING; his last one, from The Landleaguers, is TRUTH. Perhaps these subjects reflect his active and honest life.

# Novel Titles, Editions, and Alphabetical Codes

The codes to the left of each title are those used following each quotation and refer to the novel from which the quotation was taken.

AS      The American Senator.   London: Oxford University Press, 1962.   The World's Classics # 391.

AyA     Ayala's Angel.   London: Oxford University Press, 1968.   The World's Classics # 342.

BaT     Barchester Towers.   Garden City, N.Y.: Doubleday and Co., Inc., 1945.

Bel     The Belton Estate.   London: Oxford University Press, 1964.   The World's Classics # 251.

Ber     The Bertrams.   London:   John Lane: The Bodley Head, 1905. Alger Thorold, ed., The New Pocket Library, XX.

CanY    Can You Forgive Her?   Oxford:  Oxford University Press, 1973.

CasR    Castle Richmond.   New York: Garland Publishing, Inc., 1979.   A Garland Series.

Cl      The Claverings.   New York: Dover Publications, Inc., 1977.

CoH     Cousin Henry.  London: Oxford University Press, 1929. The World's Classics, CCCXLIII.

DoT     Doctor Thorne.   London:  Oxford University Press, 1963.   The World's Classics # 298.

DrW     Dr. Wortle's School.   London: Oxford University Press, 1973.   The World's Classics # 317.

DuC      The Duke's Children.  Oxford: Oxford University
         Press, 1973.

ED       The Eustace Diamonds.  Oxford: Oxford University
         Press, 1973.

EE       An Eye for an Eye.  London: Garland Publishing, Inc.,
         1979.

FiP      The Fixed Period.  Leipzig: Bernhard Tauchnitz, 1882.
         Ann Arbor,Mich.: University Microfilms International,
         1978.

FrP      Framley Parsonage.  New York: Harcourt Brace & World,
         Inc., 1962.

GLOG     The Golden Lion of Granpere.  London: J.M. Dent &
         Sons Ltd., 1924.  Everyman's Library # 761.

HHOG     Harry Heathcote of Gangoil.  Melbourne: Lansdowne
         Press, 1963.

HKHWR    He Knew He Was Right.  London: Oxford University
         Press, 1963.  The World's Classics # 507.

IHP      Is He Popenjoy?  London: Oxford University Press,
         1965.  The World's Classics # 492.

JC       John Caldigate.  London: The Zodiac Press, 1972.

Kel      The Kellys and the O'Kellys.  Oxford: Oxford
         University Press, 1978.  The World's Classics # 341.

Kept     Kept in the Dark.  New York: Dover Publications,
         Inc., 1978.

LA       Lady Anna.  London: Oxford University Press, Geoffrey
         Cumberlege, 1950.  The World's Classics # 443.

Land     The Landleaguers.  New York: Garland Publishing Co.,
         1979.

LasC     The Last Chronicle of Barset.  London: The Zodiac
         Press, 1949.

LaV      La Vendee.  London: Warwick House, Salisbury Square.
         Ann Arbor,Mich.: University Microfilms International,
         1977.

LT       Linda Tressel.  London: Oxford University Press,
         1946.  The World's Classics #505.

MB       The Macdermots of Ballycloran.  New York: Garland
         Publishing Inc., 1979.

MF       <u>Marion Fay</u>. Leipzig: Bernhard Tauchnitz, 1882. Collection of British Authors, Tauchnitz Edition, Vol. 2088.

MM      <u>Miss Mackenzie</u>. London: Oxford University Press, Geoffrey Cumberlege (no date). The World's Classics (no number) 1950.

MSF     <u>Mr. Scarborough's Family</u>. London: Chatto & Windus, 1883.

NB      <u>Nina Balatka</u>. London: Oxford University Press, 1946. The World's Classics # 505.

OML     <u>An Old Man's Love</u>. London: Oxford University Press, Humphrey Milford, 1936. The World's Classics, CDXLIV.

OrF     <u>Orley Farm</u>. London: Oxford University Press, 1963. The World's Classics # 423.

PF      <u>Phineas Finn</u>. Oxford: Oxford University Press, 1973.

PR      <u>Phineas Redux</u>. Oxford: Oxford University Press, 1973.

PrM     <u>The Prime Minister</u>. Oxford: Oxford University Press, 1973.

RacR    <u>Rachel Ray</u>. New York: Alfred A. Knopf, 1952.

RalH    <u>Ralph the Heir</u>. London: Strahan & Co., Pub., 1871; rpt. New York: Dover Publications, Inc., 1978.

SHHOH  <u>Sir Harry Hotspur of Humblethwaite</u>. London: Oxford University Press, 1950. The World's Classics # 336.

SmaH    <u>The Small House at Allington</u>. New York: Harcourt Brace & World, Inc., 1962.

Str     <u>The Struggles of Brown, Jones, and Robinson</u>. New York: Harper & Brothers, Publishers, 1870.

TC      <u>The Three Clerks</u>. Oxford: Oxford University Press, 1978. The World's Classics # 140.

VOB     <u>The Vicar of Bullhampton</u>. London: Oxford University Press, 1924. The World's Classics # 272.

War     <u>The Warden</u>. London: Oxford University Press, 1968. The World's Classics # 217.

Way     <u>The Way We Live Now</u>. Oxford: Oxford University Press, 1971. The World's Classics # 484.

# Chronological List of Novels

These are listed by date of completion. First editions are given parenthetically.

1845   The Macdermots of Ballycloran (London: Newby, 1847)

1847   The Kellys and the O'Kellys (London: Colburn, 1848)

1849   La Vendee (London: Colburn, 1850)

1853   The Warden (London: Longman, 1855)

1856   Barchester Towers (London: Longman, 1857)

1857   The Three Clerks (London: Bentley, 1858)

1858   Doctor Thorne (London: Chapman & Hall, 1858)

1858   The Bertrams (London: Chapman & Hall, 1859)

1860   Castle Richmond (London: Chapman & Hall, 1860)

1860   Framley Parsonage (London: Smith, Elder, 1860)

1861   Orley Farm (London: Chapman & Hall, 1862)

1861   The Struggles of Brown, Jones, and Robinson (London: Smith, Elder, 1870)

1863   The Small House at Allington (London: Smith, Elder, 1864)

1863   Rachel Ray (London: Chapman & Hall, 1863)

1864   Can You Forgive Her? (London: Chapman & Hall, 1864)

# TOPICAL DIGRESSIONS

## ABUSE

[T]his abuse did not pass beyond the precincts of ... [his] own breast. We all know how delightful is the privilege of abusing our nearest friends after this fashion; but we generally satisfy ourselves with that limited audience. RacR 285, XXII.

But who is there that abstains from reading that which is printed in abuse of himself? PF 73, XLVII,II.

Abuse from those who occasionally praise is considered to be personally offensive, and they who give personal offence will sometimes make the world too hot to hold them. But censure from those who are always finding fault is regarded so much as a matter of course that it ceases to be objectionable. The caricaturist, who draws only caricatures, is held to be justifiable, let him take what liberties he may with a man's face and person. It is his trade, and his business calls upon him to vilify all that he touches. But were an artist to publish a series of portraits, in which two out of a dozen were made to be hideous, he would certainly make two enemies, if not more. Way 8, I,I. See also CONTUMELY.

## ACCIDENTS

An accident, if it does no material harm, is always an inspiriting thing, unless one feels that it has been attributable to one's fault. TC 242, XXI.

A closer intimacy will occasionally be created by some accident, some fortuitous circumstance, than weeks of ordinary intercourse will produce. Walk down Bond Street in a hailstorm of peculiar severity and you may make a friend of the first person you meet, whereas you would be held to have committed an affront were you to speak to the same person in the same place on a fine day. You shall travel smoothly to York with a lady and she will look as though she would call the guard at once were you so much as to suggest that it were a fine day; but if you are lucky enough to break a wheel before you get to Darlington, she will have told you all her history and shared your sherry by the time you have reached that town. AS 152, XXIII.

## ACCUSTOMED PLACES

In how very short a time will come upon one that pleasant custom of sitting in an accustomed place. OrF 216, XXII,I.

## ACHIEVEMENTS

There are some achievements which are never done in the presence of those who hear of them. Catching salmon is one, and working all night is another. MF 128-9, XII,II.

## ACQUAINTANCES

People soon get intimate with each other at such places as Jerusalem. When you have been up the Great Pyramid with a lady, the chances are you know more about her than you would do from a year's acquaintance fostered by a dozen London parties....After a certain age, men never become really intimate, let their relations with each other be ever so close. Ber 132, VIII.

It sometimes happens to all of us in life that we become acquainted with persons intimately,--that is, with an assumed intimacy,--whom in truth we do not know at all. We meet such persons frequently, often eating and drinking in their company, being familiar with their appearance, and well-informed generally as to their concerns; but we never find ourselves holding special conversations with them, or in any way fitting the modes of our life to the modes of their life....We should probably do any little kindness for them, or expect the same from them; but there is nothing in common between us, and there is generally a mutual though unexpressed agreement that there shall be nothing in common. Bel 194-5, XV.

## ACTING

To act a part perfectly requires a consummate actor; and there are phases in life in which acting is absolutely demanded....For petty troubles the amount of acting ne-cessary is so common that habit has made it almost natural. But when great sorrows come it is hard not to show them,--and harder still not to seem to hide them. JC 213, XXIX.

There are people who, however full their hearts may be, full of anger or full of joy, can keep the fulness in abeyance till a chosen time for exhibiting it shall come.
JC 243, XXXIII.

## ADMITTANCE

Those who have thanks to return for favours received find easy admittance to the halls of the great. Such is not always the case with men, or even with women, who have favours to beg. Still less easy is access for those who demand the fulfillment of promises already made.
BaT 232, XXV.

## ADOPTION

That question of adopting is very difficult. If a man have no children of his own,--none others that are dependent on him,--he can give all, and there is an end of his trouble. But a man feels that he owes his property to his children; and, so feeling, may he take it from them and give it to others? RalH 53, VII.

## ADVENTURES

To dive among the waters in warm weather is very pleasant; there is nothing pleasanter. But when the young swimmer first feels the thorough immersion of his plunge, there comes upon him a strong desire to be quickly out again. He will remember afterwards, how joyous it was; but now, at this moment, the dry land is everything to him.
HKHWR 485, LI.

## ADVICE

There are some points on which no man can be contented to follow the advice of another--some subjects on which a man can consult his own conscience only. War 201, XVI.

[W]hen an old gentleman...is asked his advice under such circumstances [that the asker has lived beyond his means], he ought to be allowed to remark that he had prophesied all these things beforehand. 'I told you so,' is such a comfortable thing to say! And when an old gentleman has taken much fruitless trouble about a young gentleman, he ought at least not to be interrupted in his remarks as to that young gentleman's folly. RalH 63, VIII.

But a man, when he undertakes to advise another, should not be down in the mouth himself. Land 132, XL,III.

## AFFLICTIONS

But no lesson is truer than that which teaches us to believe that God does temper the wind to the shorn lamb. To how many has it not seemed, at some one period of their lives, that all was over for them, and that to them in their afflictions there was nothing left but to die! And yet they have lived to laugh again, to feel that the air was warm and the earth fair, and that God in giving them ever-springing hope had given everything. How many a sun may seem to set on an endless night, and yet rising again on some morrow.
OrF 405, LXXIX,II.

## AGE

Years do not make a man old gradually and at an even pace. Look through the world and see if this is not so always, except in those rare cases in which the human being lives and dies without joys and without sorrows, like a vegetable. A man shall be possessed of florid youthful blooming health till, it matters not what age. Thirty-- forty--fifty, then comes the nipping frost, some period of agony, that robs the fibres of the body of their succulence, and the hale and hearty man is counted among the old.
BaT 303, XXXII.

When gentlemen past sixty make love to ladies past forty, it may be supposed that they are not so dilatory in their proceedings as younger swains and younger maidens. Time is then behind them, not before them; and urges them on to quick decisions. Ber 567, XXXI.

There can be to a woman no remembrance of age so strong as that of seeing a daughter go forth to the world a married woman.  If that does not tell the mother that the time of her own youth has passed away, nothing will ever bring the tale home. CasR 69, IV,I.

And, reader, if thou hast arrived at any period of life which enables thee to count thy past years by lustrums; if thou art at a time of life, past thirty we will say, hast thou not found that thy years, which are not short enough, were long in those bygone days? CasR 216, XI,I.

Young men are so apt to think that their seniors in age cannot understand romance, or acknowledge the force of a passion.  But here they are wrong, for there would be as much romance after forty as before, I take it, were it not checked by the fear of ridicule. CasR 38, II,III.

It is sad for a man to feel, when he knows that he is fast going down the hill of life, that the experience of old age is to be no longer valued nor its wisdom appreciated....When he was in his full physical vigour he was not old enough for mental success.  He was still winning his spurs at forty. But at fifty--so does the world change--he learns that he is past his work.  By some unconscious and unlucky leap he has passed from the unripeness of youth to the decay of age, without even knowing what it was to be in his prime.
CasR 122, V[sic],III.

It is so, I believe, with most of us who have begun to turn the hill.   I myself could go on to that common that is at this moment before me, and join that game of rounders with the most intense delight.   'By George! you fellow, you've no eyes; didn't you see that he hadn't put his foot in the hole.   He'll get back now that long-backed, hard-hitting chap, and your side is done for the next half hour!'  But then they would all be awestruck for a while; and after that, when they grew to be familiar with me, they would laugh at me because I loomed large in my running, and returned to my ground scant of breath.  Alas, alas!  I know that it would not do.  So I pass by, imperious in my heavy manhood, and one of the lads respectfully abstains from me though the ball is under my very feet....
It is very hard to have had no period for rounders, not to be able even to look back to one's games, and to talk of them to one's old comrades!  ...Is it not possible that one should have one more game of rounders?  Quite impossible, O my fat friend! CasR 268-9-70, XIV,III.

There is great doubt as to what may be the most enviable time of life with a man.   I am inclined to think that it is at that period when his children have all been born but have

not yet began to go astray or vex him with disappointment;
when his own pecuniary prospects are settled, and he knows
pretty well what his tether will allow him; when the
appetite is still good and the digestive organs at their
full power; when he has ceased to care as to the length of
his girdle, and before the doctor warns him against solid
breakfasts and port wine after dinner; when his affectations
are over and his infirmities have not yet come upon him;
while he can still walk his ten miles, and feel some little
pride in being able to do so; while he has still nerve to
ride his horse to hounds, and can look with some scorn on
the ignorance of younger men who have hardly yet learned
that noble art.    As regards men, this, I think, is the
happiest time of life; but who shall answer the question as
regards women?    In this respect their lot is more liable to
disappointment.    With the choicest flowers that blow the
sweetest aroma of their perfection lasts but for a moment.
The hour that sees them at their fullest glory sees also the
beginning of their fall.    OrF 190-1, LIX,II.

There is no Medea's caldron from which our limbs can come
out young and fresh; and it were well that the heart should
grow old as does the body.    OrF 398, LXXIX,II.

I would have women, and men also, young as long as they can
be young.    It is not that a woman should call herself in
years younger than her father's family Bible will have her
to be.    Let her who is forty call herself forty; but if she
can be young in spirit at forty, let her show that she is
so.    SmaH 22, III.

There are some old people whom it is very hard to flatter,
and with whom it is, nevertheless, almost impossible to live
unless you do flatter them.    SmaH 83, IX.

Ah me!    It is the young men who receive all the reverence
that the world has to pay;--all the reverence that is worth
receiving.    When a man is turned forty and has become fat,
anybody can speak to him without awe.    RacR 90, VII.

Late hours, nocturnal cigars, and midnight drinkings,
pleasurable though they may be, consume too quickly the
free-flowing lamps of youth, and are fatal at once to the
husbanded candle-ends of age.    PR 186, XXI,I.

But how many absurdities of the kind  [two older people in a
loving attitude]    are not only held to be pleasant, but
almost holy,-- as long as they remain mysteries inspected by
no profane eyes!    It is not that Age is ashamed of feeling
passion and acknowledging it,--but that the display of it is
without the graces of which Youth is proud, and which Age
regrets.    Way 465, XCIX,II.

[M]any politicians...show, that the cares of the nation may
sit upon a man's shoulders for many years without breaking
or even bending them.    PrM 61, VII,I.

[A] man of twenty-eight is apt to regard a man of forty as very much too old for falling in love. It is a mistake which it will take him fully ten years to rectify, and then he will make a similar mistake as to men of fifty. AS 40, VI.

Young ladies of five-and-twenty, when they marry gentlemen of four-and-fifty, make up their minds for well-understood and well-recognized old age. They see that they had best declare their purpose, and they do declare it. 'Of course, Mr. Walker is old enough to be my father, but I have made up my mind that I like that better than anything else.' Then the wall has been jumped, and the thing can go smoothly. But at forty-five, there is supposed to be so much of youth left that the difference of age may possibly be tided over and not made to appear abnormal. AyA 46, V.

A man who has spouted at twenty-five becomes tired of his spouting at fifty, if nothing special has come from his spouting. MF 11, I,I.

As time runs on, such a result [thinking the older partner is not quite so wide-awake] generally takes place in all close connections between the old and the young. MSF 217, LVIII,III.

## AGREEMENT

The quarrels of lovers have ever been the renewal of love, since the day when a verb between two nominative cases first became possessed of the power of agreeing with either of them. There is something in this sweet easiness of agreement which seems to tend to such reconciliations. Ber 388-9, XXI.

They two had tacitly agreed not to be bound by common sense, not to be wise. Such tacit agreements are common enough between men, between women, and between men and women. IHP 142-3,XV,I.

## AIMLESSNESS

Has it ever been the lot of any unmarried male reader of these pages, to pass three or four days in London, without anything to do...with the additional burden of some terrible, wearing misery, away from which there seems to be no road, and out of which there is apparently no escape?...In such a condition, a man can simply walk the streets by himself, and declare to himself that everything is bad, and rotten, and vile, and worthless. He wishes himself dead, and calculates the different advantages of prussic acid and pistols. He may the while take his meals very punctually at his club, may smoke his cigars, and drink his bitter beer, or brandy-and-water;--but he is all the time wishing himself dead, making that calculation as to the best way of achieving that desirable result. Cl 220, XXVI.

It is the lack of object, of all aim, in the lives of the houseless wanderers that gives to them the most terrible element of their misery.  Think of it!  To walk forth with, say, ten shillings in your pocket,--so that there need be no instant suffering from want of bread or shelter,--and have no work to do, no friend to see, no place to expect you, no duty to accomplish, no hope to follow, no bourn to which you can draw nigher,--except that bourn which, in such circumstances, the traveller must surely regard as simply the end of his weariness!  But there is nothing to which humanity cannot attune itself.  Men can live upon poison, can learn to endure absolute solitude, can bear contumely, scorn, and shame, and never show it.  VOB 369, LII.

### AIR

Most of us have recognized the fact that a dram of spirits will create,--that a so-called nip of brandy will create hilarity, or, at least, alacrity, and that a glass of sherry will often 'pick up' and set in order the prostrate animal and mental faculties of the drinker.  But we are not sufficiently alive to the fact that copious draughts of fresh air,--of air fresh and unaccustomed,--will have precisely the same effect.  We do know that now and again it is very essential to 'change the air'; but we generally consider that to do that with any chance of advantage, it is necessary to go far afield....We are seldom aware that we may imbibe long potations of pleasure and healthy excitement without perhaps going out of our own county; that such potations are within a day's journey of most of us; and that they are to be had for half-a-crown a head, all expenses told.  HKHWR 148, XVI.

### ALONENESS

Who does not know that terrible feeling [being alone in a crowd], and the all but necessity that exists for the sufferer to pretend that he is not suffering,--which again is aggravated by the conviction that the pretence is utterly vain?  This may be bad with a man, but with woman, who never looks to be alone in a crowd, it is terrible.
ED 340, XXXVII,I.

### AMBITION

Men but seldom tell the truth of what is in them, even to their dearest friends....To be visibly eager seems childish, and is always bad policy; and men, therefore, nowadays, though they strive as hard as ever in the service of ambition--harder than ever in that of mammon--usually do so with a pleasant smile on, as though after all they were but amusing themselves with the little matter in hand.
DoT 268-9, XXII.

It is no doubt very wrong to long after a naughty thing.  But nevertheless we all do so....And ambition is a great

vice--as Mark Anthony told us a long time ago--a great vice,
no doubt, if the ambition of the man be with reference to
his own advancement, and not to the advancement of others.
But then, how many of us are there who are not ambitious in
this vicious manner?     And there is nothing viler than the
desire to know great people--people of great rank, I should
say;    nothing   worse    than    the    hunting   of   titles   and
worshipping wealth.    We all know this, and say it every day
of our lives.    But presuming that a way into the society of
Park Lane was open to us, and a way also into that of
Bedford Row, how many of us are there who would prefer
Bedford Row because it is so vile to worship wealth and
title?    FrP 30, IV.

No;  the heart of man can desire deaneries--the heart, that
is, of the man vicar; and the heart of the man dean can
desire  bishoprics;  and before the eyes of the man bishop
does there not loom the transcendental glory of Lambeth?
FrP 83, IX.

...the probable miseries of a man who begins life too high
up on the ladder,--who succeeds in mounting before he has
learned how to hold on when he is aloft.    PF 8, I,I.

[A]nd a disappointment will crush the spirit worse than a
realised calamity.     There is no actual misfortune in not
being Lord Mayor of London;--but when a man has set his
heart upon the place, has worked himself into a position
within a few feet of the Mansion House, has become alderman
with the mayoralty before him in immediate rotation, he will
suffer more at being passed over by the liverymen than if he
had lost half his fortune.    RalH 2, I.

It is easy to fill with air a half-inflated bladder.    It is
already so buoyant with its own lightness, that it yields
itself with ease to receive the generous air.
LA 389, XXXVII.

A man cannot always restrain his own doings and keep them
within the limits which he had himself planned for them.
They  will  often  fall  short  of  the  magnitude  to  which  his
ambition has aspired.    They will sometimes soar higher than
his own imagination.    Way 323, XXXV,I.

That he should have wanted an impossible brick, whether the
highest or lowest brick, was very sad.    When children cry
for impossible bricks, they must of course be disappointed.
IHP 251, LVIII,II.

## AMERICANS

An American when he has spent a pleasant day will tell you
that he has had  'a good time.'    LasC 481, LI.

American women are taught by the habits of their country to
think that men should give way to them more absolutely than

is in accordance with the practices of life in Europe. A seat in a public conveyance in the States, when merely occupied by a man, used to be regarded by any woman as being at her service as completely as though it were vacant. One woman indicating a place to another would point with equal freedom to a man or a space. It is said that this is a little altered now, and that European views on this subject are spreading themselves. HKHWR 352, XXXVII.

[A]nd with no women is a speedy intimacy so possible, or indeed so profitable, as with Americans. They fear nothing, --neither you nor themselves; and talk with as much freedom as though they were men. It may, perhaps, be assumed to be true as a rule, that women's society is always more agreeable to men than that of other men,--except for the lack of ease. It undoubtedly is so when the women be young and pretty. There is a feeling, however, among pretty women in Europe that such freedom is dangerous, and it is withheld. There is such danger, and more or less of such withholding is expedient; but the American woman does not recognise the danger; and, if she withhold the grace of her countenance and the pearls of her speech, it is because she is not desirous of the society which is proffered to her. HKHWR 373, XL.

Many American gentlemen are known for such hostility. They make anti-English speeches about the country, as though they thought that war with England would produce certain triumph to the States, certain increase to American trade, and certain downfall to a tyranny which no Anglo-Saxon nation ought to endure. But such is hardly their real opinion. There, in the States, as also here in England, you shall, from day to day hear men propounding, in very loud language, advanced theories of political action, the assertion of which is supposed to be necessary to the end which they have in view....In the States a large party, which consists chiefly of those who have lately left English rule, and who are keen to prove to themselves how wise they have been in doing so, is pleased by this strong language against England; and, therefore, the strong language is spoken. But the speakers, who are, probably, men knowing something of the world, mean it not at all; they have no more idea of war with England than they have of war with all Europe; and their respect for England and for English opinion is unbounded. In their political tones of speech and modes of action they strive to be as English as possible. HKHWR 428-9, XLVI.

That their young ladies should walk in public places with unmarried gentlemen is nothing to American fathers and guardians. American young ladies are accustomed to choose their own companions. HKHWR 517, LV.

It is to be observed that American citizens are always prone to talk of Europe. It affords the best counterpoise they know to that other term, America,--and America and the

United States are of course the same.  To speak of France
or of England as weighing equally against their own country
seems to an American to be an absurdity,--and almost an
insult to himself.  With Europe he can compare himself.
HKHWR 518, LV.

Now the peculiar nasal twang which our cousins over the
water have learned to use, and which has grown out of a
certain national instinct which coerces them to express
themselves with self-assertion;--let the reader go into his
closet and talk through his nose for awhile with steady
attention to the effect which his own voice will have, and
he will find that this theory is correct;--this intonation
...is so peculiar among intelligent Americans.
HKHWR 713, LXXVI.

We in England are not usually favourably disposed to women
who take a pride in certain antagonism to men in general,
and who are anxious to shew the world that they can get on
very well without male assistance; but there are many such
in America who have noble aspirations, good intellects, much
energy, and who are by no means unworthy of friendship.  The
hope in regard to all such women...is that they will be
cured at last by a husband and half-a-dozen children.
HKHWR 717, LXXVII.

[M]ost Americans who do not as yet know the country...come
with an inward feeling that as an American and a republican
...[they] might probably be despised.
    There is not uncommonly a savageness of self-assertion
about Americans which arises from a too great anxiety to be
admitted to fellowship with Britons.  DuC 262, XXXIII.

## AMERICANS...ENGLISHMEN

When an intelligent Japanese travels in Great Britain or an
intelligent Briton in Japan, he is struck with no wonder at
national differences.   He is on the other hand rather
startled to find how like his strange brother is to him in
many things.   Crime is persecuted, wickedness is condoned,
and goodness treated with indifference in both countries.
Men care more for what they eat than anything else, and
combine a closely defined idea of meum with a lax perception
as to tuum.   Barring a little difference of complexion and
feature the Englishman would make a good Japanese, or the
Japanese a first-class Englishman.   But when an American
comes to us, or a Briton goes to the States, each speaking
the same language, using the same cookery, governed by the
same laws, and wearing the same costume, the differences
which present themselves are so striking that neither can
live six months in the country of the other without a
holding up of the hands and a torrent of exclamations.   And
in nineteen cases out of twenty the surprise and the ejacu-
lations take the place of censure.   The intelligence of the
American, displayed through the nose, worries the Englishman.   The unconscious self-assurance of the Englishman, not

always unaccompanied by a sneer, irritates the American. They meet as might a lad from Harrow and another from Mr. Brumby's successful mechanical cramming establishment.  The Harrow boy cannot answer a question, but is sure that he is the proper thing, and is ready to face the world on that assurance.   Mr. Brumby's paragon is shocked at the other's inaptitude for examination, but is at the same time tortured by envy of he knows not what....Hate is difficult and expensive, and between individuals soon gives place to love.  'I cannot bear Americans as a rule, though I have been very lucky myself with a few friends.' Who in England has not heard that form of speech, over and over again?  And what Englishman has travelled in the States without hearing abuse of all English institutions uttered amidst the pauses of a free-handed hospitality which has left him nothing to desire?  AS 531-2, LXXVII.

...the bar of the public-house,--that everlasting resort for American loungers,--with a cigar...loafing away...time as only American frequenters of such establishments know how to do.   In England such a man would probably be found in such a place with a glass of some alcoholic mixture beside him, but such is never the case with an American.   If he wants a drink he goes to the bar and takes it standing,-- will perhaps take two or three, one after another; but when he has settled himself down to loaf, he satisfies himself with chewing a cigar, and covering a circle around him with the results.   With this amusement he will remain contented hour after hour;--nay, throughout the entire day if no harder work be demanded of him.  DrW 230-1, IX Part V.

## AMUSEMENTS

How often in the various amusements of the world is one tempted to pause a moment and ask oneself whether one really likes it!   AS 89, XIII.

## ANGER

We have most of us heard of the terrible anger of a lioness when, surrounded by her cubs, she guards her prey.  Few of us wish to disturb the mother of a litter of puppies when mouthing a bone in the midst of her young family. BaT 227, XXV.

[A]s is usual with many of us, [he] had been unable to maintain his anger about two things at the same time. PrM 348, XXXVII,I.

But real anger is a passion which few men can use with judgment.   DuC 202, XXVI.

Who does not know that words are constantly used which are intended to have no real effect?  Who does not know that an angry woman will often talk after this fashion? AyA 317, XXXIV.

It was well that a man should have the power and the courage to show his anger.  Kept 6, II.

## ANIMALS

There are animals who, when they are ailing in any way, contrive to hide themselves, ashamed, as it were, that the weakness of their suffering should be witnessed.  Indeed, I am not sure whether all dumb animals do not do so more or less.  FrP 308, XXXI.

## ANNOYANCE

You may have a fierce bull shut up.  You may muzzle a dog that will bite.  You may shoot a horse that you cannot cure of biting and tearing.  But you cannot bring yourself to spend a morning in hunting a bug or killing a flea.
MF 248, XXIII,I.

## APPEARANCES

We, all of us, read more in the faces of those with whom we hold converse, than we are aware of doing....By the face of every man and woman seen by us, whether they speak or are silent, we form a judgment,--and in nine cases out of ten our judgment is true.  It is because our tenth judgment,-- that judgment which has been wrong,--comes back upon us always with the effects of its error, that we teach ourselves to say that appearances cannot be trusted.  If we did not trust them we should be walking ever in doubt, in darkness, and in ignorance.  RacR 239, XIX.

Damp gauzes, splashed stockings, trampled muslins, and features which have perhaps known something of rouge and certainly encountered something of rain may be made, but can only, by supreme high breeding, be made compatible with good-humour.  To be moist, muddy, rumpled and smeared, when by the very nature of your position it is your duty to be clear-starched up to the pellucidity of crystal, to be spot- less as the lily, to be crisp as the ivy-leaf, and as clear in complexion as a rose,--is it not, O gentle readers, felt to be a disgrace?  DuC 258, XXXII.

There are people apparently so hard, so ungenial, so un- sympathetic, that they who only half know them expect no trait of tenderness, think that features so little alluring cannot be compatible with softness.  AyA 83, IX.

The cares of the world, the looking after shillings and their results, had given her that look of commonplace in- significance which is so frequent and so unattractive among middle-aged women upon whom the world leans heavily.
AyA 94, X.

## APPOINTMENTS

...one of those numerous appointments for which none but

clever young barristers are supposed to be fitting
candidates.  PF 4, I,I.

## APRIL

April, which for most sportsmen in England is of all seasons
the most desperate.  Hunting is over.  There is literally
nothing to shoot.  And fishing,--even if there were fishing
in England worth a man's time,--has not begun.  A gentleman
of enterprise driven very hard in this respect used to
declare that there was no remedy for April but to go and fly
hawks in Holland.  EE 171-2, IX,I.

## ARCHITECTURE

We...take this opportunity to express our surprise that so
little is known by English men and women of the beauties of
English architecture.  The ruins of the Colisseum, the
Campanile at Florence, St. Mark's, Cologne, the Bourse and
Notre Dame, are with our tourists as familiar as household
words; but they know nothing of the glories of Wiltshire,
Dorsetshire, and Somersetshire....We beg that they will go
and see.  BaT 202, XXII.

It often seems that the beauty of architecture is acci-
dental.  A great man goes to work with great means on a
great pile, and makes a great failure.  The world perceives
that grace and beauty have escaped him, and that even
magnificence has been hardly achieved.  Then there grows up
beneath various unknown hands a complication of stones and
brick to the arrangement of which no great thought seems to
have been given; and, lo, there is a thing so perfect in its
glory that he who looks at it declares that nothing could be
taken away and nothing added without injury and sacrilege
and disgrace.  SHHOH 25, III.

## ARCHITECTURE, CHURCH

Who does not know the low porch, the perpendicular Gothic
window, the flat-roofed aisles, and the noble old gray tower
of such a church as this  [low, incommodious, kept with
difficulty in repair, too often pervious to the wet, and yet
strangely picturesque, and correct, too,...built with a nave
and aisles, visibly in the form of a cross, though with its
arms clipped down to the trunk, with a seperate [sic]
chancel, with lead and irregular in its proportions]?
SmaH 6-7, I.

## ARRIVALS

...the quick rattle of a carriage and a pair of horses on
the gravel sweep.  The sound was not that of visitors, whose
private carriages are generally brought up to country-house
doors with demure propriety, but betokened rather the advent
of some person or persons who were in a hurry to reach the
house, and had no intention of immediately leaving it.

Guests invited to stay a week, and who were conscious of arriving after the first dinner bell, would probably approach in such a manner.  So might arrive an attorney with the news of a granduncle's death, or a son from college with all the fresh honours of a double first.  No one would have had himself driven up to the door of a country house in such a manner who had the slightest doubt of his own right to force an entry.  BaT 460, XLVII.

## ARROGANCE

No doubt arrogance will produce submission; and there are men who take other men at the price those other men put upon themselves....We all know men of this calibre  [those who gave their hinder parts to be kicked merely because he put up his toe],--and how they seem to grow in number.
Way 35, LIV,II.

## ART

Our modern artists, whom we style Pre-Raphaelites, have de- lighted to go back, not only to the finish and peculiar manner, but also to the subjects of the early painters.  It is impossible to give them too much praise for the elaborate perseverance with which they have equalled the minute per- fections of the masters from whom they take their inspira- tions;...It is, however, singular into what faults they fall as regards their subjects;...the lady with the stiff back and bent neck, who looks at her flower, and is still looking from hour to hour, gives us an idea of pain without grace, and abstraction without a cause.  War 175, XIV.

Where is the painter who shall paint a picture after his soul's longing though he shall get not a penny for it,-- though he shall starve as he put his last touch to it, when he knows that by drawing some duchess of the day he shall in a fortnight earn a ducal price?  Shall a wife and child be less dear to him than to a lawyer,--or to a shoemaker; or the very craving of his hunger less obdurate?  A man's self, and what he has within him and his belongings, with his outlook for this and other worlds,--let that be the first, and the work, noble or otherwise, be the second.  To be honest is greater than to have painted the San Sisto, or to have chiselled the Apollo; to have assisted in making others honest,--infinitely greater.  AyA 33, IV.

## ASSIZE WEEK

I have observed that a strong, determined, regularly set-in of bad weather usually goes the circuit in Ireland in company with the judges and barristers, making the business of those who are obliged to attend even more intolerable than from its own nature it is always sure to be.
MB 221, VI,III.

## ATTACHES

...that thorough look of self-satisfaction and conceit which attaches are much more wont to exhibit that to deserve.  For the work of an attache at Brussels is not of a nature to bring forth the highest order of intellect; but the occupations are of a nature to make a young man feel that he is not like other young men.  MSF 190, XIV,I.

## ATTACKS

It is sometimes becoming enough for a man to wrap himself in the dignified toga of silence, and proclaim himself indifferent to public attacks; but it is a sort of dignity which it is very difficult to maintain.  As well might a man, when stung to madness by wasps, endeavour to sit in his chair without moving a muscle, as endure with patience and without reply the courtesies of a newspaper opponent.  DoT 32, III.

## ATTORNEYS

Is it not remarkable that the common repute which we all give to attorneys in the general is exactly opposite to that which every man gives to his own attorney in particular? Whom does anybody trust so implicitly as he trusts his own attorney?   And yet is it not the case that the body of attorneys is supposed to be the most roguish body in existence?  MM 222, XVII.

But an attorney ought to be sharp.  IHP 256-7, XXVI,I.

## AUCTION

Now,  as  many  may  be...ignorant...respecting  an  auction  in sporting phraseology, I will, if I can, explain what it is.
    It  has  but  little  reference  or  similitude  to  those auctions from which Sir Robert Peel has removed the duty.
    Supposing  there  may  be  twenty  members,  each  having half-a-crown;  and  six  horses  to  run.   Twenty bits of paper are  placed  in  a  hat,  on  six  of  which  are  written  the  names of  the  running  horses--the  others  are  blanks--and  they  are then  drawn  like  lots  out  of  the  hat.   The  tickets  bearing the  horses'  names  are  sold  by  the  auctioneer;  the  last bidder  has  to  pay  twice  the  sum  he  bids--one  moiety  to  the man  who  drew  the  horse;  the  other  is  added  to  the  fund composed  of  the  twenty  half-crowns.   After  the  race,  the happy  man  holding  the  ticket  bearing  the  name  of  the  winning horse  receives  the  whole.   There  are,  therefore,  different winners  in  this  transaction;  the  man  drawing  the  name  of  the favourite  horse  of  course  wins  what  is  bid  for  the  ticket; any  one  drawing  the  name  of  any  horse  would  probably  win something,  as  his  chance,  if  he  had  more  than  three  legs, must  be  worth  at  least  five  shillings.   Such,  however,  is  an auction.  MB 155-6, V,II.

## AUNTS

When a girl has a mother, her aunt may be little or nothing to her. But when the mother is gone, if there be an aunt unimpeded with other family duties, then the family duties of the aunt begin--and are assumed sometimes with great vigour. Bel 10, I.

An aunt's dominion, when once well established in early years, cannot easily be thrown altogether aside,--even though a young lady have a will of her own. Bel 12, I.

## AUSTRALIAN SQUATTER

But an Australian squatter, if he have any well-grounded claim to the character of a bushman, has eyes which are not ordinary, and he has, probably, nutured within himself, unconsciously, topographical instincts which are unintelligible to the inhabitants of cities. HHOG 28, II.

## AUTHORITY

...that air of authority to which the strongest-minded policeman will always bow. TC 485, XL.

When a son is frequently called on to lend money to his father, and that father is never called on to repay it, the parental authority is apt to grow dull. Ber 336-7, XVIII.

In these days a mother even can only exercise such power over a child as public opinion permits her to use. CasR 95, V,III.

Such a message as that [you are wanted in the Board-room] in official life always strikes awe into the heart of a young man. And yet, young men generally come forth from such interviews without having received any serious damage, and generally talk about the old gentlemen whom they have encountered with a good deal of light-spirited sarcasm--or chaff, as it is called in the slang phraseology of the day....[H]ow well can I remember the terror created within me by the air of outraged dignity with which a certain fine old gentleman, now long since gone, could rub his hands slowly one on the other, and look up to the ceiling, slightly shaking his head, as though lost in the contemplation of my iniquities! I would become sick in my stomach, and feel as though my ankles had been broken. That upward turn of the eye unmanned me so completely that I was speechless as regarded any defence. I think that that old man could hardly have known the extent of his own power.
    Once upon a time a careless lad, having the charge of a bundle of letters addressed to the King--petitions and such like, which in the course of business would not get beyond the hands of some lord-in-waiting's deputy assistant--sent the bag which contained them to the wrong place; to Windsor, perhaps, if the Court were in London; or to St. James's, if

it were at Windsor.  He was summoned; and the great man of
the occasion contented himself with holding his hands up to
the heavens as he stood up from his chair, and exclaiming
twice,   'Mis-sent  the  Monarch's  pouch!    Mis-sent  the
Monarch's pouch!'  That young man never knew how he escaped
from the Board-room; but for a time he was deprived of all
power of exertion, and could not resume his work till he had
had  six  months'  leave  of  absence,  and  been  brought  round
upon rum and asses's milk.   In that instance the peculiar
use  of  the  word  Monarch  had  a  power  which  the  official
magnate  had  never  contemplated.    The  story  is  traditional;
but I believe that the circumstance happened as lately as in
the days of George the Third.  SmaH 358-9, XXXVI.

To  be  didactic  and  at  the  same  time  demonstrative  of
affection  is  difficult,  even  with  mothers  towards  their
children,  though  with  them  the  assumption  of  authority
creates no sense of injury.  SHHOH 210, XXI.

Among  such  men  and  women...  [miller  and  family],  parental
authority  must  needs  lie  much  lighter  than  it  does  with
those who are wont to give much and to receive much.   What
obedience does the lad owe who at eighteen goes forth and
earns his own bread?  What is it to him that he has not yet
reached a man's estate?  He has to do a man's work, and the
price of it is his own, in his hands, when he has earned it.
There  is  no  curse  upon  the  poor  heavier  than  that  which
comes  from  the  early  breach  of  all  ties  of  duty  between
fathers and their sons, and mothers and their daughters.
VOB 47, VII.

## AUTHORITY, EPISCOPAL

Now,  episcopal  authority  admits  of  being  stretched  or  con-
tracted according to the character of the bishop who uses
it.  It is not always easy for a bishop himself to know what
he may do, and what he may not do.  He may certainly give
advice to any clergyman in his diocese, and he may give it
in such form that it will have in it something of authority.    Such  advice  coming  from  a  dominant  bishop  to  a
clergyman with a submissive mind, has in it very much of
authority.  LasC 92, XI.

## AUTUMN

We  do  not  know  here  that  special  season  which  across  the
Atlantic is called the Indian summer,--that last glow of the
year's warmth which always brings with it a half melancholy
conviction of the year's decay,--which in itself is so delightful, would be so full of delight, were it not for the
consciousness which it seems to contain of being the immediate precursor of winter with all its horrors.   There is no
sufficient  constancy  with  us  of  the  recurrence  of  such  a
season, to make any special name needful.  RalH 245, XXXII.

## AWE

In London, perhaps, a bishop inspires more awe than a Cabinet Minister. In Killaloe, where a bishop might be seen walking about every day, the mitred dignitary of the Church, though much loved, was thought of, I fear, but lightly; whereas a Cabinet Minister coming to stay in the house of a townsman was a thing to be wondered at, to be talked about, to be afraid of, to be a fruitful source of conversation for a year to come. PF 253, LXV,II.

## B

## BABBLING

There are many men of whom everybody knows all about their belongings;--as to whom everybody knows where they live, whither they go, what is their means, and how they spend it. But there are others of whom no man knows anything.... For myself I like the open babbler the best. Babbling may be a weakness but to my thinking, mystery is a vice.
CanY 121, XII,I.

There are men who cannot communicate themselves to others, as there are also men who not only can do so, but cannot do otherwise. And it is hard to say which is the better man of the two. We do not specially respect him who wears his heart upon his sleeve for daws to peck at, who carries a crystal window to his bosom so that all can see the work that is going on within it, who cannot keep any affair of his own private, who gushes out in love and friendship to every chance acquaintance; but then, again, there is but little love given to him who is always wary, always silent as to his own belongings, who buttons himself in a suit of close reserve which he never loosens. Respect such a one may gain, but hardly love....Perhaps, after all that may be said of the weakness of the gushing and indiscreet babbler, it is pleasanter to live with such a one than with the self-constrained reticent man of iron. RalH 1, I.

## BABIES

[A]nd a baby in such a household [newly married and wealthy] is apt to make things go sweetly. HKHWR 3, I.

[W]hen age is counted by months only, almost everything may be forgotten in six weeks. HKHWR 308, XXXII.

## BABIES, FIRST

How precious are all the belongings of a first baby; how dear are the cradle, the lace-caps, the first coral, all the little duds which are made with such punctilious care and anxious efforts of nicest needlework to encircle that small lump of pink humanity!...And then how soon the change comes; how different it is when there are ten of them, and the tenth is allowed to inherit the well-worn wealth which the ninth, a year ago, had received from the eighth. There is no crimson silk basket then, I trow.

'Jane, Jane, where are my boots?' 'Mary, I've lost my trousers!' Such sounds are heard, shouted through the house from powerful lungs.

'Why, Charley,' says the mother, as her eldest hope rushes in to breakfast with dishevelled hair and dirty hands, 'you've got no handkerchief on your neck--what have you done with your handkerchief?'

'No, mamma; it came off in the hay-loft, and I can't find it.'

'Papa,' says the lady wife, turning to her lord, who is reading his newspaper over his coffee--'papa, you really must speak to Charley;--he will not mind me. He was dressed quite nicely an hour ago, and do see what a figure he has made himself.'

'Charley,' says papa, not quite relishing this disturbance in the midst of a very interesting badger-baiting-- 'Charley, my boy, if you don't mind your P's and Q's, you and I shall fall out; mind that;' and he again goes on with his sport; and mamma goes on with her teapot, looking not exactly like Patience on a monument. TC 555, XLVII.

## BALDNESS

There is a baldness that is handsome and noble, and a baldness that is peculiarly mean and despicable. RalH 163,XXII.

## BANKRUPTCY

There is no position in life in which a man receives so much distinguished attentions as when he is a bankrupt--a bankrupt, that is, of celebrity. It seems as though he had then realized the legitimate ends of trade, and was brought forth in order that those men might do him honor with whom he had been good enough to have dealings on a large scale. Str 121, XXII.

There is something inexpressibly melancholy in the idea of bankruptcy in trade, unless, indeed, when it may have been produced by absolute fraud, and in such a form as to allow of the bankrupts going forth with their pockets full. But in an ordinary way, I know nothing more sad than the fate of men who have embarked all in a trade venture and have failed....They who have struggled and lost all feel only that they have worked hard, and worked in vain; that they have thrown away their money and their energy; and that

there is an end, now and forever, to those sweet hopes of
independence with which they embarked their small boats upon
the wide ocean of commerce. The fate of such men is very
sad. Of course we hear of bankrupts who come forth again
with renewed glories, and who shine all the brighter in
consequence of their temporary obscurity. These are the men
who can manage to have themselves repainted and regilded;
but their number is not great....Of ordinary bankrupts one
hears nothing. They are generally men who, having saved a
little with long patience, embark it all and lose it with
rapid impotence. They come forward once in their lives with
their little ventures, and then retire never more to be seen
or noticed. Of all the shops that are opened year after
year in London, not above a half remain· in existence for a
period of twelve months, and not a half ever afford a
livelihood to those who open them.... When one thinks of
it, it is very sad; but the sadness is not confined to
commerce. It is the same at the bar, with the army, and in
the Church. We see only the few who rise above the wages,
and know nothing of the many who are drowned beneath the
waters. Str 123, XXII.

## BANQUETING IN A TENT

[T]he banqueting in tents loses in comfort almost more than
it gains in romance. A small picnic may be very well, and
the distance previously travelled may give to a dinner on
the ground the seeming excuse of necessity....Therefore, out
with the cold pies, out with the salads, and the chickens,
and the champagne. Since no better may be, let us recruit
human nature sitting upon this moss, and forget our
discomforts in the glory of the verdure around us. And dear
Mary, seeing that the cushion from the waggonet is small,
and not wishing to accept the too generous offer that she
should take it all for her own use, will admit a contact
somewhat closer than the ordinary chairs of a dining-room
render necessary. That in its way is very well;--but I hold
that a banquet on narrow tables in a tent is displeasing.
PF 235, LXIII,II.

## BAR

All young men I believe do [dream of the bar], who have high
abilities, a taste for labour, and scanty fortune. Senior
wranglers and double firsts, when not possessed of means for
political life, usually find their way to the bar. It is on
the bench of judges, not on the bench of bishops, that we
must look for them in after life. Ber 42, III.

## BARMAIDS

If I were about to open such a house as the Moonbeam the
first thing I should look for would be a discreet, pleasant-
visaged lady to assist me in the bar department, not much
under forty, with ringlets, who knew how to whisper little
speeches while she made a bottle of cherry-brandy serve

five-and-twenty turns at the least.    She should be honest,
patient, graceful, capable of great labour, grasping,--with
that wonderful capability of being greedy for the benefit of
another which belongs to women,--willing to accept plentiful
meals and a power of saving 20[pounds] a year as sufficient
remuneration for all hardships, with no more susceptibility
than a milestone, and as indifferent to delicacy in language
as a bargee.    There are such women, and very valuable women
they are in that trade.    RalH 344, XLVI.

## BARRISTERS

The mind of a barrister who has been for fifty years
practising in court will never be biassed by his predilections.  Ber 283, XVI.

An unblushing, wordy barrister may be very full of brass
and words, and yet be no better than an unseasoned porous
deal-board, even though he have a seat in Parliament.
Ber 819, XLVI.

At a certain point in his career, supposing his career to
have been sufficiently prosperous, it becomes natural to a
barrister to stand for some constituency, and natural for
him also to form his politics at that period of his life
with a view to his further advancement, looking, as he does
so, carefully at the age and standing of the various
candidates for high legal office....It is the way of the
profession, and thus a proper and sufficient number of real
barristers find its way into the House.   PF 225, LXIII,II.

In a sensational cause the leading barrister for the defence
is always the hero of the plot,--the actor from whom the
best bit of acting is expected,--the person who is most
likely to become a personage on the occasion.   The prisoners
are necessarily mute, and can only be looked at, not heard.
The judge is not expected to do much till the time comes for
his charge, and even then is supposed to lower the dignity
of the bench if he makes his charge with any view to effect
on his own behalf.    The barrister who prosecutes should be
tame, or he will appear to be vindictive.    The witnesses,
however interesting they may be in detail, are but episodes.
Each comes and goes, and there is an end of them.    But the
part of the defending advocate requires action through the
whole of the piece.   And he may be impassioned.   He is bound
to be on the alert.    Everything seems to depend on
him....[A]n acquittal is a matter of personal prowess, of
professional triumph, and possibly of well simulated
feeling.  JC 301-2, XLI.

## BEAUTY

[The] outward bravery is not everything with a woman.   It
may be that a man in selecting his wife rarely looks for
much else;--for that in addition, of course, to money; but
though he has looked for little else, some other things do

frequently force themselves on his attention soon after the
knot is tied. Ber 139-40, IX.

Female beauty of the sterner, grander sort may support the
burden of sixteen children, all living,--and still survive.
I have known it to do so, and to survive with much of its
youthful glory.   But that mild-eyed, soft, round, plumpy
prettiness gives way beneath such a weight as that:   years
alone tell on it quickly; but children and limited means
combined with years leave to it hardly a chance.   OrF 11, I.

I have seen in Italy and in America women perhaps as beautiful as any that I have seen in England, but in neither
country does it seem that such beauty is intended for
domestic use.   In Italy the beauty is soft, and of the
flesh.   In America it is hard, and of the mind.   Here it is
of the heart, I think, and as such is the happiest of the
three.  RacR 82, VII.

[A] woman's beauty is in one sense as free as the air in all
Christian countries.   It is a light shed for the delight,
not of one, but of many.  RalH 94, XII.

## BEAUTY, MASCULINE

[B]ut his beauty was of that regular sort which is more
pleasing in a boy than in a man.  Ber 11-12, I.

## BEDROOMS

English readers will perhaps remember that among the Vosges
mountains there is less of a sense of privacy attached to
bedrooms than is the case with us here in England.
GLOG 127, XII.

## BEGINNINGS

What had been as yet done was but the tuning of the fiddles
before the commencement of the opera.  No one likes to be in
at the tuning, but there are those who never are able to
avoid this annoyance.  RacR 84, VII.

## BELIEF

That fighting of a battle without belief is, I think, the
sorriest task which ever falls to the lot of any man.
OrF 224, LXII,II.

## BELIEVERS

[I]t is not every man who exactly knows what he does
believe.  Every man!  Is there, one may almost ask, any man
who has such knowledge?  We all believe in the resurrection
of the body; we say so at least, but what do we believe by
it?
     Men may be firm believers and yet doubt some Bible

statements--doubt the letter of such statements....Such men, if they devote their time to Scripture history, will not be arrested by the sun's standing on Gibeon. If they speak out at all, they will speak out rather as to all they do believe than as to the little that they doubt. Ber 317-8, XVIII.

## BELIEVING

No one becomes an infidel at once. A man who has really believed does not lose by a sudden blow the firm convictions of his soul. But when the work has been once commenced, when the first step has been taken, the pace becomes frightfully fast. Ber 471-2, XXVI.

## BELLS

I know full well the tone with which they toll when the soul is ushered to its last long rest. I have stood in that green churchyard when earth has been laid to earth, ashes to ashes, dust to dust--the ashes and the dust that were loved so well.

But now the scene was of another sort. How merrily they rang, those joyous marriage-bells! Youth was now to know the full delight of matured happiness....

To neither man nor woman does the world fairly begin till seated together in their first mutual home they bethink themselves that the excitement of their honeymoon is over. It would seem that the full meaning of the word marriage can never be known by those who, at their first outspring into life, are surrounded by all that money can give. It requires the single sitting-room, the single fire, the necessary little efforts of self-devotion, the inward declaration that some struggle shall be made for that other one, some world's struggle, of which wealth can know nothing. One would almost wish to be poor, that one might work for one's wife; almost wish to be ill used, that one might fight for her.

He, as he goes forth to his labour, swears within his heart that, by God's help on his endeavours, all shall go well with her. And she, as she stands musing alone in her young home, with a soft happy tear in her bright eye, she also swears in her heart that, by God's help, his home shall be to him the sweetest spot on the earth's surface. Then should not marriage-bells ring joyously? Ah, my friends, do not count too exactly your three hundreds a year--your four hundreds. Try the world. But try it with industry and truth, not with idleness and falsehood. Ber 548-50, XXX.

## BETRAYALS

It is sometimes impossible to prevent the betrayal of a confidence, when the line between betrayal and non-betrayal is finely drawn. RalH 228, XXX.

## BIOGRAPHIES

In these days a man is nobody unless his biography is kept so far posted up that it may be ready for the national breakfast-table on the morning after his demise....Of great men, full of years, who are ripe for the sickle, who in the course of Nature must soon fall, it is of course comparatively easy for an active compiler to have his complete memoir ready in his desk.  But in order that the idea of omnipresent and omniscient information may be kept up, the young must be chronicled as quickly as the old.  In some cases this task must, one would say, be difficult. Nevertheless, it is done.  DoT 297-8, XXV.

## BISHOPS

We believe, as a general rule, that either a bishop or his archdeacons have sinecures:  where a bishop works, archdeacons have but little to do, and vice versa. War 19-20, II.

The bishop did not whistle:  we believe that they lose the power of doing so on being consecrated; and that in these days one might as easily meet a corrupt judge as a whistling bishop.  War 39, III.

## BLACK SHEEP

[T]hat question of admitting black sheep into society, or of refusing them admittance, is very difficult.  In the first place, whose eyes are good enough to know whether in truth a sheep be black or not?  And then is it not the fact that some little amount of shade in the fleece of male sheep is considered, if not absolutely desirable, at any rate quite pardonable?  A male sheep with a fleece as white as a ewe-lamb, is he not considered to be, among muttons, somewhat insipid?  It was this taste of which Pope was conscious when he declared that every woman was at heart a rake.  And so it comes to pass that very black sheep indeed are admitted into society, till at last anxious fathers and more anxious mothers begin to be aware that their young ones are turned out to graze among ravenous wolves.  This, however, must be admitted, that lambs when so treated acquire a courage which tends to enable them to hold their own, even amidst wolfish dangers.  SmaH 40-1, V.

Blackness in a male sheep in regard to the other sin is venial blackness....Blackness such as that will be all condoned, and the sheep received into almost any flock, on condition, not of repentance or humiliation or confession, but simply of change of practice....
     And then there are the shades of black which come from conviviality,--which we may call table blackness,--as to which there is an opinion constantly disseminated by the moral newspapers of the day, that there has come to be altogether an end of any such blackness among sheep who are

gentlemen.   To make up for this, indeed, there has been expressed by the piquant newspapers of the day an opinion that ladies are taking up the game which gentlemen no longer care to play.   It may be doubted whether either expression has in it much of truth.   We do not see ladies drunk, certainly, and we do not see gentlemen tumbling about as they used to do, because their fashion of drinking is not that of their grandfathers.   But the love of wine has not gone out from among men; and men now are as prone as ever to indulge their loves.   SHHOH 42-3, V.

## BLACKMAIL

There is nothing so ruinous as buying the silence of a rogue who has a secret.   What you buy you never possess; and the price that is once paid must be repaid again and again, as often as the rogue may demand it.   Any alternative must be better than this.   TC 424-5, XXXIV.

## BLAME

[B]ut himself he never blamed; people never do, it is so much easier to blame others, and so much more comfortable. MB 24, III,I.

## BLOWS

But a blow!   What woman can bear a blow from a man, and afterwards return to him with love?   A wife may have to bear it and to return.   And she may return with that sort of love which is a thing of custom....But as for love,--all that we mean by love when we speak of it and write of it,--a blow given by the defender to the defenceless crushes it all!   A woman may forgive deceit, treachery, desertion,--even the preference given to a rival.   She may forgive them and forget them: but I do not think that a woman can forget a blow.   And as for forgiveness,-- it is not the blow that she cannot forgive, but the meanness of spirit that made it possible.   CanY 173-4, LVII,II.

## BLUE BLOOD

It is a point of conscience among the--perhaps not ten thousand, but say one thousand of bluest blood,--that everybody should know who everybody is....It is a knowledge which the possession of the blue blood itself produces. There are countries with bluer blood than our own in which to be without such knowledge is a crime.   DuC 278, XXXV.

## BLUSHES

We used to think, when we pretended to read the faces of our neighbours, that a rising blush betrayed a conscious false-hood.   For the most part we know better now, and have learned to decipher more accurately the outward signs which are given by the impulses of the heart.   An unmerited accusation of untruth will ever bring blood to the face of the young and innocent.  RacR 44, IV.

There is no greater mistake than in supposing that only the young blush.  But the blushes of middle life are luckily not seen through the tan which has come from the sun and the gas and the work and the wiles of the world.  DuC 326, XLI.

## BONDS

A bond of discord, if the phrase may be allowed, is often quite as strong as any bond coming from concord and agreement.  JC 243, XXXIII.

## BONNETS

[A]fter all, what is the use of a French bonnet when stuck under a side wall [of church]?  Ber 391, XXII.

## BOOK REVIEWS

There is the review intended to sell a book,--which comes out immediately after the appearance of the book, or someti es before it; the review which gives reputation, but does not affect the sale, and which comes a little later; the review which snuffs a book out quietly; the review which is to raise or lower the author a single peg, or two pegs, as the case may be; the review which is suddenly to make an author,and the review which is to crush him....When the rumour goes abroad that some notable man has been actually crushed,--been positively driven over by an entire Juggernaut's car of criticism till his literary body be a mere amorphous mass,--then a real success has been achieved, and the...[editor] of the day has done a great thing; but even the crushing of a poor... [feeble author], if it be absolute, is effective.  Such a review will not make all the world call for the 'Evening Pulpit', but it will cause those who do take the paper to be satisfied with their bargain. Whenever the circulation of such a paper begins to slacken, the proprietors should, as a matter of course, admonish their...[editor] to add a little power to the crushing department.  Way 96-7, XI,I.

## BORES

A man may endure to be bored in the course of business through the day, but it becomes dreadful when the infliction is extended to post-prandial hours.  It does not often occur that one is doomed to bear the same bore both by day and night; any change gives some ease.  TC 95, IX.

## BORROWERS

Men of this class  [those men who are always mixing up business with pleasure]  have, as a rule, no daily work, no regular routine of labour; but it may be doubted whether

they do not toil much more incessantly than those who have.
FrP 51, VI.

We all of us know that swindlers and rogues do very dirty
tricks, and we are apt to picture to ourselves a certain
amount of gusto and delight on the part of the swindlers in
the doing of them. In this, I think we are wrong. The
poor, broken, semi-genteel beggar, who borrows half-
sovereigns apiece from all his old acquaintances, knowing
that they know that he will never repay them, suffers a
separate little agony with each petition that he makes....
To get his half-sovereign with scorn is painful. To get it
with apparent confidence in his honour is almost more
painful. 'D___ it,' he says to himself on such rare
occasions, 'I will pay that fellow;' and yet as he says it,
he knows that he never will pay even that fellow. It is a
comfortless unsatisfying trade, that of living upon other
people's money. CanY 389, XXXVIII,I.

There is always a difficulty in the choice, not only of the
words with which money should be borrowed, but of the
fashion after which they should be spoken. There is the
slow deliberate manner, in using which the borrower attempts
to carry the wished-for lender along with him by force of
argument, and to prove that the desire to borrow shows no
imprudence on his own part, and that a tendency to lend will
show none on the part of the intended lender. It may be
said that this mode fails oftener than any other. There is
the piteous manner--the plea for commiseration. 'My dear
fellow, unless you will see me through now, upon my word I
shall be very badly off.' And this manner may be divided
again into two. There is the plea piteous with a lie, and
the plea piteous with a truth. 'You shall have it again in
two months as sure as the sun rises.' That is generally the
plea piteous with a lie. Or it may be as follows; 'It is
only fair to say that I don't quite know when I can pay it
back.' This is the plea piteous with a truth, and upon the
whole I think that this is generally the most successful
mode of borrowing. And there is the assured demand--which
betokens a close intimacy. 'Old fellow, can you let me have
thirty pounds? No? Just put your name, then, on the back
of this, and I'll get it done in the City.' The worst of
that manner is, that the bill so often does not get itself
done in the City. Then there is the sudden attack....That
there are other modes of borrowing by means of which youth
becomes indebted to age, and love to respect, and ignorance
to experience, is a matter of course. LasC 395, XLIV.

It is a matter of consideration whether, when important
subjects are to be brought upon the tapis, the ultimate
result will or will not depend on the manner in which they
are introduced. It ought not to be the case that they shall
be so prejudiced. 'By-the-by, my dear fellow, now I think
of it, can you lend me a couple of thousand pounds for
twelve months?' Would that generally be as efficacious as
though the would-be borrower had introduced his request with

the general paraphernalia of distressing solemnities?  The
borrower, at any rate, feels that it would not, and post-
pones the moment till the fitting solemnities can be
produced.  OML 105, X.

## BOSSES

When three men start on an enterprise together, one man must
be 'boss.'  Let the republic be as few as it may one man
must be president.  JC 82, XI.

## BOYCOTTING

To boycott a man, or a house, or a firm, or a class of men,
or a trade, or a flock of sheep, or a drove of oxen, or
unfortunately a county hunt, had become an exact science,
and was exactly obeyed.  It must be acknowledged that
throughout the south and west of Ireland the quickness and
perfection with which this science was understood and
practised was very much to the credit of the intelligence of
the people.  We can understand that boycotting should be
studied in Yorkshire, and practised,--after an experience of
many years....It would require much teaching;--many books
would have to be written, and an infinite amount of heavy
slow imperfect practice would follow.  But County Mayo and
County Galway rose to the requirements of the art almost in
a night!  Gradually we Englishmen learned to know in a dull
glimmering way what they were about; but at the first
whisper of the word all Ireland knew how to ruin itself.
This was done readily by people of the poorer class,--
without any gifts of education, and certainly the immoderate
practice of the science displays great national
intelligence.  Land 56-7, XX,II.

In a boycotted house you will always find that the gentlemen
are helped before the ladies.  It is a part of the principle
of boycotting that women shall subject themselves.
Land 239, XXVIII,II.

## BOYS

Boys, in this respect, are at least as exclusive as men, and
understand as well the difference between an inner and outer
circle.  DoT 289, XXIV.

I believe masters but seldom recognize the agony of spirit
with which boys endure being beaten in these contests.  Boys
on such subjects are very reticent; they hardly understand
their own feelings enough to speak of them, and are too much
accustomed both to ridicule and censure to look anywhere for
sympathy.  A favourite sister may perhaps be told of the
hard struggle and the bitter failure, but not a word is said
to any one else.  His father, so thinks the boy, is angry at
his failure; and even his mother's kisses will hardly be
warmed by such a subject.  We are too apt to think that if
our children eat pudding and make a noise they require no

sympathy.  A boy may fail at school, and afterwards eat much pudding, and make much noise; but, ah! how his young heart may sigh for some one to grieve with him over his failures!  Ber 13, I.

And all boys long to be allowed utterance occasionally for these soft and tender things--as also do all men, unless the devil's share in the world has become altogether uppermost with them.  CasR 87, V,III.

[B]ut what can be said of a boy who is only ten which shall be descriptive and also interesting?  Land 9, I,I.

## BRAVADO

There is nothing so easy as bravado.  The wretch who is to be hung can step lightly while multitudes are looking at him.  The woman who is about to give up all that her heart most values can declare out loud that the matter is very indifferent to her.  But when the victim of the law is lying in his solitary cell, thinking on his doom, the morning before the executioner comes to him; when the poor girl is sitting alone on her bedside, with her heart all empty--or rather not empty, only hopeless; it is very difficult then to maintain a spirit of bravado!  Ber 370-1, XX.

But when men are driven into corners--when they are hemmed in on all sides, so that they have no escape, to what else than bravado can they have recourse?  Ber 812, XLVI.

## BREAKFASTS

There could be no better breakfast than used to be given in the buffet at the railway terminus at St. Michael...We are often told in our newspapers that England is disgraced by this and by that; by the unreadiness of our army, by the unfitness of our navy, by the irrationality of our laws, by the immobility of our prejudices, and what not; but the real disgrace of England is the railway sandwich,--that whited sepulchre, fair enough outside, but so meagre, poor, and spiritless within, such a thing of shreds and parings, such a dab of food, telling us that the poor bone whence it was scraped had been made utterly bare before it was sent into the kitchen for the soup pot.  HKHWR 351, XXXVII.

## BREEDING

[T]hough whence comes such show [of higher blood], and how one discerns that appearance, few of us can tell.  VOB 6, I.

## BRIBERY, ELECTION

In these days of snow-white purity all political delinquency is abominable in the eyes of--British politicians; but no delinquency is so abominable as that of venality at elections.  The sin of bribery is damnable.  It is the one

sin for which, in the House of Commons, there can be no
forgiveness. When discovered, it should render the culprit
liable to political death, without hope of pardon. It is
treason against a higher throne than that on which the Queen
sits. It is a heresy which requires an auto-da-fe. It is
pollution to the whole House, which can only be cleansed by
great sacrifice....

Such is the language of patriotic members with regard to
bribery; and doubtless, if sincere, they are in the right.
It is a bad thing, certainly, that a rich man should buy
votes; bad also that a poor man should sell them. By all
means let us repudiate such a system with heartfelt disgust.

With heartfelt disgust, if we can do so, by all means;
but not with disgust pretended only and not felt in the
heart at all. The laws against bribery at elections are now
so stringent that an unfortunate candidate may easily become
guilty, even though actuated by the purest intentions. But
not the less on that account does any gentleman, ambitious
of the honour of serving his country in Parliament, think it
necessary as a preliminary measure to provide a round sum of
money at his banker's. A candidate must pay for no
treating, no refreshments, no band of music; he must give
neither ribbons to the girls nor ale to the men. If a huzza
be uttered in his favour, it is at his peril; it may be
necessary for him to prove before a committee that it was
the spontaneous result of British feeling in his favour, and
not the purchased result of British beer. He cannot safely
ask any one to share his hotel dinner. Bribery hides itself
now in the most impalpable shapes, and may be effected by
the offer of a glass of sherry. But not the less on this
account does a poor man find that he is quite unable to
overcome the difficulties of a contested election.

We strain at our gnats with a vengeance, but we swallow
our camels with ease. For what purpose is it that we employ
those peculiarly safe men of business--Messers. Nearthewinde and Closerstil--when we wish to win our path
through all obstacles into that sacred recess, if all be so
open, all so easy, all so much above board? Alas! the money
is still necessary, is still prepared, or at any rate,
expended. The poor candidate of course knows nothing of the
matter till the attorney's bill is laid before him, when all
danger of petitions has passed away. He little dreamed till
then, not he, that there had been banquetings and junket-
ings, secret doings and deep drinkings at his expense. Poor
candidate! Poor member! Who was so ignorant as he! 'Tis
true he has paid such bills before; but 'tis equally true
that he specially begged his managing friend, Mr. Nearthewinde, to be very careful that all was done according to
law! He pays the bill, however, and on the next election
will again employ Mr. Nearthewinde....

But Mr. Nearthewinde is a safe man, and easy to be
employed with but little danger. All these stringent
bribery laws only enhance the value of such very safe men as
Mr. Nearthewinde. To him, stringent laws against bribery
are the strongest assurance of valuable employment. Were
these laws of a nature to be evaded with ease, any

indifferent attorney might manage a candidate's affairs and enable him to take his seat with security.  DoT 265-7, XXII.

## BRIDES...GROOMS

On such occasions the part of the bride is always easily played.  It is her duty to look pretty if she can, and should she fail in that,--as brides usually do,--her failure is attributed to the natural emotions of the occasion.  The part of the bridegroom is more difficult.  He should be manly, pleasant, composed, never flippant, able to say a few words when called upon, and quietly triumphant.  This is almost more than mortal can achieve, and bridegrooms generally manifest some shortcomings at the awful moment. LA 507, XLVIII.

A girl in her old home, before she is given up to a husband, has many sources of interest, and probably from day to day sees many people.  And the man just married goes out to his work, and occupies his time, and has his thickly-peopled world around him.  But the bride, when the bridal honours of the honeymoon are over, when the sweet care of the first cradle has not yet come to her, is apt to be lonely and to be driven to the contemplation of the pretty things with which her husband and her friends have surrounded her. PrM 370, XXXIX,I.

## BRIDESMAIDS

[T]he bridesmaids' dresses were pretty,--which is all that is required of a bridesmaid.  MSF 322, LXIV,III.

## BROTHERS...SISTERS

Not does it often come to pass that the brother is the confidant of the sister's lover.  Brothers hardly like their sisters to have lovers, though they are often well satisfied that their sisters should find themselves husbands. DuC 178, XXIII.

## BUDGETS

Budgets, like babies, are always little loves when first born.  But as their infancy passes away, they also become subject to many stripes.  The details are less pleasing than was the whole in the hands of the nurse.  PrM 112, XII,I.

## BUILDINGS, NEW

We all know the abominable adjuncts of a new building,-- the squalid half-used heaps of bad mortar, the eradicated grass, the truculent mud, the scattered brick-bats, the remnants of timber, the debris of the workmen's dinners, the morsels of paper scattered through the dirt!  VOB 256, XXXVI.

## BURDENS

It is all very well to say, 'No surrender;' but when the load placed upon the back is too heavy to be borne, the back must break or bend beneath it.  OrF 196, LIX,II.

...[A] disagreeable thing to be done is a lion in one's path which should be encountered and conquered as soon as possible.  JC 106, XIV.

## BURDENS, SHARED

And such weights do thus become lighter.  A burden that will crush a single pair of shoulders will, when equally divided --when shared by two, each of whom is willing to take the heavier part--becomes light as a feather.  Is not that sharing of the mind's burdens one of the chief purposes for which a man wants a wife?  For there is no folly so great as keeping one's sorrows hidden....Whether or no a man should have his own private pleasures, I will not now say; but it never can be worth his while to keep his sorrows private. FrP 324, XXXIII.

## BUSH COUNTRY

[A]ccording to common Australian parlance, all sheep stations are in the bush, even though there should not be a tree or shrub within sight.  They who live away from the towns live a "bush life."  Small towns, as they grow up, are called bush towns--as we talk of country towns.  The "bush," indeed, is the country generally.  HHOG 20, I.

## BUSINESS

This statement [business is business]  I am not prepared to contradict, but I would recommend all men in choosing a profession to avoid any that may require an apology at every turn; either an apology or else a somewhat violent assertion of right.  FrP 442, XLVI.

What nuisance can be so great to a man busied with immense affairs, as to have to explain,--or to attempt to explain, --small details to men incapable of understanding them? Way 341, XXXVII,I.

C

## CAB FARES

...up in that cheerful locality near Harrow-on-the Hill,

called St. John's Wood Road, the cab fares to which from any
central part of London are so very ruinous.
CasR 107, V[sic],III.

## CABINET

It must be a proud day for any man when he first walks into
a Cabinet.  But when a humble-minded man thinks of such a
phase of life, his mind becomes lost in wondering what a
Cabinet is.  Are they gods that attend there or men?  Do
they sit on chairs, or hang about on clouds?  When they
speak, is the music of the spheres audible in their Olympian
mansion, making heaven drowsy with its harmony?  In what way
do they congregate?  In what order do they address each
other?  Are the voices of all the deities free and equal?
...But Jove, great Jove--old Jove, the King of Olympus, hero
among gods and men, how does he carry himself in these
councils summoned by his voice?  Does he lie there at his
ease, with his purple cloak cut from the firmament around
his shoulders?  Is his thunderbolt ever at his hand to
reduce a recreant god to order?  Can he proclaim silence in
that immortal hall?  Is it not there, as elsewhere, in all
places, and among all nations, that a king of gods and a
king of men is and will be king, rules and will rule, over
those who are smaller than himself?  FrP 190-1, XX.

A Prime Minister sometimes finds great relief in the
possession of a serviceable stick who can be made to go in
and out as occasion may require; only it generally happens
that the stick will expect some reward when he is made to go
out.   PF 278-9, LXVIII,II.

Now it is quite understood among politicians in this country
that no man should presume that he will have imposed upon
him the task of forming a Ministry until he has been called
upon by the Crown to undertake that great duty.  Let the
Gresham or the Daubeny of the day be ever so sure that the
reins of the state chariot must come into his hands, he
should not visibly prepare himself for the seat on the box
till he has actually been summoned to place himself there.
PR 315, XXXV,I.

Cabinet Councils are, of course, very secret.  What kind of
oath the members take not to divulge any tittle of the
proceedings at these awful conferences, the general public
does not know; but it is presumed that oaths are taken very
solemn, and it is known that they are very binding.
Nevertheless, it is not an uncommon thing to hear openly at
the clubs an account of what has been settled; and, as we
all know, not a council is held as to which the editor of
The People's Banner does not inform its readers next day
exactly what took place.  PR 347-8, XXXIX,I.

## CABINETS

At ... cabinets it is supposed that, let a leader be ever so autocratic by disposition and superior by intelligence, still he must not unfrequently yield to the opinion of his colleagues.  PrM 94-5, XI,I.

[W]hat is done at Cabinet meetings generally does come to be understood.  PrM 297, XXXII,I.  See also HORSES, PF 129, XIV,I.

## CABMEN

Cabmen know very well who must go fast, and who may go slow. Women with children going on board an emigrant vessel at six o'clock on a February morning may be taken very slowly. TC 536, XLIV.

## CALM

It was that dangerous serenity which so often presages a storm.  AyA 329, XXXV.

## CALUMNY

There are men who can walk about the streets with composed countenances, take their seats in Parliament if they happen to have seats, work in their offices, or their chambers, or their counting-houses with diligence, and go about the world serenely, even though everybody be saying evil of them behind their backs.  Such men can live down temporary calumny, and almost take a delight in the isolation which it will produce.  ED 265, XXIX,I.

## CANAL BOATS

I will not attempt to describe the tedium of that horrid voyage, for it has been often described before.... The vis inertiae of patient endurance, is the only weapon of any use in attempting to overcome the lengthened ennui of this most tedious transit.  Reading is out of the question.  I have tried it myself, and seen others try it, but in vain.  The sense of the motion, almost imperceptible, but still perceptible; the noises above you; the smells around you; the diversified crowd, of which you are a part; at one moment the heat this crowd creates; at the next, the draught which a window just opened behind your ears lets in on you; the fumes of punch; the snores of the man under the table; the noisy anger of his neighbour, who reviles the attendant sylph; the would-be witticisms of a third, who makes continual amorous overtures to the same overtasked damsel, notwithstanding the publicity of his situation; the loud complaints of the old lady near the door, who cannot obtain the gratuitous kindness of a glass of water; and the baby-soothing lullabies of the young one, who is suckling her infant under your elbow.  These things alike prevent one from reading, sleeping, or thinking.  All one can do is to wait till the long night gradually wears itself away, and reflect that,

Time and the hour run through the longest day.
I hardly know why a journey in one of these boats should be
much more intolerable than travelling either outside or
inside a coach; for, either in or on the coach, one has less
room for motion, and less opportunity of employment.    I
believe the misery of the canal-boat chiefly consists in a
pre-conceived and erroneous idea of its capabilities.    One
prepares oneself for occupation--an attempt is made to
achieve actual comfort--and both end in disappointment; the
limbs become weary with endeavoring to fix themselves in a
position of repose, and the mind is fatigued more by the
search after, than the want of, occupation.    Ke1 95-7, VIII.

## CANDIDNESS

But when one is specially invited to be candid, one is
naturally set upon one's guard.    Those who by disposition
are most open, are apt to become crafty when so admonished.
When a man says to you, 'Let us be candid with each other,'
you feel instinctively that he desires to squeeze you
without giving a drop of water himself.    DoT 481, XL.

## CARE

The old poet told us how Black Care sits behind the horseman, and some modern poet will some day describe to us that
terrible goddess as she takes her place with the stoker
close to the fire of the locomotive engine.    C1 228, XXVII.

It is easy for a man to say that he will banish care, so
that he may enjoy to the full the delights of the moment.
But this is a power which none but a savage possesses--or
perhaps an Irishman.    We have learned the lesson from the
divines, the philosophers, and the poets.    Post equitem
sedet atra cura.    PrM 231-2, XXV,I.

## CAREERS

'There is a tide in the affairs of men
    Which, taken at the flood, leads on to fortune.'
In nine cases out of ten, this flood-tide comes but once in
life, and then in early years.    A man may have a second or
third chance for decent maintenance, but hardly a second
chance for fortune's brighter favours....The right man is
wanted in the right place; but how is a lad of two and
twenty to surmise what place will be right for him?    And
yet, if he surmises wrong, he fails in taking his tide at
its single flood.    How many lawyers are there who should
have been soldiers! how many clergymen who should have been
lawyers! how many unsuccessful doctors who might have done
well on 'Change, or in Capel court!    Ber 33-4,II.

There is, I suppose, no young man possessed of average
talents and average education, who does not early in life
lay out for himself some career with more or less precision.
...In doing this he may not attempt, perhaps, to lay down

for himself any prescribed amount of success which he will
endeavor to reach, or even the very pathway by which he will
be successful; but he will tell himself which are the vices
which he will avoid, and what the virtues which he will
strive to attain. Cl 260-1, XXXI.

## CASTLES

[T]hose strong square, ugly castles, which, two centuries
since, were the general habitations of the landed proprietors of the country, and many of which have been inhabited
even to a much later date...now afford the strongest record
of the apparently miserable state of life, which even the
favoured of the land then endured, and of the numberless
domestic comforts which years and skill have given us, apt
as we are to look back with fond regret to the happy, bygone days of past periods. Kel 132, XI.

## CATCHING A MAN

Men in this world catch their fish by various devices; and
it is necessary that these schemes should be much studied
before a man can call himself a fisherman. It is the same
with women; and Mrs. Cox was an Izaak Walton among her own
sex. Ber 717, XL.

## CATHOLIC CHURCH, ROMAN

To what wrath and sorrow--to what indignation and vexation
has that word [College of Maynooth] lately given rise in the
minds of the truly orthodox members of the Church of
England. In that college is to be implanted the seeds, all
the piety which is to foster and instruct the religious
feeling of Ireland--which is to restrain the vice and
animate the virtue of thirty-two counties, and which not
only is to do it, but which does it; whatever religious
instructions the people of those counties do get, is from
Maynooth; but yet how horrid is it that its students should
be fattened by the contributions of Protestants, and that
the wealth of the orthodox should be squandered in enabling
them to sleep in separate beds.
    It is now pretty generally admitted that we cannot
convert these staunch Romanists to Protestantism--that they
will adhere to their old tenets and principles, and that
they are likely to remain in the errors which they love so
well--nay more, it is pretended by many that they are re-
converting us--that if any essential movement is being made
by either party, that it is the Church of Rome, which is
advancing. MB 83-5, II,III.

In Europe there is no country where the religion of Rome is
so sincerely trusted to, and acted on as in Ireland. In
France it now, where it exists, serves for little better
than amusement. In Spain so long its strong hold--its
enthusiasm has all but perished, and the church even now is
fighting against itself. In Italy, even in the Papal

States, it is considered rather as gorgeous pageantry than as a religion sent from God for the guidance of mankind. In Flanders it bears the nearest resemblance to the warm fidelity of Ireland--but even there it is among the women that its strong influence is to be found. Rarely in either of these countries one finds men of education believing in, submitting to, and guided by the religion which they possess, and allowing that by that only can they regulate their conduct in this world, and hope to meet salvation in the next.

Such is the case though in Ireland--the people have a real though sincere belief in their creed--whether they act according to its tenets or no--whether they are good or bad they no more doubt the truth of the doctrines they have learnt than they doubt their own existence. I have met no Romanist Irishman who would express the remotest doubt as to any portion of the doctrines of the creed of his church--miraculous and difficult to believe as they are--and it is this unshaken belief--this firm sincerity of trust which has kept Ireland so faithful to her church, through all the frightful means which have been taken to convert her. MB 107-8, III,III.

## CATHOLICS

His...religion was not of that bitter kind in which we in England are apt to suppose that all the Irish Roman Catholics indulge. PF 2, I,I.

There are two modes of catching these votes. This or that individual Roman Catholic may be promoted to place, so that he personally may be made secure; or the right hand of fellowship may be extended to the people of the Pope generally, so that the people of the Pope may be taught to think that a general step is being made towards the re-conversion of the nation. The first measure is the easier, but the effect is but slight and soon passes away.... But the other mode, if a step be well taken, may be very efficacious. It has now and then occurred that every Roman Catholic in Ireland and England has been brought to believe that the nation is coming round to them.... To catch the Protestant,--that is the peculiarly Protestant,--vote and the Roman Catholic vote at the same instant is a feat difficult of accomplishment. Way 49-50, LVI,II.

The fervent Romanists have always this point in their favour, that they are ready to believe. And they have a desire for the conversion of men which is honest in an exactly inverse ratio to the dishonesty of the means which they employ to produce it. Way 52, LVI,II.

When a Protestant child does go to a priest on such a mission [to do something remarkable], what can the priest do but accept him? He is bound to look upon the suppliant as a brand to be saved from the burning. "You stupid young ass!" the priest may say to himself, apostrophising the boy;

"why don't you remain as you are for the present? Why do
you come to trouble me with a matter you can know nothing
about?" But the priest must do as his Church directs him,
and the brands have to be saved from the burning.
Land 46-7, III,I.

## CAUSES

When a man will do this [give annoyance and cause a dis-
turbance] pertinaciously, and when his selected enemy is
wealthy and of high standing, he will generally succeed in
getting a party round him. AS 476, LXIX.

## CENSURE

Such censure [of the police for failing to find a
criminal], as we all know, is very common, and in nine cases
out of ten it is unjust. They who write it probably know
but little of the circumstances;--and, in speaking of a
failure here and a failure there, make no reference to the
numerous successes, which are so customary as to partake of
the nature of routine. It is the same in regard to all
public matters, army matters, navy matters, poor-law
matters, and post office matters. Day after day, and almost
every day, one meets censure which is felt to be unjust;--
but the general result of all this injustice is increased
efficiency. The coach does go the faster because of the
whip in the coachman's hand, though the horses driven may
never have deserved the thong. ED 88, XLIX,II.

You can run down a demi-god only by making him out to be a
demi-devil. Way 413, XLIV,I.

The man who will not endure censure has to take care that he
does not deserve it. DrW 82, VIII, Part III.

## CHAIRMANSHIP

A man usually receives some compensation for having gone
through the penance of the chairman's duties. For the
remainder of the evening he is entitled to the flattery of
his companions, and generally receives it till they become
tipsy and insubordinate. RacR 354, XXVII.

## CHANCE

It is a small and narrow point that turns the rushing train
to the right or to the left. The rushing man is often
turned off by a point as small and narrow. HHOG 120, IX.

## CHARACTER

Persons...so argue of those whom they meet in the real
living world, are ignorant of the twists and turns, and
rapid changes in character which are brought about by
outward circumstances. Many a youth, abandoned by his
friends to perdition on account of his folly, might have yet

prospered, had his character not been set down as gone, before, in truth, it was well formed. It is not one calf only that should be killed for the returning prodigal. Oh, fathers, mothers, uncles, aunts, guardians, and elderly friends in general, kill seven fatted calves if seven should unfortunately be necessary!  TC 336-7, XXVIII.

I am inclined to think that they [commonsense and an honest purpose] are often a sufficient counterpoise to a considerable amount of worldly experience.  If one could have the worldly experience also--!  True!  but then it is so difficult to get everything.  FrP 268, XXVIII.

So much in this world depends upon character that attention has to be paid to bad character even when it is not deserved.  In dealing with men and women, we have to consider what they believe, as well as what we believe ourselves.  The utility of a sermon depends much on the idea that the audience has of the piety of the man who preaches it.  Though the words of God should never have come with greater power from the mouth of man, they will come in vain if they be uttered by one who is known as a breaker of the Commandments;--they will come in vain from the mouth of one who is even suspected to be so.  DrW 25-6, III, Part I.

Do we not all know that if a man be under a cloud the very cloud will make him more attentive to his duties than another?  If a man, for the wages which he receives, can give to his employer high character as well as work, he will think that he may lighten his work because of his character. DrW 93, IX, Part III.

CHARACTERS, DUAL

Within the figure and frame and clothes and cuticle, within the bones and flesh of many of us, there is but one person, --a man or woman, with a preponderance either of good or evil, whose conduct in any emergency may be predicted with some assurance of accuracy by any one knowing the man or woman.  Such persons are simple, single, and, perhaps, generally, safe.  They walk along lines in accordance with certain fixed instincts or principles, and are today as they were yesterday, and will be to-morrow as they are to-day. ...But there are human beings who, though of necessity single in body, are dual in character;--in whose breasts not only is evil always fighting against good,--but to whom evil is sometimes horribly, hideously evil, but is sometimes also not hideous at all.  Of such men it may be said that Satan obtains an intermitent grasp, from which, when it is released, the rebound carries them high amidst virtuous resolutions and a thorough love of things good and noble. Such men,--or women,--may hardly, perhaps, debase themselves with the more vulgar vices.  They will not be rogues, or thieves, or drunkards,--or, perhaps, liars; but ambition, luxury, self-indulgence, pride, and covetousness will get a hold of them and in various moods will be to them virtues in lieu of vices.  ED 163-4, XVIII,I.

## CHARACTERISTICS

Thus a man who always wears a green coat does not become remarkable by a new green coat; he is only so much the more than ever, the man in the green coat.  Kel 137, XI.

## CHARITY

Not even from charity will pleasure come, if charity be taken up simply to appease remorse.  Cl 101, XII.

Men in this world would have to go naked if they gave their coats to the robbers who took their cloaks; and going naked is manifestly inexpedient.  VOB 398, LV.

## CHASTISEMENT

We all know with how light a rod a father chastises the son he loves, let Solomon have given what counsel he may to the contrary.  TC 208, XVIII.

## CHILDREN

How the aspirations, and instincts, and feeling of a household become changed as the young birds begin to flutter with feathered wings, and have half-formed thoughts of leaving the parental nest!  DoT 170, XIV.

[F]or it is hardly more than a knack, that aptitude which some men have of gaining the good graces of the young.  Such men are not always the best of fathers or the safest guardians; but they carry about with them a certain <u>duc ad</u> <u>me</u> which children recognise, and which in three minutes upsets all the barriers between five and five-and-forty. FrP 345, XXXVI.

It is of such  [a beautiful fair little thing, with long soft curls, and lips red as a rose, and large, bright blue eyes, all soft and happy and laughing, loving the friends of her childhood with passionate love, and fully expecting an equal devotion from them], children that our wives and sweethearts should be made.  OrF 221-2, XXII,I.

If no one goes the child can bear it.  But to see others go, and to be left behind, is too much for the feelings of any child.  OrF 407, XL,I.

Now the general opinion of the world is certainly quite the reverse--namely this, that children as long as they are under the control of their parents, should be hindered and prevented in those things to which they are most inclined. Of course, the world in general, in carrying out this practice, excuses it by an assertion,--made to themselves or others--that children customarily like those things which they ought not to like.  OrF 71, XLVII,II.

A child, when it is ill, has buttered toast and a picture-book instead of bread-and-milk and lessons.  PF 210,XXIII,I.

## CHILTERN HUNDREDS

The Stewardship of the Chiltern Hundreds!    Does it never occur to anyone how many persons are appointed to that valuable situation?    Or does anyone ever reflect why a Member of Parliament, when he wishes to resign his post of honour, should not be simply gazetted in the newspapers as having done so, instead of being named as the new Steward of the Chiltern Hundreds?    No one ever does think of it; resigning and becoming a steward are one and the same thing, with this difference, however, that one of the grand bulwarks of the British constitution is thus preserved.
TC 282, XXIV.
Editor's note:    A member of Parliament may not resign as long as he is qualified.    However, he may apply for the Stewardship of the Chiltern Hundreds, a fictitious office, and this appointment disqualifies him for membership in Parliament;    the Stewardship may be resigned, thus opening the fiction to the next member who needs it.    It is interesting to note that in The Three Clerks Undy Scott applied for the Stewardship and was refused.    "Her Majesty could not consent to entrust to him the duties of the situation in question--;  and in lieu thereof the House expelled him by its unanimous voice."

## CHINS

How many a face, otherwise lovely to look upon, is made mean and comparatively base, either by the lengthening or the shortening of the chin!    OML 27, III.

## CHURCH, DECORATED

I do not know of anything more pleasant to the eye than a pretty country church, decorated for Christmas-day.    The effect in a city is altogether different.    I will not say that churches there should not be decorated, but comparatively it is a matter of indifference.    No one knows who does it.    The peculiar munificence of the squire who has sacrificed his holly bushes is not appreciated.    The work of the fingers that have been employed is not recognized.    The efforts made for hanging the pendent wreaths to each capital have been of no special interest to any large number of the worshippers.    It has been done by contract, probably, and even if well done has none of the grace of association.
OrF 219, XXII,I.

## CHURCH, HIGH

A few high church vagaries do not...sit amiss on the shoulders of a young dean's wife.    It shows at any rate that her heart is in the subject; and it shows moreover that she is removed, wide as the poles asunder, from that cesspool of

abomination....Anathema maranatha!    Let   anything  else  be
held   as  blessed,  so  that  that  be  well  cursed.    Welcome
kneelings and bowings, welcome matins and complines, welcome
bell,   book,   and   candle,   so   that...dirty  surplices  and
cermonial   Sabbaths   be   held   in   due   execration!
    If  it  be  essentially  and  absolutely  necessary  to  choose
between  the  two,  we  are  inclined  to  agree...that  the  bell,
book,   and   candle   are   the   lesser   evil   of   the   two.    Let  it
however  be  understood  that  no  such  necessity  is  admitted  in
these  pages.    BaT  507,  LIII.

## CHURCH ATTENDANCE

Who  has  courage  to  remain  from  church  when  staying  at  the
clergyman's  house?    No  one  ever;  unless  it  be  the  clergyman's  wife,  or  perhaps  an  independent  self-willed  daughter.
Ber  470,  XXVI.

This   [going  to  afternoon]    church  is  not  held  to  be  de
rigueur  even  in  a  parson's  house,  unless  it  be  among  certain
of  the  strictly  low-church  clergymen.    A  very  high  churchman
may  ask  you  to  attend  at  four  o'clock  of  a  winter  morning,
but  he  will  not  be  grievously  offended  if,  on  a  Sunday
afternoon,  you  prefer  your  armchair,  and  book--probably  of
sermons;  but  that  is  between  you  and  your  conscience.
Ber  473,  XXVI.

## CHURCH SERVICE

It  appears  to  us  a  question  whether  any  clergyman  can  go
through  our  church  service  with  decorum,  morning  after
morning,  in  an  immense  building,  surrounded  by  not  more  than
a  dozen  listeners.    The  best  actors  cannot  act  well  before
empty  benches,  and  though  there  is,  of  course,  a  higher
motive  in  one  case  than  the  other,  still  even  the  best  of
clergymen  cannot  but  be  influenced  by  their  audience;  and  to
expect  that  a  duty  should  be  well  done  under  such  circumstances,  would  be  to  require  from  human  nature  more  than
human  power.    War  204,  XVI.

## CHURCH WEALTH

And  who  has  not  felt  the  same  to  condemn  those  whose  impiety
would  venture  to  disturb  the  goodly  grace  of  cathedral
institutions?...    Who  would  not  feel  charity  for  a
prebendary,  when  walking  the  quiet  length  of  that  long  aisle
at  Winchester,  looking  at  those  decent  houses,  that  trim
grassplat,  and  feeling,  as  one  must,  the  solemn,  orderly
comfort  of  the  spot!  Who  could  be  hard  upon  a  dean  while
wandering  round  the  sweet  close  of  Hereford,  and  owning  that
in  that  precinct,  tone  and  colour,  design  and  form,  solemn
tower  and  storied  window,  are  all  in  unison,  and  all
perfect!  Who  could  lie  basking  in  the  cloisters  of
Salisbury,  and  gaze  on  Jewel's  library  and  that  unequalled
spire,  without  feeling  that  bishops  should  sometimes  be
rich!...Who,  without  remorse,  can  batter  down  the  dead
branches  of  an  old  oak,  now  useless,  but,  ah!  still  so

beautiful, or drag out the fragments of the ancient forest, without feeling that they sheltered the younger plants, to which they are now summoned to give way in a tone so peremptory and so harsh?  War 54-5, V.

## CITY MEN

City men can make a budget popular or the reverse. PrM 98, XI,I.

## CITY OFFICES

[B]ut then City offices are poor places, and there are certain City occupations which seem to enjoy the greater credit the poorer are the material circumstances by which they are surrounded.  LasC 327, XXXVII.

## CIVIL SERVANTS

[A] class, not very small in numbers, who, from cultivating in their bosom a certain tendency towards suspicion, have come to think that all Government servants are idle, dilatory, supercilious, and incompetent.  That some of these faults may have existed among those who took wages from the Crown in the time of George III is perhaps true.  And the memory of those times has kept alive the accusation.  The vitality of these prejudices calls to mind the story of the Nottinghamshire farmer who, when told of the return of Charles II, asked what had become of Charles I.  Naseby, Worcester, and the fatal day at Whitehall had not yet reached him.  Tidings of these things had only been approaching him during these twelve years.  The true character of the Civil Service is only now approaching the intelligence of those who are still shaking their heads over the delinquencies of the last century.  JC 417, LVII.

The AEoluses of the Civil Service are necessarily much exercised in their minds by such irregularities [stealing a day from work].  To them personally it matters not at all whether one or another young man may be neglectful.  It may be known to such a one that a Crocker may be missed from his seat without any great injury,--possibly with no injury at all,--to the Queen's service.  There are Crockers whom it would be better to pay for their absence than their pre- sence....But there is a necessity,--almost a necessity,-- that the Crockers of the world should live.  They have mothers, or perhaps even wives, with backs to be clothed and stomachs to be fed, or perhaps with hearts to be broken. There is, at any rate, a dislike to proceed to the ultimate resort of what may be called the capital punishment of the Civil Service.  To threaten, to frown, to scold, to make a young man's life a burden to him, are all within the compass of an official AEolus.  You would think occasionally that such a one was resolved to turn half the clerks in his office out into the streets,--so loud are the threats.  In regard to individuals he often is resolved to do so at the

very next fault.  But when the time comes his heart misgives
him.  Even an AEolus is subject to mercy, and at last his
conscience becomes so callous to his first imperative duty
of protecting the public service, that it grows to be
settled thing with him, that though a man's life is to be
made a burden to him, the man is not to be actually
dismissed.  But there are men to whom you cannot make their
life a burden,--men upon whom no frowns, no scoldings, no
threats operate at all; and men unfortunately sharp enough
to perceive what is that ultimate decision to which their
AEolus had been brought.  MF 246-7, XXIII,I.

## CLEANSING

Such cleansing is to be done.  Men have sinned...and, lepers
though they have been, they have afterwards been clean.  But
that task of cleansing oneself is not an easy one;--the
waters of that Jordan in which it is needful to wash are
scalding hot.   The cool neighbouring streams of life's
pleasant valleys will by no means suffice.
OrF 233, LXIII,II.

## CLERGY

A clergyman generally dislikes to be met in argument by any
scriptual quotation; he feels as affronted as a doctor does,
when recommended by an old woman to take some favourite
dose, or as a lawyer when an unprofessional man attempts to
put him down by a quibble.  War 226, XVIII.

The nolo episcopari, though still in use, is so directly at
variance with the tendency of all human wishes, that it cannot be thought to express the true aspirations of rising
priests in the Church of England.  A lawyer does not sin in
seeking to be a judge, or in compassing his wishes by all
honest means.  A young diplomat entertains a fair ambition
when he looks forward to be the lord of a first-rate
embassy; and a poor novelist when he attempts to rival
Dickens or rise above Fitzjeames, commits no fault, though
he may be foolish.  Sydney Smith truly said that in these
recreant days we cannot expect to find the majesty of St.
Paul beneath the cassock of a curate.  If we look to our
clergymen to be more than men, we shall probably teach
ourselves to think that they are less, and can hardly hope
to raise the character of the pastor by denying to him the
right to entertain the aspirations of man.  BaT 11, I.

Some few years since, even within the memory of many who are
not yet willing to call themselves old, a liberal clergyman
was a person not frequently to be met.  Sydney Smith was
such, and was looked on as little better than an infidel; a
few others also might be named, but they were 'rarae aves,'
and were regarded with doubt and distrust by their brethren.
No man was so surely a tory as a country rector--nowhere
were the powers that be so cherished as at Oxford.
BaT 19, III.

...all such adorments as are possible to a clergyman making a morning visit, such as a clean necktie, clean handkerchief, new gloves, and a soupcon of not unnecessary scent. BaT 249-50, XXVII.

An Englishman's house is his castle. And a rector's parsonage is as much the rector's castle, his own freehold castle, as is the earl's family mansion that of the earl. But it is so with this drawback, that the moment the rector's breath is out of his body, all right and claim to the castle as regards his estate and family cease instantly. If the widow and children remain there for one night, they remain there on sufferance. Ber 456, XXV.

There are no Sabbath-breakers to be compared, in the vehemence of their Sabbath-breaking, to hard-worked parochial clergymen--unless, indeed, it be Sunday-school children who are forced on that day to learn long dark collects, and stand in dread catechismal row before their spiritual pastors and masters. Ber 469-70, XXVI.

Clergymen are subject to the same passions as other men; and, as far as I can see, give way to them, in one line or in another, almost as frequently. Every clergyman should, by canonical rule, feel a personal disinclination to a bishopric; but yet we do not believe that such personal disinclination is generally very strong. FrP 30, LV.

That the priests were to be paid from tithes of the parish produce, out of which tithes certain other goods things were to be bought and paid for, such as church repairs and education, of so much the most of us have an inkling. That a rector, being a big sort of parson, owned the tithes of his parish in full--or at any rate that part of them intended for the clergyman--and that a vicar was somebody's deputy, and therefore entitled only to little tithes, as being a little body: of so much we that are simple in such matters have a general idea. But one cannot conceive that even in this way any approximation could have been made, even in those old mediaeval days, towards a fair proportioning of the pay to the work. At any rate, it is clear enough that there is no such approximation now. And what a screech would there not be among the clergy of the Church, even in these reforming days, if any over-bold reformer were to suggest that such an approximation should be attempted? ...But, nevertheless, one may prophesy that we Englishmen must come to this, disagreeable as the idea undoubtedly is. ...Our present arrangement of parochial incomes is beloved as being time-honoured, gentlemanlike, English, and picturesque....But are there not other attributes very desirable--nay, absolutely necessary-- in respect to which this time-honoured, picturesque arrangement is so very deficient?
    How pleasant it was, too, that one bishop should be getting fifteen thousand a year, and another with an equal

cure of parsons only four!    That a certain prelate could get
twenty thousand one year and his successor in the same
diocese only five the next!    There was something in it
pleasant, and picturesque; it was an arrangement with feudal
charms, and the change which they have made was distasteful
to many of us.    A bishop with a regular salary, and no
appanage of land and land-bailiffs, is only half a bishop.
...One liked to know that there was a dean or two who got
his three thousand a year, and that old Dr. Purple held four
stalls, one of which was golden and the other three silver-
gilt!    Such knowledge was always pleasant to me!    A golden
stall!    How sweet is the sound thereof to church-loving
ears!    But bishops have been shorn of their beauty, and
deans are in their decadence.    A utilitarian age requires
the fatness of the ecclesiastical land, in order that it may
be divided out into small portions of provender, on which
necessary working clergymen can hardly live.    And the full-
blown rectors and vicars, with full-blown tithes--with
tithes when too full-blown for strict utilitarian principles
--will necessarily follow....
    I have a scheme of my own on the subject, which I will
not introduce here, seeing that neither men nor women would
read it.    FrP 136-7, XIV.

I have written much of clergymen, but in doing so I have
endeavoured to portray them as they bear on our social life
rather than to describe the mode and working of their professional careers.    Had I done the latter I could hardly
have steered clear of subjects on which it has not been my
intention to pronounce an opinion, and I should either have
laden my fiction with sermons or I should have degraded my
sermons into fiction.    Therefore I have said but little in
my narrative of this man's feelings or doings as a clergyman.    FrP 407, XLII.

There is a class of country clergymen in England...which is
so closely allied to the squirearchy, as to possess a double
identity.    Such clergymen are not only clergymen, but they
are country gentlemen also.    Cl 282, XXXIII.

No man reverences a clergyman, as a clergyman, so slightly
as a brother clergyman.    LasC 34, V.

Of all persons clergymen are the most irreverent in the
handling of things supposed to be sacred, and next to them
clergymen's wives, and after them those other ladies, old or
young, who take upon themselves semi-clerical duties.    And
it is natural that it should be so; for is it not said that
familiarity does breed contempt?    When a parson takes his
lay friend over his church on a week day, how much less of
the spirit of genuflexion and head-uncovering the clergyman
will display than the layman! The parson pulls about the
woodwork and knocks about the stonework, as though it were
mere wood and stone; and talks aloud in the aisle, and
treats even the reading-desk as a common thing; whereas the
visitor whispers gently, and carries himself as though even

in looking at a church he was bound to regard himself as
performing some service that was half divine.
LasC 137-8, XVI.

Only let us think what a comfortable excitement it would
create throughout England if it was surmised that an
archbishop had forged a deed; and how England would lose
when it was discovered that the archbishop was innocent!
LasC 684, LXXII.

I desire to be allowed to say one word of apology for
myself, in answer to those who have accused me--always without bitterness, and generally with tenderness--of having
forgotten, in writing of clergymen, the first and most
prominent characteristic of the ordinary English clergyman's
life.  I have described many clergymen, they say, but have
spoken of them all as though their professional duties,
their high calling, their daily working for the good of
those around them, were matters of no moment, either to me,
or in my opinion, to themselves.  I would plead, in answer
to this, that my object has been to paint the social and not
the professional lives of clergymen; and that I have been
led to do so, firstly, by a feeling that as no men affect
more strongly, by their own character, the society of those
around than do country clergymen, so, therefore, their
social habits have been worth the labour necessary for
painting them; and secondly, by a feeling that though I, as
a novelist, may feel myself entitled to write of clergymen
out of their pulpits, as I may also write of lawyers and
doctors, I have no such liberty to write of them in their
pulpits.  When I have done so, if I have done so, I have so
far transgressed.  There are those who have told me that I
have made all my clergymen bad, and none good.  I must
venture to hint to such judges that they have taught their
eyes to love a colouring higher than nature justifies....
Had I written an epic about clergymen, I would have taken
St. Paul for my model; but describing, as I have endeavoured
to do, such clergymen as I see around me, I could not
venture to be transcendental.  LasC 781, LXXXIV.

A bishop is as much entitled to cause inquiries to be made
into the moral conduct of a dean as of any other country
clergyman in his diocese.  IHP 91, X,I.

A clergyman's coat used to save him from fighting in fighting days; and even in these days, in which broils and
personal encounters are held to be generally disreputable,
it saves the wearer from certain remote dangers to which
other men are liable.  And the reverse of this is also
true.  It would probably be hard to extract a first blow
from a whole bench of bishops.  And deans, as a rule, are
more sedentary, more quiescent, more given to sufferance
even than bishops.  The normal dean is a goodly, sleek,
bookish man, who would hardly strike a blow under any
provocation.  IHP 90, XLI,II.

An affectionate letter from a bishop must surely be the most
disagreeable missive which a parish clergyman can receive.
Affection from one man to another is not natural in letters.
A bishop never writes affectionately unless he means to
reprove severely.   When he calls a clergyman his 'dear
brother in Christ,' he is sure to go on to show that the man
so called is altogether unworthy of the name.
DrW 154-5, II, Part V.

## CLOTHING

[W]e will not talk about clothing them  [the poor families];
it would be a mockery to call the rags with which the
labouring poor in that part of the country are partially
covered, clothes, or to attach value to them, though I
suppose they must have cost something.  MB 207, VII,II.

Many of us have often thought how severe a trial of faith
must this be to the wives of our great church dignitaries
[seeing the clerical husband dressed in a robe de nuit].
To us these men are personifications of St. Paul; their very
gait is a speaking sermon; their clean and sombre apparel
exacts from us faith and submission; and the cardinal
virtues seem to hover round their sacred hats.  A dean or
archbishop, in the garb of his order, is sure of our reverence, and a well-got-up bishop fills our very souls with
awe.  But how can this feeling be perpetuated in the bosoms
of those who see the bishops without their aprons, and the
archdeacons even in a lower state of dishabille?
    Do we not all know some reverend, all but sacred,
personage before whom our tongue ceases to be loud and our
step to be elastic?  But were we once to see him stretch
himself beneath the bed-clothes, yawn widely, and bury his
face upon his pillow, we could chatter before him as glibly
as before a doctor or a lawyer.  War 17-8, II.

Such consolations  [new clothes]  come home to the heart of
a man, and quite home to the heart of a woman.
BaT 222, XXIV.

A gentleman's costume for a hunting morning is always a slow
one--sometimes so slow and tedious as to make him think of
forswearing such articles of dress for all future ages....
And what dress that Englishmen ever wear is so handsome as
this?  Or we may perhaps say what other dress does English
custom allow them that is in any respect not the reverse of
handsome.  We have come to be so dingy,--in our taste I was
going to say, but it is rather in our want of taste,--so
careless of any of the laws of beauty in the folds and lines
and hues of our dress, so opposed to grace in the arrangement of our persons, that it is not permitted to the
ordinary English gentleman to be anything else but ugly.
Chimney-pot hats, swallow-tailed coats, and pantaloons that
fit nothing, came creeping in upon us, one after the other,
while the Georges reigned--creeping in upon us with such
pictures as we painted under the reign of West, and such

houses as we built under the reign of Nash, till the English
eye required to rest on that which was constrained, dull,
and graceless....Beauty is good in all things; and I
cannot but think that those old Venetian senators, and
Florentine men of Council, owed somewhat of their country's
pride and power to the manner in which they clipped their
beards and wore their flowing garments.

But an Englishman may still make himself brave when he
goes forth into the hunting field. Custom there allows him
colour, and garments that fit his limbs....But any man who
can look well at his club, will look better as he clusters
round the hounds; while many a one who is comely there, is
mean enough as he stands on the hearth-rug before his club
fire. In my mind men, like churches and books, and women
too, should be brave, not mean, in their outward garniture.
CasR 180-3, IX,II.

A man can hardly bear himself nobly unless his outer aspect
be in some degree noble. It may be very sad, this having to
admit that the tailor does in great part make the man; but
such I fear is undoubtedly the fact. Could the Chancellor
look dignified on the woolsack, if he had had an accident
with his wig, or allowed his robes to be torn or soiled?
Does not half the piety of a bishop reside in his lawn
sleeves, and all his meekness in his anti-virile apron?
CasR 270-1, XIV,II.

Sarcastic people are wont to say that the tailor makes the
man. Were I such a one, I might certainly assert that the
milliner makes the bride. As regarding her bridehood,...
the milliner does do much to make her. She would be hardly
a bride if the trousseau were not there....In that moment
in which she finds herself in the first fruition of her
marriage finery she becomes a bride; and in that other
moment when she begins to act upon the finest of these
things as clothes to be packed up, she becomes a wife.
FrP 385-6, XL.

Money was no object. We all know what that means; and
frequently understand, when the words are used, that a blaze
of splendour is to be attained at the cheapest possible
price. FrP 386, XL.

But any young lady who does go into society, whether it be
of county or town, will fully understand the difference
between a liberal and a stingy wardrobe. Girls with slender
provisions of millinery may be fit to go out,--quite fit in
their father's eyes; and yet all such going out may be
matter of intense pain. It is all very well for the world
to say that a girl should be happy without reference to her
clothes. Show me such a girl, and I will show you one whom
I should be very sorry that a boy of mine should choose as
his sweetheart. OrF 65-6, VII,I.

Men when they arrive from their travels now-a-days have no
strippings of greatcoats, no deposits to make of thick

shawls and double gloves, no absolutely necessary changes of raiment.  OrF 110, XI,I.

It may be said of most women who could be found in such a situation   [appearing in criminal court], that they would either give no special heed to their dress on such a morning, or that they would appear in garments of sorrow studiously unbecoming and lachrymose, or that they would attempt to outface the world, and have appeared there in bright trappings, fit for happier days.  OrF 247, LXIV, II.

It was rough, and black, and clinging,--disagreeable to the eye in its shape, as will always be the dress of any woman which is worn day after day through all hours.  RacR 5,I.

It is easy to suppose that Juan wore a Turkish cap when he sat with Haidee in Lambro's island.   But we may be quite sure that he did not wear an apron.  LasC 570, LX.

Whether trade did well or ill, whether wages were high or low, whether provisions were cheap in price, whether there were peace or war between capital and labour, still there was the Sunday magnificence.   What a blessed thing it is for women,--and for men too certainly,--that there should be a positive happiness to the female sex in the possession, and in exhibiting the possession, of bright clothing!  It is almost as good for the softening of manners, and the not permitting of them to be ferocious, as is the faithful study of the polite arts.  VOB 59, IX.

Where is the woman who, when she has been pleased, will not show her pleasure by some sign in her outward garniture? VOB 474, LXVI.

We all know the peculiar solemnity of a widow's dress,--the look of self-sacrifice on the part of the woman which the dress creates; and have perhaps recognised the fact that if the woman be deterred by no necessities of oeconomy in her toilet,--as in such material circumstances the splendour is more perfect if splendour be the object,--so also is the self-sacrifice more abject.  EE 122-3, VII,II.

...those fortunate beings to whose nature belongs a facility of being well dressed, or almost an impossibility of being ill-dressed.  We all know the man,--a little man generally who moves seldom and softly,--who looks always as though he had just been sent home in a bandbox.  PrM 5-6, I,I.

[T]he real miner, when he is away from his work, puts on his best clothes, and endeavours to look as little rough as possible.  JC 38, V.

## COACHES

[A]s all the world knows St. Michael is, or was a year or two back, the end of the railway travelling in that

direction....[T]he journey from St. Michael to Susa was
still made by the diligences....The coupe of a diligence,
or, better still, the banquette, was a luxurious mode of
travelling as compared with anything that our coaches
offered.   There used indeed to be a certain halo of glory
round the occupant of the box of a mail-coach.   The man who
had secured that seat was supposed to know something about
the world, and to be such a one that the passengers sitting
behind him would be proud to be allowed to talk to him.   But
the prestige of the position was greater than the comfort.
A night on the box of a mail-coach was but a bad time, and a
night inside a mail-coach was a night in purgatory.   Whereas
a seat up above, on the banquette of a diligence passing
over the Alps, with room for the feet, and support for the
back, with plenty of rugs and plenty of tobacco, used to be
on the Mont Cenis, and still is on some other mountain
passes, a very comfortable mode of seeing a mountain route.
For those desirous of occupying the coupe, or the three
front seats of the body of the vehicle, it must be admitted
that difficulties frequently arose; and that such difficulties were very common at St. Michael.   There would be two
or three of those enormous vehicles preparing to start for
the mountain, whereas it would appear that twelve or fifteen
passengers had come down from Paris armed with tickets
assuring them that this preferable mode of travelling should
be theirs.   And then assertions would be made, somewhat
recklessly, by the officials, to the effect that all the
diligence was coupe.   It would generally be the case that
some middle-aged Englishman who could not speak French would
go to the wall, together with his wife.   Middle-aged
Englishmen with their wives, who can't speak French, can
nevertheless be very angry, and threaten loudly, when they
suppose themselves to be ill-treated.   A middle-aged
Englishman, though he can't speak a word of French, won't
believe a French official who tells him that the diligence
is all coupe, when he finds himself with his unfortunate
partner in a round-about place behind with two priests, a
dirty man who looks like a brigand, a sick maid-servant, and
three agricultural labourers.   The attempt, however, was
frequently made, and thus there used to be occasionally a
little noise round the bureau at St. Michael.
HKHWR 348-50, XXXVII.


## COALITIONS

When one branch of a Coalition has gradually dropped off,
the other branch will hardly flourish long.   And then the
tints of a political Coalition are so neutral and unalluring
that men will only endure them when they feel that no more
pronounced colours are within their reach.   PrM 260, LXVIII.


## COLONIALS

The Foreign Office is always very civil to its next-door
neighbours of the colonies,--civil and cordial, though
perhaps a little patronising.   A minister is a bigger man

than a governor; and the smallest of the diplomatic fry are greater swells than even secretaries in quite important dependencies. The attache, though he be unpaid, dwells in a capital, and flirts with a countess. The governor's right-hand man is confined to an island, and dances with a planter's daughter. The distinction is quite understood, but is not incompatible with much excellent good feeling on the part of the superior department. HKHWR 705-6, LXXV.

## COMING OF AGE

That coming of age must be a delightful time to a young man born to inherit broad acres and wide wealth. Those full-mouthed congratulations; those warm prayers with which his manhood is welcomed by the grey-haired seniors of the county; the affectionate, all but motherly caresses of neighbouring mothers who have seen him grow up from his cradle, of mothers who have daughters, perhaps, fair enough, and good enough, and sweet enough even for him; the soft-spoken, half-bashful, but tender greetings of the girls, who now, perhaps for the first time, call him by his stern family name, instructed by instinct rather than precept that the time has come when the familiar Charles or familiar John must by them be laid aside; the 'lucky dogs,' and hints of silver spoons which are poured into his ears as each young compeer slaps his back and bids him live a thousand years and then never die; the shouting of the tenantry, the good wishes of the old farmers who come up to wring his hand, the kisses which he gets from the farmers' wives, and the kisses which he gives to the farmers' daughters; all these things must make the twenty-first birthday pleasant enough to a young heir. To a youth, however, who feels that he is now liable to arrest, and that he inherits no other privilege, the pleasure may very possibly not be quite so keen. DoT 8-9, I.

Nature often does postpone the ceremony [becoming a man] even to a much later age [than twenty-one];--sometimes, altogether forgets to accomplish it. DoT 365, XXX.

## COMMERCE

OH COMMERCE, how wonderful are thy ways, how vast thy power, how invisible thy dominion! Who can restrain thee and forbid thy farther progress? Kings are but as infants in thy hands, and emperors, despotic in all else, are bound to obey thee! Thou civilizest, hast civilized, and wilt civilize. Civilization is thy mission, and man's welfare thine appointed charge. The nation that most warmly fosters thee shall ever be the greatest in the earth; and without thee no nation shall endure for a day. Thou art our Alpha and our Omega, our beginning and our end; the marrow of our bones, the salt of our life, the sap of our branches, the corner-stone of our temple, the rock of our foundation. We are built on thee, and for thee, and with thee. To worship thee should be man's chiefest care, to know thy hidden ways his chosen study.

One maxim hast thou, oh Commerce, great and true, and profitable above all others--one law which thy votaries should never transgress:  'Buy in the cheapest market and sell in the dearest.'  Str 14, II.

When a man advertises that he has 40,000 new paletots, he does not mean that he has got that number packed up in a box....If a tradesman can induce a lady to buy a diagonal Osnabruck Cashmere shawl by telling her that he has 1200 of them, who is injured?  And if the shawl is not exactly a real diagonal Osnabruck Cashmere, what harm is done as long as the lady gets the value for her money?  And if she don't get the value for her money, who fault is that?  isn't it a fair stand-up fight?  And when she tries to buy for 4[pounds] a shawl which she thinks is worth about 8[pounds], isn't she dealing on the same principles herself?  If she be lucky enough to possess credit, the shawl is sent home without payment, and three years afterward fifty per cent. is perhaps offered for settlement of the bill.  It is a fair fight, and the ladies are very well able to take care of themselves.  Str 29, V.

## COMMERCIAL ROOMS

And here it may be well to explain that ordinary travellers are in this respect badly treated by the customs of England, or rather by the hotel-keepers.  All inn-keepers have commercial rooms, as certainly as they have taps and bars, but all of them do not have commercial rooms in the properly exclusive sense.  A stranger, therefore, who has asked for and obtained his mutton-chop in the commercial room of The Dolphin, The Bear, and The George, not unnaturally asks to be shown into the same chamber at the King's Head.  But the King's Head does a business with real commercials, and the stranger finds himself--out of his element.  OrF 49, VI,I.

At such houses the commercial room is as much closed against the uninitiated as is a first-class club in London.  In such rooms a non-commercial man would be almost as much astray as is a non-broker in Capel Court, or an attorney in a bar mess-room....Certain commercial laws are maintained in such apartments.  Cigars are not allowed before nine o'clock, except upon some distinct arrangement with the waiter. There is not, as a rule, a regular daily commercial repast; but when three or more gentlemen dine together at five o'clock, the dinner becomes a commercial dinner, and the commercial laws as to wine,&c., are enforced, with more or less restriction as circumstances may seem to demand....The commercial gentleman is of his nature gregarious, and although he be exclusive to a strong degree,...he will condescend, when the circumstances of his profession have separated him from his professional brethren, to be festive with almost any gentleman whom chance may throw in his way. VOB 202, XXIX.

## COMMUNICATION

Men never can do so [speak truly] in words, let the light
within themselves be ever so clear.   I do not think that any
man yet ever had such a gift of words as to make them a
perfect exponent of all the wisdom within him.
CanY 380, LXXVII,II.

## COMPETITION

This is undoubtedly the age of humanity--as far, at least,
as England is concerned.  A man who beats his wife is shocking to us, and a colonel who cannot manage his soldiers
without having them beaten is nearly equally so.  We are not
very fond of hanging; and some of us go so far as to recoil
under any circumstances from taking the blood of life....
     But in the inner feelings of men to men, and of one
man's mind to another man's mind, is it not an age of
extremest cruelty?
     There is sympathy for the hungry man; but there is no
sympathy for the unsuccessful man who is not hungry.  If a
fellow mortal be ragged, humanity will subscribe to mend his
clothes; but humanity will subscribe nothing to mend his
ragged hopes so long as his outside coat shall be whole and
decent.
     To him that hath shall be given; and from him that hath
not shall be taken even that which he hath.  This is the
special text that we delight to follow, and success is the
god that we delight to worship.  "Ah!   pity me.   I have
struggled and fallen--struggled so manfully, yet fallen so
utterly--help me up this time that I may yet push forward
once again!"  Who listens to such a plea as this?   "Fallen!
do you want bread?"  "Not bread, but a kind heart and a kind
hand."  "My friend, I cannot stay by you; I myself am in a
hurry; there is that fiend of a rival there even now gaining
a step on me.   I beg your pardon; but I will put my foot on
your shoulder--only for one moment.   Occupet extremum
scabies."
     Yes.   Let the devil take the hindmost; the three or
four hindmost if you will; nay, all but those strong-running
horses who can force themselves into noticeable places under
the judge's eye.   This is the noble shibboleth with which
the English youth are now spurred on to deeds of--what shall
we say?--money-making activity.  Let every place in which a
man can hold up his head be the reward of some antagonistic
struggle, of some grand competitive examination!  Let us get
rid of the fault of past ages.   With us, let the race be
ever to the swift; the victory always to the strong.   And
let us always be racing, so that the swift and strong shall
ever be known among us.   But what, then, for those who are
not swift, not strong?   Vae victis!   Let them go to the
wall.   They can hew wood probably; or, at any rate, draw
water....
     But, nevertheless, let all our work be done by
race-horses; all, at least, that shall be considered
honourable.  Let us have strength and speed.  And how shall

we know who are strong and swift if we do not train our
horses to run against each other? But this early racing
will hardly produce that humanity of spirit of which we now
deplore the want. 'The devil take the hindmost' is the very
essence of the young man's book of proverbs. The devil
assuredly will take all the hindmost. None but the very
foremost can enter the present heaven of good things.
Therefore, oh my brother, my friend, thou companion of my
youth! may the devil take thee; thee quickly, since it needs
must be thee or me.

Vae victis--alas! for these hindmost ones; there are
so many of them! The skim-milk will always be so much more
in quantity than the cream.... That milk has been skimmed;
the cream has been taken away. No matter; skim it again.
There shall be something yet which we will call cream.
Competitive examination will produce something that shall
look to be strong; that shall be swift, if it be only for a
start of twenty yards.

This is the experiment of the present day. Wise men
say that when nothing but cream is accepted, all mankind,
all boykind rather, will prepare itself for a skimming of
some sort; and that the quantity of cream produced will be
immense....

'Thompson,' says Johnson, the young poet, when he has
at last succeeded in getting the bosomest of his friends
alone into his chamber with him, 'have you happened to look
at my Iphigenia yet?'

Thompson can't say that he has. He has been busy; has
had so many water-parties; and then, somehow, he doesn't
think that he is very partial to modern poetry on subjects
of old mythology. Of course, however, he means to read it--
some of these days.

'I wish you would,' says Johnson, tendering a copy of
the thin volume. 'I really wish you would; and let me have
your candid opinion. The press certainly have not noticed
it much, and what they have said has been very lukewarm.'

'I am sorry for that,' says Thompson, looking grave.

'And I did my best with it too. You would hardly
believe how hard I worked at it. There is not a line that
has not been weighed and written, perhaps, three times over.
I do not think I am conceited; but I cannot but believe that
there is something in it. The reviewers are so jealous! if
a man has not a name, they will give him credit for nothing;
and it is so hard to begin.'

'I am sure it is,' says Thompson.

'I don't expect fame; and as for money, of course I
don't think of that. But I should like to know that it had
been read by one or two persons who could understand it. I
have given to it the best of my time, the best of my labour.
I cannot but think that there is something in it.' Thus
pleads the unsuccessful one for mercy.

And thus answers to him the successful one, with no
grain of mercy in his composition:--'My dear Johnson, my
maxim is this, that in this world every man gets in the long
run exactly what he deserves--'.

'Did Milton get what he deserved?'

'These are not the days of Milton. I don't want to hurt your feelings; but old friends as we are, I should not forgive myself if I didn't tell you what I really think. Poetry is all very well; but you can't create a taste for it if it doesn't exist. Nobody that I know of cares a d____ for Iphigenia.'

'You think I should change my subject, then?'

'To tell you the truth, I think you should change your trade. This is the third attempt, you know. I dare say they are very good in their way; but if the world like them, the world would have found it out by this time. " Vox populi, vox Dei"--that is my motto--I don't trust my own judgement; I trust that of the public. If you will take my advice, you will give up Iphigenia and the rest of them. You see you are doing nothing whatever at the bar,'&c.,& c.

And thus Johnson is left, without a scrap of comfort, a word of consolation, a spark of sympathy; and yet he had given to that Iphigenia of his best that was in him to give. Had his publisher sold ten thousand copies of it, how Thompson would have admired it! how he would have pressed the poet in his arms, and have given him champagne up at Richmond! To fail is to be disgraced. Vae victis!

There is something very painful in these races, which we English are always running, to one who has tenderness enough to think of the nine beaten horses instead of the one who has conquered. Look at that list which has just come out after our grand national struggle at Cambridge. How many wranglers are there? Thirty, shall we say? and it is always glorious to be a wrangler. Out of that thirty there is probably but one who has not failed, who is not called on to submit to the inward grief of having been beaten. The youth who is second, who has thus shown himself to be possessed of a mass of erudition sufficient to crush an ordinary mind to the earth, is ready to eat his heart with true bitterness of spirit. After all his labour, his midnight oil, his many sleepless nights, his deserted pleasures, his racking headaches, Amaryllis abandoned, and Neaera seen in the arms of another--! After all this, to be beaten by Jones! Had it been Green or Smith he could have borne it. Would it not have been better to do as others had done? he could have been contented to have gone out in the crowd; but there is nothing so base as to be second--and then second to Jones!

Out of the whole lot, Jones alone is contented; and he is told by his physician that he must spend his next two winters at Cairo. The intensity of his application has put his lungs into very serious jeopardy. Ber 1-8, I.

## COMPLEXION

For myself I am not sure that I love a clear complexion. Pink and white alone will not give that hue which seems best to denote light and life, and to tell of a mind that thinks and of a heart that feels. OrF 185, XIX,I.

## CONDOLENCES

How often are men found who can speak words on such
occasions that are not commonplaces,--that really stir the
soul, and bring true comfort to the listener?  The humble
listener may receive comfort even from commonplace words.
Bel 108, IX.

## CONDUCTORS

Why conductors of diligences should object to such relief
[letting passengers get out and walk]  to their horses the
ordinary Englishman can hardly understand.  But in truth
they feel so deeply the responsibility which attaches itself
to their shepherding of their sheep, that they are always
fearing lest some poor lamb should go astray on the mountain
side.  And though the road be broad and very plainly marked,
the conductor never feels secure that his passenger will
find his way safely to the summit.  He likes to know that
each of his flock is in his right place, and disapproves
altogether of an erratic spirit.  HKHWR 365, XXXVII.

## CONFESSION

To men such a necessity   [confession of having behaved
badly] is always grievous.  Women not infrequently like the
task.  To confess, submit, and be accepted as confession and
submitting, comes naturally to the feminine mind.  The cry
of peccavi sounds soft and pretty when made by sweet lips in
a loving voice.  But the man who can own that he has done
amiss without a pang,--who can so own it to another man, or
even to a woman,--is usually but a poor creature.
Cl 350, XLI.

## CONFIDENCES

There are some moments in life in which both men and women
feel themselves imperatively called on to make a confidence;
in which not to do so requires a disagreeable resolution and
also a disagreeable suspicion.  There are people of both
sexes who never make confidences; who are never tempted by
momentary circumstances to disclose their secrets; but such
are generally dull, close, unimpassioned spirits, 'gloomy
gnomes, who live in cold dark mines.'  BaT 397, XLI.

[B]ut as it is often difficult to obtain a confidence, so is
it impossible to stop it in the midst of its effusion.
Bel 236, XVIII.

When one is in trouble it is a great ease to tell one's
trouble to a friend; but then one should always wash one's
dirty linen at home.  HKHWR 38, IV.

[B]ut it is so hard to restrain oneself from confidence when
difficulties arise!  AS 418, LXI.

## CONFINEMENT

Poverty!--how could any man be poor who had liberty to roam the world? We all of us acknowledge that the educated man who breaks the laws is justly liable to a heavier punishment than he who has been born in ignorance, and bred, as it were, in the lap of sin; but we hardly realize how much greater is the punishment which, when he be punished, the educated man is forced to undergo. Confinement to the man whose mind has never been lifted above vacancy is simply remission from labour. Confinement, with labour, is simply the enforcement of that which has hitherto been his daily lot. But what must a prison be to him whose intellect has received the polish of the world's poetry, who has known what it is to feed more than the belly, to require other aliment than bread and meat?

And then, what does the poor criminal lose? His all, it will be said; and the rich can lose no more. But this is not so. No man loses his all by any sentence which a human judge can inflict....But the one man has too often had no self-respect to risk; the other has stood high in his own esteem, has held his head proudly before the world, has aspired to walk in some way after the fashion of a god. TC 519, XLIII.

## CONJURING

When you see a young woman read a closed book placed on her dorsal vertebrae,--if you do believe that she so reads it, you think that she is endowed with a wonderful faculty! And should you also be made to believe that the same young woman had direct communication with Abraham, by means of some in- visible wire, you would be apt to do a great many things as that young woman might tell you. Conjuring, when not known to be conjuring, is very effective. DuC 165-6, XXI.

## CONSCIENCE

We are too apt to forget when we think of the sins and faults of men how keen may be their conscience in spite of their sins. CoH 197, XVII.

## CONSERVATIVES

The Conservatives were at that time in, and were declared foes to free trade in corn. They were committed to the maintenance of a duty on imported wheat--if any men were ever politically committed to anything. Indeed, it had latterly been their great shibboleth--latterly; that is, since their other greater shibboleths had been cut from under their feet.

At that time men had not learnt thoroughly by experience, as now they have, that no reform, no innovation --experience almost justifies us saying no revolution-- stinks so foully in the nostrils of an English Tory politician as to be absolutely irreconcilable to him. When

taken in the refreshing waters of office any such pill can
be swallowed....A poor Whig premier has none but the
Liberals to back him; but a reforming Tory will be backed by
all the world--except those few whom his own dishonesty will
personally have disgusted.
   But at that time--some twelve or fifteen years since--
all this was not a part of the political A B C;...Lord
chancellorships and lord chief-justiceships, though not
enjoyed till middle life, or, indeed, till the evening of a
lawyer's days, must, in fact, be won or lost in the heyday
of his career. One false step in his political novitiate
may cost him everything. A man when known as a recognized
Whig may fight battle after battle with mercernary electors,
sit yawning year after year till twelve o'clock, ready to
attack on every point the tactics of his honourable and
learned friend on the Treasury seats, and yet see junior
after junior rise to the bench before him--and all because
at starting he decided wrongly as to his party.
Ber 281-2, XVI.

There have been backslidings...it is true; but then, in what
county have there not been such backslidings? Where, in
these pinchbeck days, can we hope to find the old agricultural virtue in all its purity? FrP 11, II.

The Conservative party now and then does put its shoulder to
the wheel, ostensibly with the great national object above
named  [to prevent the coach from being hurried along at a
destructive pace]; but also actuated by a natural desire to
keep its own head well above water and be generally doing
something, so that other parties may not suppose that it is
moribund. There are, no doubt, members of it who really
think that when some object has been achieved,...the coach
has been really stopped....The handle of the windlass has
been broken, the wheel is turning fast the reverse way, and
the rope of Radical progress is running back. Who knows
what may not be regained if the Conservative party will only
put its shoulder to the wheel and take care that the handle
of the windlass be not mended! Sticinthemud, which has ever
been a doubtful little borough, has just been carried by a
majority of fifteen! A long pull, a strong pull, and a pull
altogether,--and the old day will come back again. Vener-
able patriarchs think of Lord Liverpool and other heroes,
and dream dreams of Conservative bishops, Conservative lord-
lieutenants, and of a Conservative ministry that shall
remain in for a generation. Way 31, LIV,II. See also
TORIES.

## CONSERVATIVES...WHIGS

There is no one so devoutly resolved to admit of no superior
as your Conservative, born and bred, no one so inclined to
high domestic despotism as your thoroughgoing consistent old
Whig. DoT 240, XIX.

## CONSOLATION

This kind of consolation  [hugging a baby]  from the world's deceit is very common.
Mothers obtain it from their children, and men from their dogs.  Some men even do so from their walking-sticks, which is just as rational.  How is it that we can take joy to ourselves in that we are not deceived by those who have not attained the art to deceive us?  In a true man, if such can be found, or a true woman, much consolation may indeed be taken.  BaT 432, XLIV.

When we console ourselves by our own arguments, we are not apt to examine their accuracy with much strictness.
Bel 384, XXIX.

## CONSTITUTION

It is wonderful how much disgrace of that kind a borough or county can endure without flinching; and wonderful, also, seeing how supreme is the value attached to the Constitution by the realm at large, how very little the principles of that Constitution are valued by the people in detail.
FP 458, XLVII.

## CONSUMPTION

Oh!   consumption, thou scourge of England's beauty!   how many mothers,  grasping  with  ill-suppressed  fears,  have listened  to  such  words  as  these--have  listened  and  then hoped;  listened  again  and  hoped  again  with  fainter  hopes; have listened again, and then hoped no more!   TC 363, XXX.

Men and women, or I should rather say ladies and gentlemen, used long ago, when they gave signs of weaknes about the chest, to be sent to the south of Devonshire; after that, Madeira came into fashion; but now they are all despatched to Grand Cairo.  Cairo has grown to be so near home, that it will soon cease to be beneficial, and then the only air capable of revigorating the English lungs will be that of Labuan or Jeddo.
But at the present moment, Grand Cairo has the vogue.
Ber 666, XXXVIII.

## CONTUMELY

Let a man endure to heap contumely on his own head, and he will silence the contumely of others--for the moment.
FrP 320, XXXIII.

## CONVENTIONS

Conventions are apt to go very quickly, one after another, when the first has been thrown aside.  The man who ceases to dress for dinner soon finds it to be a trouble to wash his hands.  A house is a bore.  Calling is a bore.  Church is a

great bore.   A family is a bore.   A wife is an unendurable
bore.   All laws are bores, except those by which inferiors
can be constrained to do their work.   AyA 155, XVII.

## COUNSELLORS

A marchioness in one's family is a tower of strength, no
doubt; but there are counsellors so strong that we do not
wish to trust them, lest in trusting we ourselves be overwhelmed by their strength.  LasC 14, II.

## COURAGE

How can he who deserts his own colours at the first smell of
gunpowder expect faith in any ally.   Thou thyself hath
sought the battlefield; fight out the battle manfully now
thou art there.   Courage...courage.  BaT 148, XVII.

It is so hard to conquer when the prestige of former victories is all against one.   It is so hard for the cock who has
once been beaten out of his yard to resume his courage and
again take a proud place upon a dunghill.  BaT 237, XXVI.

Alas, alas!  how few of us there are who have within us the
courage to be great in adversity.   'Aequam memento'--&c.,
&c.!--if thou couldst but have thought of it, O... [you]
who need'st must some day die.  TC 116, X.

But then a course of crime makes such violent demands on a
man's courage.   Let any one think of the difference of
attacking a thief, and being attacked as a thief!   We are
apt to call bad men cowards without much consideration.
CasR 122-3, VI,II.

No; faint heart never won a fair lady; but they who repeat
to themselves that adage, trying thereby to get courage,
always have faint hearts for such work.  Cl 140, XVII.

But such inward boastings [of being strong]  are not altogether bad.   They preserve men from succumbing, and make at
any rate some attempt to realize themselves.   The man who
tells himself that he is brave, will struggle much before
he flies; but the man who never does so tell himself, will
find flying easy unless his heart be of nature very high.
Cl 208-9, XXV.

...courage...of that steady settled kind which enables the
possessor to remember that men who are doing deeds of darkness are ever afraid of those whom they are injuring.
VOB 20, III.

Who is there that has lived to be a man or woman, and has
not experienced a moment in which a combat has impended, and
a call for such sudden courage has been necessary? Alas!--
sometimes the combat comes, and the courage is not there.
ED 51, VI,I.

...pluck,--of that sort of hardihood which we may not quite call courage, but which in a world well provided with policemen is infinitely more useful than courage. AS 460, LXVII.

...that courage which induces a man who knows that he must be thrown over a precipice, to choose the first possible moment for his fall.   DuC 38, V.

## COURT

Never mind the bustling of eager, curious countrymen; never mind those noisy numerous policemen, with their Sunday brass-chained caps, push on through them all, make your way into the centre of the court--go down there right on to the lawyers' benches--never mind the seats being full--plunge in --if you hesitate, look timid--ask questions--or hang back-- you are lost, thrust out, expelled, and finally banished with ignominy into the tumultuous sea of damp frieze coats, which aestuates in the outer court--but go on with noise, impudence, and a full face, tread on people's toes, and thrust them back with 'by your leave,' and you will find yourself soon seated in direct view of the judge, counsel, witness and prisoner.   You will then be taken for an attorney, or, at any rate, for an influential court witness-- if you talk somewhat loud, and frown very angrily in the face of the tallest policeman, you may by the ignorant even be taken for a barrister.   MB 224-5, VI,III.

All people always are    [much too soon at court], who are brought to the court perforce, criminals for instance, and witnesses, and other such-like unfortunate wretches; whereas many of those who only go there to earn their bread are very often as much too late.   TC 475, XL.

## COURTESY

...with patronising good-nature, listening with an air of half-attention to what he said, and then not taking the slightest heed of a word of it.   Who does not know this transparent pretence of courtesies, which of all discourte- sies is the most offensive?   RalH 327, XLIV.

[B]ut there is a constrained courtesy very hard to be borne. HHOG 92, VII.

## COURTSHIP

When a man can tell a young lady what she ought to read, what she ought to do, and whom she ought to know, nothing can be easier than to assure her that, of all her duties, her first duty is to prefer himself to all the world.   And any young lady who has consented to receive lessons from such a teacher, will generally be willing to receive this special lesson among others.   HKHWR 224, XXIV.

There are few men who do not feel ashamed of being paraded before the world as acknowledged suitors, whereas ladies accept the position with something almost of triumph. The lady perhaps regards herself as the successful angler, whereas the gentleman is conscious of some similitude to the unsuccessful fish. HKHWR 294, XXXI.

When an unmarried gentleman calls upon an unmarried lady to change the fashion of her personal adornments, the unmarried lady has a right to expect that the unmarried gentleman means to make her his wife. HKHWR 447, XLVII.

Clever and well-practised must, indeed, be the hand of the fisher-woman in matrimonial waters who is able to throw her fly without showing any glimpse of the hook to the fish for whom she angles. HKHWR 531, LVI.

A girl when she is courted knows at any rate that she is thought worthy of courtship. VOB 483, LXVII.

[S]ince the world began, it has been man's province to prostrate himself at the feet of the woman he loves. DuC 471, LIX.

When a man has been successful in his wooing he is supposed to be happy....[I]t is [common] for a delinquent to cover his own delinquency by declaring it. 'Of course I am idle,' says the idle one, escaping the disgrace of his idleness by his honesty. 'I have caught you!' There is something soothing to the vanity in such a declaration from a pretty woman. That she should have wished to catch you is something;--something that the net should itself be so pleasant, with its silken meshes! But the declaration may not the less be true and the fact unpleasant. In the matter of matrimony a man does not wish to be caught. JC 65, VIII.

## COWARDS

[B]ut are not most men cowards in such matters [public ridicule] as that? MM 375, XXVIII.

## CREATIVITY

It is always easiest for the mind to work, in such emergencies [threatened loss of Parliamentary election], on some matter as to which no creative struggles are demanded from it. RalH 304, XL.

## CREDIT

When a gentleman is driven by his indebtedness to go to another tradesman, it is, so to say, 'all up with him' in the way of credit. There is nothing the tradesman dislikes so much as this, as he fears that the rival is going to get the ready money after he has given the credit. And yet what is a gentleman to do when his demand for further goods at

the old shop is met by a request for a little ready money?
RalH 57, VIII.

## CRIME

[S]afety lay in the indifference of his prosecutors,--
certainly not in his innocence. Any one prominent in
affairs can always see when a man may steal a horse and when
a man may not look over a hedge. PR 30, XLIV, II.

## CRIMINALS

...the incarnation of evil, which it is always necessary
that the novelist should have personified in one of his
characters to enable him to bring about his misfortunes, his
tragedies, and various requisite catastrophes. Scott had
his Varney and such-like; Dickens his Bill Sykes and such-
like; all of whom are properly disposed of before the end of
those volumes in which are described their respective
careers. I have ventured to introduce to my readers, as my
devil, Mr. Undy Scott, M.P. for the Tillietudlem, district
burghs; and I also feel myself bound to dispose of him,
though of him I regret I cannot make so decent an end as was
done with Sir Richard Varney and Bill Sykes.
    He deserves, however, as severe a fate as either of
those heroes. With the former we will not attempt to
compare him, as the vices and devilry of the days of Queen
Elizabeth are in no way similar to those in which we
indulge; but with Bill Sykes we may contrast him, as they
flourished in the same era, and had their points of
similitude, as well as their points of difference.
    They were both apparently born to prey on their own
species; they both resolutely adhered to a fixed rule that
they would in nowise earn their bread, and to a rule equally
fixed that, though they would earn no bread, they would
consume much. They were both of them blessed with a total
absence of sensibility and an utter disregard to the pain of
others, and had no other use for a heart than that of a
machine for maintaining circulation of the blood. It is but
little to say that neither of them ever acted on principle,
on a knowledge, that is, of right and wrong, and selection
of the right; in their studies of the science of evil they
had progressed much further than this, and had taught
themselves to believe that that which other men called
virtue was, on its own account, to be regarded as mawkish,
insipid, and useless for such purposes as the acquisition of
money or pleasure; whereas vice was, on its own account, to
be preferred, as offering the only road to those things
which they were desirous of possessing.
    So far there was a great resemblance between Bill Sykes
and Mr. Scott; but then came the points of difference, which
must give to the latter a great pre-eminence in the eyes of
that master whom they had both so worthily served. Bill
could not boast the merit of selecting the course which he
had run; he had served the Devil, having had, as it were, no

choice in the matter; he was born and bred and educated an
evil-doer, and could hardly have deserted from the colours
of his great Captain, without some spiritual interposition
to enable him to do so.  To Undy a warmer reward must surely
be due; he had been placed fairly on the world's surface,
with power to choose between good and bad, and had delib-
erately taken the latter; to him had, at any rate, been
explained the theory of meum and tuum, and he had resolved
that he liked tuum better than meum; and had learnt that
there is a God ruling over us, and a Devil hankering after
us, and had made up his mind that he would belong to the
latter.    Bread and water would have come to him naturally
without any villainy on his part, aye, and meat and milk,
and wine and oil....

And yet poor Bill Sykes...is always held as the more
detestable scoundrel.  Lady, you now know them both.  Is it
not the fact, that, knowing him as you do, you could spend a
pleasant hour enough with Mr. Scott, sitting next to him at
dinner; whereas your blood would creep within you, your hair
would stand on end, your voice would stick in your throat,
if you were suddenly told that Bill Sykes was in your
presence?

Poor Bill!  I have a sort of love for him, as he walks
about wretched with that dog of his, though I know that it
is necessary to hang him.  Yes, Bill; I, your friend, cannot
gainsay that, must acknowledge that.   Hard as the case may
be, you must be hung; hung out of the way of further
mischief; my spoons, my wife's throat, my children's brains,
demand that....I admit the hardship of your case; but still,
my Bill, self-preservation is the first law of nature.  You
must be hung.  But, while hanging you, I admit that you are
more sinned against than sinning.   There is another, Bill,
another, who will surely take account of this in some way,
though it is not for me to tell you how.

Yes, I hang Bill Sykes with soft regret; but with what
a savage joy, with what exultation of heart, with what
alacrity of eager soul, with what aptitude of mind to the
deed, would I hang my friend, Undy Scott, the member of
Parliament for the Tillietudlem burghs, if I could but get
at his throat for such a purpose!  Hang him!  aye, as high
as Haman!  In this there would be no regret, no vacillation
of purpose, no doubt as to the propriety of the sacrifice,
no feeling that I was so treating him, not for his own
desert, but for my advantage.

We hang men, I believe, with this object only, that we
should deter others from crime; but in hanging Bill we shall
hardly deter his brother.  Bill Sykes must look to crime for
his bread, seeing that he has been so educated, seeing that
we have not yet taught him another trade.

But if I could hang Undy Scott, I think I should deter
some others.  The figure of Undy swinging from a gibbet at
the broad end of Lombard Street would have an effect.  Ah!
my fingers itch to be at the rope.

Fate, however, and the laws are averse.  To gibbet him,
in one sense, would have been my privilege, had I drunk

deeper from that Castalian rill whose dark waters are tinged
with the gall of poetic indignation; but as in other sense I
may not hang him, I will tell how he was driven from his
club, and how he ceased to number himself among the legislators of his country.  TC 528-31, XLIV.

It is the small vermin and the little birds that are trapped
at once.  But wolves and vultures can fight hard before thay
are caught....When a man's frauds have been enormous there
is  a  certain  safety  in  their  very  diversity  and
proportions.  Way 106, LXII, II.

## CRISIS

...the uncontrolled expression of...feeling at the moment,--
as  one  man  squeezes  another  tightly  by  the  hand  in  any
crisis of sudden impulse.  AS 152, XXIII.

## CRITICISM

Considering how much we are all given to discuss the characters  of  others,  and  discuss  them  often  not  in  the
strictest  spirit  of  charity,  it  is  singular  how  little  we
are inclined to think that others can speak ill-naturedly of
us, and how angry and hurt we are when proof reaches us that
they have done so.  It is hardly too much to say that we all
of us occasionally speak of our dearest friends in a manner
in which those dearest friends would very little like to
hear themselves mentioned; and that we nevertheless expect
that  our  dearest  friends  shall  invariably  speak  of  us  as
though they were blind to all our faults, but keenly alive
to every shade of our virtues.  BaT 179, XX.

But nobody can, in truth, endure to be told of shortcomings,
either on his own part or on that of his country.  He himself can abuse himself, or his country; but he cannot endure
it from alien lips.  AS 349, LI.

## CROSS-GRAINEDNESS

The  cross-grainedness  of  men  is  so  great  that  things  will
often  be  forced  to  go  wrong,  even  when  they  have  the
strongest  possible  natural  tendency  of  their  own  to  go
right.  LasC 601, LXIII.

## CRUELTY

Alas!  no  evil  tendency  communictaes  itself  among  young  men
more quickly than cruelty.  TC 18, II.

Mankind in general take pleasure in cruelty, though those
who are civilized abstain from it on principle.  TC 481, XL.

## CURIOSITY

It is not easy to ask a man what he has been doing with five years of his life, when the question implies a belief that these five years have been passed badly.  DrW 26,III,Part I.

## CURSING

Men in the upper walks of life do not mind being cursed, and the women, presuming that it be done in delicate phrase, rather like it.  BaT 31, IV.

## CUSTOMS

Unusual circumstances and extraordinary excitement often cause the customary rules and practices of life to be abandoned....Such declarations [of love] are usually made in private,...but strange times made strange scenes necessary.  LaV 215, XVII.


D


## DEAFNESS

It is a terrible bore to have to talk to people who use speaking-trumpets, and who are so fidgety themselves that they won't use their speaking-trumpets properly.
Ber 529, XXIX.

## DEATH

The brave soldier goes to meet death, and meets him without a shudder when he comes.  The suffering woman patiently awaits him on her bed of sickness, and conscious of her malady dies slowly without a struggle.  A not uncommon fortitude enables them to leave their mortal coil, and take the dread leap in the dark with apparent readiness and ease --but to wait in full health and strength for the arrival of the fixed hour of certain death--to feel the moments sink from under you which are fast bringing you to the executioner's hand--to know that in twelve--ten--eight--six-- hours by the clock, which hurries through the rapid minutes, you are to become--not by God's accomplished visitation--not in any gallant struggle of your own--but through the stern will of certain powerful men--a hideous, foul, and dislocated corse, to know that at one certain ordained moment you are to be made extinct--to be violently put an end to-- to be fully aware that this is your fixed fate, and that though strong as a lion--you must at that moment die like a dog--to await the doom without fear--without feeling the blood grow cold round the heart, without a quickened pulse, and shaking muscles, exceeds the bounds of mortal courage, and requires either the ignorant apathetic unimaginative indifference of a brute or the superhuman endurance of an enthusiastic martyr.  MB  417-9, XI,III.

It is a difficult task to talk properly to a dying person about death.  Kel 310, XXV.

But sudden death is always frightful.  Ber 456, XXV.

But death closes many a long account, and settles many a bitter debt.  Ber 826-7, XLVII.

...that longing for death which terrible calamities often produce for a season.  Bel 8, I.

## DEBT

How frequent it is that men on their road to ruin feel elation such as this!  A man signs away a moiety of his substance;  nay, that were nothing; but a moiety of the substance of his children; he puts his pen to the paper that ruins him and them; but in doing so he frees himself from a score of immediate little pestering, stinging troubles; and therefore, feels as though fortune had been almost kind to him.  DoT 167, XIV.

In the first place, a man whose bill is paid for him always makes some concession to the man who pays it.  He should do so, at any rate.  Ber 199, XI.

Such companions  [men in debt yet living well]  are very dangerous.  There is no cholera, no yellow-fever, no small-pox, more contagious than debt.  If one lives habitually among embarrassed men, one catches it to a certainty. FrP 32, IV.

That feeling of over-due bills, of bills coming due, of accounts overdrawn, of tradesmen unpaid, of general money cares, is dreadful at first; but it is astonishing how soon men get used to it.  A load which would crush a man at first becomes, by habit, not only endurable, but easy and comfortable to the bearer.  The habitual debtor goes along jaunty and with elastic step, almost enjoying the excitement of his embarrassments....
     But then, at last, the time does come when the excitement is over, and when nothing but the misery is left.  If there be an existence of wretchedness on earth it must be that of the elderly, worn-out roue, who has run this race of debts and bills of accomodation and acceptances--of what, if we were not in these days somewhat afraid of good broad English, we might call lying and swindling, falsehood and fraud--and who, having ruined all whom he should have loved, having burnt up everyone who would trust him much, and scorched all who would trust him a little, is at last left to finish his life with such bread and water as these men get, without one honest thought to strengthen his sinking

heart, or one honest friend to hold his shivering hand! If a
man could only think of that, as he puts his name to the
first little bill, as to which he is so good-naturedly
assured that it can easily be renewed.  FrP 116-7, XII.

It is a remarkable thing with reference to men who are
distressed for money...that they never seem at a loss for
small sums, or deny themselves those luxuries which small
sums purchase.   Cabs, dinners, wine, theatres, and new
gloves are always at the command of men who are drowned in
pecuniary embarrassments, whereas those who don't owe a
shilling are so frequently obliged to go without them!   It
would seem that there is no gratification so costly as that
of keeping out of debt.  But then it is only fair that, if a
man has a hobby, he should pay for it.  FrP 315, XXXII.

## DECAY

There is no sign of coming decay which is so melancholy to
the eye as any which tells of a decrease in the throng of
men.  Bel 87, VII.

## DECEIT

On such occasions   [the reading of an unfavourable will],
one's face, which is made up for deceit, never does deceive
any one.  Ber 801, XLV.

But there are men made of such stuff that an angel could
hardly live with them without some deceit.  FrP 211, XXII.

Many of us daily deceive our friends, and are so far gone in
deceit that the deceit alone is hardly painful to us.   But
the need of deceiving a friend is always painful.   The
treachery is easy; but to be treacherous to those we love is
never easy,--never easy, even though it be so common.
Bel 276, XXI.

Men who can succeed in deceiving no one else will succeed at
last in deceiving themselves.  MM 371, XXVIII.

Who yet ever met a man who did not in his heart of hearts
despise an attempt made by others to deceive--himself?  They
whom we have found to be gentler in their judgement towards
attempts made in another direction have been more than one
or two.   LA 375, XXXV.

With worldly people in general, though the worldliness is
manifest enough, and is taught by plain lessons from parents
to their children, yet there is generally some thin veil
even among themselves, some transparent tissue of lies,
which, though they never quite hope to deceive each other,
does produce among them something of the comfort of deceit.
AS 80, XII.

## DECISIONS

There is nothing in the world so difficult as that task of making up one's mind. Who is there that has not longed that the power and privilege of selection among alternatives should be taken away from him in some important crisis of his life, and that his conduct should be arranged for him, either this way or that, by some divine power if it were possible,--by some patriarchal power in the absence of divinity,--or by chance even, if nothing better than chance could be found to do it? But no one dares to cast the die, and to go honestly by the hazard. There must be the actual necessity of obeying the die, before even the die can be of any use. PF 204, LX,II.

When men think much, they can rarely decide. The affairs as to which a man has once acknowledged to himself that he may be either wise or foolish, prudent or imprudent, are seldom matters on which he can by any amount of thought bring himself to a purpose which to his own eyes shall be clearly correct. When he can decide without thinking, then he can decide without a doubt, and with perfect satisfaction. SHHOH 194-5, XX.

We all know those arguments and quotations, antagonistic to prudence, with which a man fortifies himself in rashness. 'None but the brave deserve the fair.' 'Where there's a will there's a way.' 'Nothing venture nothing have.' 'The sword is to him who can use it.' 'Fortune favours the bold.' But on the other side there is just as much to be said. 'A bird in the hand is worth two in the bush.' 'Look before you leap.' 'Thrust not out your hand further than you can draw it back again.'...But what matter such revolvings? A man...always does that which most pleases him at the moment, being but poor at argument if he cannot carry the weight to that side which best satisfies his own feelings. PR 10, I,I.

When a man's mind is veering towards some decision, some conclusion which he has been perhaps slow in reaching, it is probably a little thing which at last fixes his mind and clenches his thoughts. PrM 296, XXXII,I.

It may be a question whether three days are ever much better than three minutes for such a purpose [deciding whom to marry]. A man's mind will very generally refuse to make it-self up until it be driven and compelled by emergency. The three days are passed not in forming but in postponing judgment. In nothing is procrastination so tempting as in thought. AyA 391, XLI.

## DEFENSE

One ought to take it as a matter of course that a bull should use his horns, and a wolf his teeth. AS 552, LXXX.

It [that one cannot be other than as God has made him] is

the last and poorest makeshift of a defence to which a man
can be brought in his own court!   DuC 172, XXII.

A stag, when brought to bay, will trample upon the hounds.
CoH 229, XX.

## DELICACY

Honour, honesty, and truth, out-spoken truth, self-denying
truth, and fealty from man to man, are worth more than
maiden delicacy; more, at any rate, than the talk of it.
DoT 435, XXXVI.

## DEMAGOGUES

The demagogue who is of all demagogues the most popular, is
the demagogue who is a demagogue in opposition to his
apparent nature.   The Radical Earl, the free-thinking
parson, the squire who won't preserve, the tenant who defies
his landlord, the capitalist with a theory for dividing
profits, the Moggs who loves a strike,--these are the men
whom the working men delight to follow.   RalH 122, XVI.

## "DEMOCRAT"

A sweeter-tempered people than had existed there had been
found nowhere [than in Ireland]; nor a people more
ignorant, and possessing less of the comforts of civilization.   But no evil was to be expected from them, no harm
came from them, beyond a few simple lies, which were only
harmful as acting upon their own character....The tuition
for revenge and murder had come from America!   That, no
doubt, was true; but it had come by Irish hearts and Irish
voices, by Irish longings and Irish ambition.   Nothing
could be more false than to attribute the evil to America,
unless that becomes American which has once touched American
soil.   But there does grow up in New York, or thereabouts, a
mixture of Irish poverty with American wealth, which calls
itself "Democrat," and forms as bad a composition as any
that I know from which either to replenish or to create a
people.
    A very little of it goes unfortunately a long way.   It
is like gin made of vitriol when mingled with water....A
small modicum of gin, though it does not add much spirit to
the water, will damnably defile a large quantity.   And this
gin has in it a something of flavour which will altogether
deceive an uneducated palate....These "democrats" could
never do us the mischief.   They are not sufficient, either
in intellect or in number; but there are men among us who
have taught themselves to believe that the infuriated gin
drinker is the true holder of a new gospel.
Land 229-31, XLV, III.

## DEPENDENTS

Mothers-in-law, aunts, maiden sisters, and dependent female

relatives, in all degrees, are endured with greater patience and treated with a gentler hand in patient Bavaria than in some lands farther west where life is faster, and in which men's shoulders are more easily galled by slight burdens. LT 200, I.

## DERVISHES

How the dervishes there spun and shook, going through their holy exercises with admirable perseverance, that I must tell....
But in Egypt we have caused ourselves to be better respected: we thrash the Arabs and pay them, and therefore they are very glad to see us anywhere. And even the dervishes welcome us to their most sacred rites, with excellent coffee, and a loan of rush-bottomed chairs. Now, when it is remembered that a Mahomedan never uses a chair, it must be confessed that this is very civil. Moreover, let it be said to their immortal praise, that the dervishes of Cairo never ask for backsheish. They are the only people in the country that do not. Ber 680-1, XXXVIII.

## DESERTION

Women can bear anything better than desertion. Cruelty is bad, but neglect is worse than cruelty, and desertion worse than neglect. Cl 295, XXXV.

## DESIRE

The top brick of the chimney may be very desirable, but one doesn't cry for it, because it is unattainable. DrW 181, IV, Part V.

## DESPAIR

Who has not known that frame of mind in which any postponement of the thing dreaded is acceptable? LT 380, XVII.

There are moments in the lives of most of us in which it seems to us that there will never be more cakes and ale. GLOG 143, XIII.

## DESTINY

Men and women only know so much of themselves and others as circumstances and their destiny have allowed to appear. Had it perchance fallen to thy lot, O my forensic friend, heavy laden with the wisdom of the law, to write tales such as this of mine, how charmingly might not thy characters have come forth upon the canvas--how much more charmingly than I can limn them! While, on the other hand, ignorant as thou now tellest me that I am of the very alphabet of the courts, had thy wig been allotted to me, I might have gathered guineas thick as daisies in summer, while to thee perhaps they come no faster than snowdrops in the early spring. It is all in our destiny. CasR 266-7, XIV,III.

## DETAILS...GENERALITIES

What is there that we do not find to be deteriorating around us when we consider the things in detail, though we are willing enough to admit a general improvement?   GLOG 43, IV.

## DETECTIVES

Men whose business it is to detect hidden and secret things, are very apt to detect things which have never been done. What excuse can a detective make even to himself for his own existence if he can detect nothing?   HKHWR 267-8, XXVIII.

## DETERMINATION

When we buckle on our armour in any cause, we are apt to go on buckling it, let the cause become as weak as it may. Bel 24, II.

## DEVIL

How common with us it is to repine that the devil is not stronger over us than he is.   LasC 293, XXXIII.

## DIANA'S DART

...in the back of her hair she still carried that Diana's dart which maidens wear in those parts [Prague] when they are not only maidens unmarried, but maidens also disengaged. NB 22, II.

## DIGNITY

When a man has to declare a solemn purpose on a solemn occasion in a solemn place, it is needful that he should be solemn himself.... Who can boast, who that has been versed in the ways and duties of high places, that he has kept himself free from all study of grace, or feature, of attitude, of gait--or even of dress?   For most of our bishops, for most of our judges, of our statesmen, our orators, our generals, for many even of our doctors and our parsons, even our attorneys, our tax-gatherers, and certainly our butlers and our coachmen, Mr. Turveydrop, the great professor of deportment, has done much.   But there should always be the art to underlie and protect the art;-- the art that can hide the art.   The really clever archbishop,--the really potent chief justice, the man who, as a politician, will succeed in becoming a king of men, should know how to carry his buckram without showing it....There are men who look as though they were born to wear blue ribbons.   It has come, probably, from study, but it seems to be natural....[With others] you could see a little of the paint, you could hear the crumple of the starch and the padding; you could trace something of uneasiness in the would-be composed grandeur of the brow. 'Turveydrop!' the spectator would say to himself....

For I think we must hold that true personal dignity should be achieved...without any personal effort. Though it be evinced, in part, by the carriage of the body, that carriage should be the fruit of the operation of the mind. Even when it be assisted by external garniture such as special clothes, and wigs, and ornaments, such garniture should have been prescribed by the sovereign or by custom, and should not have been selected by the wearer. In regard to speech a man may study all that which may make him suasive, but if he go beyond that he will trench on those histrionic efforts which he will know to be wrong because he will be ashamed to acknowledge them. It is good to be beautiful, but it should come of God and not of the hairdresser....A real Caesar is not to be found every day, nor can we always have a Pitt to control our debates. That kind of thing, that last touch has its effect. Of course it is all paint,--but how would the poor girl look before the gaslights if there were no paint? The House of Commons likes a little deportment on occasions. If a special man looks bigger than you, you can console yourself by reflecting that he also looks bigger than your fellows. DuC 600-2, LXXVI.

## DIMPLES

...dimple...that soft couch in which one may be always sure, when one sees it, that some little imp of Love lies hidden. VOB 8, I.

## DINNER

Let what will happen to break hearts and ruin fortunes, dinner comes as long as the means last for providing it. RalH 258, XXXIV.

## DINNERS

What is there in this world more melancholy than such a dinner? A dinner, though eaten alone, in a country hotel may be worthy of some energy; the waiter, if you are known, will make much of you; the landlord will make you a bow and perhaps put the fish on the table; if you ring you are attended to , and there is some life about it. A dinner at a London eating-house is also lively enough, if it have no other attraction. There is plenty of noise and stir about it, and the rapid whirl of voices and rattle of dishes disperses sadness. But a solitary dinner in an old, respectable, sombre, solid London inn, where nothing makes any noise but the old waiter's creaking shoes; where one plate slowly goes and another slowly comes without a sound; where the two or three guests would as soon think of knocking each other down as of speaking; where the servants whisper, and the whole household is disturbed if an order be given above the voice--what can be more melancholy than a mutton chop and a pint of port in such a place? War 197-8, XVI.

A party of six is always a talking party. Men and women are not formed into pairs, and do not therefore become dumb. Each person's voice makes another person emulous, and the difficulty felt is not as to what one shall say, but how one shall get it in. Ten, and twelve, and fourteen are the silent numbers. Ber 609, XXXIII.

How Gothic, how barbarous are we still in our habits, in that we devote our wives to such wretchedness as that [going out with the dull ladies after dinner]! O, lady, has it ever been your lot to sit out such hour as that with some Mrs. Sistick, who would neither talk, nor read, nor sleep; in whose company you could neither talk, nor read, nor sleep? And if such has been your lot, have you not asked yourself why in this civilized country, in this civilized century, you should be doomed to such a senseless, sleepless purgatory? Ber 612, XXXIII.

Who does not know the way in which a lately married couple's little dinner-party stretches itself out from the pure simplicity of a fried sole and leg of mutton to the attempt at clear soup, the unfortunately cold dish of round balls which is handed about after the sole, and the brightly red jelly, and beautifully pink cream, which are ordered, in the last agony of ambition, from the next pastrycook's shop?
    'We cannot give a dinner, my dear, with only cook and Sarah.'
    It has thus begun, and the husband has declared that he has no such idea. 'If Phipps and Dowdney can come here and eat a bit of mutton, they are very welcome; if not, let them stay away. And you might as well ask Phipps's sister; just to have someone to go with you into the drawing-room.'
    'I'd much rather go alone, because then I can read'--or sleep, we may say.
    But her husband has explained that she would look friendless in this solitary state, and therefore Phipps's sister has been asked. Then the dinner has progressed down to those costly jellies which have been ordered in a last agony. There has been a conviction on the minds of both of them that the simple leg of mutton would have been more jolly for them all. Had those round balls not been carried about by a hired man; had simple mutton with hot potatoes been handed to Miss Phipps by Sarah, Miss Phipps would not have simpered with such unmeaning stiffness when young Dowdney spoke to her. They would have been much more jolly. 'Have a bit more mutton, Phipps; and where do you like it?' How pleasant it sounds! But we all know that it is impossible. My young friend had intended this, but his dinner had run itself away to cold round balls and coloured forms from the pastrycook....
    The bride must leave the church in a properly appointed carriage, and the postboys must have wedding favours....A well-cooked rissole, brought pleasantly to you, is good eating. A gala marriage, when everything is in keeping, is excellent sport. Heaven forbid that we should have no gala marriages. But the small spasmodic attempt, made in opposi-

tion to manifest propriety, made with an inner conviction of failure--that surely should be avoided in marriages, in dinners, and in all affairs of life. SmaH 451-2, XLV.

There are houses, which, in their everyday course, are not conducted by any means in a sad or unsatisfactory manner-- in which life, as a rule, runs along merrily enough; but which cannot give a dinner-party; or, I might rather say, should never allow themselves to be allured into the attempt. The owners of such houses are generally themselves quite aware of the fact, and dread the dinner which they resolved to give quite as much as it is dreaded by their friends. They know that they prepare for their guest an evening misery, and for themselves certain long hours of purgatory which are hardly to be endured. But they will do it. Why that long table, and all those supernumerary glasses and knives and forks, if they are never to be used? That argument produces all this misery; that and others cognate to it. SmaH 540-1, LIII.

A man in such a condition [waiting while a caterer serves] measures the amount of cold which his meat may possibly endure against the future coming of the potatoes, till he falls utterly to the ground between two stools. MM 105,VIII.

Why on earth did she perplex her mind and bruise her spirit, by giving a dinner a la anything? Why did she not have the roast mutton alone, so that all her guests might have eaten and have been merry?
    She could not have answered this question herself, and I doubt whether I can do so for her. But this I feel, that unless the question can get itself answered, ordinary Englishmen must cease to go and eat dinners at each other's houses. The ordinary Englishman, of whom we are now speaking, has eight hundred a year; he lives in London; and he has a wife and three or four children. Had he not better give it up and go back to his little bit of fish and his leg of mutton? Let him do that boldly, and he will find that we, his friends, will come to him fast enough; yes, and will make a gala day of it. By Heavens, we have no gala time of it when we go to dine with Mrs. Mackenzie a la Russe! ... Money, which cannot do everything...can do some things. It will buy diamonds and give grand banquets. But paste diamonds, and banquets which are only would-be grand, are among the poorest imitations to which the world has descended. MM 106-7, VIII.

Household deficiencies--and, indeed, all deficiencies--are considerable or insignificant in accordance with the aspirations of those concerned. When a man has a regiment of servants in his dining-room, with beautifully cut glass, a forest of flowers, and an iceberg in the middle of his table if the weather be hot, his guests will think themselves ill-used and badly fed if aught in the banquet be astray....But the same guests shall be merry as the evening is long with a leg of mutton and whisky toddy, and will change their own plates, and clear their own table, and think nothing wrong, if from the beginning such has been the intention of the giver of the feast. HHOG 154, XII.

It used to be the case that when a gentleman gave a dinner he asked his own guests;--but when affairs become great, society can hardly be carried on after that simple fashion. Way 327, XXXV,I.

Who does not know the effect made by the absence of one or two from a table intended for ten or twelve,--how grievous are the empty places, how destructive of the outward harmony and grace which the hostess has endeavoured to preserve are these interstices, how the lady in her wrath declares to herself that those guilty ones shall never have another opportunity of filling a seat at her table? Way 81, LIX,II.

Who, that ever without difficulty scraped his dinner guests together, was able afterwards to obliterate the signs of the struggle? PrM 281, XXX,I.

It may be a doubt whether such tradesmen as Messrs. Stewam and Sugarscraps do ever produce good food....It is certain, I think, that the humblest mutton chop is better eating than any 'Supreme of chicken after martial manner,'-- as I have seen the dish named in a French bill of fare, translated by a French pastrycook for the benefit of his English customers,--when sent in from Messrs. Stewam and Sugarscraps even with their best exertions. PrM 73-4, XLVIII, II.

What service do you do to any one in pouring your best claret down his throat, when he knows no difference between that and a much more humble vintage,--your best claret, which you feel so sure you cannot replace? Why import canvas-back ducks for appetites which would be quite as well satisfied with those out of the next farmyard? Your soup, which has been a care since yesterday, your fish, got down with so much trouble from Bond Street on that very day, your saddle of mutton, in selecting which you have affronted every butcher in the neighbourhood, are all plainly thrown away! And yet the hospitable hero who would fain treat his friends as he would be treated himself can hardly arrange his dinners according to the palates of his different guests; nor will he like, when strangers sit at his board, to put nothing better on his table than that cheaper wine with which needful economy induces him to solace himself when alone. I,--I who write this,--have myself seen an honoured guest deluge with the pump my, ah! so hardly earned, most scarce and most peculiar vintage! There is a pang in such usage which some will not understand. AS 286, XLII.

# DINNERS, FAMILY

At such entertainments Paterfamilias is simply required to find the provender and to carve it. If he does that satisfactorily, silence on his part is not regarded as a great evil.  RacR 133, XI.

## DINNERS, PUBLIC

I venture to assert that each Liberal elector there would have got a better dinner at home, and would have been served with greater comfort; but a public dinner at an inn is the recognized relaxation of a middle-class Englishman in the provinces....He is bored frightfully by every speech to which he listens.  He is driven to the lowest depths of dismay by every speech which he is called upon to make.  He is thoroughly disgusted when he is called upon to make no speech.  He has no point of sympathy with the neighbours between whom he sits.  The wine is bad.  The hot water is brought to him cold.  His seat is hard and crowded.  No attempt is made at the pleasures of conversation.  He is continually called upon to stand up that he may pretend to drink a toast in honour of some person or institution for which he cares nothing; for the hero of the evening, as to whom he is probably indifferent; for the church, which perhaps he never enters; the army, which he regards as a hotbed of aristocratic insolence; or for the Queen, whom he reveres and loves by reason of his nature as an Englishman, but against whose fulsome praises as repeated to him ad nauseam in the chairman's speech his very soul unconsciously revolts.  It is all a bore, trouble, ennui, nastiness, and discomfort.  But yet he goes again and again,--because it is the relaxation natural to an Englishman.  The Frenchman who sits for three hours tilted on the hind legs of a little chair with his back against the window-sill of the cafe, with first a cup of coffee before him and then a glass of sugar and water, is perhaps as much to be pitied as regards his immediate misery; but the liquids which he imbibes are not so injurious to him.  RacR 352-3, XXVII.

## DIPLOMATIC SERVICE

Colonial governors at their seats of government, and Ministers Plenipotentiary in their ambassadorial residences are very great persons indeed; and when met in society at home, with the stars and ribbons which are common among them now, they are less, indeed, but still something.  But at the Colonial and Foreign Offices in London, among the assistant secretaries and clerks, they are hardly more than common men.  All the gingerbread is gone there.  His Excellency is no more than Jones, and the Representative or Alter Ego of Royalty mildly asks little favours of the junior clerks.
AS 190, XXVIII.

## DISAGREEABLENESS

Of all our capabilities this [disagreeableness] is the one which clings longest to us.  PR 94, XI,I.

## DISCIPLINE

The self-indulgences of the saints in this respect    [that stage of discipline in which ashes become pleasant eating, and sackcloth is grateful to the skin]    often exceed anything that is done by the sinners.  RacR 66, V.

## DISESTABLISHMENT

The solemnities [of a great debate]  make men think for the day that no moment of greater excitement has ever blessed or cursed the country....It is out of nature that any man should think it good that his own order should be repressed, curtailed, and deprived of its power.  If we go among cab drivers or letter-carriers, among butlers or gamekeepers, among tailors or butchers, among farmers or graziers, among doctors or attorneys, we shall find in each set of men a conviction that the welfare of the community depends upon the firmness with which they,--especially they,--hold their own.  This is so manifestly true with the Bar that no barrister in practice scruples to avow that barristers in practice are the salt of the earth.  The personal confidence of a judge in his own position is beautiful, being salutary to the country, though not unfrequently damaging to the character of the man.  But if this be so with men who are conscious of no higher influence than that exercised over the bodies and minds of their fellow creatures, how much stronger must be the feeling when the influence affects the soul!  To the outsider, or layman, who simply uses a cab, or receives a letter, or goes to law, or has to be tried, these pretensions are ridiculous or annoying, according to the ascendancy of the pretender at the moment.  But as the clerical pretensions are more exacting than all others, being put forward with an assertion that no answer is possible without breach of duty and sin, so are they more galling....What is a thoughtful man to do who acknowledges the danger of his soul, but cannot swallow his parson whole simply because he has been sent to him from some source in which he has no special confidence....In no spirit of animosity to religion he begins to tell himself that Church and State together was a monkish combination, fit perhaps for monkish days, but no longer having fitness, and not much longer capable of existence in this country.  But to the parson himself,--to the honest, hardworking, conscientious priest who does in his heart of hearts believe that no diminution in the general influence of his order can be made without ruin to the souls of men,--this opinion, when it becomes dominant, is as though the world were in truth breaking to pieces over his head.  The world has been broken to pieces in the same way often;--but extreme Chaos does not come.  The cabman and the letter-carrier always expect that Chaos will very nearly come when they are disturbed.  The barristers are sure of Chaos when the sanctity of Benchers is in question.  What utter Chaos would be promised to us could any one with impunity contemn the majesty of the House of Commons! But of all these Chaoses there can be no Chaos

equal to that which in the mind of a zealous Oxford-bred
constitutional country parson must attend that annihilation
of his special condition which will be produced by the
disestablishment of the Church.  Of all good fellows he is
the best good fellow.  He is genial, hospitable, well-
educated, and always has either a pretty wife or pretty
daughters.  But he has so extreme a belief in himself that
he cannot endure to be told that absolute Chaos will not
come at once if he be disturbed.  PR 290-2, XXXIII,I.

## DISGRACE

The higher are the branches of the tree and the wider, the
greater will be the extent of earth which its fall will
disturb.  TC 469, XXXVIII.

And it may be said that no good man who has broken down in
his goodness can carry the disgrace of his fall without some
look of shame.  When a man is able to do that, he ceases to
be in any way good.  FrP 442, XLVI.

## DISPLAY

But men and women, when they show themselves at their best,
seldom do so without an effort.  If the object be near the
heart the effort will be pleasant to him who makes it, and
it if be made well, it will be hidden; but, not the less,
the effort will be there.  CanY 45-6, V,I.

## DISSENT

In Devonshire dissent has waxed strong for many years, and
the pastors of the dissenting flocks have been thorns in the
side of the Church of England clergymen.  RacR 230, XVIII.

## DISTANCES

The East is always further than the West in the estimation
of the... [housekeepers]  of the world.  LasC 729, LXXVIII.

## DOG IN THE MANGER

Well; and are we not all dogs in the manger more or less
actively?  Is not that manger-doggishness one of the most
common phases of the human heart?  FrP 297, XXXI.

## DOCTORS

The profession of a medical man in a small provincial town
is not often one which gives to its owner in early life a
large income.  Perhaps in no career has a man to work harder
for what he earns, or to do more work without earning anything.  It has sometimes seemed to me as though the young
doctors and the old doctors had agreed to divide between
them the different results of their profession--the young
doctors doing all the work and the old doctors taking all

the money.  If this be so it may account for that appearance
of premature gravity which is borne by so many of the
medical profession.  Under such an arrangement a man may be
excused for a desire to put away childish things very early
in life.  SmaH 191, XX.

Young unmarried doctors ought perhaps to be excluded from
houses in which there are young ladies.  I know, at any
rate, that many sage matrons hold very strongly to that
opinion, thinking, no doubt, that doctors ought to get themselves married before they venture to begin working for a
living.  SmaH 192, XX.

Village apothecaries are generally wronged by the doubts
which are thrown upon them, for the town doctors when they
come always confirm what the village apothecaries have said.
SmaH 386, XXIX.

## DOMINANCE

[B]ut, as we all know, the dominant cock of the farmyard
must be ever dominant.  When he shall once have had his
wings so smeared with mud as to give him even the appearance of adversity, no other cock will ever respect him
again....A man, when he wishes to reprimand another, should
always have the benefit of his own atmosphere.
SmaH 488-9, XLVIII.

I think it  [dominance]  had come from the outward look of
the men, from the form of each, from the gait and visage
which in one was good and in the other insignificant.  The
nature of such dominion of man over man is very singular,
but this is certain, that when once obtained in manhood it
may be easily held.
     Among boys at school the same thing is even more
conspicuous, because boys have less of conscience than men,
are more addicted to tyranny, and when weak are less prone
to feel the misery and disgrace of succumbing....Nor was it,
even then, personal strength, nor always superior courage,
that gave the power of command.  Nor was it intellect, or
thoughtfulness, nor by any means such qualities as make men
and boys loveable....Here again I think the outward gait of
the boy goes far towards obtaining for him the submission of
his fellow.
     But the tyrant boy does not become the tyrant man, or
the slave boy the slave man, because the outward visage,
that has been noble or mean in the one, changes and becomes
so often mean or noble in the other.  CanY 169-70, XVI,I.

## DOOM

'A long day, my lord, a long day,' screams the unfortunate
culprit from the dock when about to undergo the heaviest
sentence of the law.  But the convicted wretch is a coward
by his profession.  Ber 543, XXX.

But the man who is to be hung, has no choice.  He cannot,
when he wakes, declare that he has changed his mind, and
postpone the hour....If one has to be hung on a given day,
would it not be well to be hung as soon after waking as
possible?   I can fancy that the hangman would hardly come
early enough.   And if one had to be hung in a given week,
would not one wish to be hung on the first day of the week,
even at the risk of breaking one's last Sabbath day in this
world?   Whatever be the misery to be endured, get it over.
The horror of every agony is in its anticipation.
Way 370-1, XXXIX,I.

## DOUBLE-FIRST

We may say that no man ever gets a double-first in anything
without an effort.  Ber 17, I.

## DOUBT

It has often been said of woman that she who doubts is
lost....But they who have said so, thinking of their words
as they were uttered, have known but little of women.  Women
doubt every day, who solve their doubts at last on the right
side, driven to do so, some by fear, more by conscience, but
most of them by that half-prudential, half-unconscious
knowledge of what is fitting, useful, and best under the
circumstances, which rarely deserts either men or women till
they have brought themselves to... [a] state of recklessness.   Men when they have fallen even to that, will still
keep up some outward show towards the world; but women in
this condition defy the world, and declare themselves to be
children of perdition.  CanY 103, L,II.

Gentlemen when they make offers to ladies, and are told by
ladies that they may come again, and that time is required
for consideration, are always disposed to think that the
difficulties of the siege are over.  MM 285, XXI.

When a lady says that she will take time to think of such a
proposition, the gentleman is generally justified in supposing that he has carried his cause.  When a lady rejects a
suitor, she should reject him peremptorily.  Anything short
of such peremptory rejection is taken for acquiescence.
MM 170, XIII.

Towns which consider, always render themselves.  Ladies who
doubt always solve their doubts in the one direction.
Way 293, XXXI,I.

When a young lady takes time to consider she has, as a rule,
given way.  IHP 8, I,I.

Words so spoken will be the sweetest that can fall into a
man's ear,--if they be believed.   But let there come but
the shadow of doubt over the man's mind, let him question
the sincerity of a tone, and the words will become untrue,
mawkish and distasteful.  Kept 44, XI.

## DREAMS

It was to her...as to some hard-toiling youth who, while roaming listlessly among the houses of the wealthy, hears, as he lingers on the pavement of a summer night, the melodies which float upon the air from the open balconies above him.    A vague sense of unknown sweetness comes upon him, mingled with an irritating feeling of envy that some favoured son of Fortune should be able to stand over the shoulders of the singing syren, while he can only listen with intrusive ears from the street below.    And so he lingers and is envious, and for a moment curses his fate,-- not knowing how weary may be the youth who stands, how false the girl who sings.    But he does not dream that his life is to be altered for him, because he has chanced to hear the daughter of a duchess warble through a window.    LA 109, XI.

It is of no use to the most fervid imagination to have a castle projected in Spain from which all possible foundation has been taken away.    In his dreams of life a man should never dream that which is altogether impossible. JC 65, VIII.

## DRINK

[A]nd, though, it may seem to be an anomaly, it will always be found, that the poorer the people are, the more they drink.    MB 44, IV,I.

For, in spite of the oft-repeated assurance that there is not a headache in a hogshead of it, whiskey punch will sicken one, as well as more expensive and more fashionable potent drinks.    Kel 81, VII.

My belief is, that when men pay this penalty [a racking headache] for drinking, they are partly absolved from other penalties.    The penalties on drink are various.    I mean those which affect the body, exclusive of those which affect the mind.    There are great red swollen noses, very disagree- able both to the wearer and his acquaintances; there are morning headaches, awful to be thought of; there are sick stomachs, by which means the offender escapes through a speedy purgatory; there are sallow cheeks, sunken eyes, and shaking shoulders; there are very big bellies, and no bellies at all; and there is delirium tremens.    For the most part a man escapes with one of the penalties.    If he have a racking headache, his general health does not usually suffer so much as though he had endured no such immediate vengeance from violated nature.    CasR 274-5, XIII,I.

That pleasure [spending nights over the wine-cup] always leaves its disgusting traces round the lips. CasR 183, IX,II.

'In vino veritas!'    The sober devil can hide his cloven hoof; but when the devil drinks he loses his cunning and grows honest.    PR 52, XLVI,II.

A drunken man always feels more anxiety about what he has
not done in his drunkenness, than about what he has.
Kel 81, VII.

## DRUNKARDS

If any father have a son whose besetting sin is a passion
for alcohol, let him take his child to the room of a drunkard when possessed by 'the horrors.' Nothing will cure him
if not that. DoT 475, XL.

How dreadful to the sight are those watery eyes; that red,
uneven, pimpled nose; those fallen cheeks; and that hanging, slobbered mouth! Look at the uncombed hair, the beard
half shorn, the weak, impotent gait of the man, and the
tattered raiment, all eloquent of gin! You would fain hold
your nose when he comes nigh you, he carries with him so
foul an evidence of his only and his hourly indulgence. You
would do so, had you not still a respect for his feelings,
which he himself has entirely forgotten to maintain....I do
not know whether such a man as this is not the vilest thing
which grovels on God's earth. There are women whom we
affect to scorn with the full power of our contempt; but I
doubt whether any woman sinks to a depth so low as that.
She also may be a drunkard, and as such may more nearly move
our pity and affect our hearts, but I do not think she ever
becomes so nauseous a thing as the man that has abandoned
all the hopes of life for gin. You can still touch her;--
ay, and if the task be in one's way, can touch her gently,
striving to bring her back to decency. But the other!...I
can only say that the task is both nauseous and
unpromising. Look at him as he stands there before the
foul, reeking, sloppy bar, with the glass in his hand, which
he has just emptied. See the grimace with which he puts it
down, as though the dram had been almost too unpalatable.
It is the last touch of hypocrisy with which he attempts to
cover the offence;--as though he were to say, 'I do it for
my stomach's sake; but you know how I abhor it.' Then he
skulks sullenly away, speaking a word to no one,--shuffling
with his feet, shaking himself in his foul rags, pressing
himself into a heap--as though striving to drive the warmth
of the spirit into his extremities! And there he stands
lounging at the corner of the street, till his short
patience is exhausted, and he returns with his last penny
for the other glass. When that has been swallowed the
policeman is his guardian.
     Reader, such as you and I have come to that, when aban-
doned by the respect which a man owes to himself. May God
in his mercy watch over us and protect us both!
OrF 172-3, LVII,II.

Most men who drink at nights, and are out till cockcrow
doing deeds of darkness, become red in their faces, have
pimpled cheeks and watery eyes, and are bloated and not
comfortable to be seen. It is a kind dispensation of
Providence who thus affords to such sinners a visible sign,

to be seen day by day, of the injury which is being done.
The first approach of a carbuncle on the nose, about the age
of thirty, has stopped many a man from drinking.  No one
likes to have carbuncles on his nose, or to appear before
his female friends with eyes which look as though they were
swimming in grog. CanY 300, XXIX,I.

I wonder whether any polite reader, into whose hands this
story may fall, may ever have possessed a drunken friend,
and have been struck by some solemn incident at the moment
in which his friend is exercising the privileges of intoxication.  The effect is not pleasant, nor conducive of good-
humour.  RalH 263, XXXIV.

It is the debauched broken drunkard who should become a tee-
totaller, and not the healthy hard-working father of a
family who never drinks a drop of wine till dinner-time.  He
need not be afraid of a glass of champagne when, on a chance
occasion, he goes to a picnic.  ED 219, XXIV,I.

There is an intoxication that makes merry in the midst of
affliction;--and there is an intoxication that banishes
affliction by producing oblivion.  But again there is an intoxication which is conscious of itself though it makes the
feet unsteady, and the voice thick, and the brain foolish;
and which brings neither mirth nor oblivion....Most of my
readers will not probably know how a man looks when he comes
home drunk at six in the morning; but they who have seen the
thing will acknowledge that a sorrier sight cannot meet a
mother's eye than that of a son in such a condition.
Way 477, L,I.

## DUCHESSES

...duchesses are scarce in Ireland.  Kel 505, XXXIX.

## DUELS

Few Englishmen fight duels in these days.  They who do so
are always reckoned to be fools.  PF 353, XXXVII,I.

## DULLNESS

It is so pleasant to receive a fillip of excitement when
suffering from the dull routine of every-day life!
BaT 52, VII.

[D]ullness is always more unendurable than sadness.
LasC 194, XXII.

E

## EAGERNESS

If you pull at your fish too hard you only break your line.
RalH 175, XXIV.

## EARLY ARRIVALS

[B]ut in truth using that form of welcome ['It is so nice
of you to come early'] which to my ears sounds always the
most ungracious.   'Ten minutes before the time named; and,
of course, you must have understood that I meant thirty
minutes after it!' That is my interpretation of the words
when I am thanked for coming early.   SmaH 90-1, IX

## EARLY DAYS

'I wonder whether you ever think of the old days when we
used to be so happy in Keppel Street?'  Ah me, how often in
after life, in those successful days when the battle has
been fought and won, when all seems outwardly to go well,--
how often is this reference made to the happy days in Keppel
Street!...The struggle, the long hot hour of the honest
fight, the grinding work--when the teeth are set, and the
skin moist with sweat and rough with dust, when all is
doubtful and sometimes desperate, when a man must trust to
his own manhood knowing that those around him trust to it
not at all,--that is the happy time of life.   There is no
human bliss equal to twelve hours of work with only six
hours in which to do it.  And when the expected pay for that
work is worse than doubtful, the inner satisfaction is so
much the greater....
    Nothing makes a man so cross as success, or so soon
turns a pleasant friend into a captious acquaintance.  Your
successful man eats too much and his stomach troubles him;
he drinks too much and his nose becomes blue.   He wants
pleasure and excitement, and roams about looking for satisfaction in places where no man ever found it.   He frets
himself with his banker's book, and everything tastes amiss
to him that has not on it the flavour of gold.  The straw
of an omnibus always stinks; the linings of the cabs are
filthy.  There are but three houses round London at which an
eatable dinner may be obtained.  And yet a few years since
how delicious was that cut of roast goose to be had for a
shilling at the eating-house near Golden Square.  Mrs. Jones
and Mrs. Green, Mrs. Walker and all the other mistresses,
are too vapid and stupid and humdrum for endurance.  The
theatres are as dull as Lethe, and politics have lost their
salt.   Success is the necessary misfortune of life, but it

is only to the very unfortunate that it comes early.
OrF 87-8, XLIX,II.

## EATING

...that thoughtful, conscious pleasure which young men never
attain in eating and drinking, and which men as they grow
older so often forget to acquire.  Cl 110, XIV.

## ECONOMY

The economy...demanded was that comfortless heart-rending
economy which nips the practiser at every turn, but does not
betray itself to the world at large.  PrM 59, XLVII,II.

## EFFORT

All men should ever be making efforts, no doubt; but those
efforts should not be conspicuous.  OrF 270, XXVII,I.

## EMOTIONS

Our finer emotions should always be encouraged with a
stomach moderately full.  Ber 97, VI.

## EMPLOYEES

Curates and ushers are generally unmarried.  An assistant
schoolmaster is not often in orders, and sometimes is not a
gentleman.  A gentleman, when he is married, does not often
wish to dispose of the services of his wife.
DrW 12, II, Part I.

## EMULATION

Half at least of the noble deeds done in this world are due
to emulation, rather than to the native nobility of the actors....Jones in the hunting-field rides at an impracticable
fence because he is told that Smith took it three years ago.
And Walker puts his name down for ten guineas at a charitable dinner when he hears Thompson's read out for five.
LasC 270, XXXI.

## ENDURANCE

But we none of us know what load we can bear, and what would
break our backs.  Way 357, LXXXVIII,II.

There is no power so useful to man as that capacity of
recovering himself after a fall, which belongs especially to
those who possess a healthy mind in a healthy body...which
power of endurance is a noble attribute.  PrM 277-8, LXX,II.

## ENEMIES

What can any man do with a recusant wife?  We have often

been told that we should build a golden bridge for a flying
enemy.  And if any one can be regarded as a man's enemy, it
is a wife who is not his friend.  Ber 809, XLV.

## ENERGY

There are men whose energies hardly ever carry them beyond
looking for the thing they want....If you lie under a tree,
and open your mouth, a plum may fall into it.
CanY 264, LXVI,II.

Let a man or a woman's vitality be ever so thoroughly
crushed and quenched by fatigue or oppression--or even by
black crape--there will always be some mode of galvanising
which will restore it for a time, some specific either of
joy or torture which will produce a return of temporary
energy.  MM 331, XXV.

## ENGAGEMENTS

A girl should never obey her lover till she is married to
him; she may comply with his wishes, but she should not
allow herself to be told to do anything.  MB 119-20, VI,I.

Who does not know the smile of triumph with which a girl
asks such a question  [recently engaged, "Are you
contented?"] at such a moment as that?  Bel 127, X.

A man who is engaged may often choose to talk to his friend
about his engaged bride; but the friend does not usually
select the lady as a topic of conversation except in
conformity with the Benedict's wishes.  Ber 339, XIX.

[T]he days of...playfulness were over....And when I think
that it is true--when I see that the sportiveness and
kitten-like gambols of girlhood should be over, and
generally are over, when a girl has given her troth, it
becomes a matter of regret to me that the feminine world
should be in such a hurry after matrimony....The hurry is
not for matrimony, but for love.  Then, the love once
attained, matrimony seizes it for its own, and the evil is
accomplished.  SmaH 49, VI.

There is nothing pleasanter than all this  [having the
privileges of a lover], although a man when so treated does
feel himself to look like a calf at the altar, ready for the
knife, with blue ribbons round his horns and neck.
SmaH 61, VII.

Girls do triumph in their lovers,--in their acknowledged and
permitted lovers, as young men triumph in their loves which
are not acknowledged or perhaps permitted.  A man's triumph
is for the most part over when he is once allowed to take
his place at the family table, as a right, next to his
betrothed.  He begins to feel himself to be a sacrificial
victim,--done up very prettily with blue and white ribbons
round his horns, but still an ox prepared for sacrifice.

But the girl feels herself to be carried along in an ovation
of which that bucolic victim, tied round with blue ribbons
on to his horns, is the chief grace and ornament.
RacR 380-1, XXIX.

On this matter [secrecy about engagements]  the practice is
various among different people.    There are families who
think it almost indelicate to talk about marriage....The
engaged young ladies only whisper the news through the very
depths of their note-paper, and are supposed to blush as
they communicate the tidings by their pens, even in the re-
tirement of their own rooms.    But there are other families
in which there is no vestige of such mystery, in which an
engaged couple are spoken of together as openly as though
they were already bound in some sort of public partnership.
In these families the young ladies talk openly of their
lovers, and generally prefer that subject of conversation to
any other....The reserve in the reserved families is usually
atoned for by the magnificence of the bridal arrangements,
when the marriage is at last solemnized; whereas, among the
other set--the people who have no reserve,--the marriage
when it comes, is customarily an affair of much less outward
ceremony.    They are married without blast of trumpet, with
very little profit to the confectioner, and do their
honeymoon, if they do it at all, with prosaic simplicity.
Cl 70, IX.

...one of those men who consider themselves entitled to see,
hear, and know every little detail of a woman's conduct, as
a consequence of the circumstances of his engagement, and
who consider themselves shorn of their privilege if anything
be kept back....I am afraid that these particular gentlemen
sometimes hear some fibs; and I often wonder that their own
early passages in the tournays of love do not warn them that
it must be so.    When James has sat deliciously through all
the moonlit night with his arm round Mary's waist and afterwards sees Mary led to the altar by John, does it not occur
to him that some John may have also sat with his arm around
Anna's waist,--that Anna whom he is leading to the altar?
These things should not be inquired into too curiously; but
...women...do not choose to be pressed beyond their own
modes of utterance. Bel 136, XI.

Now there is nothing, I take it, so irritating to an engaged
young lady as counsel from her intended husband's mama.    An
engaged young lady, if she be really in love, will take
almost anything from her lover as long as she is sure that
it comes altogether from himself.    He may take what
liberties he pleases with her dress....He may order almost
any course of reading,--providing that he supply the books.
And he may even interfere with the style of dancing, and
recommend or prohibit partners.    But he may not thrust his
mother down his future wife's throat. Bel 208, XVI.

Would they live at Perivale?   Would it be necessary to re-
furnish the house?   Should he keep any of the land on his

own hands?  These are all interesting subjects of discussion between an engaged man and the girl to whom he is engaged, but the man, if he wish to make them thoroughly pleasant to the lady, should throw something of the urgency of a determined and immediate purpose into the discussion.
Bel 334, XXV.

There is often much of reticence on the part of a woman towards a man to whom she is engaged, something also of shamefacedness occasionally.  There exists a shadow of doubt, at least of that hesitation which shows that in spite of vows the woman knows that a change may come, and that provision for such possible steps backward should always be within her reach.  LasC 494, LIII.

[T]hat feeling...must be acknowledged by all engaged young men when they first find themselves encouraged by mammas in the taking of liberties which they have hitherto regarded as mysteries to be hidden, especially from maternal eyes,--that feeling of being a fine fat calf decked out with ribbons for a sacrifice.  HKHWR 852, XC.

Perhaps there is no period so pleasant among all the pleasant periods of love-making as that in which the intimacy between the lovers is so assured, and the coming event so near, as to produce and to endure conversation about the ordinary little matters of life;--what can be done with the limited means at their mutual disposal; how that life shall be begun which they are to lead together; what idea each has of the other's duties; what each can do for the other....It is very sweet to gaze at the stars together; and it is sweet to sit out among the haycocks;...but for the girl who has made a shirt for the man that she loves, there has come a moment in the last stitch of it, sweeter than any that stars, haycocks, poetry, or superlative epithets have produced.  HKHWR 895-6, XCV.

An engagement for marriage can never be so much to a man as it is to a woman, marriage itself can never be so much, can never be so great a change, produce such utter misery, or of itself be efficient for such perfect happiness.
VOB 232, XXXIII.

...a stipulation that she should not be hurried; but we all know what such stipulations are worth.  Who is to define what is and what is not hurry?  VOB 400, LV.

To be returned as a bad shilling, which has been presented over the counter and found to be bad, must be very disagreeable to a young woman's feelings.  VOB 479, LXVII.

To be alone with the girl to whom he is not engaged is a man's delight;--to be alone with the man to whom she is engaged is the woman's.  When the thing is settled there is always present to the man something of a feeling of clipped wings; whereas the woman is conscious of a new power of ex-

panding her pinions.  The certainty of the thing is to him
repressive.  He has done his work, and gained his victory,--
and by conquering has become a slave.  To her the certainty
of the thing is the removal of a restraint which has hitherto always been on her.  ED 168-9, XVIII,I.

Who does not know the smile  [half of congratulation to the
lover,  half of congratulation to herself as a woman that
another man had been caught by the leg and made fast]?  What
man,  who has been caught and made sure, has not felt a
certain dissatisfaction at being so treated, understanding
that the smile is intended to convey to him a sense of his
own captivity?  Way 258, XXVII,I.

It is not usual that a gentleman should ask a lady to be
engaged to him '--unless something should occur to separate
them! '  JC 64, VIII.

A man when he has just engaged himself to be married is as
prone as ever to talk of other men 'escaping,' feeling that,
though other young ladies were no better than evils to be
avoided,  his young lady is to be regarded as almost a
solitary instance of a blessing.  AyA 551, LVII.

Such days can hardly be agreeable to the man of whom it is
known by all around him that he is on the eve of committing
matrimony.  There is always, on such occasions, a feeling of
weakness,  as though the man had been subdued, brought at
length into a cage and tamed, so as to be made fit for
domestic purposes,  and deprived of his ancient freedom
amongst the woods; whereas the girl feels herself to be the
triumphant conqueror, who has successfully performed this
great act of taming.  Such being the case, the man had
perhaps better keep away till he is forced to appear at the
church-door.  AyA 628, LXIV.

He is cold-hearted, almost cruel, who does not like to see
the little triumph of a girl in such circumstances [engaged
to a baronet],  who will not sympathise with her, and join
with her, if occasion come, in her exaltation.  Kept 2,I.

The greater the adoration of the girl the deeper the abyss
into which she falls,--if she be doomed to fall at all....
For a month, perhaps for six weeks, the desire to subject
herself to a newly-found superior being supports her spirit
against all trials.  Neglect when it first comes is not
known to be neglect.  The first bursts of ill-temper have
about them something of the picturesque,--or at any rate of
the grotesque.  Even the selfishness is displayed on behalf
of an object so exalted as to be excusable.  Kept 2, I.

## ENGINEERS

From this time forth, and for the next twelve months, the
country was full of engineers, or of men who were so called.
I do not say this in disparagement; but the engineers were

like the yellow meal.  When there is an immense demand, and
that  a  suddenly  immense  demand,  for  any  article,  it  's
seldom easy to get it very good.  CasR 68-9, IV,II.

## ENGLAND...ENGLISHMEN

But  the  old  symbols  remained,  and  may  such  symbols  long
remain  among  us;  they  are  still  lovely  and  fit  to  be
loved....England  is  not  yet  a  commercial  country  in  the
sense  in  which  that  epithet  is  used  for  her;  and  let  us
still  hope  that  she  will  not  soon  become  so.   She  might
surely  as  well  be  called  feudal  England,  or  chivalrous
England.   If  in  western  civilized  Europe  there  does  exist  a
nation  among  whom  there  are  high  signors,  and  with  whom  the
owners  of  the  land  are  the  true  aristocracy,  the  aristocracy
that  is  trusted  as  being  best  and  fittest  to  rule,  that
nation  is  the  English.
    England a commercial country!  Yes, as Venice was.  She
may  excel  other  nations  in  commerce,  but  yet  it  is  not  that
in  which  she  most  prides  herself,  in  which  she  most
excels....Buying  and  selling  is  good  and  necessary;...but  it
cannot  be  the  noblest  work  of  man;  and  let  us  hope  that  it
may  not  in  our  time  be  esteemed  the  noblest  work  of  an
Englishman.  DoT 11-2, I.

None  but  Englishmen  or  Englishwomen  do  such  things  as  this
[have  a  picnic  over  the  ashes  of  James  the  Just].   To  other
people  is  wanting  sufficient  pluck  for  such  enterprises;  is
wanting  also  a  certain  mixture  of  fun,  honest  independence,
and  bad  taste.   Let  us  go  into  some  church  on  the  Contin-
ent--in  Italy,  we  will  say--where  the  walls  of  the  churches
still  boast  of  the  great  works  of  the  great  masters,--Look
at  that  man  standing  on  the  very  altar-step  while  the  priest
is  saying  his  mass;  look  at  his  grey  shooting-coat,  his
thick  shoes,  his  wide-awake  hat  stuck  under  one  arm,  and  his
stick  under  the  other,  while  he  holds  his  opera-glass  to  his
eyes.   How  he  shuffles  about  to  get  the  best  point  of  sight,
quite  indifferent  as  to  clergy  or  laity!   All  that  bell-
ringing,  incense-flinging,  and  breast-striking  is  nothing  to
him;  he  has  paid  dearly  to  be  brought  thither;  he  has  paid
the  guide  who  is  kneeling  a  little  behind  him;  he  is  going
to  pay  the  sacristan  who  attends  him;  he  is  quite  ready  to
pay  the  priest  himself,  if  the  priest  would  only  signify  his
wish  that  way;  but  he  has  come  there  to  see  that  fresco,  and
see  it  he  will:   respecting  that  he  will  soon  know  more  than
either  the  priest  or  his  worshippers.   Perhaps  some  servant
of  the  church,  coming  to  him  with  submissive,  almost
suppliant  gesture,  begs  him  to  step  back  just  for  one
moment.   The  lover  of  art  glares  at  him  with  insulted  look,
and  hardly  deigns  to  notice  him  further:   he  merely  turns
his  eye  to  his  Murray,  puts  his  hat  down  on  the  altar-step,
and  goes  on  studying  his  subject.   All  the  world--German,
Frenchman,  Italian,  Spaniard--all  men  of  all  nations  know
that  that  ugly  gray  shooting-coat  must  contain  an  Englishman.   He  cares  for  no  one.   If  any  one  upsets  him,  he  can  do

much towards righting himself; and if more be wanted, has he
not Lord Malmesbury or Lord Clarendon at his back? But what
would this Englishman say if his place of worship were
disturbed by some wandering Italian? Ber 143-4, IX.

He had that strong feeling of disinclination to be brought
before the public with reference to his private affairs,
which is common to all Englishmen. MM 318, XXIV.

## ENTERTAINING

The trouble in civilised life of entertaining company...is
so great that it cannot but be matter of wonder that people
are so fond of attempting it....If they who give such
laborious parties, and who endure such toil and turmoil in
the vain hope of giving them successfully, really enjoyed
the parties given by others, the matter could be
understood. A sense of justice would induce men and women
to undergo, in behalf of others, those miseries which others
had undergone in their behalf....
     Entertain! Who shall have sufficient self-assurance,
who shall feel sufficient confidence in his own powers to
dare to boast that he can entertain his company! A clown
can sometimes do so, and sometimes a dancer in short petticoats and stuffed pink legs; occasionally, perhaps, a
singer....
     Ladies...mainly trust to wax candles and upholstery.
Gentlemen seem to rely on their white waistcoats. To these
are added, for the delight of the more sensual, champagne
and such good things of the table as fashion allows to be
still considered as comestible. Even in this respect the
world is deteriorating. All the good soups are not tabooed;
and at the houses of one's accustomed friends, small barristers, doctors, government clerks, and such like, (for we
cannot all of us always live as grandees, surrounded by an
elysium of livery servants), one gets a cold potato handed
to one as a sort of finale to one's slice of mutton. Alas!
for those happy days when one could say to one's neighbourhood, 'Jones, shall I give you some mashed turnip?--may I
trouble you for a little cabbage?' BaT 343-4, XXXVI.

## ENVY

The rising in life of our familiar friends is, perhaps, the
bitterest morsel of the bitter bread which we are called
upon to eat in life. But we do eat it; and after a while it
becomes food to us,--when we find ourselves able to use, on
behalf, perhaps, of our children, the influence of those
whom we had once hoped to leave behind in the race of life.
When a man suddenly shoots up into power few suffer from it
very acutely. The rise of a Pitt can have caused no heart-
burning. PR 284, XXXII,I.

## EQUAL MIND

The equal mind...should be as sedulously maintained when

things run well, as well as when they run hardly; and
perhaps the maintenance of such equal mind is more difficult in the former than in the latter stage of life.
OrF 99, X,I.

## ERRORS

But the errors of past years will not turn themselves into
dreams.  Ber 789, XLIV.

## ESCAPE

The leader of a forlorn hope, though he be ever so resolved
to die in the breach, still makes some preparation for his
escape.  AS 341, L.

## ESTATES

There is much in the glory of ownership,--of the ownership
of land and houses, of beeves and woolly flocks, of wide
fields and thick-growing woods, even when that ownership is
of late date, when it conveys to the owner nothing but the
realization of a property on the soil; but there is much
more in it when it contains the memories of old years; when
the glory is the glory of race as well as the glory of power
and property.  Bel 412, XXXI.

## ETERNITY

It may be doubted whether any human mind has been able to
content itself with hopes of eternity, till distress in some
shape has embittered life.  The preachers preach very well,
--well enough to leave many convictions on the minds of men;
but not well enough to leave that conviction.  And godly men
live well,--but we never see them living as though such were
their conviction.  And were it so, who would strive and moil
in this world?  When the heart has been broken, and the
spirit ground to the dust by misery, then,--such is God's
mercy--eternity suffices to make life bearable.
EE 90-1,V,I.

It is the practice of many to have their minds utterly
callous in that respect  [beliefs in another life].   To
suppose that such men think this or think the other as to
future rewards and punishments is to give them credit for a
condition of mind to which they have never risen.
MF 20-1, II,II.

## EVIDENCE

Evidence by means of torture,--thumbscrew and suchlike,--we
have for many years past abandoned as barbarous, and have
acknowledged that it is of its very nature useless in the
search after truth.  How long will it be before we shall
recognize that the other kind of torture  [bullying a wit-

ness]    is equally opposed both to truth and civilization?
OrF 316, LXXI,II.

## EVIL-DOING

Evil-doing will be spoken of with bated breath and soft
words even by policemen, when the evil-doer comes in a
carriage, and with a title.    ED 317, LXXIV,II.

## EVIL THOUGHTS

It is astonishing how quickly, though how gradually, ideas
of such a nature  [wishing someone dead]  will be developed
when entertainment has once been given to them.  The Devil
makes himself at home with great rapidity when the hall door
has been opened to him.   MF 198, XVIII,I.

## EXAMINATIONS

It was no wonder that men's minds should be disturbed.
Competitive examinations at eighteen, twenty, and twenty-two
may be very well, and give an interesting stimulus to young
men at college.  But it is a fearful thing for a married man
with a family, who has long looked forward to rise to a
certain income by the worth of his general conduct and by
the value of his seniority--it is a fearful thing for such a
one to learn that he has again to go through his school
tricks, and fill up examination papers, with all his juniors
round him using their stoutest efforts to take his promised
bread from out his mouth....The prodigy of 1857, who is now
destroying all the hopes of the man who was well enough in
1855, will be a dunce to the tyro of 1860.  TC 63, VI.

It is a dreadful task that of answering examination papers.
...A man has before him a string of questions, and he looks
painfully down them, from question to question, searching
for some allusion to that special knowledge which he has
within him.  He too often finds that no such allusion is
made....He has perhaps crammed himself with the winds and
the tides, and there is no more reference to those stormy
subjects than if Luna were extinct; but he has, unfortunately, been loose about his botany, and question after
question would appear to him to have been dictated by Sir
Joseph Paxton or the headgardener at Kew.  And then to his
own blank face and puzzled look is opposed the fast scrib-
bling of some botanic candidate, fast as though reams of
folio could hardly contain all the knowledge which he is
able to pour forth.  TC 131, XI.

## EXCUSES

When yet has there been no crisis present to a man who has
wanted an excuse?--'And therefore I may probably stay,'--and
so on.  Who does not know the false mixture of excuse and
defiance which such a letter is sure to maintain; the crafty
words which may be taken as adequate reason if the receiver

be timid enough so to receive them, or as a noisy guantlet
thrown to the ground if there be spirit there for the picking of it up?  OrF 206-7, XXI,I.

## EXERTION

O reader, have you ever known what it is to rouse yourself
and go out to the world on your daily business, when all the
inner man has revolted against work, when a day of rest has
seemed to you to be worth a year of life? OrF 232, LXIII,II.

## EXILE

We are apt to think that a man may be disposed of by being
made to go abroad; or, if he is absolutely penniless and
useless, by being sent to the Colonies,--that he may there
become a shepherd and drink himself out of the world.   To
kill the man, so that he may be no longer a nuisance, is
perhaps the chief object in both cases.  MSF 235, XXXVII,II.

## EXITS

But there are times when it is very hard to get out of a
room, at which a sudden retreat would imply a conviction
that something was wrong.   IHP 10, XXXIII,II.

## EXPLANATIONS, WRITTEN

If there be a proceeding which an official man dislikes
worse than another, it is a demand for a written explanation.  ED 145, LVI,II.

## EYES

The eyes are the poet's strongest fortress; it is for their
description that he most gathers up his forces and puts
forth all his strength.  Ber 139, IX.

How few there are among women, few perhaps also among men,
who know that the sweetest, softest, tenderest, truest eyes
which a woman can carry in her head are green in colour!
ED 18, II,I.

F

## FACES

How many faces one sees which, in ordinary circumstances,

are comfortable, self-asserting, sufficient, and even bold; the lines of which, under difficulties, collapse and become mean, spiritless, and insignificant. There are faces which, in their usual form, seem to bluster with prosperity, but which the loss of a dozen points at whist will reduce to that currish aspect which reminds one of a dog-whip. ED 253, XXVIII,I.

There are people who always look black when such applications [to attend a house party] are made to them,--who look black at any allusions to pleasures. AyA 136, XV.

## FAILURE

Let any of us, in any attempt that we may make, convince ourselves with ever so much firmness that we shall fail, yet we are hardly the less downhearted when the failure comes. Ber 582, XXXII.

Nothing softens a man's feelings so much as failure, or makes him turn so anxiously to an idea of home as buffetings from those he meets abroad.  SmaH 407, XL.

Men fail often in other things, in the pursuit of honour, fortune, or power, and when they fail they can begin again. VOB 163, XXIV.

Such cessation [losing public office due to politics], however, arising from political causes, is no disappointment to a man...but he will recognise without remorse or sorrow the fact that the Ministry to which he has attached himself must cease to be a Ministry;--and there will be nothing in his displacement to gall his pride, or to create that inner feeling of almost insupportable mortification which comes from the conviction of personal failure. RalH 2, I.

[B]ut it is so hard to bear a sorrow of which all one's neighbours are conscious. When a man is reduced by poverty to the drinking of beer instead of wine, it is not the loss of the wine that is so heavy on him, as the consciousness that those around him are aware of the reason....That a man should fail in his love seems to him to be of all failures the most contemptible.  AS 328, XLVIII.

## FAINTING

The recovery from a fainting fit, a real fainting fit I beg young ladies to understand, brings with it a most unpleasant sensation.  TC 163, XIV.

## FALLING FROM POSITION

How easy it is to be seen when any man has fallen from his pride of place, though the altitude was ever so small, and the fall ever so slight.  Where is the man who can endure such a fall without showing it in his face, in his voice, in his step, and in every motion of every limb?  SmaH 406, XL.

## FAME

Fame is a skittish jade, more fickle even than Fortune, and apt to shy, and bolt, and plunge away on very trifling causes. PR 228, XXVI,I.

## FAMILIAR, THE

Let all those who have houses and the adjuncts of houses think how considerable a part of their life's pleasures consists in their interest in the things around them. When will the sea-kale be fit to cut, and when will the crocuses come up? will the violets be sweeter than ever? and the geranium cuttings, are they thriving? we have dug, and manured, and sown, and we look forward to the reaping, and to see our garners full. The very furniture which ministers to our daily uses is loved and petted....And the faces of those who have lived around us, do we not love them too, the servants who have worked for us, and the children who have first toddled beneath our eyes and prattled in our ears, and now run their strong races, screaming loudly, splashing us as they pass--very unpleasantly?...All men love such things, more or less, even though they know it not. And women love them even more than men. CasR 55-6, III,III.

None but those who have known the charms of a country-house early in life can conceive the intimacy to which a man attains with all the various trifling objects round his own locality; how he knows the bark of every tree, and the bend of every bough; how he ha[s] marked where the rich grass grows in tufts, and where the poorer soil is always dry and bare; how he watches the nests of the rooks and the holes of the rabbits, and has learned where the thrushes build, and can show the branch on which the linnet sits. CasR 97-8, V,III.

## FAMILIARITY

It is very seldom that a young man, unless he be tipsy, assumes an unwelcome familiarity in his early acquaintance with any girl; but when acquaintance has been long and intimate, familiarity must follow as a matter of course. DoT 83-4, VI.

[O]f late there seems to have grown up in the world a habit of greater familiarity than that which I think did prevail when last I moved among men. LasC 776, LXXXIII.

## FAMILIES

But old alliances...do not allow themselves to die out easily, and it is well for us all that they should be long-lived. Bel 431, XXXII.

# FAMINE

They who were in the south of Ireland during the winter of 1846-47 will not readily forget the agony of that period. For many, many years preceding and up to that time, the increasing swarms of the country had been fed upon the potato, and upon the potato only; and now all at once the potato failed them, and the greater part of eight million human beings were left without food....

There are an infinite number of smaller bearings in which this question of the famine, and of agricultural distress in Ireland, may be regarded, and should be regarded by those who wish to understand it. The manner in which the Poor Law was first rejected and then accepted, and then, if one may say so, swallowed whole by the people; the way in which emigration has affected them; the difference in the system of labour there from that here, which in former days was so strong that an agricultural labourer living on his wages and buying food with them, was a person hardly to be found: all these things must be regarded by one who would understand the matter....

But very frightful are the flames as they rush through the chambers of the poor, and very frightful was the course of that violent remedy which brought Ireland out of its misfortunes. Those who saw its course, and watched its victims, will not readily forget what they saw.

Slowly, gradually, and with a voice that was for a long time discredited, the news spread itself through the country that the food of the people was gone. That his own crop was rotten and useless each cotter knew, and realized the idea that he must work for wages if he could get them, or else go to the poorhouse. That the crop of his parish or district was gone became evident to the priest, and the parson, and the squire; and they realized the idea that they must fall on other parishes or other districts for support. But it was long before the fact made itself known that there was no food in any parish, in any district....

I think that no portion of Ireland suffered more severely during the famine than the counties of Cork and Kerry. The poorest parts were perhaps the parishes lying back from the sea and near to the mountains.
CasR 120-7, VII,I.

It may probably be said that so large a sum of money had never been circulated in the country in any one month since money had been known there; and yet it may also be said that so frightful a mortality had never occurred there from the want of that which money brings. It was well understood by all men now that the customary food of the country had disappeared. There was no longer any difference of opinion between rich and poor, between Protestant and Roman Catholic; as to that, no man dared now to say that the poor, if left to themselves, could feed themselves, or to allege that the sufferings of the country arose from the machinations of money-making speculators. The famine was an established fact, and all men knew that it was God's doing,

--all men knew this, though few could recognize as yet with how much mercy God's hand was stretched out over the country....

At any rate, there was the famine, undoubted not by any one; and death...was busy enough...among the cabins of the poor. And now the great fault of those who were the most affected was becoming one which would not have been at first sight expected. One would think that starving men would become violent, taking food by open theft--feeling, and perhaps not without some truth, that the agony of their want robbed such robberies of its sin. But such was by no means the case....The fault of the people was apathy. It was the feeling of the multitude that the world and all that was good in it was passing away from them; that exertion was useless, and hope hopeless. 'Ah, me! your honour,' said a man to me, 'there'll never be a bit and a sup again in the county Cork! The life of the world is fairly gone!'

And it was very hard to repress this feeling. The energy of a man depends so much on the outward circumstances that encumber him! It is so hard to work when work seems hopeless--so hard to trust where the basis of our faith is so far removed from sight!...And when men were falling in the highways, and women would sit with their babes in their arms, listless till death should come to them, was it not natural to think that death was making a huge success--that he, the inexorable one, was now the inexorable indeed?...

The people, however, were conscious of God's work, and were becoming dull and apathetic. They clustered about the roads, working lazily while their strength lasted them; and afterwards, when strength failed them for this, they clustered more largely in the poor-houses. And in every town-- in every assemblage of houses which in England would be called a village, there was a poor-house. Any big barrack of a tenement that could be obtained at a moment's notice, whatever the rent, became a poor-house in the course of twelve hours;--in twelve, nay, in two hours. What was necessary but the bare walls, and a supply of yellow meal? Bad provision this for all a man's wants,--as was said often enough by irrational philanthropists; but better provision than no shelter and no yellow meal! It was bad that men should be locked up at night without any of the appliances of decency; bad that they should be herded together for day after day with no resource but the eating twice a day of enough unsavoury food to keep life and soul together;--very bad, ye philanthropical irrationalists! But is not a choice of evils all that is left to us in many a contingency? Was not even this better than that life and soul should be allowed to part, without any effort at preserving their union?

And thus life and soul were kept together, the government of the day having wisely seen what, at so short a notice, was possible for them to do, and what was absolutely impossible. It is in such emergencies as these that the watching and wisdom of a government are necessary; and I shall always think--as I did think then--that the wisdom of its action and the wisdom of its abstinence from action were very good....

Life and soul were kept together in those terrible
days;--that is, the Irish life and soul generally.  There
were many slips, in which the union was violently dissolved,
--many cases in which the yellow meal allowed was not sufficient, or in which it did not reach the sufferer in time to
prevent such dissolution,--cases which when numbered together amounted to thousands.  And then the pestilence came,
taking its victims by tens of thousands,--but that was after
the time with which we shall have concern here; and
immigration followed, taking those who were saved by
hundreds of thousands.  But the millions are still there, a
thriving people; for His mercy endureth for ever.
CasR 27-33, II,III.

But then, as long as a man found work out of the poor-house,
his wife and children would not be admitted into it....The
rule in itself was salutary, as without it a man could work,
earning such wages as were adjudged to be needful for a
family, and at the same time send his wife and children to
be supported on the rates.  But in some cases...it pressed
very cruelly.  CasR 76-7, IV,III.

Protestant clergymen in Ireland in those days had very frequently other reasons for fasting than those prescribed by
ecclesiastical canons.  A well-nurtured lady, the wife of a
parish rector in the county Cork, showed me her larder one
day about that time.  It contained two large loaves of
bread, and a pan full of stuff which I should have called
paste, but which she called porridge.  It was all that she
had for herself, her husband, her children, and her charity.
Her servants had left her before she came to that pass.  And
she was a well-nurtured, handsome, educated woman, born to
such comforts as you and I enjoy every day,--oh, my reader!
perhaps without much giving of thanks for them.  Poor lady!
the struggle was too much for her, and she died under it.
CasR 157, VIII,III.

People were beginning to believe that there would never be a
bit more to eat in the land, and that the time for hope and
energy was gone.  Land was becoming of no value, and the
only thing regarded was sufficiency of food to keep body and
soul together.  Under such circumstances it was difficult to
hope.

But energy without hope is impossible, and therefore
was there such an apathy and deadness through the
country....It was this feeling that made a residence in
Ireland at that period so very sad.

Ah me!  how little do we know what is coming to us!
Irish cakes and ale were done and over for this world, we
all thought.  But in truth the Irish cakes were only then a-
baking, and the Irish ale was being brewed....The cake is
still too new,--cakes often are; and the ale is not sufficiently mellowed.  But of this I am sure, that the cakes and
ale are there....

But if one did in truth write a tale of the famine, after that it would behove the author to write a tale of the pestilence; and then another, a tale of the exodus. These three wonderful events, following each other, were the blessings coming from Omniscience and Ominipotence by which the black clouds were driven from the Irish firmament. If one, through it all could have dared to hope, and have had from the first that wisdom which has learned to acknowledge that His mercy endureth for ever! And then the same author going on with his series would give in his last set,-- Ireland in her prosperity. CasR 282-4, XV,III.

And then there came the Irish famine, and all the bindings of all the Tories were scattered to the winds like feathers. The Irishman's potato-pot ceased to be full, and at once the great territorial magnates of England were convinced that they had clung to the horns of a false altar....With great wisdom the majority of them considered that this was enough; and so the bill for the repeal of the corn laws was brought before the House, and the world knew that it would be carried. Ber 286, XVI.

## FAMINE RELIEF

When this was understood, men certainly did put their shoulders to the wheel with a great effort. Much abuse at the time was thrown upon the government; and they who took upon themselves the management of the poor in the south-west were taken most severely to task. I was in the country, travelling always through it, during the whole period, and I have to say--as I did say at the time with a voice that was not very audible--that in my opinion the measures of the government were prompt, wise, and beneficent; and I have to say also that efforts of those who managed the poor were, as a rule, unremitting, honest, impartial, and successful.
    The feeding of four million starving people with food, to be brought from foreign lands, is not an easy job. No government could bring the food itself; but by striving to do so it might effectually prevent such bringing on the part of others. Nor when the food was there, on the quays, was it easy to put it, in due proportions, into the four million mouths. Some mouths, and they, alas! the weaker ones, would remain unfed. But the opportunity was a good one for slashing philanthropical censure; and then the business of the slashing, censorious philanthropist is so easy, so exciting, and so pleasant! CasR 127, VII,I.

How they all spent their day at the soup kitchen, which however, though so called, partook quite as much of the character of a bake-house; how they studied the art of making yellow Indian meal into puddings; how the girls wanted to add milk and sugar, not understanding at first the deep principles of political economy, which soon taught them not to waste on the comforts of a few that which was so necessary for the life of many; how the poor woman brought in their sick ailing children, accepting the proffered food,

but bitterly complaining of it because they wanted money,
with which they still thought that they could buy potatoes--
all this need not here or now be described. CasR 142,VIII,I.

Here also was an establishment for distributing food, and a
crowd of poor half-fed wretches were there....Not that at
that time things were so bad as they became afterwards.  Men
were not dying on the road-side, nor as yet had the apathy
of want produced its terrible cure for the agony of hunger.
The time had not yet come when the famished living skeletons
might be seen to reject the food which could no longer serve
to prolong their lives.
     Though this had not come as yet, the complaints of the
women with their throngs of children were bitter enough; and
it was heart-breaking too to hear the men declare that they
had worked like horses, and that it was hard upon them now
to see their children starve like dogs.  For in this earlier
part of the famine the people did not seem to realize the
fact that this scarcity and want had come from God.  Though
they saw the potatoes rotting in their own gardens, under
their own eyes, they still seemed to think that the rich men
of the land could stay the famine if they would; that the
fault was with them; that the famine could be put down if
the rich would but stir themselves to do it.  Before it was
over they were well aware that no human power could suffice
to put it down.  Nay, more than that; they had almost begun
to doubt the power of God to bring back better days....This
was a place at which Indian corn flour, that which after a
while was generally termed 'meal' in those famine days, was
sold to the poor.  At this period much of it was absolutely
given away.  This plan, however, was soon found to be injurious; for hundreds would get it who were not absolutely in
want, and would then sell it;--for the famine by no means
improved the morals of the people.
     And therefore it was found better to sell the flour; to
sell it at a cheap rate, considerably less sometimes than
the cost price; and to put the means of buying it into the
hands of the people by giving them work, and paying them
wages.  Towards the end of these times, when the full weight
of the blow was understood, and the subject had been in some
sort studied, the general rule was thus to sell the meal at
its true price, hindering the exorbitant profit of the
hucksters by the use of large stores, and to require that
all those who could not buy it should seek the means of
living within the walls of workhouses.  The regular established workhouses, unions as they were called,--were not as
yet numerous, but supernumerary houses were provided in
every town, and were crowded from the cellars to the roofs.
     It need hardly be explained that no general rule could
be established and acted upon at once.  The numbers to be
dealt with were so great, that exceptions to all rules were
overwhelming.  But such and such like were the efforts made,
and these efforts ultimately were successful.
CasR 152-5, VIII,I.

It was a settled thing at their relief committee that there

should be no giving away of money to chance applicants for alms. What money each had to bestow would go twice further by being brought to the general fund--by being expended with forethought and discrimination....But the system was impracticable, for it required frames of iron and hearts of adamant. It was impossible not to waste money in almsgiving. CasR 47-8, II,II.

At this time the famine was beginning to be systematised. The sternest among landlords and masters were driven to acknowledge that the people had not got food or the means of earning it. The people themselves were learning that a great national calamity had happened, and that the work was God's work; and the Government had fully recognized the necessity of taking the whole matter into its own hands. They were responsible for the preservation of the people, and they acknowledged their responsibility.

And then two great rules seemed to get themselves laid down--not by general consent, for there were many who greatly contested their wisdom--but by some force strong enough to make itself dominant. The first was, that the food to be provided should be earned and not given away. And the second was, that the providing of that food should be left to private competition, and not in in [sic] any way be undertaken by the Government. I make bold to say that both these rules were wise and good.

But how should the people work? That Government should supply the wages was of course an understood necessity; and it was also necessary that on all such work the amount of wages should be regulated by the price at which provisions might fix themselves. These points produced questions which were hotly debated by the Relief Committees of the different districts; but at last it got itself decided, again by the hands of Government, that all hills along the country roads should be cut away, and that the people should be employed on this work. They were so employed,--very little to the advantage of the roads for that or some following years.... The question of tools also came to a sort of understood settlement before long; and within three months of the time of which I am writing legions of wheelbarrows were to be seen lying near every hill; wheelbarrows in hundreds and thousands. The fate of those myriads of wheelbarrows has always been a mystery to me....

They were wretched-looking creatures, half-clad, discontented, with hungry eyes, each having at his heart's core a deep sense of injustice done personally upon him. They hated this work of cutting hills from the commencement to the end,--hated it, though it was to bring them wages and save them and theirs from actual famine and death. They had not been accustomed to the discomfort of being taken far from their homes to their daily work. Very many of them had never worked regularly for wages, day after day, and week after week. Up to this time such was not the habit of Irish cottiers. They held their own land, and laboured there for a spell; and then they would work for a spell, as men do in England, taking wages; and then they would be idle for a spell. It was not exactly a profitable mode of life, but it

had its comforts; and now these unfortunates who felt themselves to be driven forth like cattle in droves for the
first time, suffered the full wretchedness of their
position. They were not rough and unruly, or inclined to be
troublesome and perhaps violent, as men similarly circumstanced so often are in England;--as Irishmen are when collected in gangs out of Ireland. They had no aptitudes for
such roughness, and no spirits for such violence. But they
were melancholy, given to complaint, apathetic, and utterly
without interest in that they were doing. CasR 62-5, IV,II.

The cutting off of maimed limbs, and wrenching out from
their sockets of smashed bones, is by no means shocking to
the skilled practitioner. And dying paupers, with 'the
drag' in their face--that certain sign of coming death of
which I have spoken--no longer struck men to the heart....In
administering relief one may rob five unseen sufferers of
what would keep them in life if one is moved to bestow all
that is comfortable on one sufferer that is seen....And so
in one sense those who were the best in the county, who
worked the hardest for the poor and spent their time most
completely among them, became the hardest of heart, and most
obdurate in their denials. It was strange to see devoted
women neglecting the wants of the dying, so that they might
husband their strength and time and means for the wants of
those who might still be kept among the living.
CasR 150-1, VIII,III.

## FANTASIES

But the character of a man is not to be judged from the
pictures which he may draw or from the antics which he may
play in solitary hours. Those who act generally with the
most consummate wisdom in the affairs of the world, often
meditate very silly doings before their wiser resolutions
form themselves. Bel 181, XIV.

## FAREWELLS

The world, we think, makes a great mistake on the subject of
saying, or acting, farewell. The word or deed should
partake of the suddenness of electricity; but we all drawl
through it at a snail's pace. We are supposed to tear ourselves from our friends; but tearing is a process which
should be done quickly. What is so wretched as lingering
over a last kiss, giving the hand for the third time, saying
over and over again, 'Good-bye, John, God bless you; and
mind you write!' Who has not seen his dearest friends
standing round the window of a railway carriage, while the
train would not start, and has not longed to say to them,
'Stand not upon the order of your going, but go at once!'
And of all such farewells, the ship's farewell is the
longest and the most dreary. One sits on a damp bench,
snuffing up the odour of oil and ropes, cudgelling one's
brains to think what further word of increased tenderness
can be spoken. No tenderer word can be spoken. One returns

again and again to the weather, to coats and cloaks, perhaps
even to sandwiches and the sherry flask.  All effect is thus
destroyed, and a trespass is made even on the domain of
feeling.

I remember a line of poetry, learnt in my earliest
youth, and which I believe to have emanated from a senti-
mental Frenchman, a man of genius, with whom my parents were
acquainted.  It is as follows:--
Are you go?--Is you gone?--And I left?--Vera vell!
Now the whole business of a farewell is contained in
that line.  When the moment comes, let that be said; let
that be said and felt, and then let the dear ones depart.
TC 537-8,XLIV.

Yes, ye dear ones--it is hard to part--it is hard for the
mother to see the child of her bosom torn from her for ever;
it is cruel that sisters should be severed; it is a harsh
sentence for the world to give, that of such a separation as
this.  These, O ye loving hearts, are the penalties of love!
Those that are content to love must always be content to pay
them.  TC 538-9, XLIV.

## FARMING

...a deficiency in which knowledge  [knowing how to get the
full worth in work done for the fourteen shillings a week
paid to the labourers]  is the cause why gentlemen in
general find farming so expensive an amusement.  AS 6, I.

## FATHERS

Other fathers, since Jephtha and Agamemnon, have recognised
it as true that heaven has demanded from them their
daughters.  SHHOH 231, XXIII.

## FATHERS...SONS

It is a terrible task, that of having to provide for eleven
sons.  With two or three a man may hope, with some reasonable chance of seeing his hope fulfilled, that things will
go well with him, and that he may descend to his grave without that worst of wretchedness, that gnawing grief which
comes from bad children.  But who can hope that eleven sons
will all walk in the narrow path?  TC 83-4, VIII.

Nevertheless, one would always wish to see one's own son not
less bright than one's friend's son.  Ber 12, I.

It is a grievous thing to have to write home to one's
father, and to say that one has failed when that father has
so anxiously longed for success.  Ber 17, I.

But a son is not ill inclined to accept acts of new grace
from a father.  Ber 92, VI.

A grown-up son must be the greatest comfort a man can have,
if he be his father's best friend; but otherwise he can

hardly be a comfort.  PF 100, XI,I.

But it is natural that the father should yearn for the son,
while the son's feeling for the father is of a very much
weaker nature.  PF 150, LV,II.

As the sun is falling in the heavens and the evening lights
come on, this world's wealth and prosperity afford no
pleasure equal to this [sharing the reins of government between his own hands and those of his heir].  It is this
delight that enables a man to feel, up to the last moment,
that the goods of the world are good.  RalH 87, XI.

There is nothing in the world so cruel as the way in which
sons use the natural affections of their fathers, obtaining
from these very feelings a power of rebelling against
authority!  RalH 362, XLVIII.

## FAULTS

The world, in judging of people who are false and bad and
selfish and prosperous to outward appearances, is apt to be
hard upon them, and to forget the punishments which
generally accompany such faults.  ED 191, XXI,I.

## FEAR

[B]ut we are all inclined to magnify the bugbears which
frighten us.  BaT 395, XLI.

...that sort of fear which is produced by reverence and
habits of obedience, but which, when softened by affection,
hardly makes itself known as fear, except on troublous
occasions.  GLOG 187, XVII.

...as the guilty are always afraid of those who will have to
judge their guilt.  VOB 433, LXI.

It is all very well for a woman to tell herself that she
will encounter some anticipated difficulty without fear,--
or for a man either.  The fear cannot be overcome by will.
The thing, however, may be done, whether it be leading a
forlorn hope, or speaking to an angry husband,-- in spite of
fear.  PrM 64, XLVII,II.

## FEBRUARY

February is certainly not a warm month; but with the rich it
is generally a cosy, comfortable time.  Good fires, winter
cheer, groaning tables, and warm blankets, make a fictitious
summer, which, to some tastes, is more delightful than the
long days and the hot sun.  And some marriages are
especially winter matches.  They depend for their charm on
the same substantial attractions:  instead of heart beating
to heart in sympathetic unison, purse chinks to purse.
DoT 254-5,XXI.

## FEELINGS

...that nice appreciation of the feelings of others which belongs of right exclusively to women. BaT 503, LII.

Such feelings [near to envy] are quite involuntary, whereas one's thoughts are more or less under command. TC 54, V.

But there are positions which cannot be reached, though there be no physical or material objection in the way. It is the view which the mind takes of a thing which creates the sorrow that arises from it. If the heart were always malleable and the feelings could be controlled, who would permit himself to be tormented by any of the reverses which affection meets? Death would create no sorrow; ingratitude would lose its sting; and the betrayal of love would do no injury beyond that which it might entail upon worldly circumstances. But the heart is not malleable; nor will the feelings admit of such control. SmaH 503, L.

How wrong the world is in connecting so closely as it does the capacity for feeling and the capacity for expression... in confusing the technical art of the man who sings with the unselfish tenderness of the man who feels! But the world does so connect them; and, consequently, those who express themselves badly are ashamed of their feelings. MM 192,XV.

## FIGHTING

Who can fight strenuously in any combat in which there is no danger? BaT 331, XXXIV.

There is no personal encounter in which a young man is so sure to come by the worst as in that with a much older man. This is so surely the case that it ought to be considered cowardly in an old man to attack a young one. If an old man hit a young man over the head with a walking-stick, what can the young man do, except run away to avoid a second blow? Then the old man, if he be a wicked old man, as so many are, tells all his friends that he has licked the young man....If a woman attack a man with a knife, the man will be held to have fought fairly though he shall have knocked her down in the encounter. And so also with an old man, if he take a poker instead of a stick, the world will refuse to him the advantage of his gray hairs. RacR 170, XIII.

Dogs fight with their teeth, and horses with their heels; swans with their wings, and cats with their claws;--so also do women use such weapons as nature has provided for them. RacR 175-6, XIV.

Nothing gives a man such spirit for a fight, as the act of fighting. RacR 309, XXIV.

There is something ill-mannered, ungentlemanlike, what we now call rowdy, in personal encounters, even among laymen;

and this is of course aggravated when the assailant is a
clergymen.    IHP 115-6, XLIV,II.

## FLATTERY

Of all flattery praise is the coarsest and least efficacious.    When you would flatter a man, talk to him about
himself, and criticise him, pulling him to pieces by comparison of some small present fault with his past conduct;
--and the rule holds the same with a woman.    To tell her
that she looks well is feeble work; but complain to her wo-
fully [sic] that there is something wanting at the present
moment, something lacking from the usual high standard, some
temporary loss of beauty, and your solicitude will prevail
with her.    SHHOH 56, VI.

Ah, yes!    what other moment in a man's life is at all equal
to that in which he is being flattered to the top of his
bent by the love of the woman he loves.    To be flattered by
the love of a woman whom he does not love is almost equally
unpleasant,--if the man be anything of a man.  VOB 484,LXVII.

A man may flatter another...without preconcerted falsehood.
It suits one man to be well with another,...and in such circumstances    [trying to marry a sister]    a man is almost
justified in flattering a brother.  PrM 16, II,I.

Courtesy always flatters, and flattery is alway pleasant.
MF 232, XXI,I.

## FLAWS

There are men who always ride lame horses, and yet see as
much of the hunting as others.    ED 217-8, LXIII,II.

The boy with none of the equipment of the skilled sportsman
can make himself master of a wounded bird.    ED 362,LXXIX,II.

## FLIRTATIONS

Oh! ye ruthless swains, from whose unhallowed lips fall
words full of poisoned honey, do ye never think of the
bitter agony of many months, of the dull misery of many
years, of the cold monotony of an uncheered life, which
follow so often as the consequence of your short hour of
pastime?  TC 158, XIV.

If such things [flirting] are done in the green wood, what
will be done in the dry?  DoT 83, VI.

If young gentlemen...are allowed to amuse themselves with
young ladies, surely young ladies...should be allowed to
play their own cards accordingly.  OrF 122, LII,II.

Most of such flirtations if they were done out loud would be
very innocent.  Young men are not nearly so pointed in their

compliments as their elders, and generally confine themselves to remarks of which neither mothers nor grandmothers
could disapprove if they heard them.   The romance lies
rather in the thoughts than in the words of those concerned.
RacR 96-7, VIII.

Men won't flirt with draggled girls, smirched with dust,
weary with work, and soiled with heat; and especially they
will not do so at the rate of a shilling a word....It is not
only that men will not flirt with draggled girls, but they
will carry away with them unfortunate remembrances of what
they have seen and heard.   MM 366, XXVII.

Croquet is a pretty game out of doors, and chess is delightful in a drawing-room.   Battledore and shuttlecock and hunt-
the-slipper have also their attractions.   Proverbs are good,
and cross questions with crooked answers may be made very
amusing.   But none of these games are equal to the game of
love-making--providing that the players can be quite sure
that there shall be no heart in the matter.   Any touch of
heart not only destroys the pleasure of the game, but makes
the player awkward and incapable and robs him of his skill.
And thus it is that there are many people who cannot play
the game at all.   A deficiency of some needed internal physical strength prevents the owners of the heart from keeping
a proper control over its valves, and thus emotion sets in,
and the pulses are accelerated, and feeling supervenes.   For
such a one to attempt a game of love-making, is as though
your friend with the gout should insist on playing croquet.
A sense of the ridiculous, if nothing else, should in either
case deter the afflicted one from the attempt....Husbands
when they have been drinking are very apt to make mistakes
as to the purport of the game.   LasC 236-7, XXVI.

It is perhaps not unnatural that a sick lady, preparing to
receive a clergyman in her bedroom, should put on a clean
nightcap,--but to suspicious eyes small causes suffice to
create alarm.   HKHWR 619, LXV.

## FOREIGNERS

If a prince of our own was forced, for the good of the
country, to go among some far-distant outlandish people, and
there to be poked in the ribs, and slapped on the back all
round, the change to him could hardly be so great   [as to
the Emperor of China in London].   Way 84, LIX,II.

In these days our governments are very anxious to be civil
to foreigners, and there is nothing that a robust Secretary
of State will not do for them.   AS 533, LXXVII.

## FORGIVENESS

When women are enjoined to forgive their enemies it cannot
be intended that such wrongs [twitting about a daughter's
unfortunate marriage] as these should be included.
FrP 389, XL.

Could any woman who knew that love-letters had been written to her husband by another woman forgive that other? We are all conscious of trespassers against ourselves whom we especially bar when we say our prayers.  Forgive us our trespasses, as we forgive them who trespass against us-- excepting Jones, who has committed the one sin that we will not forgive, that we ought not to forgive.  Is there not that sin against the Holy Ghost to justify us?
IHP 306, LXIII,II.

## FORTITUDE

The carrying an external look of indifference when the heart is sinking within;--or has sunk almost to the very ground,-- is more than difficult; it is an agonizing task.  In all mental suffering the sufferer longs for solitude,--for permission to cast himself loose along the ground, so that every limb and every feature of his person may faint in sympathy with his heart.  A grandly urbane deportment over a crushed spirit and ruined hopes is beyond the physical strength of most men;--but there have been men so strong.
Way 293, LXXXI,II.

There are things which the heart of a man should bear without whimpering, but which it cannot bear in public with that appearance of stoical indifference which the manliness of a man is supposed to require.  AS 551, LXXIX.

## FORTUNE

There are very different ideas of what 'a fortune' may be supposed to consist.  DrW 2, I, Part I.

## FOXES

Gorse coverts make, no doubt, the charm of hunting, but gorse coverts will not hold foxes unless the woodlands be preserved.  The fox is a travelling animal.  Knowing well that 'home-staying youths have ever homely wits,' he goes out and sees the world.  He is either born in the woodlands, or wanders thither in his early youth....
    There is something doubtless absurd in the intensity of the worship paid to the fox by hunting communities.  The animal becomes sacred, and his preservation is a religion. His irregular destruction is a profanity, and words spoken to his injury are blasphemous.  Not long since a gentleman shot a fox running across a woodland ride in a hunting country.  He had mistaken it for a hare, and had done the deed in the presence of keepers, owner, and friends.  His feelings were so acute and his remorse so great that, in their pity, they had resolved to spare him; and then, on the spot, entered into a solemn compact that no one should be told....As the vulpicide, on the afternoon of the day of the deed, went along the corridor to his room, one maid-servant whispered to another, and the poor victim of an imperfect sight heard the words--'That's he as shot the fox!'  The gentleman did not appear at dinner, nor was he ever again seen in those parts.  PR 311-2, LXXV,II.

## FRAUD

One seems inclined to think sometimes that any fool might do
an honest business.  But fraud requires a man to be alive
and wide awake at every turn.  Way 303, XXXII,II.

## FREEDOM

We can understand how in common cases the prisoner dis-
charged on his acquittal...may feel the sweetness of his
freedom and enjoy his immunity from danger with a light
heart.  He is received probably by his wife or young woman,
--or perhaps, having no wife or young woman to receive him,
betakes himself to his usual haunts.  The interest which has
been felt in his career is over, and he is no longer the
hero of an hour;--but he is a free man, and may drink his
gin-and-water where he pleases.  Perhaps a small admiring
crowd may welcome him as he passes out into the street, but
he has become nobody before he reaches the corner.
PR 240-1, LXVII,II.

There is however a good deal to be said against it
[freedom]....There is a comfort for a young lady in having a
pied-a-terre to which she may retreat in case of need.  In
American circles, where girls congregate without their
mothers, there is a danger felt by young men that if a lady
be once taken in hand, there will be no possibility of getting rid of her,--no mamma to whom she may be taken and
under whose wings she may be dropped.  'My dear,' said an
old gentleman the other day walking through an American
ball-room, and addressing himself to a girl whom he knew
well,--'My dear--' But the girl bowed and passed on, still
clinging to the arm of the young man who accompanied her.
But the old gentleman was cruel, and possessed of a determined purpose.  'My dear,' said he again, catching the young
man tight by the collar and holding him fast.  'Don't be
afraid; I've got him; he shan't desert you; I'll hold him
here till you have told me how your father does.'  The young
lady looked as if she didn't like it, and the sight of her
misery gave rise to a feeling that, after all, mammas perhaps may be a comfort.  DuC 243, XXXI.

## FRENCH...ENGLISH

At this time the popularity of Louis Philippe was on the
wane.  The grocers of Paris were becoming sick of their
paternal citizen king....Poor grocers!  too much prosperity
had made them over-nice.  When Mr. Smith had been about six
months gone from them, how gladly would they have had him
back again!
    But they are again satisfied.  The grocer interest,
which on the whole may perhaps be looked on as predominant
in Paris, is once more swathed in rose-leaves....If a king
can so devise that chocolate shall be sold--and paid for--
what more can a grocer interest need?  What more than this,
that having sold its daily quantum of chocolate, it shall

have a theatre to go to, a spectacle to look at, ices, coffee, and eau sucree! Since the world began to open its young eyes and look about it with any understanding, what else has been desirable? What does a man and a grocer want? Panem et circenses; soup that shall not be too maigre; and a seat at the Porte St. Martin that shall not be too dear. Is it not all written in that?

England a nation of shopkeepers! No, let us hope not; not as yet, at any rate. There have been nations to whom the buying and selling of bread and honey--especially of honey--has been everything; lost nations--people deadened, whose souls were ever sleeping, whose mouths only and gastric organs attested that life was in them....But let us hope that no English people will be such as long as the roads are open to Australia, to Canada, and New Zealand.

A young man whose life was to be spent in writing politico-religious pamphlets had much to learn in Paris in those days. Indeed, Paris has ever been a school for such writers since men began to find that something was wrong, even under the reign of the great Dubarry....The secret had been hardly solved in those latter days of poor Louis Philippe. Much had certainly been done when a citizen king was thought of and set agoing; but even a citizen king required to be wound up, and the alchemist was still at his crucibles.

Now, indeed, the work has been finished....Thinking men, even thinking Frenchmen, can live contented. Chocolate is sold--and paid for. And a score and a half of daily theatres are open at the most moderate of prices.
Ber 452-4, XXV.

## FRENCHMEN

...two tall Frenchmen whose faces had been remodelled in that mould into which so large a proportion of Parisians of the present day force their heads, in order that they may come out with some look of the Emperor about them. Were there not some such machine as this in operation, it would be impossible that so many Frenchmen should appear with elongated, angular, hard faces, all as like each other as though they were brothers! The cut of the beard, the long prickly-ended, clotted moustache, which looks as though it were being continually rolled up in saliva, the sallow, half-bronzed, apparently unwashed colour--these may all, perhaps, be assumed by any man after a certain amount of labour and culture. But how it has come to pass that every Parisian has been able to obtain for himself a pair of the Emperor's long, hard, bony, cruel-looking cheeks, no Englishman has yet been able to guess. That having the power they should have the wish to wear this mask is almost equally remark- able. Can it be that a political phase, when stamped on a people with an iron hand of sufficient power of pressure, will leave its impress on the outward body as well as on the inward soul? If so, a Frenchman may, perhaps, be thought to have gained in the apparent stubborn wilfulness of his coun- tenance some recompense for his compelled loss of all political wilfulness whatever. TC 298-9, XXV.

## FRIENDS

Bertram he had known long and intimately, and held him therefore somewhat cheap in many respects, as we are all accustomed to hold our dearest friends. Ber 269, XV.

[W]ho can ever consult a friend with advantage on any subject without telling him all the circumstances? Ber 289, XVI.

"[W]hat a thing it is to have a friend", she said....But... it is of all things the most difficult to acquire--and especially difficult for both ladies and gentlemen after forty years of age. Ber 389, XXI.

There are those whose nature it is to love new-found friends at a few hours' warning. CasR 238, XII,II.

The work which a friend has to perform for a friend is so much heavier than that which comes in the way of any profession! CasR 148, VIII,II.

[W]e do make new friends when we lose our old friends, and the heart is capable of cure as is the body; were it not so, how terrible would be our fate in this world! But we are so apt to find fault with God's goodness to us in this respect, arguing, of others if not of ourselves, that the heart once widowed should remain a widow through all time. I, for one, think that the heart should receive its new spouses with what alacrity it may, and always with thankfulness. CasR 102, V,III.

It is very well to have friends to lean upon, but it is not always well to lean upon one's friends. OrF 108, LI,II.

If one's friends would as a rule refrain from action how much more strongly would real friendship flourish in the world. OrF 108, LI,II.

But it is lucky for us that we seldom know what our best friends say on our behalf, when they discuss us and our faults behind our backs. Bel 248, XIX.

One's friend has no right to decide for one what is, and what is not dangerous. HKHWR 523, LV.

To oblige a friend by inflicting an injury on his enemy is often more easy than to confer a benefit on the friend himself. PR 21, XLIII,II.

## FRIENDS, FAMILY

Every one has some quiet, old, family, confidential friend; a man given to silence, but of undoubted knowledge of the world, whose experience is vast, and who, though he has not risen in the world himself, is always the man to help others to do so. Ber 283, XVI.

[A]nd I doubt whether we in England have any more valuable English characteristic than that of having old family friends. Old family feuds are not common with us now-a-days --not so common as with some other people. Sons who now hated their father's enemies would have but a bad chance before a commission of lunacy; but an old family friend is supposed to stick to one from generation to generation. CasR 85-6, V,II.

We all know the appearance of that old gentleman, how pleasant and dear a fellow he is, how welcome is his face within the gate, how free he makes with our wine, generally abusing it, how he tells our eldest daughter to light his candle for him, how he gave silver cups when the little girls were born, and now bestows tea-services as they get married,--a most useful, safe, and charming fellow, not a year younger-looking or more nimble than ourselves, without whom life would be very blank. We all know that man. HKHWR 6, I.

## FRIENDS, NEW

[N]or is it a sign of ingratitude or heartlessness in the world that at such a period of great distress new friends should fall off. New friends, like one's best coat and polished patent-leather dress boots, are only intended for holiday wear. At other times they are neither serviceable nor comfortable; they do not answer the required purposes, and are ill adapted to give us the ease we seek. A new coat, however, has this advantage, that it will in time become old and comfortable; so much can by no means be predicted with certainty of a new friend. Woe to those men who go through the world with none but new coats on their backs, with no boots but those of polished leather, with none but new friends to comfort them in adversity.
    But not the less, when misfortune does come, are we inclined to grumble at finding ourselves deserted. TC 509,XLII.

## FRIENDSHIP

[T]hree days at Jerusalem are worth a twelvemonth in such a dull, slow place as London.  Ber 394, XXII.

But they suited each other; and this, I take it, is the secret of most of our pleasantest intercourse in the world. FrP 231, XXIV.

How often may it be observed in the fields that a high-bred, quick-paced horse will choose some lowly donkey for his close companionship, although other horses of equal birth and speed be in the same pasture!  Str 74, XIII.

The deck of an ocean steamer, is perhaps the most prolific hotbed for the growth of sudden friendships; but an hotel by the side of a Swiss lake does almost as well. CanY 344, LXXIII,II.

It is sometimes very difficult to escape from the meshes of friendship.  Cl 152, XVIII.

...a loved and loving friend who was to be made free at once to all the inmost privileges of real friendship, which are given to and are desired by so few.  PR 19, II,I.


G


## GAIN

One may as well ask what does the miser gain who hides away his gold in an old pot, or what does that other madman gain who is locked up for long long years because he fancies himself the grandmother of the Queen of England?
OrF 237, XXIII,I.

## GAMBLING

There is much that is in truth dishonest even in honest play.  A man who can keep himself sober after dinner, plays with one who flusters himself with drink.  The man with a trained memory plays with him who cannot remember a card....And then there is the man who knows the game, and plays with him who knows it not at all!  Of course, the cool, the collected, the thoughtful, the practised, they who have given up their whole souls to the study of cards, will play at a great advantage, which in their calculations they do not fail to recognise....That is all fair and acknowledged; but looking at it from a distance...you will come to doubt the honesty of making your income after such a fashion.  MSF 298-9, XLI,II.

## GAMES

There is a pleasant game, requiring much sagacity, in which, by a few answers, one is led closer and closer to a hidden word, till one is able to touch it.  CoH 103, IX.

## GARDENS

In gardens to which care and labour are given abundantly, flowerbeds will be pretty, and grass will be green, let the weather be what it may.  Cl 1, I.

## GENEROSITY

We are so apt to be generous in the hot moments of impulse, but so equally apt to be only coldly just, even if coldly

just, in the long years of our ordinary existence.
Ber 56, IV.

## GENTLEMEN

Gentlemen do not write to ladies about their tresses, unless
they are on very intimate terms indeed.  BaT 247, XXVII.

But even this receipt [Eton and Cambridge], generally as it
is recognized, will not make a gentleman.  It is hard, indeed, to define what receipt will do so, though people do
have in their own minds some certain undefined, but yet
tolerably correct ideas on the subject.  DoT 129-30, X.

May I not call it a necessary qualification [being a
gentleman] for a clergyman of any church?...I am by no means
prepared to define what I do mean,--thinking, however, that
most men and women will understand me....It is not the owner
of a good coat that sees and admires its beauty....They who
have not good coats themselves have the keenest eyes for the
coats of their better-clad neighbours.  As it is with coats,
so it is with that which we call gentility.  It is caught at
a word, it is seen at a glance, it is appreciated unconsciously at a touch by those who have none of it themselves.
It is the greatest of all aids to the doctor, the lawyer,
the member of Parliament...and to the statesman; but to the
clergyman it is a vital necessity.  RacR 77, VI.

If other things be equal, it is probably that a baronet will
be more of a gentleman and a pleasanter fellow than a manu-
facturer of oilcloth.  Who is there that doesn't feel that?
MM 71, VI.

For my part I think that there are no better judges of the
article [being a gentleman] than the grooms.  LasC 179,XX.

A perfect gentleman is a thing which I cannot define.
LasC 381, XLII.

Real gentlemen think a good deal of themselves, but not half
so much as is thought of them by men who know that they
themselves are of a different order.  RalH 126, XVI.

It is difficult, perhaps, to say what amount of misconduct
does constitute a scoundrel, or justifies the critic in saying that this or that man is not a gentleman.  There be
those who affirm that he who owes a debt for goods which he
cannot pay is not gentleman, and tradesmen when they cannot
get their money are no doubt sometimes inclined to hold that
opinion.  But the opinion is changed when the money comes at
last,--especially if it comes with interest.  RalH 312, XLI.

Johnson says that any other derivation of this difficult
word [gentleman] than that which causes it to signify 'a
man of ancestry' is whimsical....The chances are very much
in favour of the well-born man, but exceptions may exist.
PrM 3, I,I.

## GENUINENESS

You may knock about a diamond, and not even scratch it; whereas paste in rough usage betrays itself. ED 230, LXV,II.

## GIFTS

A good thing should be given away like a clap of thunder if envy, hatred, and malice are to be avoided. PrM 225,LXIV,II.

## GIRLS

[T]hey were of the age when they would have been regarded as mere boys had they belonged to the other sex....[Y]oung ladies, gifted as they are with such advantages, may perhaps be thought to require some counsel, some advice, in those first tender years in which they so often have to make or mar their fortunes. TC 27, III.

But when a young girl throws prudence to the winds, and allows herself to love where there is nothing to live on, what then is she called?  It seems to me that it is some-times very hard for young girls to be in the right.  They certainly should not be mercenary; they certainly should not marry paupers; they certainly should not allow themselves to become old maids.  They should not encumber themselves with early, hopeless loves; nor should they callously resolve to care for nothing but a good income and a good house.  There should be some handbook of love, to tell young ladies when they may give way to it without censure.  Ber 182-3, X.

It clearly is the duty of a young lady on very many occasions to be somewhat hypocritical.  Ber 500, XVII.

How cheap girls do make themselves when talking of each other!  Ber 749, XLII.

[G]irls are girls from the age of three up to forty-three. FrP 94, X.

Who has not seen some such girl when she has come down early, without the full completeness of her morning toilet, and yet nicer, fresher, prettier to the eye of him who is so favoured, than she has ever been in more formal attire?  And what man who has been so favoured has not loved her who has so favoured him, even though he may not previously have been enamoured...deeply?  Bel 74, VI.

There are girls so cold-looking,--pretty girls, too, lady-like, discreet, and armed with all accomplishments,--whom to attack seems to require the same sort of courage, and the same sort of preparation, as a journey in quest of the north-west passage....But, again, there are other girls to abstain from attacking whom is, to a man of any warmth of temperament, quite impossible.  They are like water when one is athirst, like plovers' eggs in March, like cigars when

one is out in the autumn.  No one ever dreams of denying himself when such temptation comes in the way.  It often
happens, however, that in spite of appearances, the water
will not come from the well, nor the egg from its shell, nor
will the cigar allow itself to be lit.  PF 19, II,I.

A girl would wish to look well before her lover, even when
she means to refuse him.  PF 120, LII,II.

Young ladies, when they are in love, are prone to regard
their lovers as being prizes so valuable as to be coveted
by all female comers.  RalH 53, VII.

There are among us many who tell us that no pure-minded girl
should think of finding a lover,--should only deal with him,
when he comes, as truth, and circumstances, and parental
control may suggest to her.  If there be girls so pure, it
certainly seems that no human being expects to meet them.
RalH 247, XXXII.

How often it is that Nature is unkind to a girl as she grows
into womanhood, and robs the attractive child of her charms!
How often will the sparkle of early youth get itself
quenched utterly by the dampness and clouds of the opening
world.  JC 107, XIV.

It is generally understood that there are raging lions about
the metropolis, who would certainly eat up young ladies
whole if young ladies were to walk about the streets or even
about the parks by themselves....In large continental towns,
such as Paris and Vienna, young ladies would be devoured
certainly.  Such, at least, is the creed.  In New York and
Washington there are supposed to be no lions, so that young
ladies go about free as air.  In London there is a rising
doubt, under which before long, probably, the lions will
succumb altogether....Young ladies who must go about without
mothers, brothers, uncles, carriages, or attendants of any
sort, are not often eaten or even roared at.  It is the
dainty darlings for whom the roarings have to be feared.
AyA 31, IV.

But a young lady is constrained by the exigencies of society
to live with somebody.  She cannot take a lodging by herself, as her brother may do.  AyA 576, LIX.

## GIRLS, GERMAN

But how many German girls do the like  [wear glasses
constantly], and are not accounted for that reason to be
plain?  MSF 225, XVI,I.

## GIVING

We are told by the Latin proverb that he who gives quickly
gives twice; but I say that she who gives quickly seldom
gives more than half.  PF 170, LVII,II.

## GOADS

But men who sojourn amidst savagery fear the mosquito more than they do the lion.  PF 297, LXIX, II.

## GOD

The destruction of the potato was the work of God; and it was natural to attribute the sufferings which at once overwhelmed the unfortunate country to God's anger--to his wrath for the misdeeds of which that country had been guilty.  For myself, I do not believe in such exhibitions of God's anger....I do not believe that our God stalks darkly along the clouds, laying thousands low with the arrows of death, and those thousands the most ignorant, because men who are not ignorant have displeased Him.  Nor, if in his wisdom He did do so, can I think that men's prayers would hinder that which his wisdom had seen to be good and right.

But though I do not believe in exhibitions of God's anger, I do believe in exhibitions of his mercy.  When men by their folly and by the shortness of their vision have brought upon themselves penalties which seem to be over-whelming....then God raises his hand, not in anger, but in mercy, and by his wisdom does for us that for which our own wisdom has been insufficient.

But on no Christian basis can I understand the justice or acknowledge the propriety of asking our Lord to abate his wrath in detail, or to alter his settled purpose.  If He be wise, would we change his wisdom?  If He be merciful, would we limit his mercy?  There comes upon us some strange disease, and we bid Him to stay his hand.  But the disease, when it has passed by, has taught us lessons of cleanliness, which no master less stern would have made acceptable.  A famine strikes us, and we beg that that hand may be stayed....We so beg, thinking that God's anger is hot also against us.  But, lo!  the famine passes by, and a land that had been brought to the dust by man's folly is once more prosperous and happy.

Such having been the state of the country, such its wretchedness, a merciful God sent the remedy which might avail to arrest it; and we--we deprecated his wrath.  But all this will soon be known and acknowledged; acknowledged as it is acknowledged that new cities rise up in splendour from the ashes into which old cities have been consumed by fire.  If this beneficent agency did not from time to time disencumber our crowded places, we should ever be living in narrow alleys with stinking gutters, and supply of water at the minimun.  CasR 120-6, VII, I.  See also FAMINE.

Or may it not perhaps be truer to say that in such matters there is no such thing as mercy--no special mercies--no other mercy than that fatherly, forbearing, all-seeing, per-fect goodness by which the Creator is ever adapting this world to the wants of his creatures, and rectifying the evils arising from their faults and follies? CasR 28, II, III.

## GOOD

A man who strives honestly to do good will generally do good, though seldom perhaps as much as he has himself anticipated.  OrF 173, XVII,I.

## GOOD...BAD

[I]n this world no good is unalloyed, and...there is but little evil that has not in it some seed of what is goodly. War 180, XV.

A boy is turned loose into London, and desired to choose the good and eschew the bad.  Boy as he is, he might probably do so if the opportunity came in his way.  But no such chance is afforded him.  To eschew the bad is certainly possible for him; but as to the good, he must wait till he be chosen....
     Society, an ample allowance of society, this is the first requisite which a mother should seek in sending her son to live alone in London; balls, routs, picnics, good women, pretty, well-dressed, witty, easy-mannered; good pictures, elegant drawing rooms, well got-up books, Majolica and Dresden china--these are the truest guards to protect a youth from dissipation and immorality.
     These are the books, the arts, the academes
     That show, contain, and nourish all the world,
if only a youth could have them at his disposal. TC 21-2,II.

The things that are bad are accepted because the things that are good do not come easily in his way.  How many a miserable father reviles with bitterness of spirit the low tastes of his son, who has done nothing to provide his child with higher pleasures. DoT 338, XXVIII.

But we are perhaps accustomed in judging for ourselves and of others to draw the lines too sharply, and to say that on this side lie vice, folly, heartlessness, and greed,--and on the other honour, love, truth, and wisdom,--the good and the bad each in its own domain.  But the good and the bad mix themselves so thoroughly in our thoughts, even in our as- pirations, that we must look for excellence rather in over- coming evil than in freeing ourselves from its influence. HKHWR 561, LX.

A man is never strong enough to take unmixed delight in good, so may we presume also that he cannot be quite so weak as to find perfect satisfaction in evil.  ED  , I,I.

## GOOD THINGS

Alas, good things not deserved too often lose their goodness when they come. Cl 307, XXXVI.

## GOODNESS

Such little attempts at goodness  [as having dinner early on Sunday]--proceeding half the way...on the disagreeable path towards goodness and very common with respectable people.
SmaH 350, XXV

## GOSSIP

But reports, when they reach a certain magnitude, and attain a certain importance, require to be noticed.
DrW 25,III, Part I.

When passing whispers creep into the world of fashion they are heard far and wide.  MF 16, I,I.

## GOVERNMENT

That alleged difficulty as to carrying on the Queen's Govern-ment has been frequently mooted in late years since a certain great man first introduced the idea.  Nevertheless, the Queen's Government is carried on, and the propensity and aptitude of men for this work seems to be not at all on the decrease.  If we have but few young statesmen, it is because the old stagers are so fond of the rattle of their harness.
FrP 215, XXIII.

It is easy to love one's enemy when one is making fine speeches; but so difficult to do so in the actual everyday work of life.  FrP 220, XXIII.

## GOVERNMENT, PARTIES

The giants themselves...are always advancing in some sort towards the councils of Olympus.  Their highest policy is to snatch some ray from heaven....And in this consists the wisdom of the higher giants--that, in spite of their mundane antecedents, theories, and predilections, they can see that articles of divine manufacture are necessary.  But then they never carry their supporters with them.  Their whole army is an army of martyrs.  'For twenty years I have stuck to them, and see how they have treated me!'  Is not that always the plaint of an old giant-slave?  'I have been true to my party all my life, and where am I now?' he says.  Where, indeed, my friend?  Looking about you, you begin to learn that you cannot describe your whereabouts.  I do not marvel at that.
FrP 238-9, XXV.

That  [being loud in triumph]  is the fault of the giants, who, otherwise, are not bad fellows; they are unable to endure the weight of any temporary success.  When attempting Olympus...they scratch and scramble, diligently using both toes and fingers, with a mixture of good-humoured virulence and self-satisfied industry that is gratifying to all parties.  But whenever their efforts are unexpectedly, and for themselves unfortunately, successful, they are so taken aback that they lose the power of behaving themselves with even gigantesque propriety.  FrP 269, XXVIII.

## GRANDFATHERS

It is astonishing how different are the views of grand-fathers and grandchildren on such matters   [supplying them with an income]!  Ber 258, XIV.

## GRANDMOTHERS

In the long run, grandmothers are more tender to their grand-children than their own offspring.  JC 365, L.

## GRATITUDE

One may work and not for thanks, but yet feel hurt at not receiving them;...one may be disinterested in one's good actions, and yet feel discontented that they are not recog-nised.  Charity may be given with the left hand so privily that the right hand does not know it, and yet the left hand may regret to feel that it has no immediate reward....Gentle reader, did you ever feel yourself snubbed?  Did you ever, when thinking much of your own importance, find yourself suddenly reduced to a nonentity?  War 161-2, XIII.

Gratitude;--yes!  But if the whole result of the exertion for which the receiver is bound to be grateful, is to be neutralised by the greed of the conferrer of the favour,... what ground will there be left for gratitude?  If I save a man's purse from a thief, and then demand for my work twice what that purse contained, the man had better have been left with the robbers.  LA 442, XLII.

## GREATNESS

It is often very curious to trace the sources of greatness. VOB 165, XXIV.

## GREETINGS

When one Esquimau meets another, do the two, as an invariable rule, ask after each other's health?  is it inherent in all human nature to make this obliging inquiry? Did any reader of this tale ever meet any friend or acquain-tance without asking some such question, and did any one ever listen to the reply?  Sometimes a studiously courteous questioner will show so much thought in the matter as to answer it himself, by declaring that had he looked at you he needn't have asked; meaning thereby to signify that you are an absolute personification of health:  but such persons are only those who premeditate small effects.  War 178, XV.

## GRIEF

How much kinder is God to us than we are willing to be to

ourselves!   At the loss of every dear face, at the last
going of every beloved, we all doom ourselves to an eternity
of sorrow, and look to waste ourselves away in an ever-
running fountain of tears.   How seldom does such grief
endure!   how blessed is the goodness which forbids it to do
so!   'Let me ever remember my living friends, but forget
them as soon as dead' was the prayer of a wise man who
understood the mercy of God.   BaT 17, II.

How tenfold sorrowful are our sorrows when borne in solitude!   Some one has said that grief is half removed when it
is shared.   How little that some one knew about it!   Half
removed!   When it is duly shared between two loving hearts,
does not love fly off with eight-tenths of it?   There is but
a small remainder left for the two to bear between them....
How often has a man said, when evil times have come upon
him, that he could have borne it all without complaint, but
for his wife and children?   The truth, however, has been
that, but for them, he could not have borne it at all....It
is not that we should all be ready, each to make his own
quietus with a bare bodkin; but that we should run from
wretchedness when it comes in our path.   Who fights for himself alone?   Who would not be a coward, if none but himself
saw the battle--if none others were concerned in it?
Ber 815-6, XLVI.

When those we love are dead, our friends dread to mention
them, though to us who are bereaved no subject would be so
pleasant as their names.   But we rarely understand how to
treat our own sorrow or those of others.
      There was once a people in some land...who thought it
sacrilegious to stay the course of a raging fire....For who
would dare to interfere with the course of the god?   Our
idea of sorrow is much the same.   We think it wicked, or at
any rate heartless, to put it out.   If a man's wife be dead,
he should go about lugubrious, with long face, for at least
two years, or perhaps with full length for eighteen months,
decreasing gradually during the other six.   If he be a man
who can quench his sorrow--put out his fire as it were--in
less time than that, let him at any rate not show his power!
FrP 103, XI.

Spoken grief relieves itself; and when one can give counsel,
one always hopes at least that that counsel will be
effective.   FrP 131, XIV.

It is ever so in our misery [that pride is sufficient for
support in the first hour of sorrow].   In the first flush of
our wretchedness, let the outward signs of our grief be what
they may, we promise to ourselves the support of some inner
strength which shall suffice to us at any rate as against
the eyes of the outer world.   But anon, and that inner staff
fails us; our pride yields to our tears; our dignity is
crushed beneath the load with which we have burdened it, and
then with loud wailings we own ourselves to be the wretches
which we are.   RacR 250, XX.

Let the living think of the dead, when their thoughts will
travel that way whether the thinker wish it or no.   Grief
taken up because grief is supposed to be proper, is only one
degree better than pretended grief.   When one sees it, one
cannot but think of the lady who asked her friend, in
confidence, whether hot roast fowl and bread-sauce were compatible with the earliest state of weeds; or of that other
lady,--a royal lady she,--who was much comforted in the
tedium of her trouble when assured by one of the lords about
the Court that piquet was mourning.   CanY 139-40, LIV,II.

...that well-known look of customary solemnity which is
found to be necessary on such occasions [death of a child].
Cl 182, XXII.

...that longing for death which terrible calamities often
produce for a season.   Bel 8, I.

...that blackness of funeral grief which is absolutely
necessary on such occasions....[not] stricken with any of
that agony of woe which is produced on us by the death of
those whom we have loved so well that we cannot bring ourselves to submit to part with them.   Bel 107-8, IX.

The sick birds, we are told, creep into holes, that they may
die alone and unnoticed; and the wounded beasts hide themselves that their grief may not be seen of their fellows.   A
man has the same instinct to conceal the weakness of his
sufferings; but, if he be a man, he hides it in his own
heart, keeping it for solitude and the watches of the night,
while to the outer world he carries a face on which his care
has made no marks.   Bel 199, XVI.

...that affectation of funereal gravity which is common to
all of us.   PR 254, XXIX,I.

The grief that cannot bear allusion to its causes has
generally something of affectation in its composition.
PR 168, LIX,II.

The world makes great mistakes as to that which is and is
not beneficial to those whom Death has bereaved of a
companion.   It may be, no doubt sometimes it is the case,
that grief shall be so heavy, so absolutely crushing, as to
make any interference with it an additional trouble....It
may also be, and, no doubt, often is the case, that the bereaved one chooses to affect such overbearing sorrow, and
that friends abstain, because even such affectation has its
own rights and privileges.   Way 397, XCII,II.

Appetites are good even amidst grief.   CoH 59, VI.

It was now April, and this April was a sad month in Ireland.
I do not know why the deaths of two such men as were then
murdered should touch the heart with a deeper sorrow than is
felt for the fate of others whose lot is lower in life; why

the poor widow, who has lost her husband while doing his
duty amidst outrages and unmanly revenges, is not to be so
much thought of as the sweet lady who has been robbed of her
all in the same fashion.   But so it is with human nature.
We all know how a people will weep for their Sovereign, and
it was with such tears as that, with tears as sincere as
those shed for the best of kings, that Lord Frederick Caven-
dish and Mr. Burke were lamented.   Land 109, XXXIX,III.

## GRIEVANCE

There is nothing perhaps so generally consoling to a man as
a well-established grievance; a feeling of having been
injured, on which his mind can brood from hour to hour,
allowing him to plead his own cause in his own court, within
his own heart,--and always to plead it successfully.
OrF 81, VIII,I.

To be robbed of one's grievance is the last and foulest
wrong,--a wrong under which the most enduring temper will at
last yield and become soured,--by which the strongest back
will be broken.   Bel 95, VIII.

[A]nd to some women there is nothing so charming as a little
mild ill-usage, which does not interfere with their creature
comforts, with their clothes, or their carriage, or their
sham jewels; but suffices to afford them the indulgence of a
grievance.   LasC 439, LI.

Has any irascible reader,--any reader who thoroughly enjoys
the pleasure of being in a rage,--encountered suddenly some
grievance which, heavy as it may be, has been more than com-
pensated by the privilege it has afforded of blowing-up the
offender?   AyA 278, XXX.

## GUESTS

...that tone of voice with which a guest at the house--a
guest for pleasure,--may address sometimes a guest who is a
guest on business.   In such a case the guest on pleasure
cannot be a gentlemen, and must suppose that the guest on
business is not one either.   MSF 262, XIX,I.


H


## HABIT

The minds of men and women become so tuned to certain
positions, that they go astray and won't act when those

positions are confused.    Almost every man can talk for
fifteen minutes, standing in a drawing room, before dinner;
but where is the man who can do it for an hour?...[A]t that
special point of the day he is supposed to talk for fifteen
minutes, and if any prolonged call is then made upon him,
his talking apparatus falls out of order and will not work.
You can sit still on a Sunday morning, in the cold, on a
very narrow bench, with no comfort appertaining, and listen
for half an hour to a rapid outflow of words, which for any
purpose of instruction or edification, are absolutely useless to you....Try to undergo the same thing in your own
house on a Wednesday afternoon, and see where you will be.
MM 99-100, VIII.

But we know that the drunkard, though he hates drunkenness,
cannot but drink,--that the gambler cannot keep from the
dice.  DuC 47, VI.

## HAIR

With some women it [hair] is their great charm,--Neaeras
who love to sit half sleeping in the shade--but it is a
charm that possesses no powerful eloquence.  All beauty of a
high order should speak.  OrF 185, XIX,I.

But in these days we have got to like red hair.  PF 32,IV,I.

A man with a fair burden on his back is not a grievous
sight; but when we see a small human being attached to a
bale of goods which he can hardly manage to move, we feel
that the poor fellow has been cruelly overweighted.
HKHWR 440, XLVII.

From which this lesson may surely be learned,--that though
the way down Avernus may be, and customarily is, made with
great celerity, the return journey, if made at all, must be
made slowly.    A young woman may commence in chignons by
attaching any amount of an edifice to her head; but the
reduction should be made by degrees.  HKHWR 452, XLVIII.

## HAIR POWDER

Who inquires why it is that a little greased flour rubbed in
among the hair on a footman's head--just one dab here and
another there--gives such a tone of high life to the family?
And seeing that the thing is so easily done, why do not more
people attempt it?   The tax on hair-powder is but thirteen
shillings a year.  It may, indeed, be that the slightest dab
in the world justifies the wearer in demanding hot meat
three times a day, and wine at any rate on Sundays.     I
think, however, that a bishop's wife may enjoy the privilege
without such heavy attendant expense.  LasC 158, XVIII.

## HANDS

Ladies' hands, so soft, so sweet, so delicious to the touch, so grateful to the eye, so gracious in their gentle doings, were not made to belabor men's faces.  BaT 392, XL.

## HAPPINESS

The enjoyment of one's own happiness at such windfalls depends so much on the free and freely expressed enjoyment of others!  FrP 199, XXI.

## HATE

How often does it not happen that when we come across those whom we have hated and avoided all our lives, we find that they are not quite so bad as we had thought?  That old gentleman of whom we wot is never so black as he has been painted.  CasR 81, IV,II.

## HEALING

God is good to us, and heals those wounds with a rapidity which seems to us impossible when we look forward, but which is regarded with very insufficient wonder when we look backward.  Ber 38, III.

## HEAVEN

It is when things go badly with us here, and for most of us only then, that we think that we can see through the dark clouds into the joys of heaven.  HKHWR 686-7, LXXIII.

## HEAVEN...HELL

Satan knew that heaven was better than hell; but he found himself to be fitter for the latter place.  SmaH 173-4,XVIII.

## HELL

Easy, very easy, is the slope of hell.  TC 360, XXIX.

## HEROES

The author does not so call them  [heroes and heroines]; he professes to do his work without any such appendages to his story--heroism there may be, and he hopes there is--more or less of it there should be in a true picture of most characters; but heroes and heroines, as so called, are not commonly met with in our daily walks of life.  TC 557,XLVII.

[P]eople think that heroes in books should be so much better than heroes got up for the world's common wear and tear....
[W]hat would the world come to if none but absolute true heroes were to be thought worthy of women's love?  What would the men do? and what--oh! what would become of the women?  FrP 202, XXI.

When the student at Oxford was asked what man had most benefited humanity, and when he answered "Bass," I think that he should not have been plucked.  It was a fair average answer. RacR 28, III.

Perhaps no terms have been so injurious to the profession of the novelist as those two words, hero and heroine.  In spite of the latitude which is allowed to the writer in putting his own interpretation upon these words, something heroic is still expected; whereas, if he attempt to paint from Nature, how little that is heroic should he describe! Cl 239,XXVIII.

But men as I see them are not often heroic.  Cl 240, XXVIII.

[B]ut then, if all the girls are to wait for heroes, I fear that the difficulties in the way of matrimonial arrangements, great as they are at present, will be very seriously enhanced.  LasC 713, LXXVI.

A hero is never so much a hero among women as when he has been wounded in the battle.  The very weakness which throws him into female hands imparts a moiety of his greatness to the women who for the while possess him, and creates a partnership in heroism, in which the feminine half delights to make the most of its own share.  RalH 241, XXXII.

It is thought by many critics that in the pictures of imaginary life which novelists produce for the amusement, and possibly for the instruction, of their readers, none should be put upon the canvas but the very good, who by their noble thoughts and deeds may lead others to nobility, or the very bad who by their declared wickedness will make iniquity hideous.  How can it be worth one's while, such critics will say,...to waste our imaginations, our sympathies, and our time upon such a one as Ralph, the heir of the Newton property?  The writer, acknowledging the force of these objections, and confessing that his young heroes of romance are but seldom heroic, makes his apology as follows.
     The reader of a novel,--who has doubtless taken the volume up simply for amusement, and who would probably lay it down did he suspect that instruction, like a snake in the grass, like physic beneath the sugar, was to be imposed upon him,--requires from his author chiefly this, that he shall be amused by a narrative in which elevated sentiment prevails, and gratified by being made to feel that the elevated sentiments described are exactly his own....
     It is the test of a novel writer's art that he conceals his snake-in-the-grass; but the reader may be sure that it is always there.  No man or woman with a conscience,--no man or woman with intellect sufficient to produce amusement, can go on from year to year spinning stories without the desire of teaching; with no ambition of influencing readers for their good.  Gentle readers, the physic is always beneath the sugar, hidden or unhidden.  In writing novels we novelists preach to you from our pulpits and are keenly anxious that our sermons shall not be inefficacious.  In-

efficacious they are not, unless they be too badly preached
to obtain attention. Injurious they will be unless the
lessons taught be good lessons....
    Should we not be taught to see the men and women among
whom we really live,--men and women such as we are ourselves,--in order that we should know what are the exact
failings which oppress ourselves, and thus learn to hate,
and if possible to avoid in life, the faults of character
which in life are hardly visible, but which in portraiture
of life can be made to be so transparent. RalH 424-5, LVI.

A man carried away by abnormal appetites, and wickedness,
and the devil, may of course commit murder, or forge bills,
or become a fraudulent director of a bankrupt company. And
so may a man be untrue to his troth,--and leave true love in
pursuit of tinsel, and beauty, and false words, and a large
income. But why should one tell the story of creatures so
base? One does not willingly grovel in gutters, or breathe
fetid atmospheres, or live upon garbage. If we are to deal
with heroes and heroines, let us, at any rate, have heroes
and heroines who are above such meanness as falsehood in
love....
    It is very easy to depict a hero,--a man absolutely
stainless, perfect as an Arthur,--a man honest in all his
dealings, equal to all trials, true in all his speech, indifferent to his own prosperity, struggling for the general
good, and, above all, faithful in love. At any rate, it is
as easy to do that as to tell of the man who is one hour
good and the next bad, who aspires greatly, but fails in
practice, who sees the higher, but too often follows the
lower course. There arose at one time a school of art,
which delighted to paint the human face as perfect in
beauty; and from that time to this we are discontented
unless every woman is drawn for us as a Venus, or, at least,
a Madonna....There may be made for us a pretty thing to look
at, no doubt;--but we know that that pretty thing is not
really visaged as the mistress whom we serve, and whose
lineaments we desire to perpetuate on the canvas. The winds
of heaven, or the fleshpots of Egypt, or the midnight gas,--
passions, pains, and, perhaps, rouge and powder, have made
her something different. But there still is the fire of her
eye, and the eager eloquence of her mouth, and something,
too , perhaps, left of the departing innocence of youth,
which the painter might give us without the Venus or the
Madonna touches. But the painter does not dare do it.
Indeed, he has painted so long after the other fashion that
he would hate the canvas before him, were he to give way to
the rouge-begotten roughness or to the fleshpots,--or even
to the winds. And how, my lord, would you, who are giving
hundreds, more than hundreds, for this portrait of your dear
one, like to see it in print from the art critic of the day,
that she is a brazen-faced hoyden who seems to have had a
glass of wine too much, or to have been making hay?
    And so also has the reading world taught itself to
like best the characters of all but divine men and women....
With whom are we to sympathise? says the reader, who not

unnaturally imagines that a hero should be heroic. Oh, thou, my reader, whose sympathies are in truth the great and only aim of my work, when you have called the dearest of your friends round you to your hospitable table, how many heroes are there sitting at the board? Your bosom friend,-- even if he be a knight without fear, is he a knight without reproach?...And those sweet girls whom you know, do they never doubt between the poor man they think they love, and the rich man whose riches they know they covet?

Go into the market, either to buy or sell, and name the thing you desire to part with or to get, as it is, and the market is closed against you. Middling oats are the sweepings of the granaries. A useful horse is a jade gone at every point. Good sound port is sloe juice....And yet in real life we are content with oats that are really middling, are very glad to have a useful horse, and know that if we drink port at all we must drink some that is neither good nor sound. In those delineations of life and character which we call novels a similarly superlative vein is desired. Our own friends around us are not always merry and wise, nor, alas! always honest and true. They are often cross and foolish, and sometimes treacherous and false. They are so, and we are angry. Then we forgive them, not without a consciousness of imperfection on our own part. And we know--or, at least, believe,--that though they be sometimes treacherous and false, there is a balance of good. We cannot have heroes to dine with us. There are none. And were these heroes to be had, we should not like them. But neither are our friends villains,--whose every aspiration is for evil, and whose every moment is a struggle for some achievement worthy of the devil.

The persons whom you cannot care for in a novel, because they are so bad, are the very same that you so dearly love in your life, because they are so good. To make them and ourselves somewhat better,--not by one spring heavenwards to perfection, because we cannot so use our legs,--but by slow climbing, is, we may presume, the object of all teachers, leaders, legislators, spiritual pastors, and masters. He who writes tales such as this, probably also has, very humbly, some such object distantly before him. A picture of surpassing godlike nobleness,--a picture of a King Arthur among men, may perhaps do much. But such pictures cannot do all. When such a picture is painted, as intending to show what a man should be, it is true. If painted to show what men are, it is false. The true picture of life as it is, if it could be adequately painted, would show men what they are, and how they might rise, not, indeed, to perfection, but one step first, and then another on the ladder. ED 317-20, XXXV,I.

## HEROINES

[Heroine] is the novelist's customary name for his prima donna and so I use it. But many opera companies have more than one prima donna. There is the donna prima, and if one may so say, the donna primissima. Ber 60, IV.

The heroine, so called, must by a certain fixed law be young and marriageable.  OrF 12, II,I.

## HISTORY

How little are men able to conceive what award posterity will make in judging of their actions;...and posterity is often as much in error in its indiscriminate condemnation of actions, as are the actors in presuming themselves entitled to its praise.
      When years have rolled by, and passions have cooled, the different motives and feelings of the persons concerned become known to all, and mankind is enabled to look upon public acts from every side....
      Public men are like soldiers fighting in a narrow valley; they see nothing but what is close around them, and that imperfectly, as everything is in motion.  The historian is as the general, who stands elevated on the high ground, and with telescope in hand, sees plainly all the different movements of the troops.  He would be an inconsiderate general, who would expect that his officers in action should have had as clear an idea of what was going on, as he himself had been able to obtain.  LaV 283, XXIII.

## HOBBLEDEHOYS

There is a class of young men who never get petted, though they may not be the less esteemed, or perhaps loved.  They do not come forth to the world as Apollos, nor shine at all, keeping what light they may have for inward purposes.  Such young men are often awkward, ungainly, and not yet formed in their gait; they straggle with their limbs, and are shy; words do not come to them with ease, when words are required, among any but their accustomed associates.  Social meetings are periods of penance to them, and any appearance in public will unnerve them.  They go much about alone, and blush when women speak to them.  In truth, they are not as yet men, whatever the number may be of their years; and, as they are no longer boys, the world has found for them the ungraceful name of hobbledehoy.
      Such observations, however, as I have been enabled to make on this matter have led me to believe that the hobble-dehoy is by no means the least valuable species of the human race.  When I compare the hobbledehoy of one or two and twenty to some finished Apollo of the same age, I regard the former as unripe fruit, and the latter as fruit that is ripe.  Then comes the question as to the two fruits.  Which is better fruit, that which ripens early--which is, perhaps, favoured with some little forcing apparatus, or which, at least, is backed by the warmth of a southern wall; or that fruit or slower growth, as to which nature works without assistance, on which the sun operates in its own time--or perhaps never operates if some ungenial shade has been allowed to interpose itself?  The world, no doubt, is in favour of the forcing apparatus or of the southern wall.  The fruit comes certainly, and at an assured period....But,

nevertheless, according to my thinking, the fullest flavour of the sun is given to that other fruit--is given in the sun's own good time....I like the smack of natural growth, and like it, perhaps, the better because that which has been obtained has been obtained without favour.

But the hobbledehoy, though he blushes when women address him, and is uneasy even when he is near them, though he is not master of his limbs in a ball-room, and is hardly master of his tongue at any time, is the most eloquent of beings, and especially eloquent among beautiful women....But his eloquence is heard only by his own inner ears, and these triumphs are the triumphs of his imagination....

[H]e wanders about in solitude, taking long walks, in which he dreams of those successes which are so far removed from his powers of achievement. Out in the fields, with his stick in his hand, he is very eloquent, cutting off the heads of the springing summer weeds, as he practices his oratory with energy. And thus he feeds an imagination for which those who know him give him but scanty credit, and un-consciously prepares himself for that later ripening, if only the ungenial shade will some day cease to interpose itself.

Such hobbledehoys receive but little petting, unless it be from a mother. SmaH 30-1, IV.

## HOLIDAYS

...October, a month during which few choose to own that they remain in town. For myself, I always regard May as the best month for holiday-making; but then no Londoner cares to be absent in May. SmaH 40, V.

## HOME RULE

Had some inscrutable decree of fate ordained and made it certain,--with a certainty not to be disturbed,--that no candidate could be returned to Parliament who would not assert the earth to be triangular, there would rise immediately a clamorous assertion of triangularity among political aspirants. The test would be innocent. Candidates have swallowed, and daily do swallow, many a worse one. As might be this doctrine of a great triangle, so is the doctrine of Home Rule. Why is a gentleman of property to be kept out in the cold by some O'Mullins because he will not mutter an unmeaning shibboleth? 'Triangular? Yes,--or lozenge-shaped if you please; but, gentlemen, I am the man for Tipperary.' PrM 97, XI,I.

## HONESTY

He was always true to the man whose money he had taken, and gave to his customer, with all the power at his command, that assistance which he had professed to sell. But we may give the same praise to the hired bravo who goes through with truth and courage the task which he has undertaken. I knew an assassin in Ireland who professed that during twelve years of practice in Tipperary he had never failed when he had once engaged himself....[T]ruth and honesty to their customers...are great virtues.   OrF 359, LXXV,II.

But, in truth, the artists have been so much in the habit of painting for us our friends' faces without any of those flaws and blotches with which work and high living are apt to disfigure us, that we turn in disgust from a portrait in which the roughnesses and pimples are made apparent. Bel 246-7, XIX.

You should never ask the ostler whether he greases his oats. ED 352, LXXVII,II.

It is easy for most of us to keep our hands from picking and stealing when picking and stealing plainly lead to prison diet and prison garments.  But when silks and satins come of it, and with the silks and satins general respect, the net result of honesty does not seem to be so secure.  Whence will come the reward, and when?  On whom the punishment, and where?  A man will not, surely, be damned for belonging to a Coalition Ministry!   PrM 100, XI,I.

It may be doubted whether any woman has ever been brought to such honesty as that  [trying to avoid legacy duties]. AS 203, XXX.

There are so many who act honestly from noble motives, and then feel that their honesty should be rewarded by all those gains  which  dishonesty  might  have  procured  for  them! MF 317, XXXI,II.

## HONEYMOONS

During honeymoon times the fashionable married couple is always lodged and generally boarded for nothing. That opening wide of generous hands, which exhibits itself in the joyous enthusiasm of a coming marriage, taking the shape of a  houseful  of  presents,  of  a  gorgeous  and  ponderous trousseau, of a splendid marriage feast, and not unfrequently of subsidiary presents from the opulent papa,-- presents which are subsidiary to the grand substratum of settled  dowry,--generously  extends  itself  to  luxurious provision for a month or two. AyA 114-5, XIII.

## HOPE

Young men in battle are called upon to lead forlorn hopes. Three fall, perhaps, to one who gets through; but the one who gets through will have the Victoria Cross to carry for the rest of his life.  PF 8-9, I,I.

## HORSES

...and he had that look so beautiful in a horse when running, of working at his ease, and much within his power. Kel 201, XVI.

...the vehicle stopped with that kind of plunge which is made by no other animal than a post-horse, and by him only at his arrival at the end of a stage. Kel 501, XXXIX.

A gentleman, when he has good horse in his stable, does not like to leave him there eating his head off. If he be a gig-horse, the owner of him will be keen to drive a gig; if a hunter, the happy possessor will wish to be with a pack of hounds. FrP 133, XIV.

Horses always catch the temperament of their riders, and when a man wishes to break his neck, he will generally find a horse willing to assist him in appearance, but able to save him in the performance. CanY 345, XXXIII,I.

The horse is a closely sympathetic beast, and will make his turns, and do his trottings, and comport himself generally in strict unison with the pulsation of his master's heart. When a horse won't jump it is generally the case that the inner man is declining to jump also, let the outer man seem ever so anxious to accomplish the feat. Bel 259, XX.

There are but few horses which you cannot put into harness, and those of the highest spirit will generally do your work the best. PF 129, XIV,I.

When a horse puts out what strength he has against a man's arm, a man must put out what strength he has against the horse's mouth. PF 222, XXIV,I.

Who does not know that ladies only are allowed to canter their friends' horses upon roads? A gentleman trots his horse, and his friend's horse. Way 159, XVII,I.

When a man has perhaps made fifty pounds by using a 'straight tip' as to a horse at Newmarket, in doing which he had of course encountered some risks, he feels he ought not to be made to pay the amount back into the pockets of the 'tipper' and at the same time to find himself saddled with the possession of a perfectly useless animal. DuC 48, VI.

## HOSPITALITY

It is astonishing how far a very little cake will go in this way [handed round as people stand], particularly if administered tolerably early after dinner. The men can't eat it, and the women, having no plates and no table, are obliged to abstain. Mrs Jones knows that she cannot hold a piece of crumbly cake in her hand till it be consumed without doing serious injury to her best dress....Going out to tea is not a bad thing, if one can contrive to dine early, and then be allowed to sit round a big table with a tea urn in the middle. I would, however, suggest that breakfast cups should always be provided for the gentlemen. And then with pleasant neighbours--or more especially with a pleasant neighbour--the affair is not, according to my taste, by any means the worst phase of society. But I do dislike that handing round, unless it be of a subsidiary thimbleful when the business of the social intercourse has been dinner.

And indeed this handing round has become a vulgar and an intolerable nuisance among us second-class gentry with our eight hundred a year....Friends of mine who occasionally dine at such [the Duke of Omnium] houses tell me that they get their wine quite as quickly as they can drink it, that their mutton is brought to them without delay, and that the potato bearer follows quick upon the heels of carnifer.... But we of the eight hundred can no more come up to them in this than we can in their opera-boxes and equipages. May I not say that the usual tether of this class, in the way of carnifers, cupbearers, and the rest, does not reach beyond neat-handed Phyllis and the green-grocer? and that Phyllis, neat-handed as she probably is, and the green-grocer, though he be ever so active, cannot administer a dinner to twelve people who are prohibited by a Medo-Persian law from all self-administration whatever? And may I not further say that the lamentable consequence to us eight hundreders dining out among each other is this, that we too often get no dinner at all....Seeing a lady the other day in this strait, left without a small modicum of stimulus which was no doubt necessary for her good digestion, I ventured to ask her to drink wine with me. But when I bowed my head at her, she looked at me with all her eyes, struck with amazement. Had I suggested that she should join me in a wild Indian war-dance, with nothing on but my paint, her face could not have shown greater astonishment. And yet I should have thought she might have remembered the days when Christian men and women used to drink wine with each other. God be with the good old days when I could hob-nob with my friend over the table as often as I was inclined to lift my glass to my lips, and make a long arm for a hot potato whenever the exigencies of my plate required it.

I think it may be laid down as a rule in affairs of hospitality, that whatever extra luxury or grandeur we introduce at our tables when guests are with us, should be introduced for the advantage of the guest and not for our own. If, for instance, our dinner be served in a manner different from that usual to us, it should be so served in order that our friends may with more satisfaction eat our repast than our everyday practice would produce on them.... Again, if I decorate my sideboard and table, wishing that the eyes of my visitors may rest on that which is elegant and pleasant to the sight, I act in that matter with a becoming sense of hospitality; but if my object be to kill Mrs Jones with envy at the sight of my silver trinkets, I am a very mean-spirited fellow. FrP 162-4,XVII.

But hospitality in the bush can be stayed by no such considerations as that [no more sleeping space]. Let their employments or enjoyments on hand be what they may, everything must yield to the entertainment of strangers.
HHOG 148, XI.

## HOSTS...GUESTS

The usual courtesies of society demand that there shall be civility--almost flattering civility--from host to guest and from guest to host; and yet how often does it occur that in the midst of these courtesies there is something that tells of hatred, of ridicule, or of scorn!   How often does it happen that the guest knows that he is disliked, or the host knows that he is a bore!   VOB 56, VIII.

Now, when a host questions the propriety of a guest remaining under his roof, the guest is obliged to go.
PR 256, LXIX,II.

[B]ut one cannot tell one's visitor to depart from one's house without a downright rupture.   LA 198, XIX.

But nevertheless it is a bore when a gentleman dies in your house,--and a worse bore if he dies from an accident than if from an illness for which his own body may be supposed to be responsible.   Though the gout should fly to a man's stomach in your best bedroom, the idea never strikes you that your burgundy has done it!   AS 154, XXIII.

But a host expects that his corns should be respected.
JC 426, LVIII.

There are some injuries for which a host cannot abuse his guest.   If your best Venetian decanter be broken at table you are bound to look as though you liked it.   But if a horse be damaged a similar amount of courtesy is hardly required.   The well-nurtured gentleman, even in that case, will only look unhappy and not say a word.   AyA 278-9, XXX.

## HOTELS

Happy the man at such a period [assize week], who enjoys a bed-room which he can secure with a key--for in other cases the rightful possessor is not at all unlikely, on entering his own premises, to find three or four somewhat rough looking strangers, perhaps liberated jurors, or witnesses just escaped from the fangs of a counsel, sitting in most undisturbed ease on his bed, eating bread and butter, and drinking bottled porter; some huge farmer with dripping frieze coat squatted on his pillow, his towel spread as table cloth on the little deal table, which has been allotted to him as the only receptacle for his jug, basin, looking glass, brushes, and every other article of the toilet, and his carpet bag, dressing gown, and pantaloons chucked unceremoniously into a corner, off the chairs which they had occupied, to make way for the damp friends of the big farmer, who is seated on the bed.   This man is now drawing a cork from a bottle of porter, the froth of which you are quite sure from the manner in which the man holds the bottle will chiefly fall upon the sheets between which you are destined to sleep, unless some half drunken ruffian,

regardless of rights of possession and negligent of
etiquette, deposits himself there before the hour at which
you may think good to retire to rest.  MB 222-4, VI,III.

I speak not now with reference to the excellent establishment which has been named [the Great Western Hotel], but to
the nature of such tables [one of those tables which are so
comfortable to the eye, but which are so comfortless in
reality] in general.  A solitary mutton-chop in an hotel
coffee-room is not a banquet to be envied by any god; and if
the mutton-chop be converted into soup, fish, little dishes,
big dishes, and the rest, the matter becomes worse and not
better.  What comfort are you to have, seated alone on that
horsehair chair, staring into the room and watching the
waiters as they whisk about their towels?  No one but an
Englishman has ever yet thought of subjecting himself to
such a position as that!  SmaH 601, LIX.

Hotel people always are civil before the crowds come.
Way 435, XLVI,I.

## HOTELS, EGYPTIAN

For be it known that at these hotels in Egypt, a man cannot
order his dinner when he pleases.  He must breakfast at
nine, and dine at six, as others do--or go without.  And
whether he dine, or whether he do not, he must pay.  The
Medes and Persians were lax and pliable in their laws in
comparison with these publicans.  Ber 691, XXXIX.

## HOTELS, LONDON

There never are resident landlords in London hotels.
IHP 93, XLI,II.

## HOUSES

But I fancy that our ideas of rural grandeur have altered
since many of our older country seats were built.  To be
near the village, so as in some way to afford comfort,
protection, and patronage, and perhaps also with some view
to the pleasantness of neighbourhood for its own inmates,
seemed to be the object of a gentleman when building his
house in the old days.  A solitude in the centre of a wide
park is now the only site that can be recognised as
eligible.  No cottage must be seen unless the cottage orne
of the gardener.  The village, if it cannot be abolished,
must be got out of sight.  The sound of the church bells is
not desirable, and the road on which the profane vulgar
travel by their own right must be at a distance.  SmaH 6,I.

[B]ut old houses are often like old ladies, who require more
care in their dressing than they who are younger.  MM 73,VI.

The showing of a house in such circumstances [where the
owner is wealthy and the girl bringing nothing to the

marriage] is very trying, both to the man and to the woman.
He is weighted by a mixed load of pride in his possession
and of assumed humility.    She, to whom every detail of the
nest is so vitally important, is almost bound to praise,
though every encomium she pronounces will be a difficulty in
the way of those changes which she contemplates.    VOB 361,L.

[A] house not grand enough for a squire's mansion, and too
large for a farmer's homestead?    Such houses throughout
England are much more numerous than Englishmen think....It
is especially so in the eastern counties, and may be taken
as one proof among many that the broad-acred squire, with
his throng of tenants, is comparatively a modern invention.
The country gentleman of two hundred years ago farmed the
land he held.    As years have rolled on, the strong have
swallowed the weak,--one strong man having eaten up half-a-
dozen weak men.    And so the squire has been made.    Then the
strong squire becomes a baronet and a lord, till he lords it
a little too much, and a Manchester warehouseman buys him
out.    The strength of the country probably lies in the fact
that the change is ever being made, but is never made
suddenly.    RalH 371, XLIX.

## HOUSE MOVING

Who does not know how terrible are those preparations for
house-moving;--how infinite in number are the articles which
must be packed, how inexpressibly uncomfortable is the
period of packing, and how poor and tawdry is the aspect of
one's belongings while they are thus in a state of dis-
location?    Nowadays people who understand the world, and
have money commensurate with their understanding, have
learned the way of shunning all these disasters, and of
leaving the work to the hands of persons paid for doing it.
The crockery is left in the cupboards, the books on the
shelves, the wine in the bins, the curtains on their poles,
and the family that is understanding goes for a fortnight to
Brighton.    At the end of that time the crockery is comfortably settled in other cupboards, the books on other
shelves, the wine in other bins, the curtains are hung on
other poles, and all is arranged.    SmaH 495, XLIX.

## HOUSE OF COMMONS

...argumentative philosophical Radicals,--men of standing
and repute, who are always in doubtful times individually
flattered by Ministers, who have great privileges accorded
to them of speaking and dividing, and who are not unfrequently even thanked for their rods by the very owners of
the backs which bear the scourges.    PrM 107, XII,I.

...Ministers...[going] through their course of baiting with
that equanimity and air of superiority which always belongs
to a well-trained occupant of the Treasury bench.
DuC 199, XXVI.

Is it not possible that as much may be said for others, who from day to day so violently excite our spleen, as to make us feel that special Irishmen selected for special constituencies are not worthy to be ranked with men? You shall take the whole House of Commons,...and will find in conversation that the nature of the animal, the absurdity, the selfishness, the absence of all good qualities, are taken for granted as matters admitting of no dispute.
Land 51-2, XXXV,III.

There seldom is need in the House of Commons for independent eloquence. The few men who have acquired for themselves at last the power of expressing it, not to empty benches, not amidst coughings and hootings, and loud conversation, have had to make their way to that point either by long efficient service or by great gifts of pachydermatousness.
Land 172-3, XLII,III.

## HOUSEHOLD TOPICS

It generally happens, that in every household, one subject of importance occupies it at a time. DoT 466, XXXIX.

## HOUSING

There are certain items of the cost of living for which the greatest proficient in the art of tick must pay, or he will come to a speedy end;--and a man's lodging is one of them. If indeed the spendthrift adapts himself to the splendour of housekeeping, he may, provided his knowledge of his business be complete, and his courage adequate, house himself gloriously for a year or two with very small payment in ready money. He may even buy a mansion with an incredibly small outlay, and, when once in it, will not easily allow himself to be extruded. SHHOH 94, X.

## HUMAN NATURE

Flesh is flesh after all, and human nature no stronger than human nature. Kept 10, III.

## HUMILITY

A man may indeed measure small things by great, but the measurer should be careful to declare his own littleness when he illustrates his position by that of the topping ones of the earth. PrM 307, LXXII,II.

## HUMOUR

How pleasantly young men and women of fifty or thereabouts can joke and flirt and poke their fun about, laughing and holding their sides, dealing in little innuendos and rejoicing in nicknames, when they have no Mentors of twenty-five or thirty near them to keep them in order! FrP 52, VI.

With the young the love of fun is gratified generally by
grotesque movement.    It is not till years are running on
that the grotesqueness of words and ideas is appreciated.
EE 86-7, V,I.

## HUNTING

[F]or in every field there are two classes of men.    Those
who go out to get the greatest possible quantity of riding,
and those whose object is to get the least.    Those who go to
work their nags, and those who go to spare them.    The former
think that the excellence of the hunt depends on the horses;
the latter, on the dogs.    The former go to act, and the
latter to see.    And it is very generally the case that the
least active part of the community know the most about the
sport.
     They, the less active part above alluded to, know every
high-road and bye-road; they consult the wind, and calculate
that a fox won't run with his nose against it; they remember
this stream and this bog, and avoid them; they are often at
the top of eminences, and only descend when they see which
way the dogs are going; they take short cuts, and lay
themselves out for narrow lanes; they dislike galloping, and
eschew leaping; and yet, when a hard-riding man is bringing
up his two hundred guinea hunter, a minute or two late for
the finish, covered with foam, trembling with his exertion,
not a breath left in him--he'll probably find one of these
steady fellows there before him, mounted on a broken-down
screw, but as cool and as fresh as when he was brought out
of the stable; and what is, perhaps, still more amazing, at
the end of the day, when the hunt is canvassed after dinner,
our dashing friend, who is in great doubt whether his
thoroughbred steeplechaser will ever recover his day's work,
and who has been personally administering warm mashes and
bandages before he would venture to take his own boots off,
finds he does not know half as much about the hunt, or can
tell half as correctly where the game went, as our quiet-
going friend, whose hack will probably go out on the following morning under the car, with the mistress and children.
Kel 284-5, XXII.

Neither for gods nor men must he  [the fox]  be left, as
long as his skin was whole above ground.    There is an importance attaching to the pursuit of a fox, which gives it a
character quite distinct from that of any other amusement
which men follow in these realms.    It justifies almost anything that men can do, and that at any place and in any
season....A man in a hunting county who opposes the county
hunt must be a misanthrope, willing to live in seclusion,
fond of being in Coventry, and in love with the enmity of
his fellow-creatures.    There are such men, but they are
regarded as lepers by those around them.    All this adds to
the nobleness of the noble sport, and makes it worthy of a
man's energies.  CasR 207-8, X,II.

Foxes will not do well in any country which is not provided

with their natural food.  Rats they eat, and if rats be
plentiful it is so far good.  But one should not begrudge
them occasional geese and turkeys, or even break one's heart
if they like a lamb in season.  A fox will always run well
when he has come far from home seeking his breakfast....
     The huntsman in looking after his game is as wily as
the fox himself.  Men do not talk at the covert side--or at
any rate they ought not.  And they should stand together
discreetly at the nonrunning side.  All manner of wiles and
silences and discretions are necessary.
CasR 192-3; 195, X,III.

Indeed it was one of those hunting-days got up rather for
the ladies than for the sport.  Great nuisances they are to
steady, middle-aged hunting men; but the young fellows like
them because they have thereby an opportunity of showing off
their sporting finery, and of doing a little flirtation on
horseback.  FrP 32, IV.

[The clergy]  always show a special aptitude for the
pursuit, as though hunting were an employment peculiarly
congenial with a cure of souls in the country.  FrP 117,XII.

Sure there is no sound like it  [the music of the dogs]  for
filling a man's heart with an eager desire to be at work.
What may be the trumpet in battle I do not know, but I can
imagine it has the same effect.  OrF 286, XXVIII,I.

And let it be understood that in hunting those who are in
advance generally do ride on.  The lame and the halt and the
wounded, if they cannot pick themselves up, have to be
picked up by those who come after them.  OrF 289, XXIX,I.

I don't know any feeling more disagreeable than that produced by being left alone in a field, when out hunting, with
a man who has been very much hurt and who is incapable of
riding or walking.  The hurt man himself has the privilege
of his infirmities and may remain quiescent; but you, as his
only attendant, must do something.  You must for the moment
do all, and if you do wrong the whole responsibility lies on
your shoulders.  If you leave a wounded man on the damp
ground, in the middle of winter, while you run away, five
miles perhaps, to the next doctor, he may not improbably--as
you then think--be dead before you come back.  You don't
know the way; you are heavy yourself, and your boots are
very heavy.  You must stay therefore; but as you are no
doctor you don't in the least know what is the amount of the
injury.  In your great trouble you begin to roar for assistance; but the woods re-echo your words, and the distant
sound of the huntsman's horn, as he summons his hounds at a
check, only mocks your agony.  OrF 290, XXIX,I.

That riding back over fences in cold blood is the work that
really tries a man's nerve.  And a man has to do it too when
no one is looking on.  How he does crane and falter and look
about for an easy place at such a moment as that!  But when
the blood is cold no places are easy.  OrF 294-5, XXIX,I.

[S]uch men [who know what they are about] are always welcome. It is the man who does not know how to ride that is made uncomfortable in the hunting field by cold looks or expressed censure. And yet it is very rarely that such men do any real harm....Many such complaints are made; but in truth the too forward man, who presses the dogs, is generally one who can ride, but is too eager or too selfish to keep in his proper place. The bad rider, like the bad whist player, pays highly for what he does not enjoy, and should be thanked. But at both games he gets cruelly snubbed. CanY 162, XVI,I.

Of all sights in the world there is, I think, none more beautiful than that of a pack of fox-hounds seated, on a winter morning, round the huntsman, if the place of meeting has been chosen with anything of artistic skill. It should be in a grassy field, and the field should be small. It should not be absolutely away from all buildings, and the hedgerows should not have been clipped and pared, and made straight with reference to modern agricultural economy. There should be trees near, and the ground should be a little uneven, so as to mark some certain small space as the exact spot where the dogs and servants of the hunt should congregate.
      There are well-known grand meets in England, in the parks of noblemen, before their houses, or even on what are called their lawns; but these magnificent affairs have but little of the beauty of which I speak. Such assemblies are too grand and too ornate, and, moreover, much too far removed from true sporting proprieties....As regards my own taste, I do not know that I do like beginning a day with a great wood,--and if not beginning it, certainly not ending it. It is hard to come upon the cream of hunting, as it is upon the cream of any other delight....A man has usually to work through much mud before he gets his nugget. It is so certainly in hunting, and a big wood too frequently afflicts the sportsman, as the mud does the miner. The small gorse cover is the happy, much-envied bit of ground in which the gold is sure to show itself readily. But without the woods the gorse would not hold the foxes, and without the mud the gold would not have its resting place. CanY 171-2, XVII,I.

No hunting man ever wants to jump if he can help it.... CanY 178, XVII,I.

Such is the lot of men who hunt. A man pays five or six pounds for his day's amusement, and it is ten to one that the occurrences of the day disgust rather than gratify him! CanY 180, XVII,I.

A double rail is a nasty fence always if it has been made in any way strong, and one which a man with a wife and a family is justified in avoiding. CanY 181, XVII,I.

[B]ut it was devoutly desired by all of them that the fox might soon come to the end of his tether. Ah! that intense longing that the fox may fail, when the failing powers of the horse begin to make themselves known,--and the consciousness comes on that all that one has done will go for nothing unless the thing can be brought to a close in a field or two!  So far you have triumphed, leaving scores of men behind; but of what good is all that, if you also are to be left behind at the last?  CanY 184, XVII,I.

For myself, I think it as well that clergymen should not hunt; but had I been the parson of Clavering, I should, under those circumstances, have hunted double.  Cl 12, II.

A crowd in a fast run no doubt quickly becomes small by degrees and beautifully less; but it is very difficult, especially for a stranger, to free himself from the rush at the first start.  PF 220, XXIV,I.

When a run is over, men are very apt to regret the termination, who a minute or two before were anxiously longing that the hounds might pull down their game.  To finish well is everything in hunting.  To have led for over an hour is nothing, let the pace and country have been what they might, if you fall away during the last half mile....To ride to hounds is very glorious; but to have ridden to hounds is more glorious still.  PF 223, XXIV,I.

[A]s a rule, of all sports, cub-hunting is the sorriest. RalH 205, XXVII.

And then there were the hunters.  Every sportsman knows, and the wives and daughters of all sportsmen know, how important a month in the calendar is the month of October....But it is needful to know, down to a single line on the form, whether this or that animal wants more exercise,--and if so, of what nature.  We hold that for hunters which are worked regularly throughout the season, and which live in loose boxes summer and winter, but little exercise is required except in the months of September and October.  Let them have been fed on oats throughout the year, and a good groom will bring them into form in two months....What good sportsman is too proud, or even too much engaged to inspect his horse's gear,--and his own?  Only let his horse's gear stand first in his mind!  Let him be sure that the fit of a saddle is of more moment than the fit of a pair of breeches;--that in riding the length, strength, and nature of the bit will avail more,-- should at least avail more,--than the depth, form, and general arrangement of the flask; that the question of boots, great as it certainly is, should be postponed to the question of shoes; that a man's seat should be guarded by his girths rather than by his spurs!  that no run has ever been secured by the brilliancy of the cravat, though many a run has been lost by the insufficiency of the stirrup-leather.  RalH 231, XXXI.

Anybody may see a fox found at the gorses who will simply take the trouble to be with the hounds when they go into the covert; but in the wood it becomes a great question with a sportsman whether he will stick to the pack or save his horse and loiter about till he hears that a fox has been found.   The latter is certainly the commoner course, and perhaps the wiser.   And even when the fox has been found it may be better for the expectant sportsman to loiter about till he breaks, giving some little attention to the part of the wood in which the work of hunting may be progressing. There are those who systematically stand still or roam about very slowly;--others, again, who ride and cease riding by spurts, just as they become weary or impatient;--and others who, with dogged perserverance, stick always to the track of the hounds.   RalH 236, XXXI.

A huntsman at the beginning of any day or at the end of a good day is so different from a huntsman at the end of a bad day!   A huntsman often has a very bad time out hunting, and it is sometimes a marvel that he does not take the advice which Job got from his wife.   ED 349, XXXVIII,I.

A man who likes hunting but hunts only once a year is desirous of doing the best he can with his day. ED 350, XXXVIII,I.

In hunting, to have ridden is the pleasure;--and not simply to have ridden well, but to have ridden better than the others.   ED 354, XXXVIII,I.

The worst of doing a big thing out hunting is the fact that in nine cases out of ten they who don't do it are as well off as they who do....When you have nearly broken your neck to get to hounds, or made your horse exert himself beyond his proper power, and then find yourself, within three minutes, overtaking the hindmost ruck of horsemen on a road because of some iniquitous turn that the fox has taken, the feeling is not pleasant.   And some man who has not ridden at all, who never did ride at all, will ask you where you have been; and his smile will give you the lie in your teeth if you make any attempt to explain the facts.   Let it be suffi- cient for you at such a moment to feel that you are not ashamed of yourself.   Self-respect will support a man even in such misery as this.   ED 356-7, XXXVIII,I.

When we give a guinea for a stall at the opera we think that we pay a large sum; but we are fairly sure of having our music.   When you go to Copperhouse Cross  [a popular meet] you are by no means sure of your opera.   PR 139, XVI,I.

Hunting men will know that all this was not quite comfor- table  [to be told that a horse sometimes won't jump].   When you ride your own horse, and know his special defects, you know also how far that defect extends, and what real prospect you have of overcoming it....But when you are told that your friend's horse is perfect,--only that he does this or that,--there comes a weight on your mind from which you are unable to release it.   You cannot discount your trouble

at any percentage.  It may amount to absolute ruin, as far
as that day is concerned; and in such a circumstance you
alway look forward to the worst.  PR 141, XVI,I.

Most hounds will lie occasionally....To get away well is so
very much!  And to get away well is often so very difficult!
There are so many things of which the horseman is bound to
think in that moment.  Which way does the wind blow?  And
then, though a fox will not long run up wind, he will break
covert up wind, as often as not....When you hear some wild
halloa, informing you that one fox has gone in the direction
exactly opposite to that in which the hounds are hunting,
are you sure that the noise is not made about a second fox?
On all these matters you are bound to make up your mind
without losing a moment; and if you make up your mind
wrongly the five pounds you have invested in that day's
amusement will have been spent for nothing.  PR 142-3,XVI,I.

But to go back in such circumstances  [being thrown into a
ditch]  is a terrible disaster.  It amounts to complete
defeat; and is tantamount to a confession that you must go
home, because you are unable to ride to hounds.  A man, when
he is compelled to do this, is almost driven to resolve at
the spur of the moment that he will give up hunting for the
rest of his life.  And if one thing be more essential than
any other to the horseman in general, it is that he, and not
the animal which he rides, shall be the master.
PR 144-5, XVI,I.

When a man hunts five days a week, regardless of distances,
and devotes a due proportion of his energies to the necessary circumstances of hunting, the preservation of foxes,
the maintenance of good humour with the farmers, the proper
compensation for poultry really killed by four-legged
favourites, the growth and arrangements of coverts, the
lying-in of vixens, and the subsequent guardianship of
nurseries, the persecution of enemies, and the warm protection of friends,--when he follows the sport, accomplishing all the concomitant duties of a true sportsman, he
has not much time left for anything.  Such a one...finds
that his off day is occupied from breakfast to dinner with
grooms, keepers, old women with turkeys' heads, and
gentlemen in velveteens with information about wires and unknown earths.  His letters fall naturally to the Sunday
afternoon, and are hardly written before sleep overpowers
him.  Many a large fortune has been made with less of true
devotion to the work than is given to hunting by so genuine
a sportsman.  PR 111, LIII,II.

Is a landed proprietor bound, or is he not, to keep foxes
for the amusement of his neighbours?  To ordinary thinkers,
to unprejudiced outsiders,--to Americans, let us say, or
Frenchmen,--there does not seem to be room even for an
argument.  But what law of God of man can a man be bound to
maintain a parcel of injurious vermin on his property, in
the pursuit of which he finds no sport himself, and which

are highly detrimental to another sport in which he takes, perhaps, the keenest interest?...But a good deal had been said which, though not perhaps capable of convincing the unprejudiced American or Frenchman, had been regarded as cogent arguments to country-bred Englishmen....Many things are, no doubt, permissible under the law, which, if done, would show the doer of them to be the enemy of his species, --and this destruction of foxes in a hunting country may be named as one of them.  PR 310-1, LXXV,II.

There is always a doctor in the field--sent there by some benignity of Providence,--who always rides forward enough to be near to accidents, but never so forward as to be in front of them....All public institutions have, or ought to have, their doctor; but in no institution is the doctor so invariably at hand, just when he is wanted, as in the hunting-field.  IHP 76-7, VIII,I.

[A]nd a huntsman is not entitled to beer till he has found a fox.  AS 61, IX.

There are some men who can crush their hats, have their boots and breeches full of water, and be covered with dirt from their faces downwards, and yet look as though nothing were amiss, while, with others, the marks of a fall are always provocative either of pity or ridicule.  AS 72, XI.

The hunting-field is by no means a place suited for real love-making.  Very much of preliminary conversation may be done there in a pleasant way, and intimacies may be formed. But when lovers have already walked with arms round each other in a wood, riding together may be very pleasant, but can hardly be ecstatic.  AS 265, XXXIX.

When a Master has been deserted on any day by the choice spirits of his hunt he is always apt to boast to them that he had on that occasion the run of the season. AS 330, XLVIII.

What hunting man or woman does not know the gloom which comes over a hunting county when one Master goes before another is ready to step into his shoes?...A Master does appear at last, though for a time it appears that the kingdom must come to an end because no one will consent to sit on the throne.  AS 555, LXXX.

...there was a suggestion as to a committee of three,--than which nothing for hunting purposes can be much worse. AS 556, LXXX.

There is often someone in a hunting country who never becomes a master of hounds himself, but who has almost as much to say about the business as the master himself.  Sometimes at hunt meetings he is rather unpopular, as he is always inclined to talk.  But there are occasions on which his services are felt to be valuable.  DuC 454, LVII.

[A] check,--as there is generally after a short spurt, when fox, hounds, and horsemen get off together, and not always in the order in which they have been placed here. There is too much bustle, and the pack becomes disconcerted. DuC 504, LXIII.

It was...as when a hunter has hunted a fox after the approved laws of venery. There have been a dozen ways of killing the animal of which he has scorned to avail himself. He has been careful to let him break from his covert, regarding all who would stop him as enemies to himself....Let all be done by hunting law,--in accordance with those laws which give so many chances of escape. But when the hounds have run their quarry, not all the eloquence of all the gods should serve to save that doomed one's life. JC 431, LIX.

Hunting from home coverts rarely exacts much jumping from ladies. The woods are big, and the gates are numerous. It is when the far-away homes of wild foxes are drawn,--those secluded brakes and gorses where the noble animal is wont to live at a distance from carriage-roads and other weak refuges of civilisation,--that the riding capacities of ladies must be equal to those of their husbands and brothers. AyA 214-5, XXIII.

'Always to excel and to go ahead of everybody' should, the present writer thinks, be in the heart of every man who rides to hounds. AyA 230, XXIV.

It never occurs to a hunting-man to suppose that either a lady, or a bishop, or a political economist, can be indifferent to hunting. There is something beyond millinery,-- beyond the interests of the church,--beyond the price of wheat,--in that great question whether the hounds did or did not change their fox in Gobblegoose Wood. AyA 472-3, XLIX.

For the rudiments of love-making, for little endearing attentions, for a few sweet words to be whispered with shortened breath as one horse gallops beside another, perhaps for a lengthened half-hour together, amidst the mazes of a large wood when opportunities are no doubt given for private conversion, hunting may be very well. But for two persons who are engaged, with the mutual consent of all their friends, a comfortable sofa is perhaps preferable. AyA 540, LVI.

I hold that nothing is so likely to be permanently prejudicial to the interest of hunting in the British Isles as a certain flavour of tip-top fashion which has gradually enveloped it. There is a pretence of grandeur about that and, alas, about other sports also, which is, to my thinking, destructive of all sport itself....In all these cases [rowing, cricket, hockey, tennis] the fashion of the game is much more cherished than the game itself. But in nothing is this feeling so predominant as in hunting. For the management of a pack, as packs are managed now, a huntsman needs

must be a great man himself, and three mounted subordinates
are necessary, as at any rate for two of these servants a
second horse is required.    A hunt is nothing in the world
unless it goes out four times a week at least.    A run is
nothing unless the pace be that of a steeplechase....A bold
huntsman who can make a dash across country from one covert
to another, and who can so train his hounds that they shall
run as though game were before them, is supposed to have
provided good sport.    If a fox can be killed in covert
afterwards so much the better for those who like to talk of
their doings....But the worst of all is the attention given
by men to things altogether outside the sport.    Their coats
and waistcoats, their boots and breeches, their little
strings and pretty scarfs, their saddles and bridles, their
dandy knick-knacks, and, above all, their flasks, are more
to many men then [sic] aught else in the day's proceedings.
I have known girls who thought that their first appearance
in the ball-room, when all was fresh, unstained, and perfect
from the milliner's hand, was the one moment of rapture for
the evening.    I have sometimes felt the same of young
sportsmen at a Leicestershire or Northamptonshire meet.    It
is not that they will not ride when the occasion comes.
They are always ready enough to break their bones.    There is
no greater mistake than to suppose that dandyism is
antagonistic to pluck.    The fault is that men train
themselves to care for nothing that is not as costly as
unlimited expenditure can make it.    Thus it comes about that
the real love of sport is crushed under a desire for
fashion.  MF 140-2, XIII,I.

To have seen the hounds as they start, and to see them again
as they are clustering round the huntsman after eating their
fox, is a great deal to some men.   MF 148, XIII,I.

The misery of sportsmen on these days is sometimes so great
that we wonder that any man, having experienced the bitterness of hunting disappointment, should ever go out again....
"Things have come to such a pass," says Walker to Watson,
"that I mean to give it up.   There's no good keeping horses
for this sort of thing."   All this is very sad....
    It is certainly true as to hunting that there are so
many hours in which the spirit is vexed by a sense of
failure, that the joy when it does come should be very great
to compensate the evils endured.    It is not simply that
foxes will not dwell in every spinney, or break as soon as
found, or always run when they do break.    These are the
minor pangs.  But when the fox is found, and will break, and
does run, when the scent suffices, and the hounds do their
duty, when the best country which the Shires afford is open
to you, when your best horse is under you, when your nerves
are even somewhat above the usual mark,--even then there is
so much of failure!  You are on the wrong side of the wood,
and getting a bad start are never with them for a yard; or
your horse, good as he is , won't have that bit of water; or
you lose your stirrup-leather, or your way; or you don't see
the hounds turn, and you go astray with others as blind as

yourself; or, perhaps, when there comes the run of the
season, on that very day you have taken a liberty with your
chosen employment and lain in bed.  Look back upon your
hunting lives, brother sportsmen, and think how few and how
far between the perfect days have been.  MF 78-80, VII,II.

But when a man is too forward to be seen, he is always
supposed to be somewhere behind.  MF 80, VII,II.

It is, perhaps, on such occasions as these  [the immediate
finding of a fox]  that riders are subjected to the worst
perils of the hunting field.   There comes a sudden rush,
when men have not cooled themselves down by the process of
riding here and there and going through the usual preliminary prefaces to a run.  They are collected in crowds, and
the horses are more impatient even than their riders....A
sportsman who could at such a moment have kept his blood
perfectly cool, might have remembered his duties well enough
to have abstained from pressing into the field in order that
the fox might have his fair chance.  MF 84-5, VIII,II.

Ever so many hindrances have been created to bar the killing
of a fox,--as for instance that you shouldn't knock him on
the head with a brickbat....The laws of hunting are so many,
that most men who hunt cannot know them all.
MSF 93,XXVIII,II.

Now, it is well known that you may follow a hunted fox
through whatever country he may take you to, if only your
hounds are hunting him continuously.  And one hound for that
purpose is as good as thirty, and if a hound can only "show
a line" he is held to be hunting.  MSF 98, XXVIII,II.

No one who has not ridden with the hounds regularly can
understand the effect of such an order  [that the hounds
should be withdrawn for the remainder of the season].
Land 211, XII,I.

## HUSBANDS

Husbands, when they give their wives a talking, should do it
out of hand, uttering their words hard, sharp, and quick,--
and should then go.  There are some works that won't bear a
preface, and this work of marital fault-finding is one of
them.  CanY 185, LVIII,II.

A member of Parliament, with a small house near Eaton
Square, with a moderate income, and a liking for committees,
who would write a pamphlet once every two years, and read
Dante critically during recess, was, to her, the model for a
husband....Her model may not appear, when thus described, to
be a very noble one; but I think it is the model most
approved among ladies of her class in England.  Bel 129, XI.

If husbands would only be complaisant, how much nicer it
would be for everybody.  IHP 146, XLVII,II.

## HUSBAND HUNTING

We are apt to abuse mothers for wanting high husbands for
their daughters;--but can there be any point in which the
true maternal instinct can shew itself with more affectionate enthusiasm?...Husband hunting mothers may be
injudicious; but surely they are maternal and unselfish.
HKHWR 724-5, LXXVII.

## HUSBANDS...WIVES

There are men--may we not rather say monsters?--who do such
things [leave for a visit without consulting a wife]; and
there are wives--may we not rather say slaves?--who put up
with such usage.  BaT 233-4, XXV.

It would be useless here to repeat the arguments that were
used on each side, and needless to record the result.  Those
who are married will understand very well how the battle was
lost and won; and those who are single will never understand
it till they learn the lesson which experience alone can
give.  BaT 234, XXV.

Oh!  my aspiring pastors, divines to whose ears nolo
episcopari are the sweetest of words, which of you would be
a bishop on such terms as these [the wife waiting until the
husband comes to bed]?  BaT 245, XXVI.

But it can be taken for granted that no husband can carry on
such dealings [money] long without some sort of cognizance
on his wife's part as to what he is doing; a woman who is
not trusted by her lord may choose to remain in apparent
darkness, may abstain from questions, and may consider it
either her duty or her interest to assume an ignorance as to
her husband's affairs; but the partner of one's bed and
board, the minister who soothes one's headaches, and makes
one's tea, and looks after one's linen, can't but have the
means of guessing the thoughts which occupy her companion's
mind and occasionally darken his brow.  TC 184-5, XVII.

There are those who boast that a gentleman must always be a
gentleman; that a man, let him marry whom he will, raises or
degrades his wife to the level of his own condition....[But]
a man from the ordinary ranks of the upper classes, who has
had the nurture of a gentleman, prepares for himself a hell
on earth in taking a wife from any rank much below his own--
a hell on earth, and, alas!  too often another hell elsewhere also.  He must either leave her or loathe her.  She
may be endowed with all those moral virtues which should
adorn all women;...but he will have to endure habits,
manners, and ideas, which the close contiguity of married
life will force upon his disgusted palate, and which must
banish all love.  Man by instinct desires in his wife something softer, sweeter, more refined than himself; and though
in failing to obtain this, the fault may be all his own, he
will not on that account the more easily reconcile himself
to the want.  TC 383-4, XXXI.

But even duty may pall on an exigeant husband, and a man may be brought to wish that his wife would cross him.
Ber 604, XXXIII.

A man does not willingly accuse his wife of even the first germ of infidelity; does not willingly suggest to her that any one is of more moment to her than himself.
Ber 624, XXXIII.

A man does not like to be told by a beautiful woman that every hair of his head is odious to her, while the very footsteps of another are music to her ears. Perhaps it does not mend the matter when the hated man is the husband.
Ber 653-4, XXXVI.

'What shall we do if he has not dined?' That, I believe, is always the first thought in the mind of a good wife when her husband returns home. Has he had his dinner? What can I give him for dinner? Will he like his dinner? Oh dear, oh dear! there is nothing in the house but cold mutton.
FrP 257-8, XXVI.

Men who had risen in the world...do find it sometimes difficult to dispose of their wives. It is not that the ladies are in themselves more unfit for rising than their lords, or that if occasion demanded they would not as readily adapt themselves to new spheres. But they do not rise, and occasion does not demand it. A man elevates his wife to his own rank, and when Mr. Brown, on becoming solicitor-general, becomes Sir Jacob, Mrs. Brown also becomes my lady. But the whole set among whom Brown must be more or less thrown do not want her ladyship. On Brown's promotion she did not become part of the bargain. Brown must henceforth have two existences--a public and a private existence....
    If Lady B. can raise herself also, if she can make her own occasion--if she be handsome and can flirt, if she be impudent and can force her way, if she have a daring mind and can commit great expenditure, if she be clever and can make poetry, if she can in any way create a separate glory for herself, then, indeed, Sir Jacob with his blue nose may follow his own path, and all will be well. Sir Jacob's blue nose seated opposite to her will not be her summum bonum.
OrF 104-5, XI,I.

An angry ill-pleased wife is no pleasant companion for a gentleman on a long evening. For those who have managed that things shall run smoothly over the domestic rug there is no happier time of life than these long candlelight hours of home and silence....The fact that is felt is enough for peace. But when the fact is not felt;...when bitter grievances from one to the other fill the heart, rather than memories of mutual kindness; then, I say, those long candlelight hours of home and silence are not easy of endurance.
OrF 205-6, XXI,I.

Let the master be ever so much master, what is he to do? Say that his wife is wrong from the beginning to the end of the quarrel,--that in no way improves the matter.   His anxiety is that the world abroad shall not know he has ought amiss at home; but she, and her hot sense of injury, and her loud revolt against supposed wrongs, cares not who hears it. 'Hold your tongue, madam,' the husband says.   But the wife, bound though she be by an oath of obedience, will not obey him, but only screams the louder.   OrF 214, XXI,I.

Those who would hang by the letter of the law in such matters [as when a wife refuses to live with her husband] may say that he should have rung the bell, sent for his wife, explained to her that obedience was a necessary duty on her part, and have finished by making her understand that she must and would continue to live wherever he chose that she should live.   There be those who say that if a man be anything of a man, he can always insure obedience in his own household.   He has the power of the purse and the power of the law; and if, having these, he goes to the wall, it must be because he is a poor creature.   Those who so say have probably never tried the position.   OrF 411, XLI,I.

The theory of man and wife--that special theory in accordance with which the wife is to bend herself in loving submission before her husband--is very beautiful; and would be good altogether if it could only be arranged that the husband should be the stronger and the greater of the two. The theory is based upon that hypothesis;--and the hypothesis sometimes fails of confirmation.   In ordinary marriages the vessel rights itself, and the stronger and the greater takes the lead, whether clothed in petticoats, or in coat, waistcoat, and trousers; but there sometimes comes a terrible shipwreck, when the woman before marriage has filled herself full with ideas of submission, and then finds that her golden-headed god has got an iron body and feet of clay.   Bel 132, XI.

A young husband may dislike the too-friendly bearing of a friend, and may abstain from that outrage on his own dignity and on his wife, which is conveyed by a word of suspicion. HKHWR 7, I.

We all know what a husband means to think when he resolves to be round with his wife.   HKHWR 13, II.

[B]ut we may almost say that the man who is really generous in such matters [to his wife's family]   is unconscious of his own generosity.   The giver who gives the most, gives, and does not know that he gives....In that matter of giving between a man and his wife, if each gives all, the two are equal, let the things given be what they may!   HKHWR 42, V.

Let a man have any such friendships [with the opposite sex],--what friendships he may,--he does not disgrace his wife.   HKHWR 42-3, V.

Let a man be ever so much his wife's master, he cannot maintain his masterdom by any power which the law places in his
hands.  HKHWR 43, V.

Wives are bound to obey their husbands, but obedience cannot
be exacted from wives, as it may from servants, by aid of
law and with penalties, or as from a horse, by punishments,
and manger curtailments.  A man should be master in his own
house, but he should make his mastery palatable, equitable,
smooth, soft to the touch, a thing almost unfelt.
HKHWR 44, V.

How many husbands have come to the same resolution  [to
speak to his wife in the morning]; and how few of them have
found the words of wisdom to be efficacious!  HKHWR 86, IX.

A husband who is also an eager lover must be delightful to a
young bride.  PrM 234, XXV, I.

When a husband declares that his wife shall not know a man,
that edict must be obeyed,--or, if disobeyed, must be sub-
verted by intrigue.  PrM 178, LIX, II.

[A]nd how can a man be a real lord over a woman when he has
had to confess his fault to her, and to beg her to forgive
him?  A wife's position with her husband may be almost
improved by such asking for pardon.  It will enhance his
tenderness.  But the man is so lowered that neither of them
can ever forget the degradation.  IHP 179-80, XIX, I.

I do not know whether a husband's comfort is ever perfect
till some family peccadilloes have been conclusively proved
against him.  I am sure that a wife's temper to him is
sweetened by such evidence of human imperfection.  A woman
will often take delight in being angry; will sometimes wrap
herself warm in prolonged sullenness; will frequently revel
in complaint--but she enjoys forgiving better than aught
else.  She never feels that all the due privileges of her
life have been accorded to her till her husband shall have
laid himself open to the caressess of a pardon.  Then, and
not till then, he is her equal; and equality is necessary
for comfortable love.  But the man, till he be well used to
it, does not like to be pardoned.  He has assumed divine
superiority, and is bound to maintain it.  Then, at last, he
comes home some night with a little too much wine, or he
cannot pay the weekly bills because he has lost too much
money at cards, or he has got into trouble at his office and
is in doubt for a fortnight about his place, or perhaps a
letter from a lady falls into wrong hands.  Then he has to
tell himself that he has been 'found out'.  The feeling is
at first very uncomfortable; but it is, I think, a step
almost necessary in reaching true matrimonial comfort.  Hunting men say that hard rain settles the ground.  A good scold
with a 'kiss and be friends' after it, perhaps, does the
same.  IHP 315-6, XXXII, I.

A man, if his mind be given that way, may perhaps with
safety whisper into a woman's ear that her husband is untrue
to her.   Such an accusation may serve his purpose.   But the
woman, on her side, should hold her peace about the man's
wife.   A man must be very degraded indeed if his wife be not
holy to him.   IHP 31, XXXV,II.

A young wife when she is sure of her husband, will readily
forgive all offences committed before marriage, and will
almost be thankful for the confidence placed in her when
offences are confessed.   But she could understand that a
brother could not be thankful, and she would naturally
exaggerate in her own mind the horror which he would feel at
such a revelation.   JC 185, XXV.

What comfort does a woman get out of her husband unless she
may be allowed to talk to him about everything?
DrW 178, IV, Part V.

No gentleman wishes another to assure him that his wife is
one in a thousand.   An old mother might say so, or an old
aunt; hardly any one else near and less intimate could be
allowed to do so.   Kept 54, XIV.

## HYPOCRISY

Available hypocrisy is a quality very difficult of attainment and of all hypocrisies, epistolatory hypocrisy is perhaps the most difficult.   A man or woman must have studied
the matter very thoroughly, or be possessed of great natural
advantages in that direction, who can so fill a letter with
false expressions of affection, as to make any reader
believe them to be true.   MM 71, VI.

[B]ut there was no hypocrisy in this, as the world goes.
Women in such matters  [going to the Low Church]  are absolutely false if they be not sincere; but men, with political
views, and with much of their future prospects in jeopardy
also, are allowed to dress themselves differently for
different scenes.   Whatever be the peculiar interest on
which a man goes into Parliament, of course he has to live
up to that in his own borough.   Whether malt, the franchise,
or teetotalism be his rallying point, of course he is full
of it when among his constituents.   But it is not desirable
that he should be full of it also at his club.   Bel 14, I.

...with that special hypocrisy which belongs to women, and
is allowed to them.   Bel 203, XVI.

## HYPOCRITES

What hypocrites women are!   Even Ophelia in her madness
would pretend that she raved for her murdered father, when
it was patent to all the world that she was mad for love for
Hamlet....But then, what is the use of a lady's speech but
to conceal her thoughts?   Ber 484, XXVII.

A man is no more a hypocrite because his manner and gait
when he is alone are different from those which he assumes
in company, than he is for wearing a dressing-gown in the
morning, whereas he puts on a black coat in the evening.
OrF 230, LXIII,II.


I


## IGNORANCE

To the conductor of an omnibus on the Surrey side of the
river, the man who does not know what 'The Castle' means is
ignorant.   The outsider who is in a mist as to the 'former
question,' or 'the order of the day,' is ignorant to the
member of Parliament.   To have no definite date conveyed by
the term 'Rogation Sunday' is to the clerical mind gross
ignorance.   The horsey man thinks you have been in bed all
your life if the 'near side' is not as descriptive to you
'the left hand.'   JC 348-9, XLVII.

## IMAGINATION

A man requires some power of imagination to enable him to
look forward to the circumstances of an untried existence.
LT 257-8, V.

## IMPRESSIONS

It is seldom that a bad person expects to be accounted good.
It is the general desire of such a one to conquer the existing evil impression; but it is generally presumed that the
evil impression is there.   ED 84, IX,I.

We seldom think how much is told to us of the owner's
character by the first or second glance of a man or woman's
face.   Is he a fool, or is he clever; is he reticent or out-
spoken;  is he passionate or long-suffering;-nay, is he
honest or the reverse; is he malicious or of a kindly
nature?   Of all these things we form a sudden judgment
without any thought; and in most of our sudden judgments we
are roughly correct.   OML 20, II.

## INDEPENDENCE

The tamest animal will turn when driven too hard.
War 230, XIX.

It is all very well for a man or woman to boast that he,-or
she,-may do what he likes with his own,-or with her own.
But there are circumstances in which such self-action is

ruinous to so many that coercion from the outside becomes
absolutely needed.   PF 215, LXII,II.

In most parishes there are some who think it well to let the
parson know that they are independent and do not care for
him, though they profess to be of his flock.   VOB 393, LV.

## INEQUALITIES

...one of those whose lot in life drives us to marvel at the
inequalities of human destiny, and to inquire curiously
within ourselves whether future compensation is to be given.
     It is said of those who are small and crooked-backed in
their bodies, that their minds are equally cross.
Bel 156, XIII.

## INFORMERS

That such characters...[as informers] should exist and find
employment in a country, is a fact which must shock and disgust; but that it is a fact in great parts of Ireland, those
who are  most conversant with the country will not pretend
to deny.   It is true, that by paid spies and informers, real
criminals may not unfrequently be brought to justice; but...
are by no means atoned for by the occasional detection and
punishment of a criminal.
     Let the police use such open means as they have--and,
God knows, in Ireland they are effective enough; but I cannot but think the system of secret informers...has greatly
increased crime in many districts of Ireland....
     A very few years since I was walking with a gentleman
in the immediate employment of the Government, on a fair
day, through the crowd collected in a small town a very few
miles from the scene of my story; the dusk was fast
commencing, and he pointed out to me two or three men, who
had come in from the country like the others, telling me
that they were waiting till it was dark to speak to him--
that they did not dare speak to him during the light--that
they were in his pay--and that they had information to give
him respecting illegal societies, and hidden arms.    He
ridiculed me when I questioned the propriety of his system;
in fact he was so accustomed to it, that he could not
conceive the possibility of going on without it.   In the
same way I have had men pointed out to me by the officer
leading a party of revenue police, in quest of illicit
stills, who were dressed as policemen, though not belonging
to the force, and who were brought in that disguise that
they might not be known by their neighbours, whose haunts
they were going to disclose.
     The monetary success no doubt reconciles this usage to
the officer employing it; but the result must be to create
suspicion of each other among the poor, and fearfully to
increase, instead of diminishing crime.   MB 282-5, XI,I.

## INHERITANCE

What man, let alone what lawyer, will ever believe in the
sincerity of such a wish [that the possessor may live a long
time] as that expressed by the heir to a property? And yet
where is the man who will not declare to himself that such,
under such circumstances, would be his own wish? Bel 9, I.

A life-interest in a property is, perhaps, as much as a man
desires to have when he for whose protection he is debarred
from further privileges of ownership is a well-loved son;--
but an entail that limits an owner's rights on behalf of an
heir who is not loved, who is looked upon as an enemy, is
very grievous....As the sun is falling in the heavens and
the evening lights come on, this world's wealth and prosperity afford no pleasure equal to this  [sharing with the
son]. It is this delight that enables a man to feel, up to
the last moment, that the goods of the world are good.
RalH 87, XI.

Oh,--what salvation or destruction there may be to an
English gentleman in the sex of an infant!  PrM 277, LXX,II.

The British world regards the position of heirship to acres
as the most desirable which a young man could hold.
JC 17, II.

## INJUSTICE

When people complain of some cruel shame, which does not
affect themselves personally, the complaint is generally
accompanied by an unexpressed and unconscious feeling of
satisfaction. Bel 116, X.

Who does not know the sense of aggravated injustice which
comes upon a sufferer when redress for an acknowledged evil
is delayed? The wronged one feels that the whole world must
be out of joint in that all the world does not rise up in
indignation. JC 416, LVII.

There are not many more painful things in life than when an
honest gallant young fellow has to look about him in such a
frame of mind  [to see if his old friends will cut him].
MSF 92, XXVIII,II.

## INNKEEPERS

It is wonderful what love an innkeeper has for his bill in
its entirety. An account, with a respectable total of five
or six pounds, is brought to you, and you complain but of
one article; that fire in the bedroom was never lighted; or
that second glass of brandy and water was never called for.
You desire to have the shilling expunged, and all your
host's pleasure in the whole transaction is destroyed.  Oh!
my friends, pay for the brandy and water, though you never
drank it; suffer the fire to pass, though it never warmed

you.  Why make a good man miserable for such a trifle?
DoT 214-5, XVII.

Innkeepers like such visitors    [rich widowed countesses
respecting whom...strange tales were told].  The more
venomous are the stores told against them, the more they are
apt to spend, and the less likely they are to examine their
bills.  A rich woman altogether without a character is a
mine of wealth to an innkeeper.  Cl 228, XXVII.

## INNOCENCE

[B]ut even innocence may be dangerous.  BaT 357, XXXVII.

There is a bloom on the flower which may rest there till the
flower has utterly perished, if the handling of it be sufficiently delicate;--but no care, nothing that can be done by
friends on earth, or even by better friendship from above,
can replace that when once displaced.  VOB 195, XXVIII.

## INNS, ENTERING

There is a great difference between the entrance into an inn
of men who are not known there and of men who are known.
The men who are not known are shy, diffident, doubtful, and
anxious to propitiate the chambermaid by great courtesy.
The men who are known are loud, jocular, and assured;--or
else, in case of deficient accommodations, loud, angry, and
full of threats.  OrF 49-50, VI,I.

## INSANITY

There is perhaps no great social question so imperfectly
understood among us at the present day as that which refers
to the line which divides sanity from insanity.  That this
man is sane and that other unfortunately mad we do know
well enough; and we know also that one man may be subject to
various hallucinations,--may fancy himself to be a teapot,
or what not,--and yet be in such a condition of mind as to
call for no intervention either on behalf of his friends, or
of the law; while another may be in possession of intellec-
tual faculties capable of lucid exertion for the highest
purposes, and yet be so mad that bodily restraint upon him
is indispensable.  We know that the sane man is responsible
for what he does, and that the insane man is irresponsible;
but we do not know,--we only guess wildly, at the state of
mind of those, who now and again act like madmen....The same
juryman who would find a man mad who has murdered a young
woman, would in private life express a desire that the same
young man should be hung, crucified, or skinned alive, if he
had moodily and without reason broken his faith to the young
woman in lieu of killing her.  HKHWR 361, XXXVIII.

Thought deep, correct, continued, and energetic is quite
compatible with madness.  HKHWR 786, LXXXIV.

But who can tell how busy and how troubled are the thoughts of a madman!  HKHWR 881, XCIII.

One does not become angry with a madman; but while a man has power in his hands over others, and when he misuses that power grossly and cruelly, who is there that will not be angry?  The misery of the insane more thoroughly excites our pity than any other suffering to which humanity is subject; but it is necessary that the madness should be acknowledged to be madness before the pity can be felt.
HKHWR 919-20, XCVIII.

## INSTINCT

Men hunt foxes by the aid of dogs, and are aware that they do so by the strong organ of smell with which the dog is endowed.  They do not, however, in the least comprehend how such a sense can work with such acuteness.  The organ by which women instinctively, as it were, know and feel how other women are regarded by men, and how also men are re-garded by other women, is equally strong, and equally in-comprehensible.  A glance, a word, a motion, suffices.
BaT 368, XXXVIII.

## INSULTS

In these days...personal insolence to one man in a company seems almost to constitute an insult to every one present. When men could fight readily, an arrogant word or two between two known to be hostile to each other was only an invitation to a duel, and the angry man was doing that for which it was known that he could be made to pay....But a different feeling prevails at present;--a feeling so different, that we may almost say that a man in general society cannot speak even roughly to any but his intimate comrades without giving offence to all around him.  Men have learned to hate the nuisance of a row, and to feel that their comfort is endangered if a man prone to rows gets among them.  Of all candidates at a club a known quarreller is more sure of blackballs now than even in the times when such a one provoked duels.  Of all bores he is the worst; and there is always an unexpressed feeling that such a one exacts more from his company than his share of attention.
PR 52-3, XLVI.

Not true is as bad as 'false.'  'False,' applied to a gentleman in a club, must be matter either of an apology or expulsion.  AYA 393, XLI.

A man shall tell you you are a thief and a scoundrel in such a manner as to make it impossible for you to take him by the throat.  "You, of course, are not a thief and a scoundrel," he shall say to you, but shall say it in such a tone of voice as to make you understand that he conceives you to be both.  We all know the parliamentary mode of giving an opponent the lie so as to make it impossible that the Speaker shall interfere.  MSF 228, XVII,I.

## INTEREST

We all know that look of true interest which the countenance
of a real friend will bear when the welfare of his friend is
in question. There are doubtless some who can assume it
without feeling,-as there are actors who can personate all
passions. But in ordinary life we think that we can trust
such a face, and that we know the true look when we see it.
PF 316, LXXII,II.

## INTERFERENCE

If it be a recognized fact in society that young ladies are
in want of husbands, and that an effort on their part
towards matrimony is not altogether impossible, it must be
recognised also that failure will be disagreeable, and
interference regarded with animosity....It may be that the
theory of womanhood is right which forbids to women any such
attempts,--which teaches them that they must ever be the
pursued, never the pursuers. As to that there shall be no
discourse at present. But it must be granted that whenever
the pursuit has been attempted, it is not in human nature to
abandon it without an effort. HKHWR 336-7, XXXV.

## INTERLOPERS

It is to be feared that men in general do not regret as they
should do any temporary ill-feeling, or irritating jealousy
between husbands and wives, of which they themselves have
been the cause....When such suspicion rises in the bosom of
a wife, some woman intervening or being believed to intervene between her and the man who is her own, that woman who
has intervened or been supposed to intervene, will either
glory in her position or bewail it bitterly, according to
the circumstances of the case. We will charitably suppose
that, in a great majority of such instances, she will bewail
it. But when such painful jealous doubts annoy the husband,
the man who is in the way will...say to himself probably,
unconsciously indeed, and with no formed words, that the
husband is an ass, an ass if he be in a twitter either for
that which he has kept or for that which he has been unable
to keep, that the lady has shewn a good deal of appreciation....If he be allowed to buy a present or two, or to
pay a few shillings here or there, he has achieved much.
Terrible things now and again do occur, even here in
England; but women, with us, are slow to burn their household gods. It happens, however, occasionally, as we are all
aware, that the outward garments of a domestic deity will be
a little scorched; and when this occurs, the man who is the
interloper, will generally find a gentle consolation in his
position, let its interest be ever so flaccid and unreal.
HKHWR 86-7, X.

## INTERNATIONAL CONGRESSES

[A]ll this palaver that was going on in the various tongues

of Babel would end as it began--in words.  'Vox et praeterea nihil.'  To practical Englishmen most of these international congresses seem to arrive at nothing else.  Men will not be talked out of the convictions of their lives.  No living orator would convince a grocer that coffee should be sold without chicory; and no amount of eloquence will make an English lawyer think that loyalty to truth should come before loyalty to his client....

And indeed one cannot understand how the bent of any man's mind should be altered by the sayings and doings of such a congress.  OrF 165, XVII,I.

...as that country is supposed to be most honoured which is selected as the meeting-ground for plenipotentiaries when some important international point requires to be settled.  RalH 294, XXXIX.

## INTIMACY

These intimacies will sometimes grow up in five days, though an acquaintance of twenty years will often not produce them.  Ber 484, XXVII.

The idea of cousinly intimacy to girls is undoubtedly very pleasant....In America a girl may form a friendly intimacy with any young man she fancies....A dozen such intimacies do not stand in her way when there comes some real adorer who means to marry her and is able to do so.  She rides with these friends, walks with them, and corresponds with them. She goes out to balls and picnics with them, and afterwrds lets herself in with a latchkey, while her papa and mamma are a-bed and asleep, with perfect security....Girls on the other hand, on the continent of Europe, do not dream of making friendship with any man.  A cousin with them is as much out of the question as the most perfect stranger.  In strict families, a girl is hardly allowed to go out with her brother; and I have heard of mothers who thought it indis-creet that a father should be ssen alone with his daughter at a theatre.  All friendships between the sexes must, under such a social code, be looked forward to as post-nuptial joys.  Here in England there is a something betwixt the two. The intercourse between young men and girls is free enough to enable the latter to feel how pleasant it is to be able to forget for awhile conventional restraints, and to acknowledge how joyous a thing it is to indulge in social intercourse in which the simple delight of equal mind meeting equal mind in equal talk is just enhanced by the unconscious remembrance that boys and girls when they meet together may learn to love.  There is nothing more sweet in youth than this, nothing more natural, nothing more fitting, nothing, indeed, more essentially necessary for God's purposes with his creatures.  Nevertheless, here with us, there is the restriction, and it is seldom that a girl can allow herself the full flow of friendship with a man who is not old enough to be her father, unless he is her lover as well as her friend.  But cousinhood does allow some escape

from the hardship of this rule.  Cousins are Tom and Jack,
and George, and Dick.  Cousins probably know all or most of
your little family secrets.  Cousins, perhaps, have romped
with you, and scolded you, and teased you, when you were
young.  Cousins are almost the same as brothers, and yet
they may be lovers.  There is certainly a great relief in
cousinhood.  VOB 93-4, XIV.

## INTRIGUE

The spirit of intrigue with women, as to which men will
flatter themselves, is customarily so vile, so mean, so
vapid a reflection of a feeling, so aimless, resultless, and
utterly unworthy!  Passion exists and has its sway....But
the commonest folly of man in regard to women is a weak
taste for intrigue, with little or nothing on which to feed
it....Such men have their glory in their own estimation.  We
remember how Falstaff flouted the pride of his companion
whose victory in the fields of love had been but little
glorious.  But there are victories going now-a-days so
infinitely less glorious, that Falstaff's page was a
Lothario, a very Don Juan, in comparison with the heroes
whose praises are too often sung by their own lips.  There
is this recompense,--that their defeats are always sung by
lips louder than their own.  HKHWR 784, LXXXIII.

## INVALIDS

And then, creeping on tiptoe, as men do in such houses, to
the infinite annoyance of the invalids whom they wish to
spare....Ber 732, XLI.

## INVESTIGATIONS

In all such cases [the investigation of an election
petition] the singular part of the matter is that everybody,
those who are concerned and those who are not concerned,
really know the whole truth which is to be investigated; and
yet, that which everybody knows cannot be substantiated.
RalH 335, XLIV.

## INVITATIONS

It is not always easy to decline invitations so given  [at
the end of an entertainment].  It may, I think, be doubted
whether any man or woman has a right to give an invitation
in this way, and whether all invitations so given should not
be null and void, from the fact of the unfair advantage that
has been taken.  The man who fires at a sitting bird is
known to be no sportsman.  Now, the dinner-giver who catches
his guest in an unguarded moment, and bags him when he has
had no chance to rise upon his wing, does fire at a sitting
bird.  Cl 84, X.

When various details of hospitality have been offered by a
comparative stranger a man hardly likes to accept them all.
AS 116, XVII.

## IRELAND

...the ugliest part of Ireland, in fact, a more uninteresting road than that from Boyle to Dublin it would be
impossible to find.   The country is mostly flat and
unproductive--the bogs numerous--the villages poor--the
gentlemen's residences few and far between--the towns
dirty--and the prospects barren.   The first idea that
strikes a stranger on passing through this portion of
Ireland is astonishment that Erin should have had the
epithet green applied to it--for certainly in most of the
central counties, it is, generally speaking, as brown a
country as ever the eye rested on.  MB 71-2, II,III.

I do not know that we need lean too heavily on the stupidity
of the country's side in not having perceived that this
would be so  [better to go back to the police and
magistrates than wholesale murder].   The country's side is
very slow in perceiving the course which things will take.
Land 270, XLVIII,III.

## IRELAND, LAND LAWS

[Trollope reviews the land laws in Ireland in an entire
chapter.  The reader is directed to Land 142-68, XLI, III.]

## IRISH AGENTS

I do not think that any person is to be found, as a rule,
attached to English estates whose position is analogous to
that of an Irish agent....I believe that, as a class, the
agents on Irish properties do their duty in a manner
beneficial to the people....
      The duties towards an estate which an agent performs in
Ireland are, I believe, generally shared in England between
three or four different persons.  The family lawyer performs
part, the estate steward performs part, and the landlord himself performs part;--as to small estates, by far the greater
part.
      In Ireland, let the estate be ever so small--eight
hundred a year we will say--all the working of the property
is managed by the agent.  It is he who knows the tenants,
and the limits of their holdings; it is he who arranges
leases, and allows--or much more generally does not allow--
for improvements.  He takes the rent, and gives the order
for the ejection of tenants if he cannot get it.
      I am far from saying that it would not be well that
much of this should be done by the landlord himself;--that
all of it should be so done on a small property.  But it is
done by agents; and, as a rule is, I think, done honestly.
CasR 251-3, XII,I.

## IRISH BISHOPS

Bishops in Ireland, if they live at home, even in these
days, are very warm men.  PF 1, I,I.

## IRISH CHILDREN

[T]he very poor Irish children will never speak to you.
MB 8-9, I,I.

## IRISH COUNTRYSIDE

Perhaps the most interesting, and certainly the most beautiful part of Ireland is that which lies down in the extreme
south-west, with fingers stretching far out into the
Atlantic Ocean.    This consists of the counties Cork and
Kerry, or a portion, rather, of those counties.    It contains
Killarney, Glengarriffe, Bantry, and Inchigeela; and is
watered by the Lee, the Blackwater, and the Flesk.    I know
not where is to be found a land more rich in all that
constitutes the loveliness of scenery. CasR 3, I,I.

## IRISH COVERED CAR

An inside-covered car is an equipage much given to shaking,
seeing that it has a heavy top like a London cab, and that
it runs on a pair of wheels.    It is entered from behind, and
slopes backwards.    The sitter sits sideways, between a
cracked window on one side and a cracked doorway on the
other; and as a draught is always going in at the ear next
the window, and out at the ear next the door, it is about as
cold and comfortless a vehicle for winter as may be well
imagined. CasR 258-9, XIII,I.

## IRISH CRIMINAL LAW

It would be useless here to refer to that Bill which was to
have been passed for trying certain prisoners in Ireland
without the intervention of a jury, and of the alteration
which took place in it empowering the Government to alter
the venue, and to submit such cases to a selected judge, to
selected juries, to selected counties.    The Irish judges had
remonstrated against the first measure, and the second was
to be first tried, so that should it fail the judges might
yet be called upon to act.
    Such was the law under which criminals were tried in
1882, and the first capital convictions were made under
which the country began to breathe freely.
Land 127-8,XXXIX,III.

## IRISH CUSTOMS

In England no one would think of taking his steed into a
poor man's cottage, and would hardly put his beast into a
cottager's shed without leave asked and granted; but people
are more intimate with each other, and take greater
liberties in Ireland.    It is no uncommon thing on a wet
hunting-day to see a cabin packed with horses, and the
children moving about among them, almost as unconcernedly as
though the animals were pigs.    But then the Irish horses are
so well-mannered and good-natured. CasR 70, IV,III.

## IRISH FAREWELLS

O, my reader, have you ever seen a railway train taking its departure from an Irish station, with a freight of Irish emigrants? if so, you know how the hair is torn, and how the hands are clapped, and how the low moanings gradually swell into notes of loud lamentation. It means nothing. I have heard men say,--men and women too. But such men and women are wrong. It means much; it means this: that those who are separated, not only love each other, but are anxious to tell each other that they so love....For myself I am inclined to think that such speaking out has its good ends. 'The faculty of silence! is it not of all things the most beautiful?' That is the doctrine preached by a great latter-day philosopher; for myself, I think that the faculty of speech is much more beautiful--of speech if it be made but by howlings, and wailings, and loud clappings of the hand. What is in a man, let it come out and be known to those around him; if it be bad it will find correction; if it be good it will spread and be beneficent.
CasR 60-1, III, III.

## IRISH FEATURES

It is strange how various are the kinds of physical development among the Celtic peasantry in Ireland. In many places they are singularly beautiful, especially as children; and even after labour and sickness shall have told on them as labour and sickness will tell, they still retain a certain softness and grace which is very nearly akin to beauty. But then again in a neighbouring district they will be found to be squat, uncouth, and in no way attractive to the eye. The tint of the complexion, the nature of the hair, the colour of the eyes, shall be the same. But in one place it will seem as though noble blood had produced delicate limbs and elegant structure, whereas in the other a want of noble blood had produced the reverse. The peasants of Clare, Limerick, and Tipperary are, in this way, much more comely than those of Cork and Kerry. CasR 42-3, II,II.

## IRISH GIRLS

No girls know better how to dress themselves than Irish girls, or can do it with less assistance or less expence; but they are too much given to morning dishabilles. If they would only remember that the change in a man's opinion and mind respecting a girl will often take place as quick as that in her appearance, and that the contrast will be quite as striking, they would be more particular; and they never can be sure of themselves, take what precautions they will. Lovers will drop in at most unseasonable hours; they can never be kept out with certainty, and all the good done by a series of brilliant evenings--satin dresses, new flowers for the hair, expensive patterns, and tediously finished toilets--may be, and often is, suddenly counteracted by one untidy head, greasy dress, or dirty stocking.
MB 169-70, VIII,I.

## IRISH KITCHENS

The difference of the English and Irish character is nowhere more plainly discerned than in their respective kitchens. With the former, this apartment is probably the cleanest, and certainly the most orderly, in the house. It is rarely intruded into by those unconnected, in some way, with its business. Everything it contains is under the vigilant eye of its chief occupant, who would imagine it quite impossible to carry on her business, whether of an humble or important nature, if her apparatus was subjected to the hands of the unauthorised. An Irish kitchen is devoted to hospitality in every sense of the word. Its doors are open to almost all loungers and idlers; and the chances are that Billy Bawn, the cripple, or Judy Molloy, the deaf old hag, are more likely to know where to find the required utensil than the cook herself. It is usually a temple dedicated to the goddess of disorder; and, too often joined with her, is the potent deity of dirt. It is not that things are out of their place, for they have no place. It isn't that the floor is not scoured, for you cannot scour dry mud into anything but wet mud. It isn't that the chairs and tables look filthy, for there are none. It isn't that the pots, and plates, and pans don't shine, for you see none to shine. All you see is a grimy, black ceiling, an uneven clay floor, a small darkened window, one or two unearthly-looking recesses, a heap of potatoes in the corner, a pile of turf against the wall, two pigs and a dog under the single dresser, three or four chickens on the window-sill, an old cock moaning on the top of a rickety press, and a crowd of ragged garments, squatting, standing, kneeling, and crouching, round the fire, from which issues a babel of strange tongues, not one word of which is at first intelligible to ears unaccustomed to such eloquence.

And yet, out of these unfathomable, unintelligible dens, proceed in due time dinners, of which the appearance of them gives no promise. Kel 54-5, IV.

## IRISH LAWYERS

It would, I think, astonish a London attorney in respectable practice, to see the manner in which his brethren towards the west of Ireland get through their work....[The] office was open to all the world; the front door of the house...was never closed, except at night; nor was the door of the office, which opened immediately into the hall.
Kel 226, XVIII.

## IRISH NAMES

It must be understood that among the poorer classes in the south and west of Ireland it is almost rare for a married woman to call herself or to be called by her husband's name. CasR 44, II,II.

...omitting all mention of that Christian name, which the poor Irishman is generally so fond of using. 'Mister Blake' sounds cold and unkindly in his ears. It is the 'Masther,' or 'His honour,' or if possible 'Misther Thady.' Or if there be any handle, that is used with avidity. Pat is a happy man when he can address in his landlord as 'Sir Patrick.' CasR 34, II,III.

## IRISH NOVELS

I wonder whether the novel-reading world--that part of it, at least, which may honour my pages--will be offended if I lay the plot of this story in Ireland! That there is a strong feeling against things Irish it is impossible to deny. Irish servants need not apply; Irish acquaintances are treated with limited confidences; Irish cousins are regarded as being decidedly dangerous; and Irish stories are not popular with the booksellers.

For myself, I may say that if I ought to know anything about any place, I ought to know something about Ireland; and I do strongly protest against the injustice of the above conclusions. Irish cousins I have none. Irish acquaintances I have by dozens; and Irish friends, also, by twos and threes, whom I can love and cherish--almost as well, perhaps, as though they had been born in Middlesex. Irish servants I have had some in my house for years, and never had one that was faithless, dishonest, or intemperate. I have travelled all over Ireland, closely as few other men can have done, and have never had my portmanteau robbed or my pocket picked. At hotels I have seldom locked up my belongings, and my carelessness has never been punished. I doubt whether as much can be said for English inns.

Irish novels were once popluar enough. But there is a fashion in novels, as there is in colours and petticoats; and now I fear they are drugs on the market. It is hard to say why a good story should not have a fair chance of success whatever may be its bent; why it should not be reckoned to be good by its own intrinsic merits alone; but such is by no means the case. I was waiting once, when I was young at the work, in the back parlour of an eminent publisher, hoping to see his eminence on a small matter of business touching a three-volumed manuscript which I held in my hand. The eminent publisher, having probably larger fish to fry, could not see me, but sent his clerk or foreman to arrange the business.

'A novel, is it, sir?' said the foreman.

'Yes,' I answered; 'a novel.'

'It depends very much on the subject,' said the foreman, with a thoughtful and judicious frown--'upon the name, sir, and the subject;--daily life, sir; that's what suits us; daily English life. Now your historical novel, sir, is not worth the paper it's written on.'

I fear that Irish character is in these days considered almost as unattractive as historical incident; but, nevertheless, I will make the attempt. I am now leaving the Green Isle and my old friends, and would fain say a word of

them as I do so.    If I do not say that word now it will
never be said.
        The readability of a story should depend, one would
say, on its intrinsic merit rather than on the site of its
adventures.    No one will think that Hampshire is better for
such a purpose than Cumberland, or Essex than Leistershire.
What abstract objection can there then be to the county
Cork?  CasR 1-3, I,I.

## IRISH PEASANTS

The miserable appearance of Irish peasants, when in the very
lowest poverty, strikes one more forcibly in the towns than
in the open country.
        The dirt and filth around them seems so much more
oppressive on them--they have no escape from it.    There is a
good deal, too, in ideas and associations.    On a road side,
or on the borders of a bog, the dusty colour of the cabin
walls, the potatoe patch around it, the green scraughs or
damp brown straw which forms its roof, all appurtenances, in
fact, of the cabin, seem suited to the things around it;
but, in a town, this is not so....Poverty, to be
picturesque, should be rural.    Suburban misery is as hideous
as it is pitiable.
        But it is not only in appearance that the poverty of
the inhabitant of town cabins is more oppressive than that
of his fellow-sufferer in the country, but it actually is
so.    And woe to the poor country labourer who comes into a
town, leaving his little holding, under the impression, that
where so many of the--comparatively speaking--wealthy live,
money must be to be had--work and wages must be going.
        This may be true for those who have some smattering in
mechanic lore, be it ever so humble; who have some acquired
knowledge, besides that of merely working the soil.    For him
whose only trade is such--what should he do in a town?    The
land from which he must draw his support is twice as dear on
him; his vexations are multiplied, and his means of
subsistence lessened.    Besides, should chance miraculously
favour him, should he now and again earn a solitary
sixpence, the very money he has so hardly earned leads him
into mischief.    Those who have so often disturbed Ireland,
and who have given her so bad a name through the world--
Whiteboys, Terryalts, Ribbonmen, and the rest--will be found
to have been originally dwellers in towns, and not in the
country.  MB 204-6, IX,I.

## IRISH PRIESTS

Irish priests have been made by chroniclers of Irish story
to do marvellous things.  EE 35, II,II.

There has come a change among the priests in Ireland during
the last fifty years, as has been natural....When an entire
country has been left unmoved by the outside world, so as to
seem to have been left asleep while others have been awake,
the different classes will seem to be the same at the end of

every half century.  A village lawyer in Spain will be as
was a village lawyer fifty years ago.  But a parish priest
in Ireland will be an altered personage, because the country
generally has not been sleeping.
    There used to be two distinct sorts of priests; of whom
the elder, who had probably been abroad, was the better
educated; whereas the younger, who was home-nurtured had
less to say for himself on general topics.  He was generally
the more zealous in his religious duties, but the elder was
the better read in doctrinal theology.  As to the political
question of the day, they were both apt to be on the list
against the Government, though not so with such violence as
to make themselves often obnoxious to the laws.  It was
natural that they should be opposed to the Government, as
long as the Protestant Church claimed an ascendency over
them.  But their feelings and aspirations were based then on
their religious opinions.  Now a set of men has risen up,
with whom opposition to the rulers of the country is
connected chiefly with political ideas.  A dream of Home
Rule has made them what they are, and thus they have been
roused into waking life, by the American spirit, which has
been imported into the country.  There is still the old
difference between the elder and the younger priests.  The
parish priest is not so frequently opposed to the law, as is
his curate.  The parish priest is willing that the landlord
shall receive his rents, is not at least anxious, that he
shall be dispossessed of his land.  But the curate has ideas
of peasant proprietors; is very hot for Home Rule, is less
obedient to the authority of the bishops than he was of
yore, and thinks more of the political, and less of the
religious state of his country.  Land 42-4, III,I.

## IRISH QUESTION

It had been all very well to put down Fenianism, and
Ribandmen, and Repeal,--and everything that had been put
down in Ireland in the way of rebellion for the last seventy-
five years.  England and Ireland had been apparently joined
together by laws of nature so fixed, that even...[liberal
politicians] could not trust themselves to think that
disunion could be for the good of the Irish.  They had
taught themselves that it certainly could not be good for
the English.  But if it was incumbent on England to force
upon Ireland the maintenance of the Union for her own sake,
and for England's sake, because England could not afford
independence established so close against her own ribs,--it
was at any rate necessary to England's character that the
bride thus bound in a compulsory wedlock should be endowed
with all the best privileges that a wife can enjoy....But
let there be that good understanding at bottom.  What about
this Protestant Church; and what about this tenant-right?...
[T]he subject of the Protestant endowments in Ireland was so
difficult that it would require almost more than human
wisdom to adjust it.  PF 180-1, LVIII,II.

...that terribly unintelligible subject, a tenant-right proposed for Irish farmers, no English reader will desire to know much. Irish subjects in the House of Commons are interesting or are dull, are debated before a crowded audience composed of all who are leaders in the great world of London, or before empty benches, in accordance with the importance of the moment and the character of the debate. PF 341, LXXV,II.

## IRISH SERVANTS

All Irish servants especially love to pay respect to the 'young masther.' CasR 98, V,III.

## IRISH WEATHER

Such cold, drizzling rain is the commonest phase of hard weather during Irish winters, and those who are out and about get used to it and treat it tenderly. They are euphemistical as to the weather, calling it hazy and soft, and never allowing themselves to carry bad language on such a subject beyond the word dull. And yet at such a time one breathes the rain and again exhales it, and become as it were oneself a water spirit, assuming an aqueous fishlike nature into one's inner fibres. It must be acknowledged that a man does sometimes get wet in Ireland; but then a wetting there brings no cold in the head, no husky voice, no need for multitudinous pocket-handkerchiefs, as it does here in this land of catarrhs. It is the east wind and not the rain that kills; and of east wind in the south of Ireland they know nothing. CasR 215-6, XI,II.

## IRISH WOMEN

Why can no woman walk like an Irish-woman? all nations have different female graces, but an Irish-woman alone can walk. MB 17, II,I.

## IRISHMEN

An Irishman as a rule will not come regularly to his task. It is a very difficult thing to secure his services every morning at six o'clock; but make a special point,--tell him that you want him very early, and he will come to you in the middle of the night. Breakfast every morning punctually at eight o'clock is almost impossible in Ireland; but if you want one special breakfast, so that you may start by a train at 4 A.M., you are sure to be served. No irregular effort is distasteful to an Irishman of the lower classes, not if it entails on him the loss of a day's food and the loss of a night's rest; the actual pleasure of the irregularity repays him for all this, and he never tells you that this or that is not his work. He prefers work that is not his own. Your coachman will have no objection to turn the mangle, but heaven and earth put together won't persuade him to take the horses out to exercise every morning at the same hour. CasR 67-8, IV,II.

The love which a poor Irishman feels for the gentleman whom
he regards as his master--'his masther,' though he has
probably never received from him, in money, wages for a
day's work, and in all his intercourse has been the man who
has paid money and not the man who received it--the love
which he nevertheless feels, if he has been occasionally
looked on with a smiling face and accosted with a kindly
word, is astonishing to an Englishman. I will not say that
the feeling is altogether good. Love should come of love.
Where personal love exists on one side, and not even
personal regard on the other, there must be some mixture of
servility. That unbounded respect for human grandeur cannot
be altogether good; for human greatness, if the greatness be
properly sifted, it may be so. CasR 214-5, XI,II.

## IRISHMEN v. ENGLISHMEN

[A]n Englishman would have put down the barrow while he was
speaking, making some inner calculation about the waste of
his muscles; but an Irishman would despise himself for such
low economy. CasR 220, XI,II.

## IRISHMEN IN LONDON

...though an Irishman did not as a rule herd with other
Irishmen. PF 200, XXII,I.


**J**


## JEALOUSY

The advantages of matrimony are many and great--so many and
so great, that all men, doubtless, ought to marry. But even
matrimony may have its drawbacks; among which unconcealed
and undeserved jealousy on the part of the wife is perhaps
as disagreeable as any. What is a man to do when he is
accused before the world, of making love to some lady of his
acquaintance? What is he to say? What way is he to look?
'My love, I didn't. I never did, and wouldn't think of it
for worlds. I say it with my hand on my heart. There is
Mrs. Jones herself, and I appeal to her.' He is reduced to
that! But should any innocent man be so reduced by the wife
of his bosom?
     I am speaking of undeserved jealousy. OrF 123, XIII,I.

...that strange jealousy which could exist even when he who
was jealous did not love the woman who caused it.
DuC 472, LIX

## JEWS

It is thus, thou great family of Sidonia--it is thus that we Gentiles treat thee, when, in our extremest need, thou and thine have aided us with mountains of gold as big as lions, --and occasionally with wine-warrants and orders for dozens of dressing-cases.  BaT 162-3, XIX.

He had heard of Jews in Vienna, in Paris, and in London, who were as true to their religion as any Jew of Prague, but who did not live immured in a Jews' quarter, like lepers separate and alone in some loathed corner of a city other-wise clean.   These men went abroad into the world as men, using the wealth with which their industry had been blessed, openly as the Christians used it.   And they lived among Christians as one man should live with his fellow-men--on equal terms, giving and taking, honouring and honoured.   As yet it was not so with the Jews of Prague, who were still bound to their old narrow streets, to their dark houses, to their mean modes of living, and who, worst of all, were still subject to the isolated ignominy of Judaism.    In Prague a Jew was still a Pariah.  NB 69, VI.

Strangers who come to Prague visit the Jews' quarter as a matter of course, and to such strangers the Jews of Prague are invariably courteous.   But the Christians of the city seldom walk through the heart of the Jews' locality, or hang about the Jews' synagogue, or are seen among the houses un-less they have special business.  The Jews' quarter, though it is a banishment to the Jews from the fairer portions of the city, is also a separate and somewhat sacred castle in which they may live after their old fashion undisturbed. NB 81, VII.

## JILTING

Everybody would know it!   I doubt whether that must not be one of the bitterest drops in the cup which a girl in such circumstances  [having been jilted]   is made to drain. SmaH 304, XXX.

Men when they are jilted can hardly be vain of the conquest which has led to such a result.  Cl 261, XXXI.

Damnable arguments!   [that not to jilt would be deceitful]. False cowardly logic, by which all male jilts seek to excuse their own treachery to themselves and others!   Cl 209, XXV.

## JOY

Ah!  how much joy is there in this mortal, moribund world if one will but open one's arms to take it!   Ber 631, XXXV.

[I]t is to be remembered that but very little complete and unalloyed joy is allowed to sojourners in this vale of tears, even though they have been but two months married. PrM 246, XXVI,I.

## JUDGES

It was understood...that no allusion could with propriety be made to it in the presence of the judge before whom the cause was now pending, and the ground was considered too sacred for feet to tread upon it. Were it not that this feeling is so general an English judge and English counsellors would almost be forced to subject themselves in such cases to the close custody which jurymen are called upon to endure. But, as a rule, good taste and good feeling are as potent as locks and walls. OrF 293, LXIX,II.

It is odd that it never occurs to judges that a witness who is naturally timid will be made more so by being scolded. When I hear a judge thus use his authority, I always wish that I had the power of forcing him to some very uncongenial employment,--jumping in a sack, let us say; and then when he jumped poorly, as he certainly would, I would crack my whip and bid him go higher and higher. The more I bade him, the more he would limp; and the world looking on, would pity him and execrate me. It is much the same thing when a witness is sternly told to speak louder. OrF 311, LXXI,II.

We are all aware how impassionately grand are the minds of judges, when men accused of crimes are brought before them for trial; but judges after all are men. PR 31, XLIV,II.

But men, when they become judges, are apt to change their ideas. And Judge Parry was known to be a firm man, whom nothing would turn from the execution of his duty....A man is at liberty to indulge what vagaries he pleases, as long as he is simply a Member of Parliament. But a judge is not at liberty. Land 270-1, XXXI,II.

## JURIES

There are many ludicrous points in our blessed constitution, but perhaps nothing so ludicrous as a juryman praying to a judge for mercy. He has been caught, shut up in a box, perhaps, for five or six days together, badgered with half a dozen lawyers till he is nearly deaf with their continual talking, and then he is locked up until he shall find a verdict. Such at least is the intention of the constitution. The death, however, of three of four jurymen from starvation would not suit the humanity of the present age, and therefore, when extremeties are nigh at hand, the dying jurymen, with medical certificates, are allowed to be carried off. It is devoutly to be wished that one juryman might be starved to death while thus serving the constitution; the absurdity then would cure itself, and a verdict of a majority would be taken. TC 502, XLI.

## JUSTICE

If even-handed justice were done throughout the world, some apology could be found for most offences. Not that the

offences would thus be wiped away, and black become white;
but much that is now very black would be reduced to that
sombre, uninviting shade of ordinary brown which is so
customary to humanity....
   Were we all turned inside out, as is done with ladies
and gentlemen in novels, some of us might find some little
difficulty in giving good apologies for ourselves.   Our
shade of brown would often be very dark.   Ber 343; 346, XIX.

How can one plead one's cause justly before a tribunal which
is manifestly unjust,--which is determined to do injustice?
LT 242, IV.

The crooked places of the world, if they are to be made
straight at all, must be made straight after a sterner and a
juster fashion    [than because of the crooked one's
prettiness].   VOB 281, XL.

[F]or generosity is less efficacious towards permanent good
than justice, and tender speaking less enduring in its beneficial results than truth.   MF 165, XV,I.

## JUNE

June passed away,--as Junes do pass in London,--very gaily
in appearance, very quickly in reality, with a huge outlay
of money and an enormous amount of disappointment.   Young
ladies would not accept, and young men would not propose.
Papas became cross and stingy, and mamas insinuated that
daughters were misbehaving.   The daughters fought their own
battles, and became tired in the fighting of them, and many
a one had declared to herself before July had come to an end
that it was all vanity and vexation of spirit.
SHHOH 62, VII.

# K

## KEEPSAKES

Oh, the misery of packing such a parcel!   The feeling with
which a woman does it is never encountered by a man.   He
chucks the things together in wrath,--the lock of hair, the
letters in the pretty Italian hand that have taken so much
happy care in the writing, the jewelled shirt-studs, which
were first put in by the fingers that gave them.   They are
thrown together, and given to some other woman to deliver.
But the girl lingers over her torture.   She reads the
letters again.   She thinks of the moments of bliss which
each little toy has given.   She is loth to part with
everything.   She would fain keep some one thing,--the

smallest of them all.    She doubts,--till a feeling of
maidenly reserve constrains her at last, and the coveted
trifle, with careful, painstaking fingers, is put with the
rest, and the parcel is made complete, and the address is
written with precision.  Cl 273-5, XXXII.

## KINDNESS

A little kindness after continued cruelty will always win a
dog's heart; some say, also a woman's.    IHP 238, XXIV,I.

## KISSING

A kiss to be joyful should be stolen, with a conviction on
the part of the offender that she who has suffered the loss
will never prosecute the thief.  VOB 361, L.

Other young ladies have, perhaps, before now made such a
mistake [as to think that kissing and proposing are the
same thing].  AS 271, XL.

## KNAVERY

There are knaves in this world, and no one can suppose that
he has a special right to be exempted from their knavery
because he himself is honest.  It is on the honest that the
knaves prey.  Cl 273, XXXII.

## KNEELING

Such kneeling on the part of lovers used to be the fashion
because lovers in those days held in higher value than they
do now that which they asked their ladies to give,--or
because they pretended to do so.  The forms at least of
supplication were used; whereas in these wiser days Augustus
simply suggests to Caroline that they two might as well make
fools of themselves together,--and so the thing is settled
without the need of much prayer.  Bel 379, XXIX.

## KNIGHT OF THE GARTER

A minister is not bound to bestow a Garter the day after it
becomes vacant.    There are other Knights to guard the
throne, and one may be spared for a short interval....A
broad blue ribbon across the chest is of all decorations the
most becoming, or, at any rate, the most desired.
PrM 225, LXIV,II.

## KNOWLEDGE, PUBLIC

There is a wide difference in the qualities of knowledge
regarding such matters.  In affairs of public interest we
often know, or fancy that we know, down to every exact
detail, how a thing has been done,--who have given the
bribes and who have taken them,--who has told the lie and
who has pretended to believe it,--who has peculated and how

the public purse has suffered,--who was in love with such a
one's wife and how the matter was detected, then smothered
up, and condoned; but there is no official knowledge, and
nothing can be done.  LA 473, XLV.

## L

### LADIES, GREETING

There are ladies who always kiss their female friends, and
always call them 'dear.'  In such cases one cannot but pity
her who is so bekissed.  OrF 135, XIV,I.

### LAKES

A lake should, I think, be small, and should be seen from
above, to be seen in all its glory.  The distance should be
such that the shadows of the mountains on its surface may
just be traced, and that some faint idea of the ripple on
the waters may be present to the eye.  And the form of the
lake should be irregular, curving round from its base among
the lower hills, deeper and still deeper into some close
nook up among the mountains from which its head waters
spring.  CanY 327, XXXI,I.

### LANDLORDS

A landlord if he wishes to be popular should be seen frequently.  If he lives among his farmers they will swear by
him, even though he raises his rental every ten or twelve
years and never puts a new roof to a barn for them.  AS 5,I.

### LAW

Lincoln's Inn itself is dingy, and the Law Courts therein
are perhaps the meanest in which Equity ever disclosed herself....And the study of the Chancery law itself is not an
alluring pursuit till the mind has come to have some insight
into the beauty of its ultimate object.  PF 64, VII,I.

But with us the law is the same for an Italian harlot and an
English widow; and it may well be that in its niceties it
shall be found kinder to the former than to the latter.
LA 20,II.

### LAWSUITS

Many men have threatened to spend a property upon a lawsuit
who have afterwards felt grateful that their threats were
made abortive.  OrF 406, LXXIX,II.

A lawsuit will sometimes make a man extremely pleasant company to his wife and children. Even a losing lawsuit will sometimes do so, if he be well backed in his pugnacity by his lawyer, and if the matter of the battle be one in which he can take a delight to fight. "Ah," a man will say, "though I spend a thousand pounds over it, I'll stick to him like a burr. He shan't shake me off." And at such times he is almost sure to be in a good humour, and in a generous mood. Then let his wife ask him for money for a dinner-party, and his daughters for new dresses. He has taught himself for the moment to disregard money, and to think that he can sow five-pound notes broadcast without any inward pangs. RacR 279, XXII.

## LAWYERS

A lawyer has always a sort of affection for a scoundrel,--such affection as a hunting man has for a fox. He loves to watch the skill and dodges of the animal, to study the wiles by which he lives, and to circumvent them by wiles of his own, still more wily. It is his glory to run the beast down; but then he would not for worlds run him down, except in conformity with certain laws, fixed by old custom for the guidance of men in such sports. And the two-legged vermin is adapted for pursuit as is the fox with four legs. He is an unclean animal, leaving a scent upon his trail, which the nose of your acute law hound can pick up over almost any ground. And the more wily the beast is, the longer he can run, the more trouble he can give in the pursuit, the longer he can stand up before a pack of legal hounds, the better does the forensic sportsman love and value him. There are foxes of so excellent a nature, so keen in their dodges, so perfect in their cunning, so skilful in evasion, that a sportsman cannot find it in his heart to push them to their destruction unless the field be very large so that many eyes are looking on. And the feeling is I think the same with lawyers....
     Much as the sportsman loves the fox, it is a moment to him of keen enjoyment when he puts his heavy boot on the beast's body,--the expectant dogs standing round demanding their prey--and there both beheads and betails him. 'A grand old dog,' he says to those around him. 'I know him well. It was he who took us that day from Poulnarer, through Castlecor, and right away to Drumcollogher.' And then he throws the heavy carcass to the hungry hounds. CasR 190-2, X,III.

In what Medea's caldron is it that the great lawyers so cook themselves, that they are able to achieve half an immor-tality, even while the body still clings to the soul?...The men who think of superannuation at sixty are those whose lives have been idle, not they who have really buckled them-selves to work. It is my opinion that nothing seasons the mind for endurance like hard work. Port wine should perhaps be added. CasR 233-4, XII,III.

'Is it meum or is it tuum?'  To answer which question justly
should be the end and object of every lawyer's work.
OrF 115, XII,I.

In the ordinary intercourse of the world when one man seeks
advice from another, he who is consulted demands in the
first place that he shall be put in possession of all the
circumstances of the case.  How else will it be possible
that he should give advice?  But in matters of law it is
different.  If I, having committed a crime, were to confess
my criminality to the gentleman engaged to defend me, might
he not be called on to say:  'Then, O my friend, confess it
also to the judge; and so let justice be done.  Ruat coelum,
and the rest of it?'  But who would pay a lawyer for counsel
such as that?  OrF 118, XII,I.

I cannot understand how any gentleman can be willing to use
his intellect for the propagation of untruth, and to be paid
for so using it.  OrF 165, LVI,II.

But lawyers endure these troubles, submitting themselves to
the extravagances, embarrassments, and even villainy of the
bad subjects among their clients' families, with a good-
humoured patience that is truly wonderful.  Bel 168, XIV.

It may be observed that ladies belonging to the families of
solicitors always talk about lawyers, and never about
attorneys or barristers.  LasC 675, LXXI.

The broad landmarks between the respectable and the disreputable may guide the tone of a lawyer somewhat, when he
has a witness in his power; but the finer lines which
separate that which is at the moment good and true from that
which is false and bad cannot be discerned amidst the
turmoil of a trial, unless the eyes, and the ears, and the
inner touch of him who has the handling of the victim be of
a quality more than ordinarily high.  VOB 486, LXVIII.

There is nothing in the world so brisk as the ways and
manners of lawyers when in any great case they come to that
portion of it which they know to be the real bone of the
limb and kernel of the nut.  The doctor is very brisk when
after a dozen moderately dyspeptic patients, he comes on
some unfortunate gentleman whose gastric apparatus is gone
altogether.  The parson is very brisk when he reaches the
minatory clause in his sermon.  The minister is very brisk
when he asks the House for a vote, telling his hoped-for
followers that this special point is absolutely essential to
his government....But the briskness of none of these is
equal to the briskness of the barrister who has just got
into his hands for cross-examination him whom we may call
the centre witness of a great case. He plumes himself like
a bullfinch going to sing.  He spreads himself like a pea-
cock on a lawn.  He perks himself like a sparrow on a
paling.  He crows amidst his attorneys and all the satellites of the court like a cock among his hens.  He puts

his hands this way and that, settling even the sunbeams as they enter, lest a mote should disturb his intellect or dull the edge of his subtlety. There is a modesty in his eye, a quiescence in his lips, a repose in his limbs, under which like half-concealed,--not at all concealed from those who have often watched him at his work,--the glance, the tone, the spring, which are to tear that unfortunate witness into pieces, without infringing any one of those conventional rules which have been laid down for the guidance of successful well-mannered barristers. RalH 331-2, XLIV.

It may, perhaps, be the case that a barrister is less likely to be influenced by personal convictions in taking his side in politics than any other man who devotes himself to public affairs.    No slur on the profession is intended by this suggestion....The highest work of a lawyer can only be reached through political struggle.    As a large-minded man of the world, peculiarly conversant with the fact that every question has two sides, and that as much may often be said on one side as on the other, he has probably not become violent in his feelings as a political partisan.    Thus he sees that there is an opening here or an opening there, and the offence in either case is not great to him.
ED 34-5, IV,I.

...that pleasing animosity between rival lawyers, which is so gratifying to the outside world, and apparently to themselves also.  LA 290-1, XXVIII.

It is always satisfactory to see the assurance of a cock crowing in his own farmyard, and to admire his easy familiarity with things that are awful to a stranger bird. If you, O reader, or I were bound to stand up in that court, dressed in wig and gown, and to tell a story that would take six hours in the telling, the one or the other of us knowing it to be his special duty so to tell it that judge, and counsellors, and jury, should all catch clearly every point that was to be made,--how ill would that story be told, how would those points escape the memory of the teller, and never come near the intellect of the hearers!  And how would the knowledge that it would be so, confuse your tongue or mine,--and make exquisitely miserable that moment of rising before the audience!  LA 291, XXVIII.

The 'scolding'...in the guise of that advice which a lawyer so often feels himself justified in giving.  CoH 49, V.  See also BARRISTERS.

## LAWYERS' CHAMBERS

There is, I think, no sadder place in the world than the waiting-room attached to an attorney's chambers in London. MM 217, XVII.

## LAWYERS, ECCLESIASTICAL

Those gentlemen, two or three of whom are to be seen in

connexion with every see-who seem to be hybrids--half-lay,
half-cleric.   They dress like clergymen, and affect that
mixture of clerical solemnity and clerical waggishness which
is generally to be found among minor canons and vicars
choral of a cathedral.   They live, or at least have their
offices, half in the Close and half out of it--dwelling as
it were just on the borders of holy orders.   They always
wear white neck-handkerchiefs and black gloves; and would be
altogether clerical in their appearance, were it not that as
regards the outward man they impinge somewhat on the
characteristics of the undertaker.   They savour of the
church, but the savour is of the church's exterior.   Any
stranger thrown into chance contact with one of them would,
from instinct, begin to talk about things ecclesiastical
without any reference to things theological or things
religious.   They are always most worthy men, much respected
in the society of the Close, and I never heard of one of
them whose wife was not comfortable or whose children were
left without provision.   LasC 299, XXXIV.

## LEARNING

[F]or there be so many things which we could find out ourselves by search, but which we never do find out unless they
be specially told us.   FrP 57, VI.

## LECTURES

All persons who have a propensity to lecture others have a
strong constitutional dislike to being lectured themselves.
TC 51, V.

## LECTURES, FREE

And then the lecture was gratis, a fact which is always
borne in mind by an Englishman when he comes to reckon up
and calculate the way in which he is treated.   When he pays
his money, then he takes his choice; he may be impatient or
not as he likes.   His sense of justice teaches him so much,
and in accordance with that sense he usually acts.
FrP 55,VI.

## LEGAL BUSINESS

Gentlemen when at law, or in any way engaged in matters
requiring legal assistance, are very apt to go to their
lawyers without much absolute necessity;--gentlemen when
doing so, are apt to describe such attendance as quite
compulsory, and very disagreeable.   The lawyers, on the
other hand, do not at all see the necessity, though they
quite agree as to the disagreeable nature of the visit;--
gentlemen when so engaged are usually somewhat gravelled at
finding nothing to say to their learned friends; they
generally talk a little politics, a little weather, ask some
few foolish questions about their suit, and then withdraw,
having passed half an hour in a small dingy waiting-room, in

company with some junior assistant-clerk, and ten minutes with the members of the firm; the business is then over for which the gentleman has come up to London, probably a distance of a hundred and fifty miles.  To be sure he goes to the play, and dines at his friend's club, and has a bachelor's liberty and bachelor's recreation for three or four days; and he could not probably plead the desire of such gratifications as a reason to his wife for a trip to London.

Married ladies, when your husbands find they are positively obliged to attend their legal advisers, the nature of the duty to be performed is generally of this description....

[A]nd I think it may be taken for granted, that whatever the cause may be that takes a gentleman to a lawyer's chambers, he never goes there to pay his bill.  War 240,XIX.

## LEGAL PROFESSION

The best of the legal profession consists in this;--that when you get fairly at work you may give over working.  An aspirant must learn everything; but a man may make his fortune at it, and know almost nothing.  He may examine a witness with judgment, see through a case with precision, address a jury with eloquence,--and yet be altogether ignorant of law.  But he must be believed to be a very pundit before he will get a chance of exercising his judgment, his precision, or his eloquence.  The men whose names are always in the newspapers never look at their Stone and Toddy,--care for it not at all,--have their Stone and Toddy got up for them by their juniors when cases require that reference shall be made to precedents.  But till that blessed time has come, a barrister who means success should carry his Stone and Toddy with him everywhere.
ED 207-8, XXIII,I.

## LEGISLATION

In the fabrication of garments for the national wear, the great thing is to produce garments that shall, as far as possible, defy hole-picking.  It may be, and sometimes is, the case, that garments so fabricated will be good also for wear.  PF 134, LIII,II.

## LEPERS

In the town, but not of it, within the walls, but forbidden all ingress to the streets, there they dwell, a race of mournfullest Pariahs.  From father to son, from mother to daughter, dire disease, horrid, polluting, is handed down, a certain legacy, making the body loathsome, and likening the divine face of man to a melancholy ape.  Oh!  the silent sadness, the inexpressible melancholy of those wan, thoughtless, shapeless, boneless, leaden faces!  To them no happy daily labour brings rest and appetite; their lot forbids them work, as it forbids all other blessings.  No; on their

dunghills outside their cabins there they sit in the sun,
the mournfullest sight one might look on, the leper parents
with their leper children, beggars by inheritance, paupers,
outcasts, mutilated victims,--but still with souls, if they
or any round them did but know it.  Ber 112, VII.

## LETTERS

He did, moreover, what so many wise people are accustomed to
do in similar circumstances; he immediately condemned the
person to whom the letter was written, as though she were
necessarily a <u>particeps</u> <u>criminis</u>.  BaT 260, XXVIII.

Letters from one young lady to another are doubtless written
in this [dashed off without changes] manner, and even with
them it might sometimes be better if more patience had been
taken.  DoT 507, XLIII.

An angry letter, especially if the writer be well loved, is
so much fiercer than any angry speech, so much more unendurable!   There the words remain, scorching, not to be explained away, not to be atoned for by a kiss, not to be
softened down by the word of love that may follow so quickly
upon spoken anger.   Heaven defend me from angry letters!
They should never be written, unless to schoolboys and men
at college; and not often to them if they be anyway tender-
hearted.   This at least should be a rule through the letter-
writing world:   that no angry letter be posted till four-
and-twenty hours shall have elapsed since it was written.
We all know how absurd is that other rule, that of saying
the alphabet when you are angry.   Trash!  Sit down and write
your letter; write it with all the venom in your power; spit
out your spleen at the fullest; 'twill do you good; you
think you have been injured; say all that you can say with
all your poisoned eloquence, and gratify yourself by reading
it while your temper is still hot.   Then put it in your
desk; and, as a matter of course, burn it before breakfast
the following morning.  Believe me that you will then have a
double gratification.
    A pleasant letter I hold to be the pleasantest thing
that this world has to give.   It should be good-humoured;
witty it may be, but with a gentle diluted wit.   Concocted
brilliancy will spoil it altogether.   Not long, so that it
be tedious in the reading; nor brief, so that the delight
suffice not to make itself felt.   It should be written
specially for the reader, and should apply altogether to
him, and not altogether to any other.   It should never
flatter.   Flattery is always odious.   But underneath the
visible stream of pungent water there may be the slightest
under-current of eulogy, so that it be not seen, but only
understood.   Censure it may contain freely, but censure
which in arraigning the conduct implies no doubt as to the
intellect.   It should be legibly written, so that it may be
read with comfort; but no more than that.  Caligraphy betokens caution, and if it be not light in hand it is
nothing.   That it be fairly grammatical and not ill spelt

the writer owes to his schoolmaster; but this should come of
habit, not of care.    Then let its page be soiled by no
business; one touch of utility will destroy it all.
     If you ask for examples, let it be as unlike Walpole as
may be.    If you can so write it that Lord Byron might have
written it, you will not be very far from high excellence.
     But, above all things, see that it be good-humoured....
Ber 326-8, XVIII.

That habit of bringing in letters at the breakfast-table has
its good points, certainly.    It is well that one should have
one's letters before the work or pleasure of the day
commences:    it is well to be able to discuss the different
little subjects of mutual interest as they are mentioned....
This is all very convenient; but the plan has its drawbacks.
Some letters will be in their nature black and brow-com-
pelling.    Tidings will come from time to time at which men
cannot smile....One would fain receive such letters in
private.    Ber 460, XXV.

It is a great thing for young ladies to live in a household
in which free correspondence by letter is permitted.    'Two
for mamma, four for Amelia, three for Fanny, and one for
papa.'    When the postman has left his budget they should be
dealt out in that way, and no more should be said about
it,--except what each may choose to say.    Papa's letter is
about money of course, and interests nobody.    Mamma's
contain the character of a cook and an invitation to dinner.
But Fanny's letters and Amelia's should be private; and a
well-bred mamma of the present day scorns even to look at
the handwriting of the addresses.    OrF 261, LXVI,II.

The question of the management of letters for young ladies
is handled very differently in different houses.    In some
establishments the post is as free to young ladies as it is
to the reverend seniors of the household.    In others it is
considered to be quite a matter of course that some experienced discretion should sit in judgment on the correspondence of the daughters of the family.    HKHWR 497,LIII.

Who is there that can write letters to all his friends, or
would not find it dreary work to do so even in regard to
those whom he really loves?    When there is something pal-
pable to be said, what a blessing is the penny post!    To
one's wife, to one's child, one's mistress, one's steward if
there be a steward; one's gamekeeper, if there be shooting
forward; one's groom,if there be hunting; one's publisher,
if there be a volume ready or money needed; or one's tailor
occasionally, if a coat be required, a man is able to
write.    But what has a man to say to his friend, --or for
that matter, what has a woman?...Distance in time and place,
but especially in time, will diminish friendship.    It is a
rule of nature that it should be so, and thus the friendships which a man most fosters are those which he can best
enjoy.    If your friend leave you, and seek a residence in
Patagonia, make a niche for him in your memory, and keep him

there as warm as you may.    Perchance he may return from
Patagonia and the old joys may be repeated.    But never think
that those joys can be maintained by the assistance of ocean
postage, let it be at never so cheap a rate.    PR 23-4, II,I.

It is certainly a part of the new dispensation that young
women shall send and receive letters without inspection.
Way 454, XLVIII,I.

But there are many reasons strong against such written
communications.    A man may desire that the woman he loves
should hear the record of his folly,--so that, in after
days, there may be nothing to detect:    so that, should the
Mrs. Hurtle of his life at any time intrude upon his
happiness, he may with a clear brow and undaunted heart say
to his beloved one,--'Ah, this is the trouble of which I
spoke to you.'    And then he and his beloved one will be in
one cause together.    But he hardly wishes to supply his
beloved one with a written record of his folly.    And then
who does not know how much tenderness a man may show to his
own faults by the tone of his voice, by half-spoken
sentences, and by an admixture of words of love for the lady
who has filled up the vacant space once occupied by the
Mrs. Hurtle of his romance?    But the written record must go
through from beginning to end, self-accusing, thoroughly
perspicuous, with no sweet, soft falsehoods hidden under the
half-expressed truth.    The soft falsehoods which would be
sweet as the scent of violets in a personal interview, would
stand in danger of being denounced as deceit added to
deceit, if sent in a letter.    Way 242-3, LXXVI,II.

The secrecy which some correspondence requires certainly
tends to make a club a convenient arrangement.    'Why don't
you come as you said you would?--A.'    In olden times,
fifteen or twenty years ago, when telegraph-wires were still
young, and messages were confined to diplomatic secrets,
horse-racing, and the rise and fall of stocks, lovers used
to indulge in rapturous expressions which would run over
pages; but the pith and strength of laconic diction has now
been taught to us by the self-sacrificing patriotism of the
Post Office.    We have all felt the vigour of telegrammatic
expression, and, even when we do not trust the wire, we
employ the force of wiry language.    'Wilt thou be mine?--
M.N.,' is now the ordinary form of an offer of marriage by
post; and the answer seldom goes beyond 'Ever thine--P.Q.'
IHP 90-1, XX,I.

There was still that 'locus poenitentiae' which should be
accorded to all letters written in anger.    DuC 404, LI.

When a man has written a letter, and has taken some trouble
with it, and more especially when he has copied it several
times himself so as to have made many letters of it,--when
he has argued his point successfully to himself, and has
triumphed in his own mind,...he does not like to make waste
paper of his letters.    DrW 259, XI, Conclusion.

Who does not know how odious a letter will become by being shoved on one side day after day? Answer it at the moment, and it will be nothing. Put it away unread, or at least un-digested, for a day, and it at once begins to assume ugly proportions. When you have been weak enough to let it lie on your desk, or worse again, hidden in your breast-pocket, for a week or ten days, it will have become an enemy so strong and so odious that you will not dare to attack it. It throws a gloom over all your joys. It makes you cross to your wife, severe to the cook, and critical to your own wine-cellar....You think of destroying it and denying it, dishonestly and falsely....And yet you must bear yourself all the time as though there were no load lying near your heart. MF 299-300, XXIX,II.

...a subject on which the practice of the English world has been much altered during the last thirty or forty years,-- perhaps we may say fifty or sixty years. Fifty years ago young ladies were certainly not allowed to receive letters as they chose, and to write them, and to demand that this practice should be carried on without any supervision from their elder friends. It is now usually the case that they do so....Practically the use of the post-office is in her own hands. And as this spirit of self-conduct has grown up, the morals and habits of our young ladies have certainly not deteriorated. In America they carry latch-keys, and walk about with young gentlemen as young gentlemen walk about with each other. In America the young ladies are as well-behaved as with us....Whether the latch-key system, or that of free correspondence, may not rob the flowers of some of that delicate aroma which we used to appreciate, may be a question; but then it is also a question whether there does not come something in place of it which in the long run is found to be more valuable. MSF 56-7, XLVII,III.

## LETTERS, LOVE

Now I put it to all lovers whether, when they wish to please, they ever write in such manner ['My dearest Caroline'] to their sweethearts. Is it not always, 'My own love?' 'Dearest love?' 'My own sweet pet?' But that use of the the Christian name, which is so delicious in the speaking during the first days of intimacy, does it not always betoken something stern at the beginning of a lover's letter? Ah, it may betoken something very stern! 'My dearest Jane, I am sorry to say it, but I could not approve of the way in which you danced with Major Simkins last night.' 'My dearest Lucy, I was at Kensington-garden gate yesterday at four, and remained absolutely till five. You really ought--' Is not that always the angry lover's tone? Ber 328-9, XVIII.

[A]s all lovers seem to think that no lovers have done before themselves [using sweet appellations], with appel-lations which are so sweet to those who write, and so musical to those who read, but which sound so ludicrous when

barbarously made public in hideous law courts by brazen-
browed lawyers with mercernary tongues.
CasR 262-3, XIII,II.

I believe there is no bliss greater than that which a
thorough love-letter gives to a girl who knows that in
receiving it she commits no fault--who can open it before
her father and mother with nothing more than the slight
blush which the consciousness of her position gives her.
And of all love-letters the first must be the sweetest!
What a value there is in every word!  How each expression is
scanned and turned to the best account!   With what
importance are all those little phrases invested, which too
soon become mere phrases, used as a matter of course.
SmaH 200, XXI.

It does not promise well for any of the parties concerned
when a young woman with two lovers can bring herself to show
the love-letters of him to whom she is engaged to the other
lover whom she has refused!  Bel 296, XXIII.

A man does not write a love-letter easily when he is in
doubt himself whether he does or does not mean to be a
scoundrel.  ED 323, XXXV,I.

To a girl who really loves, the first love letter is a thing
as holy as the recollection of the first kiss.  EE 167,IX,I.

LIBEL

Now they who are concerned in the manufacture of newspapers
are well aware that censure is infinitely more attractive
than eulogy,--but they are quite as well aware that it is
more dangerous.  No proprietor or editor was ever brought
before the courts at the cost of ever so many hundred
pounds,--which if things go badly may rise to thousands,--
because he had attributed all but divinity to some very poor
specimen of mortality.   No man was ever called upon for
damages because he had attributed grand motives....Censure
on the other hand is open to very grave perils.   Let the
Editor have been ever so conscientious, ever so beneficent,
--even ever so true,--let it be ever so clear that what he
has written has been written on behalf of virtue, and that
he has misstated no fact, exaggerated no fault, never for a
moment been allured from public to private matters,--and he
may still be in danger of ruin.  A very long purse, or else
a very high courage is needed for the exposure of such
[bad]  conduct.  Way 415-6, XLIV,I.

LIBERALS...CONSERVATIVES

There is probably more of the flavour of political aristocracy to be found still remaining among our liberal leading
statesmen than among their opponents.  A conservative
Cabinet is, doubtless, never deficient in dukes and lords,
and the sons of such; but conservative dukes and lords

are recruited here and there, and as recruits, are new to
the business, whereas among the old Whigs a halo of state-
craft has, for ages past, so strongly pervaded and enveloped
certain great families, that the power in the world of
politics thus produced still remains, and is even yet
efficacious in creating a feeling of exclusiveness.  They
say that 'misfortune makes men acquainted with strange
bedfellows'. The old hereditary Whig Cabinet ministers must,
no doubt, by this time have learned to feel themselves at
home with strange neighbours at their elbows.   But still
with them something of the feeling of high blood, of rank,
and of living in a park with deer about it, remains.
PR 358, XL,I.   See also Whigs.

## LIBRARIES

But then, how few of those who live in flashy new houses in
the west require to have libraries in London!
CasR 116, V[sic], III.

## LIES

We English gentlemen hate the name of a lie; but how often
do we find public men who believe each other's words?
BaT 315, XXXII.

Few liars can lie with the full roundness and self-
sufficiency of truth.  SmaH 226, XXIII.

There are men who fib with so bad a grace and with so little
tact that they might as well not fib at all.  They not only
never arrive at success, but never even venture to expect
it.  Cl 119, XV.

A lie on such a subject  [about marriage to one who has not
proposed]  from a woman under such circumstances is hardly
to be considered a lie at all.  It is spoken with no mean
object, and is the only bulwark which the woman has ready at
her need to cover her own weakness.  Bel 96, VIII.

[N]ature does not require by any of its laws that self-
preservation should be aided by falsehood.  Bel 275, XXI.

When you have used your lie gracefully and successfully, it
is hard to bury it and get it well out of sight.  It crops
up here and there against you, requiring more lies; and at
last, too often, has to be admitted as a lie, most usually
so admitted in silence, but still admitted,--to be forgiven
or not, according to the circumstances of the case.   The
most perfect forgiveness is that which is extended to him
who is known to lie in everything.   The man has to be taken,
lies and all, as a man is taken with a squint, or a harelip,
or a bad temper.  He has an uphill game to fight, but when
once well known, he does not fall into the difficulty of
being believed.  SHHOH 74, VIII.

It is so hard, when you have used a lie commodiously, to bury it, and get well rid of it.  SHHOH 92, IX.

Now, when there have been such tender passages, and the gentleman is cross-examined by the lady...,the gentleman usually teaches himself to think that a little falsehood is permissible.  A gentleman can hardly tell a lady that he has become tired of her, and has changed his mind.  He feels the matter, perhaps, more keenly even than she does; and though, at all other times he may be a very Paladin in the cause of truth, in such strait as this he does allow himself some latitude.  HKHWR 338, XXXV.

The general belief which often seizes upon the world in regard to some special falsehood is very surprising.  Everybody on a sudden adopts an idea that some particular man is over head and ears in debt, so that he can hardly leave his house for fear of the bailiffs;--or that some ill-fated woman is cruelly-used by her husband;--or that some eldest son has ruined his father; whereas the man doesn't owe a shilling, the woman never hears a harsh word from her lord, and the eldest son in question has never succeeded in obtaining a shilling beyond his allowance.  ED 152, XVII,I.

When a young man has behaved badly about a woman, when a young man has been beaten without returning a blow, when a young man's pleasant vices are brought directly under a mother's eyes, what can he do but lie?...In such cases the liar does not expect to be believed.  He knows that his disgrace will be made public, and only hopes to be saved from the ignominy of declaring it with his own words.
Way 209, LXXII,II.

A liar has many points to his favour,--but he has this against him, that unless he devote more time to the management of his lies than life will generally allow, he cannot make them tally.  Way 254-5, LXXVII,II.

[B]ut a man doesn't lie when he exaggerates an emphasis, or even when he gives by a tone a meaning to a man's words exactly opposite to that which another tone would convey.  Or, if he does lie in doing so, he does not know that he lies.  PrM 68, VIII,I.

Could you call your friend a liar more plainly than by saying to him that you would not say that he lied?
PrM 177, XIX,I.

## LIFE

To live with one's hands ever daubed with chalk from a billiard-table, to be always spying into stables and rubbing against grooms, to put up with the narrow lodgings which needy men encounter at race meetings, to be day after day on the rails running after platers and steeplechasers, to be conscious on all occasions of the expediency of selling your

beast when you are hunting, to be counting up little odds at
all your spare moments;--these things do not, I think, make
a satisfactory life for a young man. And for a man that is
not young, they are the very devil! Better have no
digestion when you are forty than find yourself living such
a life as that! Cl 161, XIX.

Each created animal must live and get its food by the gifts
which the Creator has given to it, let those gifts be as
poor as they may....The rat, the toad, the slug, the flea,
must each live according to its appointed mode of existence.
Animals which are parasites by nature can only live by
attaching themselves to life that is strong.
HKHWR 446, XLVII.

The change from a life of fevered, though most miserable,
excitement, to one of dull, pleasureless, and utterly uninteresting propriety, is one that can hardly be made without
the assistance of binding control. VOB 283, XL.

## LIFESTYLE

There are certain modes of life which, if once adopted, make
contentment in any other circumstances almost an impossibility. In old age a man may retire without repining;...
but in youth, with all the faculties still perfect, with the
body still strong, with the hopes still buoyant, such a
change as that which had been made by Phineas Finn was more
than he, or than most men, could bear with equanimity....To
the palate accustomed to high cookery, bread and milk is
almost painfully insipid. PR 6-7, I,I.

## LIPS

No man with thin lips ever seems to me to be genially human
at all points. CasR 85, V,II.

## LISTENERS

There are listeners who show by their mode of listening that
they listen as a duty,--not because they are interested.
ED 25, III,I.

## LOCATIONS

I never could understand why anybody should ever have begun
to live at...[a particular town], or why the population
there should have been at any time recruited by newcomers.
That a man with a family should cling to a house in which he
has once established himself is intelligible. The butcher
who supplied,...or the baker, or the ironmonger, though he
might not drive what is called a roaring trade,
nevertheless found himself probably able to live, and might
well hesitate before he would encounter the dangers of a
more energetic locality. But how it came to pass that he
first got himself...[there] or his father, or his grand-

father before him, has always been a mystery to me.    AS 1,I.

## LODGINGS

Lodgings in London are always gloomy.    Gloomy colours wear
better than bright ones for curtains and carpets, and the
keepers of lodgings in London seem to think that a certain
dinginess of appearance is respectable.    I never saw a
London lodging in which any attempt at cheerfulness had been
made, and I do not think that any such attempt, if made,
would pay.    The lodging-seeker would be frightened and
dismayed, and would unconsciously be led to fancy that something was wrong.    Ideas of burglars and improper persons
would present themselves.    This is so certainly the case
that I doubt whether any well-conditioned lodging-house
matron could in induced to show rooms that were prettily
draped or pleasantly coloured.    LasC 404, XLV.

## LODGINGS KEEPERS

Few positions in life could be harder to bear than hers
[keeping lodgers]!    To be ever tugging at others for money
that they could not pay; to desire respectability for its
own sake, but to be driven to confess that it was a luxury
beyond her means; to put up with disreputable belongings for
the sake of lucre, and then not to get the lucre, but be
driven to feel that she was ruined by the attempt!    How many
Mrs. Ropers there are who from year to year sink down and
fall away, and no one knows whither they betake themselves!
One fancies that one sees them from time to time at the
corners of the streets in battered bonnets and thin gowns,
with the tattered remnants of old shawls upon their
shoulders, still looking as though they had within them a
faint remembrance of long-distant respectability.    With
anxious eyes they peer about, as though searching in the
streets for other lodgers.    Where do they get their daily
morsels of bread, and their poor cups of thin tea--their
cups of thin tea, with perhaps a penny-worth of gin added to
it, if Providence be good!    SmaH 518, LI.

## LONDON

In days gone by the house had been the habitation of some
great rich man, who had there enjoyed the sweet breezes from
the river before London had become the London of the present
days, and when no embankment had been need for the Thames.
Cl 52, VII.

In all the world around us there is nothing more singular
than the emptiness and the fullness of London.
VOB 488, LXVIII.

## LONDON, NEW TENEMENTS

Of such streets    [built, as yet, only on one side of the
way, with the pavement only one third finished, and the

stones in the road as yet unbroken and untrodden]  there are
thousands now round London.  They are to be found in every
suburb, creating wonder in all thoughtful minds as to who
can be their tens of thousands of occupants.  The houses are
a little too good for artisans, too small and too silent to
be the abode of various lodgers, and too mean for clerks who
live on salaries.  They are as dull-looking as Lethe itself,
dull and silent, dingy and repulsive.  But they are not dis-
creditable in appearance, never have that Mohawk look which
by some unknown sympathy in bricks and mortar attaches itself to the residences of professional ruffians.
CasR 196, X,III.

## LONDON SEASON

It was now May, and London was bright with all the exotic
gaiety of the season.  The Park was crowded with riders at
one, and was almost impassable at six.  Dress was outvying
dress, and equipage equipage.  Men and women, but
principally woman, seemed to be intent on finding out new
ways of scattering money.  Tradesmen no doubt knew much of
defaulters, and heads of families might find themselves
pressed for means; but to the outside west-end eye looking
at the outside west-end world, it seemed as though wealth
were unlimited and money a drug.  To those who had known the
thing for years, to young ladies who were now entering on
their seventh or eighth campaign, there was a feeling of
business about it all which, though it buoyed them up by
its excitement, robbed amusement of most of its pleasure.  A
ball cannot be very agreeable in which you may not dance
with the man you like and are not asked by the man you want;
at which you are forced to make a note that that full-blown
hope is futile, and that this little bud will surely never
come to flower.  And then the toil of smiles, the pretence
at flirtation, the long-continued assumption of fictitious
character, the making of oneself bright to the bright,
solemn to the solemn, and romantic to the romantic, is work
too hard for enjoyment.  IHP 259, XXVII,I.

## LONDON SUBURBS

It is very difficult nowadays to say where the suburbs of
London come to an end, and where the country begins.  The
railways, instead of enabling Londoners to live in the
country, have turned the country into a city.  London will
soon assume the shape of a great starfish.  The old town,
extending from Poplar to Hammersmith, will be the nucleus,
and the various railway lines will be the projecting rays.
    There are still, however, some few nooks within reach
of the metropolis which have not been be-villaed and be-
terraced out of all look of rural charm, and the little
village of Hampton, with its old-fashioned country inn, and
its bright, quiet, grassy river, is one of them, in spite of
the triple metropolitan waterworks on the one side, and the
close vicinity on the other of Hampton Court, that well-
loved resort of cockneydom.  TC 22, III.

## LORD CHANCELLOR

[F]or legal offices have a signification differing much from
that which attaches itself to places simply political.    A
Lord Chancellor becomes a peer, and on going out of office
enjoys a large pension.  When the woolsack has been reached
there comes an end of doubt, and a beginning of ease.
PrM 64, VIII,I.

## LORD PRIVY SEAL

...Lord Privy Seal,--a Lordship of State which does carry
with it a status and a seat in the Cabinet, but does not
necessarily entail any work.   PR 156, LVIII,II.

## LOSS OF HIGH OFFICE

We are told that it is a bitter moment with the Lord Mayor
when he leaves the Mansion House and becomes once more
Alderman Jones, on No. 75, Bucklersbuty.   Lord Chancellors
going out of office have a great fall though they take
pensions with them for their consolation.   And the President
of the United States when he leaves the glory of the White
House and once more becomes a simple citizen must feel the
change severely.   PF 350, LXXVI,II.

## LOSS, LOVERS

Oh, my sensitive reader!    have you ever performed the
process [of removing a loved one]?   It is by no means to be
done with rose-water appliances and gentle motherly
pressure.  The whole force of the hospital has to be brought
out to perform this operation.  Ber 371, XX.

## LOVE

[B]ut in matters of love men do not see clearly in their own
affairs.  They say that faint heart never won fair lady; and
it is amazing to me how fair ladies are won, so faint are
often men's hearts!  Were it not for the kindness of their
nature, that seeing the weakness of our courage they will
occasionally descend from their impregnable fortresses, and
themselves aid us in effecting their own defeat, too often
would they escape unconquered if not unscathed, and free of
body if not of heart.  War 83-4, VII.

How many shades there are between love and indifference, and
how little the graduated scale is understood. BaT 217,XXIV.

It is, we believe, common with young men of five and twenty
to look on their seniors--on men of, say, double their own
age--as so many stocks and stones,--stocks and stones, that
is, in regard to feminine beauty.  There never was a greater
mistake.  Women, indeed, generally know better; but on this
subject men of one age are thoroughly ignorant of what is
the very nature of mankind of other ages....Men of fifty

don't dance mazurkas, being generally too fat and wheezy,
nor do they sit for the hour together on river banks at
their mistresses' feet, being somewhat afraid of rheumatism.
But for real true love, love at first sight, love to
devotion, love that robs a man of his sleep, love that 'will
gaze an eagle blind,' love that 'will hear the lowest sound
when the suspicious tread of theft is stopped,' love that is
'like a Hercules, still climbing trees in the Hesperides,'--
we believe the best age is from forty-five to seventy; up to
that, men are generally given to mere flirting.
BaT 363-4, XXXVII.

And how great that luxury [to enjoy the assurance of the
other's love]  is!  How far it surpasses any other pleasure
which God has allowed to his creatures!   And to a woman's
heart how doubly delightful!
    When the ivy has found its tower, when the delicate
creeper has found its strong wall, we know how the parasite
plants grow and prosper.   They were not created to stretch
forth their branches alone, and endure without protection
the summer's sun and the winter's storm.   Alone they but
spread themselves on the ground, and cower unseen in the
dingy shade.    But when they have found their firm supporters, how wonderful is their beauty; how all pervading
and victorious! What is the turret without its ivy, or the
high garden-wall without the jasmine which gives it its
beauty and fragrance?   The hedge without the honeysuckle is
but a hedge.
    There is a feeling still half existing, but now half
conquered by the force of human nature, that a woman should
be ashamed of her love till the husband's right to her
compels her to acknowledge it.   We would fain preach a
different doctrine.   A woman should glory in her love; but
on that account let her take the more care that it be such
as to justify her glory. BaT 478-9, XLIX.

But love, gratified love, will, we believe, keep out even an
English east wind.  If so, it is certainly the only thing
that will.  TC 174, XV.

It is so little flattering to be loved when such love is the
offspring of gratitude.   And then when that gratitude is
unnecessary, when it has been given in mistake for supposed
favours, the acceptance of such love is little better than a
cheat!  TC 321-2, XXVI.

There is, undoubtedly, a propensity in human love to attach
itself to excellence; but it has also, as undoubtedly, a
propensity directly antagonistic to this, and which teaches
it to put forth its strongest efforts in favour of inferiority.  Watch any fair flock of children in which there may
be one blighted bud, and you will see that that blighted one
is the mother's darling.  What filial affection is ever so
strong as that evinced by a child for a parent in misfortune?...and what is so sweet as to be able to protect?...

It seldom happens that a woman's love is quenched by a man's crime. Women in this respect are more enduring than men; they have softer sympathies, and less acute, less selfish, appreciation of the misery of being joined to that which has been shamed. TC 461, XXXVIII.

A housemaid, not long since, who was known in the family in which she lived to be affianced to a neighbouring gardener, came weeping to her mistress.

'Oh, ma'am!'

'Why, Susan, what ails you?'

'Oh, ma'am!'

'Well, Susan--what is it?--why are you crying?'

'Oh, ma'am--John!'

'Well--what of John? I hope he is not misbehaving.'

'Indeed, ma'am, he is then; the worst of misbehaviour; for he's gone and got hisself married.' And poor Susan gave vent to a flood of tears.

Her mistress tried to comfort her, and not in vain. She told her that probably she might be better as she was; that John, seeing what he had done, must be a false creature, who would undoubtedly have used her ill; and she ended her good counsel by trying to make Susan understand that there were still as good fish in the sea as had ever yet been caught out of it.

'And that's true too, ma'am,' said Susan, with her apron to her eyes.

'Then you should not be downhearted, you know.'

'Nor I han't down'arted, ma'am, for thank God I could love any man, but it's the looks on it, ma'am; it's that I mind.'

How many of us are there, women and men too, who think most of the 'looks of [sic] it' under such circumstances; and who, were we as honest as poor Susan, ought to thank God, as she did, that we can love anyone; anyone, that is, of the other sex. We are not all of us susceptible of being torn to tatters by an unhappy passion; not even all those of us who may be susceptible of a true and honest love. And it is well that it is so. It is one of God's mercies; and if we were as wise as Susan, we should thank God for it. TC 179-80, XVI.

Yes, they are commonplaces when we read of them in novels; common enough, too, to some of us when we write them; but they are by no means commonplace when first heard by a young girl in the rich, balmy fragrance of a July evening stroll.

Nor are they commonplaces when so uttered for the first or second time at least, or perhaps the third. 'Tis a pity that so heavenly a pleasure should pall upon the senses. DoT 274, XXIII.

To love thoroughly, truly, heartily, with her whole body, soul, heart, and strength; should not that be counted for a merit in a woman? And yet we are wont to make a disgrace of it. We do so most unnaturally, most unreasonably; for we expect our daughters to get themselves married off our hands.    When the period of that step comes, then love is proper enough; but up to that--before that--as regards all those preliminary passages which must, we suppose, be necessary--in all those it becomes a young lady to be icy-hearted as a river-god in winter.

    'O whistle and I'll come to you, my lad!
    O whistle and I'll come to you, my lad!
    Tho'father and mither and a'should go mad,
    O whistle and I'll come to you, my lad!'

This is the kind of love which a girl should feel before she puts her hand proudly in that of her lover, and consents that they two shall be made one flesh. DoT 275, XXIII.

A girl may scold a man in words for rashness in his love, but her heart never scolds him for such offence as that. DoT 488, XLI.

It is one thing for a young lady to make prudent, heart-breaking suggestions, but quite another to have them accepted. DoT 541, XLV.

Is it not always so,   [every word he spoke was gospel to her]--should it not be so always, when love first speaks to loving ears? CasR 48, III,I.

According to my ideas woman's love should be regarded as fair prize of war,--as long as the war has been carried on with due adherence to the recognized law of nations.    When it has been fairly won, let it be firmly held. CasR 92,V,III.

One worships that which one feels, through the inner and unexpressed conviction of the mind, to be greater, better, higher than oneself. OrF 228, XXII,I.

But girls, I think, have no objection to this   [the man having had previous loves]. They do not desire the first fruits, or even early fruits, as men do.  Indeed, I am not sure whether experience on the part of a gentleman in his use of his heart is not supposed by most young ladies to enhance the value of the article. OrF 411, LXXX,II.

What has the world to offer equal to the joy of gratified love?   What triumph is there so triumphant as that achieved by valor over beauty?

    'Take the goods the gods provide you.
    The lovely Thais sits beside you.'

Was not that the happiest moment in Alexander's life?  Was it not the climax of all his glories, and the sweetest drop which Fortune poured into his cup?  Str 73, XIII.

There is a silent love which women recognise, and which in some silent way they acknowledge--giving gracious but silent thanks for the respect which accompanies it. SmaH 33, IV.

To think of one's absent love is very sweet; but it becomes monotonous after a mile or two of a towing-path, and the mind will turn away to Aunt Sally, or the Cremorne Gardens, and financial questions. I doubt whether any girl would be satisfied with her lover's mind if she knew the whole of it. SmaH 35, IV.

How wonderful in its nature is that passion of which men speak when they acknowledge to themselves that they are in love. Of all things, it is, under one condition, the most foul, and under another, the most fair. As that condition is, a man shows himself either as a beast or as a god! SmaH 58, VI.

Where is the girl who will not sympathise with such love and such grief, if it be shown only because it cannot be concealed, and be declared against the will of him who declares it? SmaH 81, IX.

I think there is nothing in the world so pretty as the conscious little tricks of love played off by a girl towards the man she loves, when she has made up her mind boldly that all the world may know that she has given herself away to him. SmaH 83, IX.

Why is it that girls so constantly do this--so frequently ask men who have loved them to be present at their marriages with other men? There is no triumph in it. It is done in sheer kindness and affection. They intend to offer something which shall soften and not aggravate the sorrow that they have caused. 'You can't marry me yourself,' the lady seems to say. 'But the next greatest blessing which I can offer you shall be yours--you shall see me married to somebody else.' I fully appreciate the intention, but in honest truth, I doubt the eligibility of the proffered entertainment. SmaH 90-1, IX.

Most young men have to go through that disappointment [rejection in love], and are enabled to bear it without much injury to their prospects of happiness. And in after-life the remembrance of such love is a blessing rather than a curse, enabling the possessor of it to feel that in those early days there was something within him of which he had no cause to be ashamed. SmaH 133-4, XIV.

A girl, when she is thoroughly in love,...likes to receive hints as to her future life from the man to whom she is devoted; but she would, I think, prefer that such hints should be short, and that the lesson should be implied rather than declared;--that they should, in fact, be hints and not lectures. SmaH 139, XV.

A man will dine, even though his heart be breaking. SmaH 285, XXVIII.

But then a woman in such a contest  [where she is **determined**

to trap the man]    has so many points in her favour.
SmaH 294, XXIX.

Love does not follow worth, and is not given to excellence;
--nor is it destroyed by ill-usage, nor killed by blows and
mutilation.  SmaH 306, XXX.

But such signs among such people  [the ungentlemanly clergy]
do not bear the meaning which they have in the outer world.
These people are demonstrative and unctuous,--whereas the
outer world is reticent and dry.  They are perhaps too free
with their love, but the fault is better than that other
fault of no love at all.  RacR 79-80, VI.

Nor is it often that a man's love is like a woman's,--rest-
less, fearful, uncomfortable, sleepless, timid, and all-
pervading.  Not the less may it be passionate, constant, and
faithful.  RacR 333, XXVI.

When an unmarried gentleman of forty tells an unmarried lady
of thirty-six that she is the dearest friend he has in the
world, he must surely intend that they shall, neither of
them, remain unmarried any longer.  MM 135-6, X.

When a lady who is thinking about getting married is asked
by a gentleman who is frequently in her thoughts whether she
does not want some one to love, it is natural that she
should presume that he means to be particular; and it is
natural also that she should be in some sort gratified by
that particularity.  MM 147, XI.

[S]uch sufferings are seldom perpetual.  Cl 30, IV.

No man need cease to love without a cause.  A man may
maintain his love, and nourish it, and keep it warm by
honest manly effort, as he may his probity, his courage, or
his honour.  Cl 210, XXV.

A man, you say, delicate reader, a true man can love but one
woman,--but one at a time.  So you say, and are so
convinced; but no conviction was ever more false.  When a
true man has loved with all his heart and all his soul,--
does he cease to love,--does he cleanse his heart of that
passion when circumstances run against him, and he is forced
to turn elsewhere for his life's companion?...No; the first
love, if that was true, is ever there; and should she and he
meet after many years, though their heads be gray and their
cheeks wrinkled, there will still be a touch of the old
passion as their hands meet for a moment.  Methinks that
love never dies, unless it be murdered by downright ill-
usage.  It may be so murdered, but even ill-usage will more
often fail than succeed in that enterprise.  Cl 239, XXVIII.

A man, though he may love many, should be devoted only to
one.  The man's feelings to the woman whom he is to marry
should be this;...he will be prepared always, and at all
hazards, to defend her from every misadventure, to struggle

ever that she may be happy, to see that no wind blows upon
her with needless severity, that no ravening wolf of a
misery shall come near her, that her path be swept clean for
her,--as clean as may be, and that her roof-tree be made
firm upon a rock.   There is much of this which is quite
independent of love,--much of it that may be done without
love.   This is devotion, and it is this which a man owes to
the woman who has once promised to be his wife, and has not
forfeited her right.  Cl 239, XXVIII.

We rarely, I fancy, love those whose love we have not either
possessed or expected,--or at any rate for whose love we
have not hoped; but when it has once existed, ill-usage will
seldom destroy it.  Cl 299, XXXV.

But in moments such as those,  [a family suicide]  soft
words may be spoken and hands may be pressed without any of
that meaning which soft words and the grasping of hands
generally carry with them.  Bel 16, I.

But all young ladies are apt to talk to themselves in such
phrases  [safe from love-making]  about gentlemen with whom
they are thrown into chance intimacy;--as though love-making
were in itself a thing injurious and antagonistic to happiness, instead of being, as it is, the very salt of life.
Safe against love-making!  Bel 42-3, IV.

...those tendernesses, which need not imperatively be made
to mean anything, though they do often mean so much.
Bel 68,VI.

What is there that any man desires,--any man or any woman,--
that does not lose half its value when it is found to be
easy of access and easy of possession?  Wine is valued by its
price, not its flavour.  Open your doors freely to Jones and
Smith, and Jones and Smith will not care to enter them.
Shut your doors obdurately against the same gentlemen, and
they will use all their little diplomacy to effect an
entrance.  Bel 126, X.

Much is said of the rashness of women in giving away their
hearts wildly; but the charge when made generally is, I
think, an unjust one.   I am more often astonished by the
prudence of girls than by their recklessness.   A woman of
thirty will often love well and not wisely; but the girls of
twenty seem to me to like propriety of demeanor, decency of
outward life, and a competence.   It is, of course, good
that it should be so; but if it is so, they should not also
claim a general character for generous and passionate in-
discretion, asserting as their motto that Love shall still
be Lord of All.  Bel 128-9, XI.

They used to say in the nursery that cold pudding is good to
settle a man's love.  Bel 165, XIII.

Women are so good and kind that those whom they love they

love almost the more when they commit offences, because of the offences so committed.  Bel 321, XXIV.

A women who really loves will hardly allow that her love should be forfeited by any fault.  True love breeds forgiveness for all faults.  Bel 329, XXV.

Men may know all that they require to know on that subject [being loved]  without any plainly spoken words. LasC 240, XXVII.

Nothing reopens the springs of love so fully as absence, and no absence so thoroughly as that which must needs be endless.  We want that which we have not; and especially that which we can never have.  LasC 639, LXVII.

To struggle in vain always hurts the pride; but the wound made by the vain struggle for a woman is sorer than any wound so made.  LasC 742, LXXX.

A maiden who has been wooed and won, generally thinks that it is she who has conquered, and chooses to be triumphant accordingly.  LasC 765, LXXXII.

[A]nd they who talk best of love protest that no man or woman can be in love with two persons at once.  PF 107,L,II.

...that painful, irritating affection which...a girl...can show to...a man when she will not give him that other affection for which his heart is pining.  PF 119, LI,II.

For women such episodes in the lives of their lovers [previous love affairs]  have an excitement which is almost pleasurable, whereas each man is anxious to hear his lady swear that until he appeared upon the scene her heart had been fancy free.  PF 267, LXVI,II.

There is nothing so flattering as the warm expression of the confidence of a woman's love.  PF 288, LXIX,II.

I am not sure that it is well that a man should have any large number from whom to select a best; as, in such circumstances, he is so very apt to change his judgment from hour to hour.  The qualities which are the most attractive before dinner sometimes becomes the least so in the evening. PF 313, LXXII,II.

How is a man not to tell such tales when he has on his arm, close to him, a girl who tells him her little everything of life, and only asks for his confidence in return?...For all that he has to tell she loves him the better and still the better.  A man desires to win a virgin heart, and is happy to know,--or at least to believe,--that he has won it.  With a woman every former rival is an added victim to the wheels of the triumphant chariot in which she is sitting.  'All these has he known and loved, culling sweets from each of them.  But now he has come to me, and I am the sweetest of them all.'  PF 353, LXXVI,II.

When a girl says that she will try to reconcile herself to a man's overtures, she has almost yielded.  GLOG 55, V.

Perhaps it may be said of every human heart in a sound condition that it must be specially true to some other one human heart; but it may certainly be so said of every female heart.  The object may be changed from time to time,--may be changed very suddenly, as when a girl's devotion is transferred with the consent of all her friends from her mother to her lover; or very slowly, as when a mother's is transferred from her husband to some favourite child; but, unless self-worship be predominant, there is always one friend to whom the woman's breast is true,--for whom it is the woman's joy to offer herself in sacrifice.  GLOG 101, IX.

...the agony which a passionate man feels when the woman whom he loves is to be given into the arms of another. GLOG 112, X.

Let things go as they may with a man in an affair of love, let him be as far as possible from the attainment of his wishes, there will always be consolation to him if he knows that he is loved.  GLOG 135, XII.

To declare a passion to the girl he loves may be very pleasant work to the man who feels almost sure that his answer will not be against him....The very possession of the passion,--or even its pretence,--gives the man a liberty which he has a pleasure and a pride in using.  But this is the case when the man dashes boldly at his purpose without preconcerted arrangements.  VOB 27, IV.

There is something mean to a man in the want of success in love.  If a man lose a venture of money he can tell his friends; or if he be unsucessful in trying for a seat in parliament; or be thrown out of a run in the hunting-field; or even if he be blackballed for a club; but a man can hardly bring himself to tell his dearest comrade that his Mary has preferred another man to himself.  VOB 160-1,XXIII.

Now men in love, let their case be ever so bad, must dine or die.  So much no doubt is not admitted by the chroniclers of the old knights who went forth after their ladies; but the old chroniclers, if they soared somewhat higher than do those of the present day, are admitted to have been on the whole less circumstantially truthful.  VOB 203, XXIX.

We are apt to suppose that love should follow personal acquaintance; and yet love at third sight is probably as common as any love at all, and it takes a great many sights before one human being can know another.  Years are wanted to make a friendship, but days suffice for men and women to get married.  VOB 216, XXI.

Is a man to know no joy because he has an ache at his heart?
    In this matter of disappointed and, as it were, dis-
jointed affection, men are very different from women, and
for the most part, much more happily circumstanced.  Such
sorrow a woman feeds;--but a man starves it....But, in
truth, the difference comes not so much from the inner
heart, as from the outer life.  It is easier to feed a
sorrow upon needle-and-thread and novels, than it is upon
lawyers' papers, or even the out-a-door occupations of a
soldier home upon leave who has no work to do....When a girl
asks herself that question,--what shall she do with her
life?  it is so natural that she should answer it by saying
that she will get married, and give her life to somebody
else.  It is a woman's one career--let women rebel against
the edict as they may; and though there may be
word-rebellion here and there, women learn the truth early
in their lives.  And women know it later in life when they
think of their girls; and men know it, too, when they have
to deal with their daughters.  Girls, too, now acknowledge
aloud that they have learned the lesson; and Saturday
Reviewers and others blame them for their lack of modesty in
doing so,--most unreasonably, most uselessly, and, as far as
the influence of such censors may go, most perniciously.
Nature prompts the desire, the world acknowledges its
ubiquity, circumstances show that it is reasonable, the
whole theory of creation requires it; but it is required
that the person most concerned should falsely repudiate it,
in order that a mock modesty may be maintained, in which no
human being can believe!  Such is the theory of the censors
who deal heavily with our Englishwomen of the present day.
Our daughters should be educated to be wives, but, forsooth,
they should never wish to be wooed!  The very idea is but a
remnant of the tawdry sentimentality of an age in which the
mawkish insipidity of the women was the reaction from the
vice of that preceding it.  That our girls are in quest of
husbands, and know well in what way their lines in life
should be laid, is a fact which none can dispute.  Let men
be taught to recognise the same truth as regards themselves,
and we shall cease to hear of the necessity of a new career
for women.  VOB 259-60, XXXVII.

There was never a woman to whom the idea of being loved was
not the sweetest thought that her mind could produce.
VOB 378, LIII.

The man who becomes divine in a woman's eyes, has generally
achieved his claim to celestial honours by sudden assault.
And, alas!  the qualities which carry him through it and
give the halo to his head may after all be very ungodlike.
SHHOH 15, II.

It is so hard to have to bid a girl, and a good girl too,
not to fall in love with a particular man!  There is left
among us at any rate so much of reserve and assumed delicacy
as to require us to consider, or pretend to consider on the
girl's behalf, that of course she won't fall in love.  We

know that she will, sooner or later;...and the propensity
has been planted in her for wise purposes. But as to this
or that special sample of the genus girl, in reference to
this or that special sample of the genus young man, we
always feel ourselves bound to take it as a matter of course
that there can be nothing of the kind, till the thing is
done. Any caution on the matter is therefore difficult and
disagreeable, as conveying almost an insult. Mothers in
well-regulated families do not caution their daughters in
reference to special young men. SHHOH 69, VIII.

But evils such as that [falling in love] do admit of
remedy. It is not every girl that can marry the man whom
she first confesses that she loves. SHHOH 136, XIV.

There is nothing in the first flush of acknowledged love
that is sweeter to the woman than this [a reversal of those
social rules by which the man is ordered to wait upon the
woman]. All the men around her are her servants; but in
regard to this man she may have the inexpressibly greater
pleasure of serving him herself. RalH 353, XLVII.

Now that [knowing that she 'possessed a divinity which made
the ground she stood upon holy ground for him'] is a conviction very pleasant to a young woman....It is so much for
a girl to be sure that she is really loved!
RalH 364, XLVIII.

A homely brow, and plain features, and locks of hair that
have not been combed by Love's attendant nymphs into soft
and winning tresses, seems to tell us that Love is not
wanted by the bosom that owns them. We teach ourselves to
regard such a one, let her be ever so good, with ever so
sweet temper, ever so generous in heart, ever so affectionate among her friends, as separated alike from the
perils and the privileges of that passion without which they
who are blessed or banned with beauty would regard life but
as a charred and mutilated existence. It is as though we
should believe that passion springs from the rind, which is
fair or foul to the eye, and not in the heart, which is
often fairest, freshest, and most free, when the skin is
dark and the cheeks are rough. RalH 429, LVII.

It is a great nuisance, a loss that maims the whole life,--
[unrequited love] a misfortune to be much regretted. But
because the leg is gone, everything is not gone. A man with
a wooden leg may stump about through much action, and may
enjoy the keenest pleasures of humanity. He has his eyes
left to him, and his ears, and his intellect. He will not
break his heart for the loss of that leg. ED 26, III,I.

To be in love, as an absolute, well-marked, acknowledged
fact, is the condition of a woman more frequently and more
readily than of a man. Such is not the common theory on the
matter, as it is the man's business to speak, and the
woman's business to be reticent. And the woman is presumed

to have kept her heart free from any load of love, till she
may accept the burthen with an assurance that it shall
become a joy and a comfort to her. But such presumptions,
though they may be very useful for the regulation of
conduct, may not be always true. It comes more within the
scope of a woman's mind, than that of a man's, to think
closely and decide sharply on such a matter. With a man it
is often chance that settles the question for him. He
resolves to propose to a woman, or proposes without
resolving, because she is close to him....
     Moreover, it frequently happens with men that they fail
to analyse these things, and do not make out for themselves
any clear definition of what their feelings are or what they
mean....It is simply friendship. And yet were his friend to
tell him that she intended to give herself in marriage elsewhere, he would suffer all the pangs of jealousy, and would
imagine himself to be horribly ill-treated. To have such a
friend,--a friend whom he cannot or will not make his wife,
--is no injury to him. To him it is simply a delight, an
excitement in life, a thing to be known to himself only and
not talked of to others, a source of pride and inward
exultation....It is, indeed, death to her;--but he does not
know it. ED 31-2, IV,I.

No girl likes to be warned against falling in love, whether
the warning be needed or not needed. ED 58, VII,I.

A woman never so dearly loves a man as when he confesses
that he has been on the brink of a great crime,--but has re-
frained, and has not committed it. ED 111, XII,I.

There are many men, and some women, who pass their lives
without knowing what it is to be or to have been in love.
They not improbably marry,--the men do, at least,--and make
good average husbands. Their wives are useful to them, and
they learn to feel that a woman, being a wife, is entitled
to all the respect, protection, and honour which a man can
give, or procure for her. Such men, no doubt, often live
honest lives, are good Christians, and depart hence with
hopes as justifiable as though they had loved as well as
Romeo. But yet, as men, they have lacked a something, the
want of which has made them small and poor and dry. It has
never been felt by such a one that there would be triumph in
giving away everything belonging to him for one little
whispered, yielding word, in which there should be
acknowledgment that he had succeeded in making himself
master of a human heart. And there are other men,--very
many men,--who have felt this love, and have resisted it,
feeling it to be unfit that Love should be Lord of all.
ED 120, XIII,I.

If it were to be asserted here that a young man may be
perfectly true to a first young woman while he is falling in
love with a second, the readers of this story would probably
be offended. But undoubtedly many men believe themselves to
be quite true while undergoing this process, and many young

women expect nothing else from their lovers.  If only he
will come right at last, they are contented.  And if he
don't come right at all,--it is the way of the world, and
the game has to be played over again.  ED 218-9, XXIV,I.

There are men in whose love a good deal of hatred is mixed;
--who love as the huntsman loves the fox, towards the
killing of which he intends to use all his energies and
intellects.  ED 12, XLI,II.

Love will excuse roughness.  Spoken love will palliate even
spoken roughness.  ED 223, LXIV,II.

But of such stealing [of a heart in love]  it is always
better that no mention should be made till the theft has
been sanctified by free gift.  Till the loss has been spoken
of and acknowledged, it may in most cases be recovered.
EE 118, VII,I.

Let sorrow be ever so deep, and love ever so true, a man
will be cold who travels by winter, and hungry who has
travelled by night.  And a woman, who is a true, genuine
woman, always takes delight in ministering to the natural
wants of her friend.  To see a man eat and drink, and wear
his slippers, and sit at ease in his chair, is delightful to
the feminine heart that loves.  When I heard the other day
that a girl had herself visited the room prepared for a man
in her mother's house, then I knew that she loved him,
though I had never before believed it.  PR 95-6, XI,I.

There are both men and women to whom even the delays and
disappointments of love are charming, even when they exist
to the detriment of hope.  It is sweet to pine, sweet to
feel that they are now wretched after a romantic fashion as
have been those heroes and heroines of whose sufferings they
have read in poetry.  Way 74, VIII,I.

It is very hard for a woman to tell a lie to a man when she
loves him.  She may speak the words.  She may be able to
assure him that he is indifferent to her.  But when a woman
really loves a man,...there is a desire to touch him which
quivers at her fingers' ends, a longing to look at him which
she cannot keep out of her eyes, an inclination to be near
him which affects every motion of her body.  She cannot
refrain herself from excessive attention to his words.  She
has a god to worship, and she cannot control her admiration.
PrM 256, LXVII,II.

When a young man tells a young woman that she is the most
charming human being in the world, he is certainly using
peculiar language.  In most cases the young man would be
supposed to be making love to the young woman.
IHP 9, XXXIII,II.

...that affectation of love and anger which some women know

how to assume, and which so few men know how to withstand.
IHP 24, XXXV,II.

But still, still it is so poor a thing to miss your plum
because you do not dare to shake the tree! It is especially
so if you are known as a professional stealer of plums!
IHP 113, XLIII,II.

For such love as that   [a man thoroughly earnest in his
love]  it is impossible that a girl should not be grateful.
AS 174, XXVI.

Men may often do much   [by way of making girls fall in love]
without knowing that they do anything.   AS 202, XXX.

I doubt whether men ever are in love with girls who throw
themselves into their arms.  A man's love, till it has been
chastened and fastened by the feeling of duty which marriage
brings with it, is instigated mainly by the difficulty of
pursuit.  'It is hardly possible that anything so sweet as
that should ever be mine; and yet, because I am a man, and
because it is so heavenly sweet, I will try.'  That is what
men say to themselves.  AS 273, XL.

A man cannot walk when he has broken his ankle-bone, let him
be ever so brave in the attempt.  AS 363, LIII.

How is it possible that a man should tell a girl that he has
not loved her, when he has embraced her again and again?  He
may know it, and she may know it;--and each may know that
the other knows it;--but to say that he does not and did not
then love her is beyond the scope of his audacity,--unless
he be a heartless Nero.  AS 464, LXVII.

It is not without a pang that anyone can be told that she
who is of all the dearest has some other one who to her is
the dearest.   Such pain fathers and mothers have to
bear....The mother knows that it is good that her child
should love some man better than all the world beside, and
that she should be taken away to become a wife and a
mother.  And the father, when that delight of his eyes
ceases to assure him that he is her nearest and dearest,
though he abandon the treasure of that nearestness and
dearestness with a soft melancholy, still knows that it is
as it should be.  Of course that other 'him' is the person
she loves best in the world.  Were it not so how evil a
thing it would be that she should marry him!  Were it not so
with reference to some 'him,' how void would her life be!
DuC 66-7, VIII.

When a man's love goes well with him,--so well as to be in
some degree oppressive to him even by its prosperity,--when
the young lady has jumped into his arms and the father and
mother have been quite willing, then he wants no confidant.
He does not care to speak very much of the matter which

among his friends is apt to become a subject for raillery.
DuC 182, XXIII.

When men in such matters have two strings to their bow, much
inconvenience is felt when the two become entangled.
DuC 319, XL.

[A]ffection,--of that kind of love which most of us have
been happy enough to give and receive, without intending to
show more than true friendship will allow at special
moments.  DuC 472, LIX.

Where is the young man who cannot do so  [transfer his heart
as well as his allegiance when told to];--how few are there
who do not do so when their first fit of passion has come on
them at one-and-twenty?  DuC 607, LXXVII.

To one who has thus entered in upon the heroism of romance
his own daily work, his dinners, clothes, income, father and
mother, sisters and brothers, his own street and house are
nothing.   Hunting, shooting, rowing, Alpine-climbing, even
speeches in Parliament,--if they perchance have been
attained to,--all become leather or prunella.   The heavens
have been opened to him, and he walks among them like a god.
DuC 618, LXXVIII.

What is a young man to say in such a position  [maneuvered
into a declaration by an ambitious mama]?   'I do not love
the young lady after that fashion, and therefore I must
decline.'   It requires a hero, and a cold-blooded hero, to
do that.  JC 14, I.

It shames no man to swear that he loves a woman when he has
ceased to love her;--but it does shame him to drop off from
the love which he has promised.  JC 90, XII.

A girl with large ankles is, one may suppose, as liable to
die for love as though she were as fine about her feet as a
thorough-bred filly; and there is surely no reason why a
true heart and a pair of cherry cheeks should not go
together.   But our imagination has created ideas in such
matters so fixed, that it is useless to contend against
them.   In our endeavours to produce effects, these ideas
should be remembered and obeyed.  JC 121, XVI.

It is so hard for a young man to speak of love, if there be
real love,--so impossible that a girl should do so!
AyA 34, IV.

[B]ut then perhaps the young men who do fall most absolutely
into love do not look like it.  AyA 59, VII.

It is not always like to like in love.   Titania loved the
weaver Bottom with the ass's head.   Bluebeard, though a bad
husband, is supposed to have been fond of his last wife.
The Beauty has always been beloved by the Beast. AyA 59,VII.

A girl loves most often because she is loved,--not from choice on her part. She is won by the flattery of the man's desire. AyA 154-5, XVII.

The merit is to despair and yet to be constant. When a man has reason to be assured that a young lady is very fond of him, he may always hope that love will follow,--unless indeed the love which he seeks has been already given away elsewhere. AyA 594, LXI.

There is no barrier in a girl's heart so strong against love as the feeling that the man in question stands in awe of her. MF 46, IV,I.

It is not the girl that the man loves, but the image which imagination has built up for him to fill the outside covering which has pleased his senses. MF 230, XXI,I.

But, as it will sometimes be that a man shall in his flesh receive a fatal injury, of which he shall for awhile think that only some bruise has pained him, some scratch annoyed him; that a little time, with ointment and a plaister, will give him back his body as sound as ever; but then after a short space it becomes known to him that a deadly gangrene is affecting his very life; so will it be with a girl's heart. MF 234, XXI,I.

When a young man has it in him to make love to a young lady, and is earnest in his intention, no duty, however paramount, should be held as a restraint. MSF 207-8, XV,I.

## LOVE, OLD MAN'S

Young man, young friend of mine, who art now filled to the overflowing of thy brain with poetry, with chivalry, and love, thou seest seated opposite to thee there that grim old man, with long snuffy nose, with sharp piercing eyes, with scanty frizzled hairs. He is rich and cross, has been three times married, and has often quarrelled with his children. He is fond of his wine, and snores dreadfully after dinner. To thy seeming he is a dry, withered stick, from which all the sap of sentiment has been squeezed by the rubbing and friction of years. Poetry, the feeling if not the words of poetry,--is he not dead to it, even as the pavement is dead over which his wheels trundle? Oh, my young friend! thou art ignorant in this--as in most other things. He may not twitter of sentiment, as thou doest; nor may I trundle my hoop along the high road as do the little boys. The fitness of things forbids it. But that old man's heart is as soft as thine, if thou couldst but read it. The body dries up and withers away, and the bones grow old; the brain, too, becomes decrepit, as do the sight, the hearing, and the soul. But the heart that is tender once remains tender to the last. OrF 264-5, XXVI,I.

It is seldom that a young man may die from a broken heart;

but if an old man have a heart still left to him, it is **more**
fragile.   OrF   373, LXXVI,II.

## LOVE MAKING

Young men in such matters  [making love]   are so often without any fixed thoughts!   They are such absolute moths.   They
amuse themselves with the light of the beautiful candle,
fluttering about, on and off, in and out of the flame with
dazzled eyes, till in a rash moment they rush in too near
the wick, and then fall with singed wings and crippled legs,
burnt up and reduced to tinder by the consuming fire of
matrimony.   FrP 195, XX.

Nature had given him that art  [love making easily], as she
does give to some, withholding it from many.  Cl 130, XVI.

Making love to a sweet, soft, blushing, willing, though
silent girl is a pleasant employment; but the task of
declaring love to a stony-hearted, obdurate, ill-conditioned
Diana is very disagreeable for any gentleman.  And it is the
more so when the gentleman really loves,--or thinks that he
loves,--his Diana.  PR 118, LIII,II.

There is an obligation on a man to persevere when a woman
has encouraged him in love-making.  It is like riding at a
fence.  When once you have set your horse at it you must go
on, however impracticable it may appear as you draw close to
it.   If you have never looked at the fence at all,--if you
have ridden quite the other way, making for some safe gate
or clinging to the dull lane,--then there will be no excitement, but also there will be no danger and no disgrace.
JC 62, VIII.

## LOVERS

Oaths between lovers are but Cupid's phrases, made to enable
them to talk of love.  They are the playthings of love, as
kisses are.  When lovers trust each other they are sweet
bonds; but they will never bind those who do not trust....
Never know a gentleman's moods, never understand his
feelings till, in the plain language of his mother-tongue,
he has asked you to be mistress of them.  Ber 72, IV.

[S]o few men ever do acknowledge till the words that they
have said make it necessary that they should ask themselves
whether those words are true.  Ber 173, X.

There are certainly some privileges which an accepted lover
may take in a house, and no one but an accepted lover.
Ber 270, XV.

How very many young gentlemen have made the same soliloquy
[saying that she is cold as she is beautiful]  when their
mistresses have not been so liberal as they would have had
them!  Ber 300, XVII.

We--speaking for the educated male sex in England--do not
like to think that any one should tamper with the ladies
whom we love.  Ber 348, XIX.

How is it that girls are so potent to refuse such favours
[as kisses]   at one time, and so impotent in preventing
their exaction at another?  Ber 507, XXVIII.

Oh, those lovers' rambles!   A man as he grows old can
perhaps teach himself to regret but few of the sweets which
he is compelled to leave behind him....The polka and the
waltz were once joyous; but he sees now that the work was
warm, and that one was often compelled to perform it in
company for which one did not care.   Those picnics too were
nice; but it may be a question whether a good dinner at his
own dinner-table is not nicer.   Though fat and over forty he
may still ride to hounds, and as for boating and cricketing,
after all they were but boy's play.   For those things one's
soul does not sigh.   But, ah!  those lovers' walks, those
loving lovers' rambles....If there be an Elysium on earth,
it is this.   They are done and over for us, oh, my
compatriots!   Never again, unless we are destined to rejoin
our houris in heaven, and to saunter over fields of asphodel
in another and a greener youth--never again shall those joys
be ours!   And what can ever equal them?   'Twas then, between
sweet hedgerows, under green oaks, with our feet rustling on
the crisp leaves, that the world's cold reserve was first
thrown off, and we found that those we loved were not
goddesses made of buckram and brocade, but human beings like
ourselves, with blood in their veins, and hearts in their
bosoms--veritable children of Adam like ourselves.
      'Gin a body meet a body comin' through the rye.'   Ah,
how delicious were those meetings!...[A]ll that is done and
over for us.  We shall never gang that gait' again.
      There is a melancholy in this that will tinge our
thoughts, let us draw ever so strongly on our philosophy.
We can still walk with our wives;--and that is pleasant too,
very--of course.   But there was more animation in it when we
walked with the same ladies under other nanes.   Nay, sweet
spouse, mother of dear bairns, who hast so well done thy
duty; but this was so let thy brows be knit never so
angrily.   That lord of thine has been indifferently good to
thee, and thou to him hast been more than good.   Up-hill
together have ye walked peaceably labouring; and now arm-in-
arm ye shall go down the gradual slope which ends below
there in the green churchyard.   'Tis good and salutary to
walk thus.   But for the full cup of joy, for the brimming
spring-tide of human bliss, oh, give me back, give me back
-- -- --!   Well, well, well, it is nonsense; I know it; but
may not a man dream now and again in his evening nap and yet
do no harm?...
      Dost thou not envy that smirk young knave with his five
lustrums, though it goes hard with him to purchase his kid-
gloves?   He dines for one-and-twopence at an eating-house;
but what cares Maria where he dines?   He rambles through the
rye with his empty pockets, and at the turn of the field-

path Maria will be there to meet him.  Envy him not; thou
hast had thy walk; but lend him rather that thirty shillings
that he asks of thee.  So shall Maria's heart be glad as she
accepts his golden brooch.  Ber 512-4, XXVIII.

I believe there is no period of life so happy as that in
which a thriving lover leaves his mistress after his first
success....But when the promise has once been given to him,
and he is able to escape into the domain of his own heart,
he is as a conqueror who has mastered half a continent by
his own strategy.
   It never occurs to him, he hardly believes, that his
success is no more than that which is the ordinary lot of
mortal man.  He never reflects that all the old married
fogies whom he knows and despises, have just as much ground
for pride, if such pride were enduring; that every fat,
silent, dull, somnolent old lady whom he sees and quizzes,
has at some period been deemed as worthy a prize as his
priceless galleon; and so deemed by as bold a captor as
himself.
   Some one has said that every young mother, when her
first child is born, regards the babe as the most wonderful
production of that description which the world has yet seen.
And this too is true.  But I doubt even whether that
conviction is so strong as the conviction of the young
successful lover, that he has achieved a triumph which
should ennoble him down to late generations.  As he goes
along he has a contempt for other men; for they know nothing
of such glory as his.  As he pores over his 'Blackstone,' he
remembers that he does so, not so much that he may acquire
law, as that he may acquire Fanny; and then all other porers
over 'Blackstone' are low and mean in his sight--are
mercernary in their views and unfortunate in their ideas,
for they have no Fanny in view.  CasR 229-30, XII,I.

But then do not all despondent lovers hold that opinion
[that she will not change her mind]   of their own
mistresses?  OrF 383, XXXVIII,I.

The sorrows of Lydia*in the play when she finds that her
passion meets with general approbation are very absurd, but,
nevertheless, are quite true to nature.  Lovers would be
great losers if the path of love were always to run smooth.
Under such a dispensation, indeed, there would probably be
no lovers.  The matter would be too tame.  [*The Rivals,
Sheridan]   OrF 170, LVII,II.

There are men who are much too forward in believing that
they are regarded with favour; but there are others of whom
it may be said that they are as much too backward.  The
world hears most of the former, and talks of them the most,
but I doubt whether the latter are not the more numerous.
OrF 297, LXIX,II.

There are cases in which lovers present themselves in so un-
mistakable guise, that the first word of open love uttered

by them tells their whole story, and tells it without the possibility of a surprise. And it is generally so when the lover has not been an old friend, when even his acquaintance has been of modern date. SmaH 392, XXXIX.

There is your bold lover, who knocks his lady-love over as he does a bird, and who would anathematise himself all over, and swear that his gun was distraught, and look about as though he thought the world was coming to an end, if he missed to knock over his bird. And there is your timid lover, who winks his eyes when he fires, who has felt certain from the moment in which he buttoned on his knicker-bockers that he at any rate would kill nothing, and who, when he hears the loud congratulations of his friends, cannot believe that he really did bag that beautiful winged thing by his own prowess. The beautiful winged thing which the timid man carries home in his bosom, declining to have it thrown into a miscellaneous care, so that it may never be lost in a common crowd of game, is better to him than are the slaughtered hecatombs to those who kill their birds by the hundred. SmaH 393, XXXIX.

But Jove smiles at lovers' perjuries;--and it is well that he should do so, as such perjuries can hardly be avoided altogether in the difficult circumstances of a successful gentleman's life. PF 145, XVI,I.

I am afraid that he did not doubt her answer,--as it would be good that all lovers should do. PF 267, LXVI,II.

It is the instinct of the lover to know that his mistress has given him her heart heartily, when she does not deny the gift with more than sternness,--with cold cruelty.
LT 273, VI.

A month is quite long enough to realise the pleasure of a new lover, but it may be doubted whether the intimacy of a brother does not take a very much longer period for its creation. VOB 108, XVI.

When it comes to this, that a pair of lovers are content to sit and rub their feathers together like two birds, there is not much more need of talking. VOB 129, XVIII.

A man is bound to take a woman's decision against him, bear it as he may, and say as little against it as possible. He is bound to do so when he is convinced that a woman's decision is final! and there can be no stronger proof of such finality than the fact that she has declared a preference for some other man. VOB 200, XXIX.

In such cases [pursuing a rival lover], the knight who is to be the deliverer desires above all things that he may be near his enemy. VOB 201-2, XXIX.

...leaning upon him somewhat heavily for a minute, as girls

do when they want to show that they claim the arm that they lean on as their own.    VOB 217, XXXI.

In ordinary cases it is probably common for a lady, when she has yielded to a gentleman's entreaties for the gift of herself, to yield also something further for his immediate gratification, and to submit herself to his embrace. VOB 358, L.

On all such occasions interviews are bad.    The teller of this story ventures to take the opportunity of recommending parents in such cases always to refuse interviews, not only between the young lady and the lover who is to be excluded, but also between themselves and the lover.    The vacillating tone...is perceived and understood, and at once utilized, by the least argumentative of lovers, even by lovers who are obtuse.    The word 'never' may be so pronounced as to make the young lady's twenty thousand pounds full present value for ten in the lover's pocket.    There should be no arguments, no letters, no interviews; and the young lady's love should be starved by the absence of all other mention of the name, and by the imperturbable good humour on all other matters of those with whom she comes in contact in her own domestic circle.    If it be worth anything, it won't be starved; but if starving to death be possible, that is the way to starve it.    SHHOH 188-9, XIX.

An unmarried man who is willing to sacrifice himself is, in feminine eyes, always worthy of ribbons and a chaplet. ED 348, LXXVII,II.

The Adelaide Pallisers of the world have a way of making themselves uncommonly unpleasant to a man when they refuse him for the third or fourth time.    They allow themselves sometimes to express a contempt which is almost akin to disgust, and to speak to a lover as though he were no better than a footman.    And then the lover is bound to bear it all, and when he has borne it, finds it so very difficult to get out of the room.    PR 116, LIII,II.

When young ladies quarrel with their lovers it is always presumed, especially in books, that they do not wish to get them back.    It is to be understood that the loss to them is as nothing.    Miss Smith begs that Mr. Jones may be assured that he is not to consider her at all.    If he is pleased to separate, she will be at any rate quite as well pleased,-- probably a great deal better.    No doubt she had loved him with all her heart, but that will make no difference to her, if he wishes,--to be off.    Upon the whole Miss Smith thinks that she would prefer such an arrangement, in spite of her heart.    PR 258, LXIX,II.

When a girl once hesitates with a lover, she has as good as surrendered.    To say even that she will think of it, is to accept the man.    LA 252-3, XXIV.

The English girl living in a town--or even in what we call
the country--has no need to think of any special man till
some special man thinks of her. Men are fairly plentiful,
and if one man does not come another will....But in the bush
the thing is very different. It may be that there is no
young man available within fifty miles--no possible lover or
future husband, unless Heaven should interfere almost with a
miracle. To those to whom lovers are as plentiful as black-
berries it may seem indelicate to surmise that the thought
of such a want should ever enter a girl's head.
HHOG 150, XII.

There are a thousand little silly softnesses which are
pretty and endearing between acknowledged lovers, with which
no woman would like to dispense, to which even men who are
in love submit sometimes with delight; but which in other
circumstances would be vulgar,--and to the woman distasteful. There are closenesses and sweet approaches, smiles and
nods, and pleasant winkings, whispers, innuendos and hints,
little mutual admirations and assurances that there are
things known to those two happy ones of which the world
beyond is altogether ignorant. Much of this comes of
nature, but something of it sometimes comes by art.
Way 260, XXVII,I.

There are rejected lovers who, merely because they are
lovers, become subject to the scorn and even to the disgust
of the girls they love. But again there are men who, even
when they are rejected, are almost loved, who are considered
to be worthy of all reverence, almost of worship;--and yet
the worshippers will not love them. PrM 154, XVII,I.

[B]ut we know that for 'lovers lacking matter, the clean-
liest shift is to kiss.' In such moments silence charms,
and almost any words are unsuitable except those soft, bird-
like murmurings of love which, sweet as they are to the ear,
can hardly be so written as to be sweet to the reader.
PrM 222, XXIII,I.

I don't know how a gentleman is to do so [speak to his
lover] in the presence of her father, and mother, and
sisters. AS 19, III.

To a girl whose life is full of delights her lover need not
be so very much,--need not, at least, be everything. Though
he be a lover to be loved at all points, her friends will be
something, her dancing, her horse, her theatre-going, her
brothers and sisters, even her father and mother. AyA 35,IV.

Who does not know the way in which a man may set himself at
work to gain admission into a woman's heart without
addressing hardly a word to herself? And who has not noted
the sympathy with which the woman has unconsciously accepted
the homage? That pressing of the hand, that squeezing of
the arm, that glancing of the eyes, which are common among
lovers, are generally the developed consequences of former

indications which have had their full effect, even though
they were hardly understood, and could not have been acknowledged, at the time.  MF 221-2, XX,I.

But still a lover can hardly be satisfied with the world unless he can see some point in his heaven from which light
may be expected to break through the clouds. MF 231-2,XXI,I.

What woman is there will not forgive her lover for coming,
even though he certainly should not have come?  What woman
is there will fail to receive a stranger with hard looks
when a stranger shall appear to her instead of an expected
lover?  MF 250, XXIII,I.

A lover in China, or waging wars in Zululand or elsewhere
among the distant regions, is a misfortune.  A lover ought
to be at hand, ready at the moment, to be kissed or scolded,
to wait upon you, or, so much sweeter still, to be waited
upon, just as the occasion may serve.  But the lover in
China is better than one in the next street or the next
parish,--or only a few miles off by railway,--whom you may
not see.  The heart recognizes the necessity occasioned by
distance with a sweet softness of tender regrets, but is
hardened by mutiny, or crushed by despair in reference to
stern parents or unsuitable pecuniary circumstances.
MF 35-6, III,II.

The happiness and pride of a girl in her lover is something
wonderful to behold.  He is surely the only man, and she the
only woman born worthy of such a man.  She is to be the
depository of all his secrets, and the recipient of all his
thoughts.  That other young ladies should accept her with
submission in this period of her ecstasy would be surprising
were it not that she is so truly exalted by her condition as
to make her for a short period an object to them of genuine
worship.  Kept 1,I.

When a girl really loves her lover, the very atmosphere
tells of his wherabouts.  MSF 264, LXI,III.

A lover who is anxious to prevail with a lady should always
hold up his head.  Where is the writer of novels, or of
human nature, who does not know as much as that?  And yet
the man who is in love, truly in love, never does hold up
his head very high.  It is the man who is not in love who
does so.  Nevertheless it does sometimes happen that the
true lover obtains his reward.  MSF 312, LXIV,III.

How is it that a girl understands to a certainty the state
of a man's heart in regard to her,--or rather, not his
heart, but his purpose?  A girl may believe that a man loves
her, and may be deceived; but she will not be deceived as to
whether he wishes to marry her.  OML 28-9, III.

## LUNCH

A convivial lunch I hold to be altogether bad, but the worst of its many evils is that vacillating mind which does not know when to take its owner off.  DuC 503-4, LXX.

The rising and getting away from luncheon is always a great difficulty,--so great a difficulty when there are guests that lunch should never be much a company festival.  There is no provision for leaving the table as there is at dinner. AA 179, XIX.

## LUTHERANS

Nuremberg is one of those German cities in which a stranger finds it difficult to understand the religious idiosyncrasies of the people.  It is in Bavaria, and Bavaria, as he knows, is Roman Catholic.  But Nuremberg is Protestant, and the stranger, when he visits the two cathedrals--those of St. Sebald and St. Lawrence--finds it hard to believe that they should not be made to resound with masses, so like are they in all respects to other Romanist cathedrals which he has seen.  But he is told that they are Lutheran and Protestant, and he is obliged to make himself aware that the prevailing religion of Nuremberg is Lutheran, in spite of what to him are the Catholic appearances of the churches. LT 201, I.

## LUXURIES

There were ornaments about, and pretty toys, and a thousand knick-knacks which none but the rich can possess, and which none can possess even among the rich unless they can give taste as well as money to their acquisition.  Cl 54-5, VII.

## M

## MAGISTRATES

County magistrates, as a rule, are more conspicuous for common sense and good instincts than for sound law. VOB 130, XIX.

## MAHOMEDAN

I believe that, as a rule, a Mahomedan hates a Christian: regarding him merely as Christian, he certainly does so.... In Syria no Christian is admitted within a mosque, for his foot and touch are considered to carry pollution. Ber 681, XXXVIII.

## MALADIES

There are certain maladies which make the whole body sore. The patient, let him be touched on any point--let him even be nearly touched--will roar with agony as though his whole body had been bruised. So it is with maladies of the mind. SmaH 323, XXXIII.

## MAN

A perfect man, we are told, would be a monster. LaV 3, I.

## MAN...MEN

A man cannot change as men change. Individual men are like the separate links of a rotatory chain. The chain goes on with continuous easy motion as though every part of it were capable of adapting itself to a curve, but not the less is each link as stiff and sturdy as any other piece of wrought iron. RacR 228, XVIII.

## MANHOOD

Who was ever called upon for a stronger proof of manhood than this [finding out that one is illegitimate]? In nine cases out of ten it is not for oneself that one has to be brave....But we are all so mixed up and conjoined with others--with others who are weaker and dearer than ourselves, that great sorrows do require great powers of endurance.
CasR 152, VIII,II.

## MANLINESS

The property of manliness is a great possession, but perhaps there is none that is less understood....The woman's error, occasioned by her natural desire for a master, leads her to look for a certain outward magnificence of demeanour, a pretended indifference to stings and little torments, a would-be superiority to the bread-and-butter side of life, an unreal assumption of personal grandeur....That personal bravery is required in the composition of manliness must be conceded, though, of all the ingredients needed, it is the lowest in value. But the first requirement of all must be described by a negative. Manliness is not compatible with affectation....The self-conscious assumption of any outward manner, the striving to add,--even though it be but a tenth of a cubit to the height,--is fatal, and will at once banish the all but divine attribute. Before the man can be manly, the gifts which make him so must be there, collected by him slowly, unconsciously, as are his bones, his flesh, and his blood. They cannot be put on like a garment for the nonce, --as may a little learning. A man cannot become faithful to his friends, unsuspicious before the world, gentle with women, loving with children, considerate to his inferiors, kindly with servants, tender-hearted with all,--and at the

same time be frank, of open speech, with springing eager
energies,--simply becasue he desires it.  These things,
which are the attributes of manliness, must come of training
on a nature not ignoble.  But they are the very opposites,
the antipodes, the direct antagonism, of that staring,
posed, bewhiskered and bewigged deportment, that nil admirari, self-remembering assumption of manliness, that endeavour of twopence halfpenny to look as high as threepence,
which, when you prod it through, has in it nothing deeper
than deportment.  We see the two things daily, side by side,
close to each other.  Let a man put his hat down, and you
shall say whether he has deposited it with affectation or
true nature.  The natural man will probably be manly.  The
affected man cannot be so.  PR 251-2, LXVIII,II.

## MANNERS, ENGLISH

In this respect we Englishmen might certainly learn much
from the manners of our dear allies  [paying the greater
share of attention to the elder ladies].  We know well
enough how to behave ourselves to our fair young country-
women; we can be civil enough to young women--nature teaches
us that; but it is so seldom that we are sufficiently complaisant to be civil to old women.  And yet that, after all,
is the soul of gallantry.  It is to the sex that we profess
to do homage.  Our theory is, that feminine weakness shall
receive from man's strength humble and respectful service.
But where is the chivalry, where the gallantry, if we only
do service in expectation of receiving such guerdon as rosy
cheeks and laughing eyes can bestow.  TC 297, XXV.

## MANOEUVRES

But in such a matter  [finding the opportunity to allow a
man to propose]  it is so hard to act without seeming to
act!  She who can manoeuvre on such a field without dis-
playing her manoeuvres is indeed a general.  RalH 427, LVII.

## MARQUISES

Marquises, though they may have large properties, are not
always in possession of any number of loose hundreds which
they can throw away without feeling the loss. VOB 521,LXXII.

## MARRIAGE

Oh, husbands, oh, my marital friends, what great comfort is
there to be derived from a wife well obeyed!  BaT 417,XLIII.

It may be a question whether men, in marrying, do not become
too prudent.  A single man may risk anything, says the
world; but a man with a wife should be sure of his means.
Why so?  A man and a woman are but two units.  A man and a
woman with ten children are but twelve units.  It is sad to

see a man starving--sad to see a woman starving--very sad to
see children starving. But how often does it come to pass
that the man who will work is seen begging his bread? we
may almost say never--unless, indeed, he be a clergyman.
Let the idle man be sure of his wife's bread before he
marries her; but the working man, one would say, may generally trust to God's goodness without fear. TC 391, XXXI.

And then the marriage was again put off. This, in itself,
was a great misery, as young ladies who have just been
married, or who may now be about to be married, will surely
own. The words 'put off' are easily written, the necessity
of such a 'put off' is easily arranged in the pages of a
novel;...but, nevertheless, a matrimonial 'put off' is,
under any circumstances, a great grief. To have to counter-
write those halcyon notes which have given glad promise of
the coming event; to pack up and put out of sight, and, if
possible, out of mind, the now odious finery with which the
house has for the last weeks been strewed; to give the
necessary information to the pastry-cook, from whose counter
the sad tidings will be disseminated through all the neighbourhood; to annul the orders which have probably been given
for rooms and horses for the happy pair;...all these things
in themselves make up a great grief, which is hardly
lightened by the knowledge that they have been caused by a
still greater grief. TC 460, XXXVII.

We may imagine that eagles find it difficult to pair when
they become scarce in their localities; and we all know how
hard it has sometimes been to get comme il faut husbands
when there has been any number of Protestant princesses on
hand. DoT 461, XXXIX.

There never was a fox yet without a tail who would not be
delighted to find himself suddenly possessed of that
appendage. Never; let the untailed fox have been ever so
sincere in his advice to his friends! We are all of us, the
good and the bad, looking for tails--for one tail, or for
more than one; we do so too often by ways that are mean
enough; but perhaps there is no tail-seeker more mean, more
sneakingly mean, than he who looks out to adorn his bare
back with a tail by marriage. DoT 545, XLVI.

No educated woman, we may suppose, stands at the altar as a
bride, without having read and re-read those words till they
are closely fixed on her memory. It is a great oath, and a
woman should know well what that is to which she is about to
pledge herself. Ber 551, XXX.

It is reported that unmarried ladies...generally regret the
forlornness of their own condition. If so, the fault is not
their own, but must be attributed to the social system to
which they belong. The English world is pleased to say that
an unmarried lady past forty has missed her hit in life--has
omitted to take her tide at the ebb; and what can unmarried
ladies do but yield to the world's dictum? That the English

world may become better informed, and learn as speedily as
may be to speak with more sense on the subject, let us all
pray.  Ber 586, XXXII.

[O]rdinary young ladies are merely married, but those of
real importance are established....Mothers sometimes depre-
ciate their wares by an undue solicitude to dispose of them.
FrP 106, XI.

It is certainly the fact that high contracting parties do
sometimes allow themselves a latitude which would be considered dishonest by contractors of a lower sort.
FrP 164, XVII.

As for feast of reason and for flow of soul, is it not a
question whether any such flows and feasts are necessary between a man and his wife?...But a handsome woman at the head
of your table, who knows how to dress, and how to sit, and
how to get in and out of her carriage--who will not disgrace
her lord by her ignorance, or fret him by her coquetry, or
disparage him by her talent--how beautiful a thing it is!
FrP 464, XLVIII.

I will not say that the happiness of marriage is like the
Dead Sea fruit--an apple which, when eaten, turns to bitter
ashes in the mouth.   Such pretended sarcasm would be very
false.   Nevertheless, is it not the fact that the sweetest
morsel of love's feast has been eaten, that the freshest,
fairest blush of the flower has been snatched and has passed
away, when the ceremony at the altar has been performed, and
legal possession has been given?   There is an aroma of love,
an undefinable delicacy of flavour, which escapes and is
gone before the church portal is left, vanishing with the
maiden name, and incompatible with the solid comfort appertaining to the rank of wife.   To love one's own spouse, and
to be loved by her, is the ordinary lot of man, and is a
duty exacted under penalties.   But to be allowed to love
youth and beauty that is not one's own...can it be that a
man is made happy when a state of anticipation such as this
is brought to a close?   No; when the husband walks back from
the altar, he has already swallowed the choicest dainties of
his banquet.   The beef and pudding of married life are then
in store for him;--or perhaps only the bread and cheese.
Let him take care lest hardly a crust remain--or perhaps not
a crust.   FrP 465-6, XLVIII.

The idea that their fathers and mothers should marry and
enjoy themselves is always a thing horrible to be thought of
in the minds of the rising generation.   OrF 364, XXXVI,I.

It is the first rumpus of the thing, or rather the fear of
that, which keeps together many a couple.   OrF 6, XLI,II.

[S]he had stoutly declared her opinion that it was a young
woman's duty to get married.   For myself, I am inclined to
agree with her.   OrF 179, LVIII,II.

People often say that marriage is an important thing, and
should be much thought of in advance, and marrying people
are cautioned that there are many who marry in haste and
repent at leisure. I am not sure, however, that marriage
may not be pondered over too much; nor do I feel certain
that the leisurely repentance does not as often follow the
leisurely marriages as it does the rapid one. That some
repent no one can doubt; but I am inclined to believe that
most men and women take their lots as they find them,
marrying as the birds do by force of nature, and going on
with their mates with a general, though not perhaps an undisturbed satisfaction, feeling inwardly assured that
Providence, if it have not done the very best for them, has
done for them as well as they could do for themselves with
all the thought in the world. I do not know that a woman
can assure to herself, by her own prudence and taste, a good
husband any more than she can add two cubits to her stature;
but husbands have been made to be decently good,--and wives
too, for the most part, in our country,--so that the thing
does not require so much thinking as some people say.
CanY 109, XI,I.

I believe that a desire to get married is the natural state
of a woman at the age of--say from twenty-five to thirty-
five, and I think also that it is good for the world in
general that it should be so....There is, I know, a feeling
abroad among women that this desire is one of which it is
expedient that they should become ashamed; that it will be
well for them to alter their natures in this respect, and
learn to take delight in the single state. Many of the most
worthy women of the day are now teaching this doctrine, and
are intent on showing by precept and practice that an unmarried woman may have as sure a hold on the world, and a
position within it as ascertained, as may an unmarried man.
But I confess to an opinion that human nature will be found
to be too strong for them. Their school of philosophy may
be graced by a few zealous students--by students who will be
subject to the personal influence of their great masters--
but it will not be successful in the outer world. The truth
in the matter is too clear. A woman's life is not perfect
or whole till she has added herself to a husband.
     Nor is a man's life perfect or whole till he has added
to himself a wife; but the deficiency with the man, though
perhaps more injurious to him than its counterpart is to
the woman, does not, to the outer eye, so manifestly unfit
him for his business in the world....It is infinitely for
his advantage that he should be tempted to take to himself a
wife; and, therefore, for his sake if not for her own, the
philosophic preacher of single blessedness should break up
her classrooms, and bid her pupils go and do as their
mothers did before them.
     They may as well give up their ineffectual efforts, and
know that nature is too strong for them. The desire is
there; and any desire which has to be repressed with an
effort, will not have itself repressed unless it be in
itself wrong. MM 136-7, XI.

[B]ut a man of fifty should not be made to marry a woman by muslin and starch, if he be not prepared to marry her on other considerations.  MM 389, XXIX.

[G]entlemen, when they get married at fifty, are not expected to be graceful.  MM 401, XXX.

No man likes to be talked out of his marriage by his mother, and especially not so when the talking takes the shape of threats.  Bel 368, XXVIII.

What reader is there, male or female, of such stories as is this, who has not often discussed in his or her own mind the different sides of this question of love and marriage?  On either side enough may be said by any arguer to convince at any rate himself.  It must be wrong for a man, whose income is both insufficient and precarious also, not only to double his own cares and burdens, but to place the weight of that doubled burden on other shoulders besides his own,--on shoulders that are tender and soft, and ill adapted to the carriage of any crushing weight.  And then that doubled burden,--that burden of two mouths to be fed, of two backs to be covered, of two minds to be satisfied, is so apt to double itself again and again.  The two so speedily become four, and six!...As a man thinks of all this, if he chooses to argue with himself on that side, there is enough in the argument to make him feel that not only as a wise man but as an honest man, he had better let the young lady alone.  She is well as she is, and he sees around him so many who have tried the chances of marriage and who are not well!...
    But arguments on the other side are equally cogent, and so much more alluring!...Only the former line of thoughts occurred to him on a Saturday, when he was ending his week rather gloomily, and this other way of thinking on the same subject has come upon him on a Monday, as he is beginning his week with renewed hope.  Does this young girl of his heart love him?  And if so, their affection for each other being thus reciprocal, is she not entitled to an expression of her opinion and her wishes on this difficult subject?  And if she be willing to run the risk and to encounter the dangers,--to do so on his behalf, because she is willing to share everything with him,--is it becoming in him, a man, to fear what she does not fear?  If she be not willing let her say so.  If there be any speaking, he must speak first;--but she is entitled, as much as he is, to her own ideas respecting their great outlook into the affairs of the world.  And then is it not manifestly God's ordinance that a man should live together with a woman?...Of course there is a risk; but what excitement is there in anything in which there is none?  So on the Tuesday he speaks his mind to the young lady, and tells her candidly that there will be potatoes for the two of them,--sufficient, as he hopes, of potatoes, but no more.  As a matter of course the young lady replies that she for her part will be quite content to take the parings for her own eating.  Then they rush deliciously into each other's arms and the matter is settled.  For,

though the convictions arising from the former line of argument may be set aside as often as need be, those reached from the latter are generally conclusive. That such a settlement will always be better for the young gentleman and the young lady concerned than one founded on a sterner prudence is more than one may dare to say; but we do feel sure that that country will be most prosperous in which such leaps in the dark are made with the greatest freedom. HKHWR 314-6, XXXIII.

The old women are right in their views on this matter [that it be much best that young women should get themselves married]; and the young women, who on this point are not often refractory, are right also....But old women are never selfish in regard to the marriage of young women....The belief is so thorough that the woman would cease to be a woman, would already have become a brute, who would desire to keep any girl belonging to her out of matrimony for the sake of companionship to herself....A dependant, distant in blood, or a paid assistant, may find here and there a want of the true feminine sympathy; but in regard to a daughter, or one held as a daughter, it is never wanting. 'As the pelican loveth her young do I love thee; and therefore will I give thee away in marriage to some one strong enough to hold thee, even though my heartstrings be torn asunder by the parting.' Such is always the heart's declaration of the mother respecting her daughter. The match-making of mothers is the natural result of mother's love; for the ambition of one woman for another is never other than this,--that the one loved by her shall be given to a man to be loved more worthily. VOB 477-9, LXVII.

Whether marriages should be made in heaven or on earth, must be a matter of doubt to observers;--whether, that is, men and women are best married by chance, which I take to be the real fashion of heaven-made marriages; or should be brought into that close link and loving bondage to each other by thought, selection, and decision. That the heavenly mode prevails the oftenest there can hardly be a doubt. It takes years to make a friendship; but a marriage may be settled in a week,--in an hour. If you desire to go into partnership with a man in business, it is an essential necessity that you should know your partner; that he be honest,--or dis-honest, if such be your own tendency,--industrious, instructed in the skill required, and of habits of life fit for the work to be done. But into partnerships for life, of a kind much closer than any business partnership,--men rush without any preliminary inquiries....But in other respects everything is taken for granted. Let the woman, if possible, be pretty;--or if not pretty let her have style. Let the man, if possible, not be a fool; or, if a fool, let him not show his folly too plainly. As for knowledge of character, none is possessed, and none is wanted. The young people meet each other in their holiday dresses, on holiday occasions, amidst holiday pleasures,--and the thing is arranged. Such matches may be said to be heaven-made.

It is a fair question whether they do not answer better than those which have less of chance,--or less of heaven,--in their manufacture. If it be needful that a man and woman take five years to learn whether they will suit each other as husband and wife, and that then, at the end of the five years, they find that they will not suit, the freshness of the flower would be gone before it could be worn in the buttonhole. There are some leaps which you must take in the dark if you mean to jump at all. We can all understand well that a wise man should stand on the brink and hesitate; but we can understand also that a very wise man should declare to himself that with no possible amount of hesitation could certainty be achieved. Let him take the jump or not take it,--but let him not presume to think that he can so jump as to land himself in certain bliss. It is clearly God's intention that men and women should live together, and therefore let the leap in the dark by made. RalH 419-20, LVI.

All earls' daughters are not married at St. George's, Hanover Square, nor is it absolutely necessary that a bishop should tie the knot, or that the dresses should be described in a newspaper. LA 505, XLVIII.

Nothing perhaps is so efficacious in preventing men from marrying as the tone in which married women speak of the struggles made in that direction by their unmarried friends. Way 304, XXXII,I.

The mutual assent which leads to marriage should no doubt be spontaneous. Who does not feel that? Young love should speak from its first doubtful unconscious spark,--a spark which any breath of air may quench or cherish,--till it becomes a flame which nothing can satisfy but the union of the two lovers. No one should be told to love, or bidden to marry, this man or that woman. The theory of this is plain to us all, and till we have sons or daughters whom we feel imperatively obliged to control, the theory is unassailable. But the duty is so imperative! DuC 271, XXXIV.

King Copheta married the beggar's daughter....King Copheta probably had not a father; and the beggar, probably, was not high-minded. DuC 426, LIII.

Will the world of British young ladies be much scandalised if I say that such [the general desirability of marriage] is often an actuating motive? They would be justly scandalised if I pretended that many of its members were capable of...speedy transitions. AyA 573, LIX.

Faith, honesty, steadiness of purpose, joined to the warmest love and the truest heart, will not enable a husband to maintain the sweetness of that aroma which has filled with delight the senses of the girl who has leaned upon his arm as her permitted lover. AyA 630, LXIV.

The feeling is uncommon  [that a husband should supply all

that is needed and a wife should owe everything to the
husband]   just at present,--except with the millions who
neither have nor expect other money than what they earn.  If
you are told that the daughter of an old man who has earned
his own bread is about to marry a young man in the same
condition of life,  it is spoken of as a misfortune.
MF 286, XXVIII,II.

The threats of a single life made by pretty girls with good
fortunes never go for much in this world.  Kept 8, III.

To a girl, when it is proposed to her suddenly to change
everything in life, to go altogether away and place herself
under the custody of a new master, to find for herself a new
home, new pursuits, new aspirations, and a strange companion, the change must be so complete as almost to frighten
her by its awfulnes.  And yet it has to be always thought
of, and generally done.  MSF 126, X,I.

It is very hard for a young girl to have to be firm with her
mother in declining a proposed marriage, when all the circumstances of the connection are recommended to her as being
peculiarly alluring.  MSF 128, X,I.

## MARRIAGE BONDS

Many a man who is prone enough to escape from the bonds
which he has undertaken to endure,--to escape from them
before they are riveted,--is mild enough under their
endurance, when they are once fastened upon him.
Cl 236, XXVIII.

## MARRYING FOR MONEY

Such a feeling  [securing a comfortable income for the benefit of the family]   as this is very bitter when it first
impresses itself on a young mind.  To the old such plots and
plans, such matured schemes for obtaining the goods of this
world without the trouble of earning them, such long-headed
attempts to convert 'tuum' into 'meum,' are the ways of life
to which they are accustomed.  'Tis thus that many live, and
it therefore behoves all those who are well to do in the
world to be on their guard against those who are not.  With
them it is the success that disgusts, not the attempt.
BaT 413, XLII.

There is no doubt but that the privilege of matrimony offers
opportunities to money-loving young men which ought not to
be lightly abused.  Too many young men marry without giving
any consideration to the matter whatever.  It is not that
they are indifferent to money, but that they recklessly mis-
calculate their own value, and omit to look around and see
how much is done by those who are more careful.  A man can
be young but once, and, except in cases of a special interposition of Providence, can marry but once.  The chance once
thrown away may be said to be irrecoverable!  How, in after-

life, do men toil and turmoil through long years to attain
some prospect of doubtful advancement! Half that trouble,
half that care, a tithe of that circumspection would, in
early youth, have probably secured to them the enduring
comfort of a wife's wealth....
    [T]his might have been spared had the men made adequate
use of those opportunities which youth and youthful charms
afford once--and once only. There is no road to wealth so
easy and respectable as that of matrimony; that is, of
course, provided that the aspirant declines the slow course
of honest work. But then, we can so seldom put old heads on
young shoulders!  DoT 223-4, XVIII.

That marriage without love is a perilous step for any woman
who has a heart within her bosom. For those who have none--
or only so much as may be necessary for the ordinary blood-
circulating department--such an arrangement may be convenient enough.  Ber 637-8, XXXV.

Ah! young ladies, sweet young ladies, dear embryo mothers
of our England as it will be, think not overmuch of your
lovers' incomes. He that is true and honest will not have
to beg his bread--neither his nor yours....If a wholesome
loaf on your tables, and a strong arm round your waists, and
a warm heart to lean on cannot make you happy, you are not
the girls for whom I take you.  Ber 641, XXXV.

Miss Fitzgerald had strongly planted within her bosom the
prudent old-world notion, that young gentlefolks should not
love each other unless they have plenty of money; and that,
if unfortunately such did love each other, it was better
that they should suffer all the pangs of hopeless love than
marry and trust to God and their wits for bread and cheese.
To which opinion...I cannot subscribe myself an an adherent.
CasR 42, XLII,III.

That girls should not marry for money we are all agreed. A
lady who can sell herself for a title or an estate, for an
income or a set of family diamonds, treats herself as a
farmer treats his sheep and oxen--makes hardly more of herself, of her own inner self, in which are comprised a mind
and soul, than the poor wretch of her own sex who earns her
bread in the lowest stage of degradation. But a title, and
an estate, and an income, are matters which will weigh in
the balance with all Eve's daughters--as they do with all
Adam's sons. Pride of place, and the power of living well
in front of the world's eye, are dear to us all;--are,
doubtless, intended to be dear. Only in acknowledging so
much, let us remember that there are prices at which these
good things may be too costly.  FrP 202, XXI.

Did any man in love ever yet find himself able to tell the
lady whom he loved that he was very much disappointed on
discovering that she had got no money? If so, his courage,
I should say, was greater than his love.  SmaH 115, XII.

When a man marries an heiress for her money, if that money
be within her own control...it is generally well for the
speculating lover that the lady's friends should quarrel
with him and with her.  She is thereby driven to throw herself entirely into the gentleman's arms, and he thus becomes
possessed of the wife and the money without the abominable
nuisance of stringent settlements.  CanY 2, I,I.

Were not all men and women mercenary upon whom devolved the
necessity of earning their bread?  Cl 25, III.

Such a man almost naturally looks to marriage as an assistance in the dreary fight.  It soon becomes clear to him
that he cannot marry without money, and he learns to think
heiresses have been invented exactly to suit his case....He
has got himself, his position, and, perhaps, his title to
dispose of, and they are surely worth so much per annum.  As
for giving anything away, that is out of the question.  He
has not been so placed as to be able to give.  But, being an
honest man, he will, if possible, make a fair bargain.
ED 75-6, IX,I.

A man born to great wealth may,--without injury to himself
or friends,--do pretty nearly what he likes in regard to
marriage, always presuming that the wife he selects be of
his own rank.  He need not marry for money, nor need he
abstain from marriage because he can't support a wife without money.  And the very poor man....His wife's fortune will
consist in the labour of her hands, and in her ability to
assist him in his home.  But between these there is a middle
class of men, who, by reason of their education, are peculiarly susceptible to the charms of womanhood, but who
literally cannot marry for love, because their earnings will
do no more than support themselves.  ED 329, LXXVI,II.

It is only when we read of such men  [those who marry for
love without money]  that we feel that truth to his sweetheart is the first duty of man.  I am afraid that it is not
the advice which we give to our sons.  ED 330, LXXVI,II.

In such families, when such results have been achieved, it
is generally understood that matters shall be put right by
an heiress.  It has become an institution, like primogen-
iture, and is almost as serviceable for maintaining the
proper order of things.  Rank squanders money; trade makes
it;--and then trade purchases rank by re-gilding its splendour.  The arrangement, as it affects the aristocracy
generally, is well understood, and...quite approved of.
Way 59, LVII,II.

Now a young woman entering the world cannot make a greater
mistake than not to know her own line, or, knowing it, not
to stick to it.  Those who are thus weak are sure to fall
between two stools.  If a girl chooses to have a heart, let
her marry the man of her heart, and take her mutton-chops
and bread and cheese, her stuff gown and her six children,

as they may come.  But if she can decide that such horrors
are horrid to her, and that they must at any cost be
avoided, then let her take her Houghton when he comes, and
not hark back upon feelings and fancies, upon liking and
loving, upon youth and age.  If a girl has money and beauty
too, of course she can pick and choose.  IHP 114, XII,I.

Fifty years ago young men used to encounter the misery of
such questions,  [about income, prospects, and occupation]
and to live afterwards often in the enjoyment of the stern
questioner's money and daughters.  But there used in those
days to be a bad quarter of an hour while the questions were
being asked, and not unfrequently a bad six months afterwards, while the stern questioner was gradually undergoing a
softening process under the hands of the females of the
family.  But the young man of to-day has no bad quarter of
an hour.  'You are a mercantile old brick, with money and a
daughter.   I am a jeunesse doree,--gilded by blood and
fashion, though so utterly impecunious!   Let us know your
terms.  How much is it to be, and then I can say whether we
can afford to live upon it.'  The old brick surrenders himself more readily and speedily to the latter than to the
former manner;--but he hardly surrenders himself quite at
once.  AyA 126, XIV.

He must be a brave man who can stand up before a girl and
declare that he will love her for ever,--on condition that
she shall have so many thousand pounds; but he must be more
than brave, he will be heroic, who can do so in the presence
not only of the girl but of the girl's mother and married
sister as well.  AyA 567, LVIII.

## MASTER OF HOUNDS

But a master of hounds, if he have long held the country,
...obtains a power which that of no other potentate can
equal.  He may say and do what he pleases, and his tyranny
is always respected.  No conspiracy against him has a chance
of success; no sedition will meet with sympathy; --that is,
if he be successful in showing sport.  If a man be sworn at,
abused, and put down without cause, let him bear it and
think that he has been a victim for the public good.  And let
him never be angry with the master.  That rough tongue is
the necessity of the master's position.  They used to say
that no captain could manage a ship without swearing at his
men.  But what are the captain's troubles in comparison with
those of the master of hounds?  The captain's men are under
discipline, and can be locked up, flogged, or have their
grog stopped.  The master of hounds cannot stop the grog of
any offender, and he can only stop the tongue, or horse, of
such an one by very sharp words.  CanY 174, XVII,I.

A master of fox hounds is a necessity of the period....
    It is essential that a Master of Hounds should be some-
what feared by the men who ride with him.  There should be
much awe mixed with the love felt for him.  He should be a

man with whom other men will not care to argue; an irrational, cut and thrust, unscrupulous, but yet distinctly
honest man; one who can be tyrannical, but will tryrannise
only over the evil spirits; a man capable of intense cruelty
to those alongside of him, but who wil know whether his
victim does in truth deserve scalping before he draws his
knife.   He should be savage and yet good-humoured; severe
and yet forbearing; truculent and pleasant in the same
moment.   He should exercise unflinching authority, but
should do so with the consciousness that  he can support it
only by his own popularity.   His speech should be short,
incisive, always to the point, but never founded on argument.   His rules are based on no reason, and will never bear
discussion.   He must be the most candid of men, also the
most close;--and yet never a hypocrite.   He must condescend
to no explanation, and yet must impress men with an
assurance that his decisions will certainly be right.    He
must rule all as though no man's special welfare were of any
account, and yet must administer all so as to offend none.
Friends he must have, but not favourites.   He must be self-
sacrificing, diligent, eager, and watchful.   He must be
strong in health, strong in heart, strong in purpose, and
strong in purse.   He must be economical and yet lavish;
generous as the wind and yet obdurate as the frost.    He
should be assured that of all human pursuits hunting is the
best, and that of all living things a fox is the most valuable.   He must so train his heart as to feel for the fox a
mingled tenderness and cruelty which is inexplicable to
ordinary men and women.   His desire to preserve the brute
and then to kill him should be equally intense and passionate.   And he should do it all in accordance with a code of
unwritten laws, which cannot be learnt without profound
study.   PR 60-2, VII,I.

To a Master of Hounds the poisoning of one of his pack is
murder of the deepest dye.    There probably never was a
Master who in his heart of hearts would not think it right
that a detected culprit should be hung for such an offence.
And most Masters would go further than this, and declare
that in the absence of such detection the owner of the
covert in which the poison had been picked up should be held
to be responsible.   PR 121, XIV,I.

When the end of August comes, a Master of Hounds,--who is
really a master,--is wanted at home.   PR 315, LXXV,II.

## MASTERS

[B]ut, like other such imperious masters, he now found that
when trouble came the privilege of dictatorship brought with
it an almost insupportable burden.   HHOG 65, V.

## MATURITY

The flower that blows the quickest is never the sweetest.
The fruit that ripens tardily has ever the finest flavour.

It is often the same with men and women.  The lad who talks at twenty as men should talk at thirty, has seldom much to say worth hearing when he is forty; and the girl who at eighteen can shine in society with composure, has generally given over shining before she is a full-grown woman.
HKHWR 911, XCVII.

## MEALS, SICK HOUSE

...one of those sad sick-house meals which he or she who has not known must have been lucky indeed.  MM 181, XIV.

...such a dinner as is served in a house of invalids.
VOB 419, LVIII.

## MEANS...ENDS

[F]or human ends must be attained by human means.
BaT 54, VII.

...a belief as erroneous as, alas, it is common,--that first-rate results might be achieved by second-rate means.
PrM 347, XXXVII,I.

Many a man can fight his battle with good courage, but not with a doubting conscience.  War 51, V.

## MEN

Whatever man may have reached the age of forty unmarried without knowing something of such feelings  [regret at losing a woman to someone else]  must have been very successful or else very cold hearted.  BaT 283, XXX.

There are such men; men who can endure no taint on their personal self-respect, even from a woman;--men whose bodies are to themselves such sacred temples, that a joke against them is desecration, and a rough touch downright sacrilege.
BaT 392, XL.

He was exigeant, and perhaps even selfish in his love.  Most men are so.  Ber 350, XX.

There are some men who are so specially good at rearranging the domestic disarrangements of others.  Ber 436, XXIV.

A man who lives before the world in London, and lives chiefly among men of fortune, can hardly be economical.
Ber 509, XXVIII.

But men running hither and thither in distress do not well calculate their chances.  They are too nervous, too excited to play their game with judgment.  Ber 729-30, XLI.

To be in advance of other men, that is the desire which is

strongest in the hearts of all strong men.    CasR 217, XI,II.

But an unreasonable man, though he is one whom one would fain conquer by arguments were it possible, is the very man on whom arguments have no avail.  A madman is mad because he is mad.  CasR 17, I,III.

If a man of fifty have his wits about him, and be not too prosy, he can generally make himself master of the occasion, when his companions are under thirty.  FrP 189, XIX.

There are men who are old at one-and-twenty;...but there are others who at that age are still boys,--whose inner persons and characters have not begun to clothe themselves with the 'toga virilis.'  I am not sure that those whose boyhoods are so protracted have the worst of it, if in this hurrying and competitive age they can be saved from being absolutely trampled in the dust before they are able to do a little trampling on their own account.  Fruit that grows ripe the quickest is not the sweetest....The days have not yet come, though they are no doubt coming, when 'detur digniori' shall be the rule of succession to all titles, honours, and privileges whatsoever.  Only think what a life it would give to the education of the country in general, if any lad from seventeen to twenty-one could go in for a vacant dukedom; and if a goodly inheritance could be made absolutely incompatible with incorrect spelling and doubtful proficiency in rule of three!  OrF 30-1, III,I.

There are men of this sort, men slow in their thoughts but very keen in their memories; men who will look for the glance of a certain bright eye from a window-pane, though years have rolled on since last they saw it....But when the bright eyes do glance, such men pass by abashed; and when the occasion offers, their wit is never at hand.  Nevertheless they are not the least happy of mankind, these neverreadies; they do not pick up sudden prizes, but they hold fast by such good things as the ordinary run of life bestows upon them.  OrF 13, XLII,II.

Let us never forget that 'an honest man is the noblest work of God.'  Str 18, II.

The man who tells you how much his wine costs a dozen, knows that he is wrong while the words are in his mouth; but they are in his mouth, and he cannot restrain them. RacR 123-4,X.

There are men who rarely think well of women,--who hardly think well of any woman.  They put their mothers and sisters into the background,--as though they belonged to some sex or race apart,--and then declare to themselves and to their friends that all women are false,--that no woman can be trusted unless her ugliness protect her; and that every woman may be attacked as fairly as may game in a cover, or deer on a mountian.  What man does not know men who have so thought?  CanY 117, LI,II.

[A]nd in such matters   [avoiding publicity]   such men are
weak and foolish, and often cowardly.  MM 386, XXIX.

[B]ut there may be a question whether as much evil would not
be known of most men, let them be heroes or not be heroes,
if their characters were, as to say, turned inside out
before our eyes.  Cl 79, X.

...one of those men to whom love-making comes so readily
that it is a pity that they should ever marry.  Cl 123, XV.

...[T]hey do weigh themselves, and know their own weight,
and shove themselves aside as being too light for any real
service in the world.  This they do, though they may fluster
with their voices, and walk about with their noses in the
air, and swing their canes, and try to look as large as they
may.  They do not look large, and they know it; and consequently they ring the bells, and look after the horses, and
shove themselves on one side, so that the heavier weights
may come forth and do the work.  Cl 140, XVII.

[N]or is the heart of any man made so like a weathercock
that it needs must turn itself hither and thither, as the
wind directs, and be altogether beyond the man's control.
Cl 209, XXV.

A man rarely carries himself meanly whom the world holds
high in esteem.  LasC 3, I.

There are men who, though they have not sense enough to be
true, have nevertheless sense enough to know that they cannot expect to be believed in by those who are near enough to
them to know them.  LasC 348, XXXIX.

Many men, fickle as weathercocks, are ready to marry at the
moment--are ready to marry at the moment, because they are
fickle, and think so little about it.  LasC 718, LXXVII.

A man who desires to soften another man's heart should
always abuse himself.  In softening a woman's heart, he
should abuse her.  LasC 397, XLIV.

A man must live, even though his heart be broken, and living
he must dine.  PF 135, LIII,I.

[A]nd danger and dangerous men are always more attractive
than safety and safe men.  PF 154, XVII,I.

There are men who cannot guard themselves from the assertion
of marital rights at most inappropriate moments.
PF 24,XL,II.

He was one of those men who, in spite of their experience of
the world, of their experience of their own lives, imagine

that lips that have once lied can never tell the truth.
PF 127, LII,II.

There are men to whom release from the constraint imposed by
family ties will be, at any rate for a time, felt as a
release.  HKHWR 174, XIX.

There be men, and not bad men either, and men neither uneducated, or unintelligent, or irrational in ordinary matters,
who seem to be absolutely unfitted by nature to have the
custody or guardianship of others.  A woman in the hands of
such a man can hardly save herself or him from endless
trouble.  It may be that between such a one and his wife,
events shall flow on so evenly that no ruling, no constraint
is necessary,--that even the giving of advice is never
called for by the circumstances of the day.  If the man be
happily forced to labour daily for his living till he be
weary, and the wife be laden with many ordinary cares, the
routine of life may run on without storms;--but for such a
one, if he be without work, the management of a wife will be
a task full of peril.  The lesson may be learned at last; he
may after years come to perceive how much and how little of
guidance the partner of his life requires at his hands; and
he may be taught how that guidance should be given;--but in
the learning of the lesson there will be sorrow and gnashing
of teeth.  HKHWR 257, XXVII.

But there are men so awkward that it seems to be their
especial province to say always the very worst thing at the
very worst moment.  HKHWR 448, XLVII.

There is nothing that a man may not do, nothing that he may
not achieve, if he have only pluck enough to go through with
it.  HKHWR 781, LXXVII.

There are men who can raise such sparks [of sympathy], the
pretence of fire, where there is no heat at all;--false,
fraudulent men.  SHHOH 28, III.

When one man is wise and another foolish, the foolish man
knows generally as well as does the wise man in what lies
wisdom and in what folly....We may almost say that a man is
only as strong as his weakest moment.  RalH 207, XXVII.

There are men who never dream of great work,...but who themselves never fail in accomplishing those second-class tasks
with which they satisfy their own energies.  Men these are
who to the world are very useful.  Some few there are, who
seeing the beauty of a great work and believing in its
accomplishment within the years allotted to man, are contented to struggle for success, and struggling, fail.  Here
and there comes one who struggles and succeeds.  But the men
are many who see the beauty, who adopt the task, who promise
themselves the triumph, and then never struggle at all.  The
task is never abandoned; but days go by and weeks;--and then
months and years,--and nothing is done.  The dream of youth

becomes the doubt of middle life, and then the despair of age. In building a summer-house it is so easy to plant the first stick, but one does not know where to touch the sod when one begins to erect a castle. RalH 301, XL.

There is a misery in this [not attacking a planned life's work] which only they who have endured it can understand. There are idle men who rejoice in idleness....They revel in it, look forward to it, and almost take a pride in it....And there are men who love work, who revel in that, who attack it daily with renewed energy, almost wallowing in it, greedy of work, who go to it almost as the drunkard goes to his bottle, or the gambler to his gaming-table. These are not unhappy men, though they are perhaps apt to make those around them unhappy....And again there are men, fewer in number, who will work though they hate it, from sheer conscience and from conviction that idleness will not suit them or make them happy. Strong men these are....But there will ever be present to the mind of the ambitious man the idea of something to be done over and above the mere earning of his bread;--and the ambition may be very strong, though the fibre be lacking. Such a one will endure an agony protracted for years, always intending, never performing, self-accusing through every wakeful hour, self-accusing almost through every sleeping hour. The work to be done is close there by the hand, but the tools are loathed, and the paraphernalia of it become hateful. And yet it can never be put aside. It is to be grasped to-morrow, but on every morrow the grasping of it becomes more difficult, more impossible, more revolting. There is no peace, no happiness for such a man. RalH 388, LI.

There are men who may doubt, who may weigh the evidence, who may venture to believe or disbelieve in compliance with their own reasoning faculties,--who may trust themselves to think it out. RalH 393, LI.

It is true, indeed, that men are merciless as wolves to women,--that they become so, taught by circumstances and trained by years; but the young man who begins by meaning to be a wolf must be bad indeed. EE 104, VI,I.

Who does not remember that horrible Turk, Jacob Asdrubal, the Old Bailey barrister, the terror of witnesses, the bane of judges,--who was gall and wormwood to all opponents. It was said of him that 'at home' his docile amiability was the marvel of his friends, and delight of his wife and daughters. PR 318, XXXV,I.

Let a man doubt ever so much his own capacity for some public exhibition which he has undertaken; yet he will always prefer to fail,--if fail he must,--before a large audience. PR 322, XXXVI,I.

There are men who exercise dominion, from the nature of their disposition, and who do so from their youth upwards,

without knowing, till advanced life comes upon them, that
any power of dominion belongs to them.  Men are persuasive,
and imperious withal, who are unconscious that they use
burning words to others, whose words to them are never even
warm.  LA 117, XII.

When one man says that he has been hard to another he almost
boasts that, on that occasion, he got the better of him.
HHOG 93-4, VII.

It is a small and narrow point that turns the rushing train
to the right or to the left.  The rushing man is often
turned off by a point as small and narrow.  HHOG 120, IX.

There are men who, of their natures, do not like women, even
though they may have wives and legions of daughters, and be
surrounded by things feminine in all the affairs of their
lives.  Others again have their strongest affinities and
sympathies with women, and are rarely altogether happy when
removed from their influence.  Way 260, XXVII,I.

Throughout the world, the more wrong a man does, the more
indignant is he at wrong done to him.  Way 186, LXX,II.

It is said that if you were to take a man of moderate parts
and make him Prime Minister out of hand, he might probably
do as well as other Prime Ministers, the greatness of the
work elevating the man to its own level.  Way 288, LXXXI,II.

There are men who cannot conceive of themselves that anything should be difficult for them, and again others who
cannot bring themselves so to trust themselves as to think
that they can ever achieve anything great.  Samples of each
sort from time to time rise high in political life, carried
thither apparently by Epicurean concourse of atoms; and it
often happens that the more confident samples are by no
means the most capable.  PrM 358, XXXVIII,I.

[A] dishonest man cannot begin even to sweep a crossing
honestly till he have in very truth repented of his former
dishonesty.  The lazy man may become lazy no longer, but
there must have been first a process through his mind where-
by laziness has become odious to him.  PrM 190, LX,II.

There are men whose very eyes glance business, whose every
word imports care, who step as though their shoulders were
weighted with thoughtfulness, who breathe solicitude, and
who seem to think that all the things of life are too
serious for smiles....And then there are men who are always
playfellows with their friends, who--even should misfortune
be upon them--still smile and make the best of it, who come
across one like sunbeams, and who, even when tears are
falling, produce the tints of a rainbow.  IHP 115, XII,I.

There are men, who do not seem at first sight very susceptible to feminine attractions, who nevertheless are dom-

inated by the grace of flounces, who succumb to petticoats unconsciously, and who are half in love with every woman merely for her womanhood.  DuC 589, LXXIV.

But among such  [men who during the course of a successful life have contrived to repress their original roughness, and who make a not ineffectual attempt to live after the fashion of those with whom their wealth and successes have thrown them]  will occasionally be found one whose roughness does not altogether desert him, and who can on an occasion use it with a purpose.  Such a one will occasionally surprise his latter-day associates by the sudden ferocity of his brow, by the hardness of his voice, and by an apparently unaccustomed use of violent words.  The man feels that he must fight, and, not having learned the practice of finer weapons, fights in this way.  Unskilled with foils or rapier he falls back upon the bludgeon with which his hand has not lost all its old familiarity.  AyA 118, XIII.

When a man is compelled by some chance circumstance to address another man whom he does not know, and whom by inspection he feels he shall never wish to know, he always hardens his face, and sometimes also his voice.
AyA 342, XXXVI.

When a man has been thoroughly ill-used in greater matters it is almost a consolation to him to feel that he has been turned out into the street to get wet through without his dinner,--even though he may have turned himself out.
AyA 419, XLIV.

There is a class of men who always choose to show by their outward appearance that they belong to horses, and they succeed.  MSF 201, XXXV, II.

But the horsey man is generally on the alert to take care that no secret of his trade escapes from him unawares.
MSF 203, XXXV, II.

There are men who can't walk upstairs as though to do so were an affair of ordinary life.  They perform the task as though they walked upstairs once in three years.  It is to be presumed that such men always sleep on the ground floor, though where they find their bedrooms it is hard to say.
MSF 204, XXXV, II.

A man's sorrows of that kind  [having his loved one love someone else first]  do not commence, or at any rate are not acutely felt, while the knowledge of the matter from which they grow is confined altogether to his own bosom.
OML 89, VIII.

It is necessary to be stern and cruel and determined, a man shall say to himself.  In this particular emergency of my life I will be stern and cruel.  General good will come out of such a line of conduct.  But unless he be stern and cruel in other matters also,--unless he has been born stern and cruel, or has so trained himself,--he cannot be stern and cruel for that occasion only. OML 117, XI.

Who does not know the "got up" look of the gentleman from the other side of the water, who seems to know himself to be much better than his father, and infinitely superior to his grandfather; who is always ready to make a speech on every occasion, and who feels himself to be fit company for a Prime Minister as soon as he has left school. Probably he is. Land 100, VI,I.

Let a man undertake what duty he will in life, if he be a good man he will desire success; and if he be a brave man he will long for victory. Land 128, XXXIX,III.

## MEN BUTTERFLY

He was one of those butterfly beings who seem to have been created that they may flutter about from flower to flower in the summer hours of such gala times as those now going on at Chiswick, just as other butterflies do. What the butter- flies were last winter, or what will become of them next winter, no one but the naturalist thinks of inquiring. How they may feed themselves on flowerjuice, or on insects small enough to be their prey, is matter of no moment to the general world. It is sufficient that they flit about in the sunbeams, and add bright glancing spangles to the beauty of the summer day. TC 296, XXV.

## MEN, OLD

[T]he tears of an old man are bitter. War 255, XX.

Rich old men, when they wish to be cordial on such occasions [engagements], have but one way of envincing cordiality. It is not by a pressure of the hand, by a kind word, by an approving glance. Their embrace conveys no satisfaction; their warmest words, if unsupported, are very cold. An old man, if he intends to be cordial on such an occasion, must speak of thousands of pounds. "My dear young fellow, I approve altogether. She shall have twenty thousand pounds the day she becomes yours." Then is the hand shaken with true fervour; then is real cordiality expressed and felt. "What a dear old man grandpapa is! Is there any one like him! Dear old duck! He is going to be so generous to Harry." Ber 508-9, XXVIII.

There are things no elderly man can learn, and there are lessons which are full of light for the new recruit, but dark as death to the old veteran. Str 29, V.

It is a mistake, I think, to suppose that men become greedy as they grow old. The avaricious man shall show his avarice as he gets into years, because avarice is a passion com- patible with old age,--and will become more avaricious as

his other passions fall off from him.    And so will it be
with the man that is open-handed.    RalH 7,I.

...that love for himself for which an old man is always hankering, for which the sick man breaks his heart; but which
the old and sick find it so difficult to get from the young
and healthy.    It is in nature that the old man should keep
the purse in his own pocket, or otherwise he will have so
little to attract.    He is weak, querulous, ugly to look at,
apt to be greedy, cross, and untidy.    Though he himself can
love, what is his love to anyone?    Duty demands that one
shall smooth his pillow, and someone does smooth it,--as a
duty.    But the old man feels the difference, and remembers
the time when there was one who was anxious to share it.
MSF 205-6, LVII,III.

## MEN, PUBLIC

Public men in England have so much to do that they cannot
give time to the preparation of speeches for such meetings
as these [international congresses].    OrF 172, XVII,I.

## MEN, WORTHY

A man may be very imperfect and yet worth a great deal....If
not, how many of us are unworthy of the mothers and wives we
have!    It is my belief that few young men settle themselves
down to the work of the world, to the begetting of children,
and carving and paying and struggling and fretting for the
same, without having first been in love with four or five
possible mothers for them, and probably with two or three at
the same time.    And yet these men are, as a rule, worthy of
the excellent wives and that ultimately fall to their lot.
FrP 297, XXXI.

## MEN, YOUNG

How can any youth of nineteen or twenty do other than
consort himself with the daily companions of his usual avoca-
tions?    Once and again, in one case among ten thousand, a
lad may be found formed of such stuff, that he receives
neither the good nor the bad impulses of those around him.
But such a one is a lapsus naturae.    He has been born without the proper attributes of youth, or at any rate, brought
up so as to have got rid of them.    TC 17, II.

But if it be hard for a young man to keep in the right path
when he has not as yet strayed out of it, how much harder is
it to return to it when he has long since lost the track!...
It is not by our virtues or our vices that we are judged,
even by those who know us best; but by such credit for
virtues or vices as we may have acquired.    TC 18-9, II.

Who could expect that a young man...should sit for hours and
hours alone in a dull London lodging, over his book and tea-
cup?    Who should expect that any young man will do so?    And

yet mothers, and aunts, and anxious friends, do expect it--
very much in vain.  TC 120, XI.

It is so difficult for a young man to enumerate senten-
tiously a principle of morality, or even an expression of
ordinary good feeling, without giving himself something of a
ridiculous air, without assuming something of mock grandeur.
DoT 50, IV.

Now nothing on earth can be more difficult than bringing up
well a young man who has not to earn his own bread, and who
has no recognized station among other young men similarly
circumstanced.   Juvenile dukes, and sprouting earls, find
their duties and their places as easily as embryo clergymen
and sucking barristers.   Provision is made for their peculiar positions:  and, though they may possibly go astray,
they have a fair chance given to them of running within the
posts.  Dot 290-1, XXIV.

But marquises are usually obeyed; especially when they have
livings to give away, and when their orders are given to
young clergymen....[A]t twenty-four the east wind does not
penetrate deep, the traches is all but invulnerable, and the
left shoulder knows no twinges.  Ber 44-5, III.

There are subjects on which young men talk freely with each
other, but on which they hesitate to speak to their elders
without restraint....[o]f wine and women, of cards and
horses, of money comforts and money discomforts....There is
always some compliment implied when an old man unbends
before a young one, and it is this which makes the vicious-
ness of old men so dangerous.  Ber 203, XI.

When I hear of a young man sitting down by himself as the
master of a household, without a wife, or even without a
mother or sister to guide him, I always anticipate danger.
If he does not go astray in any other way, he will probably
mismanage his money matters.   And then there are so many
other ways.  A house, if it be not made pleasant by domestic
pleasant things, must be made pleasant by pleasure.  And a
bachelor's pleasures in his own house are always dangerous.
There is too much wine drunk at his dinner parties.   His
guest sit too long over their cards.  The servants know that
they want a mistress; and, in the absence of that mistress,
the language of the household becomes loud and harsh--and
sometimes improper.   Young men among us seldom go quite
straight in their course, unless they are, at any rate
occasionally, brought under the influence of tea and small
talk....
     It is undoubtedly a very dangerous thing for a young
man of twenty-two to keep house by himself, either in town
or country.  CasR 12-3, I,I.

Where is the young man who has not in his early years been
half in love with some woman older, much older than himself,
who has half conquered his heart by her solicitude for his

welfare?--with some woman who has whispered to him while
others were talking, who has told him in such gentle, loving
tones of his boyish follies, whose tenderness and experience
together have educated him and made him manly?...Such
liaisons have the interests of intrigue, without--I was
going to say its dangers. Alas! it may be that it is not
always so. CasR 29, II,I.

For men of three and twenty, though they are so fond of the
society of woman older than themselves, understand so little
the hearts and feeling of such women. CasR 30, II,I.

Young men...are more inclined to be earnest and thoughtful
when alone than they ever are when with others, even though
those others be their elders. I fancy that, as we grow old
ourselves, we are apt to forget that it was so with us; and,
forgetting it, we do not believe that it is so with our
children. We constantly talk of the thoughtlessness of
youth. I do not know whether we might not more appropriately speak of its thoughtfulness. It is, however, no
doubt, true that thought will not at once produce wisdom.
It may almost be a question whether such wisdom as many of
us have in our mature years has not come from the dying out
of the power of temptation, rather than as the results of
thought and resolution. Men, full fledged and at their
work, are, for the most part, too busy for much thought; but
lads, on whom the work of the world has not yet fallen with
all its pressure--they have time for thinking. SmaH 133,XIV.

It seems to me that in this respect the fathers and mothers
of the present generation understand but little of the inward nature of the young men for whom they are so anxious.
They give them credit for so much that it is impossible they
should have, and then deny them credit for so much that they
possess! They expect from them when boys the discretion of
men--that discretion which comes from thinking; but will not
give them credit for any of that power of thought which
alone can ultimately produce good conduct. Young men are
generally thoughtful--more thoughtful than their seniors;
but the fruit of their thought is not as yet there. And
then so little is done for the amusement of lads who are
turned loose into London at nineteen or twenty. Can it be
that any mother really expects her son to sit alone evening
after evening in a dingy room drinking bad tea and reading
good books? And yet it seems that mothers do so expect--the
very mothers who talk about the thoughtlessness of youth! O
ye mothers who from year to year see your sons launched
forth upon the perils of the world, and who are so careful
with your good advice, with flannel shirting, with books of
devotion and tooth-powder, does it never occur to you that
provision should be made for amusement, for dancing , for
parties, for the excitement and comfort of women's society?
That excitement your sons will have, and if it be not provided by you of one kind, will certainly be provided by
themselves of another kind. If I were a mother sending lads
out into the world, the matter most in my mind would be this

--to what houses full of nicest girls could I get them admission, so that they might do their flirting in good company.  SmaH 511-2, LI.

But be it always remembered that there are two modes in which a young man may be free and easy with his elder and superior--the mode pleasant and the mode offensive. SmaH 329, XXXIII.

Young men given to sigh are generally attracted by some outward and visible sign of softness which may be taken as an indication that sighing will produce some result, however small.  VOB 9, I.

Fathers, guardians, and the race of old friends generally, hardly ever give sufficient credit to the remorse which young men themselves feel when they gradually go astray. They see the better as plainly as do their elders, though they so often follow the worse,--as not unfrequently do the elders also.  RalH 61, VIII.

When young men are anxious to indulge the spirit of adventure, they generally do so by falling in love with young women of whom their fathers and mothers would not approve. In these days a spirit of adventure hardly goes further than this, unless it take a young man to a German gaming table. EE 32-3, II,I.

When young men will run into such difficulties [meeting and courting an unsuitable girl], it is, alas, so very difficult to interfere with them!  EE 41, III,I.

To take delight in beauty is assumed to be the nature of a young man.  EE 105, VI,I.

The young man who would not so feel  [happy to find himself the heir to a title]  might be the better philosopher, but one might doubt whether he would be the better young man. PrM 256, LXVII,II.

Nothing crushes a young man so much as an assurance that his presence can be dispensed with without loss to any one. MF 329, XXX,I.

There are at present a number of young men about who think that few girls are worth the winning, but that any girl is to be had, not by asking,--which would be troublesome,--but simply by looking at her.  You can see the feeling in their faces.  They are for the most part small in stature, well-made little men, who are aware that they have something to be proud of, wearing close-packed shining little hats, by which they seem to add more than a cubit to their stature, men endowed with certain gifts of personal,--dignity, I may perhaps call it, though the word rises somewhat too high. They look as though they would be able to say a clever thing; but their spoken thoughts seldom rise above a small acrid sharpness. They respect no one; above all, not their elders. To such a one his horse comes first, if he have a horse; then a dog; and then a stick; and after that the mistress of his affections. But their fault is not altogether of their own making. It is the girls themselves who spoil them and endure their inanity, because of that assumed look of superiority which to the eyes of the outside world would be a little offensive were it not a little foolish. But they do not marry often. Whether it be that the girls know better at last, or that they themselves do not see sufficiently clearly their future dinners, who can say?...The first instinct with such a young man as those of whom I have spoken teaches him, the moment he has committed himself, to begin to consider how he can get out of the scrape. It is not much of a scrape, for when an older man comes this way, a man verging towards baldness, with a good professional income, our little friend is forgotten and he is passed by without a word. MSF 1-3, XXII,II.

The mind of a young man so circumstanced  [educated but taught to be idle]  turns always first to the bar and then to literature. MSF 4, XXII,II.

Young men, who are the heirs to properties, and are supposed to be rich because they are idle, do get themselves asked about, here and there--and think a great deal of themselves in consequence. "There's young Jones. He is fairly good-looking, but hasn't a word to say for himself. He will do to pair off with Miss Smith, who'll talk for a dozen. He can't hit a haystack, but he's none the worse for that. We haven't got too many pheasants. He'll be sure to come when you ask him--and he'll be sure to go." So Jones is asked, and considers himself to be the most popular man in London. MSF 88, XXVIII,II.

### MEN...WOMEN

[F]emales travelling in stage coaches never eat breakfast--men always do if they have eighteen-pence to pay for it--sometimes even when they have not--from this I am led to believe that females generally are more powerful than the nobler sex in resisting strong temptation, and I know none stronger than that of a good breakfast after travelling four hours on a cold March morning. MB 74-5, II,III.

Ladies are sometimes less nice in their appreciation of physical disqualification; and, provided that a man speak to them well, they will listen, though he speak from a mouth never so deformed and hideous. BaT 53, VII.

What chance has dead knowledge with experience in any of the transactions between man and man?  What possible chance between man and woman?  BaT 257, XXVII.

Few men do understand the nature of a woman's heart, till years have robbed such understanding of its value. And it is well that it should be so, or men would triumph too easily.  BaT 291, XXX.

But the tears of a man bring with them no comfort as do those of the softer sex.  TC 146, XII.

Nothing is so painful to a woman as a man in tears. TC 377, XXX.

Now, here a very useful moral may be deduced.  Ladies, take care how you permit yourselves to fall into intimacies with unknown gentlemen on your travels.  Ber 169, IX.

And what man was ever worthy, perfectly worthy, of a pure, true, and honest girl?  Man's life admits not of such purity and honesty; rarely of such truth.  But one would not choose that such flowers should remain unplucked because no hands are fit to touch them.  Ber 824, XLVII.

[A]nd why should we think that personal excellence is to count for nothing in female judgment, when in that of men it ranks so immeasurably above all other excellences? CasR 215, XI,I.

There are such men  [who shake in their shoes as though the majesty of womanhood were too great], and many of them, who carry this dread to the last day of their long lives.  I have often wondered what women think of men who regard women as too awful for the free exercise of open speech. CasR 299, XIV,I.

Men and women when they are written about are always supposed to have fixed resolves, though in life they are so seldom found to be thus armed.  CasR 23, II,II.

A man never should forgive a woman unless he has her absolutely in his power.  When he does so, and thus wipes out all old scores, he merely enables her to begin again. Str 45, VIII.

It  [to fall to the ground between two stools...lose both men]  is a truth terrible to a woman.  There is no position in a man's life of the same aspect.  A man may fail in business, and feel that no farther chance of any real success can ever come in his way; or he may fail in love, and in the soreness of his heart may know that the pleasant rippling waters of that fountain are for him dried forever. But with a woman the two things are joined together.  Her battle must be fought all in one.  Her success in life and her romance must go together, hand in hand.  She is called upon to marry for love, and if she marry not for love, she disobeys the ordinance of nature, and must pay the penalty. But, at the same time, all her material fortune depends upon the nature of that love.  An industrious man may marry a silly, fretful woman, and may be triumphant in his counting-house though he be bankrupt in his drawing-room.  But a woman has but the one chance.  She must choose her life's companion because she loves him; but she knows how great is the ruin of loving one who can not win for her that worldly success which all in the world desire to win.  Str 114, XXI.

But men are cowards before women until they become tyrants; and are easy dupes, till of a sudden they recognise the fact that it is pleasanter to be the victimiser than the victim-- and as easy.  There are men, indeed, who never learn the latter lesson.  SmaH 134, XIV.

None but the worst and most heartless of women know the extent of their own power over men;--as none but the worst and most heartless of men know the extent of their power over women.  SmaH 287, XXIX.

Women are more accustomed than men to long, dull, unemployed hours.  SmaH 326, XXXIII.

If a man takes a dog with him from the country up to town, the dog must live a town life without knowing the reason why;--must live a town life or die a town death.  But a woman should not be treated like a dog.  CanY 233, LXIII,II.

In such contests, a woman has ever the best of it at all points.  The man plays with a button to his foil, while the woman uses a weapon that can really wound.
CanY 278, LXVII,II.

She had treated him de haut en bas with all that superiority which youth and beauty give to a young woman over a very young man.  Cl 9, II.

The tact of women excels the skill of men.  Cl 352, XLI.

Women in such matters [religion] are absolutely false if they be not sincere; but men, with political views, and with much of their future prospects in jeopardy also, are allowed to dress themselves differently for different scenes.  Whatever be the peculiar interest on which a man goes into Parliament, of course he has to live up to that in his own borough.  Whether malt, the franchise, or teetotalism be his rallying point, of course he is full of it when among his constituents. But it is not desirable that he should be full of it also at his club.  Bel 14, I.

There are calamities which, by their natural tendencies, elevate the character of women and add strength to the growth of feminine virtues;--but then, again, there are other calamities which few women can bear without some degradation....In this, I think, the world is harder to women than to men; that a woman often loses much by the chance of adverse circumstances which a man only loses by his own misconduct.  Bel 274, XXI.

...those little attentions, amounting almost to worship,

with which such men...are prone to treat all women in exceptionable circumstances, when the ordinary routine of life has been disturbed!  Bel 297, XXIII.

A man's heart must be very hard when it does not become softened by the trouble of a woman with whom he finds himself alone.  Bel 341, XXVI.

Men succeed often by the simple earnestness of their prayers.  Women cannot refuse to give that which is asked for with so much of the vehemence of true desire.
Bel 378, XXVIII.

...a certain look of ferocity to him, which was apt to make men afraid of him at first sight.  Women are not actuated in the same way, and are accustomed to look deeper into men at the first sight than other men will trouble themselves to do.  PF 98, XI,I.

Women can work so much harder in this way  [conciliatory conversation]  than men find it possible to do!  HKHWR 55,VI.

When such tempests occur in a family, a woman will generally suffer the least during the thick of the tempest.  While the hurricane is at the fiercest, she will be sustained by the most thorough conviction that the right is on her side, that she is aggrieved, that there is nothing for her to acknowledge, and no positon that she need surrender.  Whereas her husband will desire a compromise, even amidst the violence of the storm.  But afterwards, when the wind has lulled, but while the heavens around are still all black and murky, then the woman's sufferings begin.  When passion gives way to thought and memory, she feels the loneliness of her positon, --the loneliness, and the possible degradation.  It is all very well for a man to talk about his name and his honour; but it is the woman's honour and the woman's name that are, in truth, placed in jeopardy.  Let the woman do what she will, the man can, in truth, show his face in the world; and, after awhile, does show his face.  But the woman may be compelled to veil hers, either by her own fault or by his.  HKHWR 93-4, XI.

There is no question more difficult than this for a gentleman to answer....'If I, a woman, can dare, for your sake, to encounter the public tongue, will you, a man, be afraid?' The true answer, if it could be given, would probably be this; 'I am afraid, though a man, because I have much to lose and little to get.  You are not afraid, though a woman, because you have much to get and little to lose.'  But such an answer would be uncivil, and is not often given.  Therefore men shuffle and lie and tell themselves that in love,-- love here being taken to mean all antenuptial contests between man and woman,--everything is fair....
HKHWR 445-6, XLVII.

The world in general says such things  [hinting romance]   to

ladies more openly than it does to men, and the probability
of a girl's success in matrimony is canvassed in her hearing
by those who are nearest to her with a freedom which can seldom be used in regard to a man.    A man's most intimate
friend hardly speaks to him of the prospect of his marriage
till he himself has told that the engagement exists.
HKHWR 513, LV.

Men...find themselves subjected to criticism, and under the
necessity of either defending themselves or of succumbing.
If, indeed, a man neither speaks, nor writes,--if he be dumb
as regards opinion,--he passes simply as one of the crowd,
and is in the way neither of convincing nor of being
convinced; but a woman may speak, and almost write, as she
likes, without danger of being wounded by sustained
conflict.  HKHWR 719, LXXVII.

There is nothing that a woman will not forgive a man, when
he is weaker than she is herself.  HKHWR 883-4, XCIII.

When there is illness in a house, the feminine genius and
spirit predominates the male.   If the illness be so severe
as to cause a sense of danger, this is so strongly the case
that the natural position of two is changed.   VOB 418,LVIII.

...that undemonstrative, unexpressed, almost unconscious
affection which, with men, will often make the greatest
charm of their lives, but which is held by women to be quite
unsatisfactory and almost nugatory....Women, who love each
other as well, will always be expressing their love, always
making plans to be together, always doing little things each
for the gratification of the other, constantly making
presents backwards and forwards.  VOB 439-40, LXII.

There is no matter of doubt at all but that on all such subjects   [love]   an average woman can write a better letter
than an average man.   SHHOH 182, XVIII.

A man cannot bear himself gracefully under the weight of a
pardon as a woman may do.   A man chooses generally that it
shall be assumed by those with whom he is closely connected
that he has done and is doing no wrong; and, when wronged,
he professes to forgive and to forget in silence.   To a
woman the act of forgiveness, either accepted or bestowed,
is itself a pleasure.  SHHOH 208, XXI.

A vain attachment in a woman's heart must ever be a weary
load, because she can take no step of her own towards the
consummation by which the burden may be converted into a
joy.   A man may be active, may press his suit even a tenth
time, may do something towards achieving success.   A woman
can only be still and endure.  RalH 307, XLI.

There are men by whom a woman, if she have wit, beauty, and
no conscience, cannot be withstood....A man so weak and so
attacked may sometimes run; but even the poor chance of run-

ning is often cut off from him.   ED 176-7, XIX,I.

Woman, when they are fond of men, do think much of men's
comfort in small matters, and men are apt to take the good
things provided almost as a matter of course.
ED 206, XXIII, I.

When a man has shown himself to be so far amenable to feminine authority as to have put himself in the way of matrimony, ladies will bear a great deal from him.
ED 33-4, XLIII,II.

But women, perhaps, feel less repugnance than do men at
using ignoble assistance in the achievement of good
purposes.   ED 178, LIX,II.

It is almost impossible for a man,--a man under forty and
unmarried, and who is not a philosopher,--to have familiar
and affectionate intercourse with a beautiful young woman,
and carry it on as he might do with a friend of the other
sex.   ED 229-30, LXV,II.

Is it not the fate of women to play the tunes which men
dictate,--except in some rare case in which the woman can
make herself the dictator?   ED 333, LXXVI,II.

Girls are undoubtedly better prepared to fall in love with
men whom they have never seen, than are men with girls.   It
is a girl's great business in life to love and to be loved.
Of some young men it may almost be said that it is their
great business to avoid such a catastrophe.   EE 46-7, III,I.

Perhaps there is nothing so generally remarkable in the conduct of young ladies in the phase of life of which we are
now speaking as the facility,--it may almost be said
audacity,-- with which they do make up their minds.   A young
man seeks a young woman's hand in marriage, because she has
waltzed stoutly with him, and talked pleasantly between the
dances;--and the young woman gives it, almost with gratitude.   As to the young man, the readiness of his action is
less marvellous than hers.   He means to be master, and, by
the very nature of the joint life they propose to lead, must
take her to his sphere of life, not bind himself to hers.
If he worked before he will work still.   If he was idle
before he will be idle still; and he probably does in some
sort make a calculation and strike a balance between his
means and the proposed additional burden of a wife and
children.   But she, knowing nothing, takes a monstrous leap
in the dark, in which everything is to be changed, and in
which everything is trusted to chance.   PR 156-7, XVIII.

Men will love to the last, but they love what is fresh and
new.   A woman's love can live on the recollection of the
past, and clings to what is old and ugly.   PR 225, XXV,I.

Men who make women a prey, prey also on themselves.
LA 12,II.

There is, perhaps, no condition of mind more difficult for
the ordinary well-instructed inhabitant of a city to realise
than that of such a girl as Ruby Ruggles.   The rural day
labourer and his wife live on a level surface which is comparatively open to the eye.   Their aspirations, whether for
good or evil...--are, if looked at at all, fairly visible.
And with the men of the Ruggles class one can generally find
out what they would be at, and in what direction their minds
are at work.   But the Ruggles woman,--is better educated,
has higher aspirations and a brighter imagination, and is
infinitely more cunning than the man.   If she be good-
looking and relieved from the pressure of want, her thoughts
soar into a world which is as unknown to her as heaven is to
us, and in regard to which her longings are apt to be infinitely stronger than are ours for heaven.   Her education has
been much better than that of the man.   She can read,
whereas he can only spell words from a book.   She can write
a letter after her fashion, whereas he can barely spell
words out on a paper.   Her tongue is more glib, and her
intellect sharper.   But her ignorance as to the reality of
things is much more gross than his.   By such contact as he
has with men in markets, in the streets of towns he
frequents, and even in the fields, he learns something
unconsciously of the relative condition of his countrymen,--
and, as to that which he does not learn, his imagination is
obtuse.   But the woman builds castles in the air, and
wonders, and longs.   To the young farmer the squire's
daughter is a superior being very much out of his way.   To
the farmer's daughter the young squire is an Apollo, whom to
look at is a pleasure,--by whom to be looked at is a
delight.   The danger for the most part is soon over.   The
girl marries after her kind, and then husband and children
put the matter at rest forever.   Way 169-70, XVIII,I.

But it is very difficult for a young lady to have done with
her family!   A young man may go anywhere, and may be lost at
sea; or come and claim his property after twenty years.   A
young man may demand an allowance, and has almost a right to
live alone.   The young male bird is supposed to fly away
from the paternal nest.   But the daughter of a house is compelled to adhere to her father till she shall get a husband.
Way 267, LXXVIII,II.

A young man generally regards it as his destiny either to
succeed or to fail in the world, and he thinks about that.
To him marriage, when it comes, is an accident to which he
has hardly as yet given a thought.   But to the girl the
matrimony which is or is not to be her destiny contains
within itself the only success or failure which she antici-
pates.   The young man may become Lord Chancellor, or at any
rate earn his bread comfortably as a county court judge.
But the girl can look forward to little else than the chance
of having a good man for her husband;--a good man, or if her

tastes lie in that direction, a rich man.  PrM 39-40, V,I.

[N]or was it expected that any of the gentlemen would do so
[attend afternoon church]; but women are supposed to require
more church than men.  AS 253, XXXVIII.

The lady in such a case  [telling a proposal]  can always
tell her story, with what exaggeration she may please to
give, and can complain.  The man can never do so.  When
inquired into, he cannot say that he has been pursued.  He
cannot tell her friends that she began it, and, in point of
fact, did it all.  'She would fall into my arms; she would
embrace me; she persisted in asking me whether I loved her!'
Though a man have to be shot for it, or kicked for it, or
even though he have to endure perpetual scorn for it, he
cannot say that let it be ever so true.  And yet is a man to
be forced into a marriage which he despises?  AS 307, XLV.

A girl if she has had a former love passage says nothing of
it to her new lover; but a man is not so reticent.
DuC 225, XXIX.

[A] woman with a misfortune is condemned by the general
voice of the world, whereas for a man to have stumbled is
considered hardly more than a matter of course.
DrW 43, IV, Part II.

There is something so sad in the condition of a girl who is
known to be in love, and has to undergo the process of being
made ashamed of it by her friends, that one wonders that any
young woman can bear it....A young man who has got into
debt, or been plucked,--or even when he has declared himself
to be engaged to a penniless young lady, which is worse,--is
supposed merely to have gone after his kind, and done what
was to be expected of him.  The mother never looks at him
with that enduring anger by which she intends to wear out
the daughter's constancy.  The father frets and fumes, pays
the debts, prepares the way for a new campaign, and merely
shrugs his shoulders about the proposed marriage, which he
regards simply as an impossibility.  But the girl is held
to have disgraced herself.  Though it is expected of her, or
at any rate hoped, that she will get married in due time,
yet the falling in love with a man,--which is, we must
suppose, a preliminary step to marriage,--is a wickedness....
      There are heroines who live through it all, and are
true to the end.  There are many pseudo-heroines who intend
to do so, but break down.  The pseudo-heroine generally
breaks down when young Smith,--not so very young,--has been
taken in as a partner by Messrs.  Smith and Walker, and
comes in her way, in want of a wife.  The persecution is, at
any rate, so often efficacious as to make fathers and
mothers feel it to be their duty to use it.  MF 40-1, IV,I.

With a girl, at any early age, all her outlookings into the
world have something to do with love and its consequences.

When a young man takes his leaning either towards Liberalism or Conservatism he is not at all actuated by any feeling as to how some possible future young woman may think on the subject. But the girl, if she entertains such ideas at all, dreams of them as befitting the man whom she may some day hope to love. Should she, a Protestant, become a Roman Catholic and then a nun, she feels that in giving up her hope for a man's love she is making the greatest sacrifice in her power for the Saviour she is taking to her heart. If she devotes herself to music, or the pencil, or to languages, the effect which her accomplishments may have on some beau ideal of manhood is present to her mind. From the very first she is dressing herself unconsciously in the mirror of a man's eyes. MF 44-5, IV,I.

Was there ever a young man who, when he first found a girl to be pleasant to him, has intended to fall in love with her? Girls will intend to fall in love, or, more frequently perhaps, to avoid it; but men in such matters rarely have a purpose. MF 226, XXI,I.

When a woman is bad a man can generally get quit of her from his heartstrings;--but a woman has no such remedy. She can continue to love the dishonoured one without dishonour to herself,--and does so. MF 116, XI,II.

There is in a man a pride of which a woman knows nothing. Or rather a woman is often subject to pride the every opposite. The man delights to think that he has been the first to reach the woman's heart; the woman is rejoiced to feel that she owns permanently that which has been often reached before....His Mary may have liked some other one, but it has not gone farther. Or if she has been engaged as a bride there has been no secret about it. Or it has been a thing long ago, so that there has been time for new ideas to form themselves. The husband when he does come knows at any rate that he has no ground of complaint, and is not kept specially in the dark when he takes his wife. Kept 69,XVIII.

A man always dines, let his sorrow be what it may. A woman contents herself with tea, and mitigates her sorrow, we must suppose, by an extra cup. OML 93, IX.

It seems to be almost a shame to tell the truth of what modest girls may think of any man whom they may chance to meet. They would never tell it to themselves. Even two sisters can hardly do so. And when the man comes before them, just for once or twice, to be judged and thought of at a single interview, the girl...can hardly tell it to herself. Land 249-50, XV,I.

Under such misfortunes [poverty and death], when continued, men do become more weary than women. Land 69-70, XXXVI,III.

## MERCY

But to some is given and to some is denied that cruse of heavenly balm with which all wounds can be assuaged and sore hearts ever relieved of some portion of their sorrow.  Of all the virtues with which man can endow himself surely none other is so odious as that justice which can teach itself to look down upon mercy almost as a vice!  OrF 356-7, LXXV,II.

## MIDDLEMEN

...one of the middlemen as they were formerly named,--though by the way I never knew that word to be current in Ireland; it is familiar to all, and was I suppose common some few years since, but I never heard the peasants calling such persons by that title.  CasR 74, IV,II.

## MILLSTONES

Well; it may be questioned whether even that  [beginning the swimming-match of life with a slight millstone round the neck]  is not better than an air-puffed swimming-belt. Ber 40, III.

## MIND

There are certain phases of mind in which a man can neither ride nor shoot, nor play a stroke at billiards, nor remember a card at whist.  SmaH 64, VII.

Oh, how vile is the mastery which matter still has over mind in many of the concerns of life!  How can a man withstand the assault of a bull?  Str 21, III.

## MINISTERS

A Minister can always give a reason; and, if he be clever, he can generally when doing so punish the man who asks for it.  The punishing of an influential enemy is an indis-cretion; but an obscure questioner may often be crushed with good effect.  PR 180, XX,I.

## MINISTRY

It can never be a very easy thing to form a Ministry.  The one chosen chief is readily selected.  Circumstances, in-deed, have probably left no choice in the matter....The Prime Minister is elected by the nation, but the nation, except in rare cases, cannot go below that in arranging details, and the man for whom the Queen sends is burdened with the necessity of selecting his colleagues.  It may be, --probably must always be the case,--that this, that, and the other colleagues are clearly indicated to his mind, but then each of these colleagues may want his own inferior coadjutors, and so the difficulty begins, increases, and at length culminates.  PR 355, XL,I.

## MISFORTUNE

The man must be made of very sterling stuff, whom continued and undeserved misfortune does not make unpleasant. FrP 141, XV.

But misfortune masters all but the great men, and upsets the best-learned lesson of even a long life.   PrM 174, LVIII,II.

## MISTAKES

The putting right of mistakes is never pleasant.Bel 405,XXX.

## MODESTY

...all the mawkish modesty which usually marks such speeches [those of congratulations]--or, rather, with modesty which would be mawkish were it not so completely a matter of course.  Ber 30, II.

## MONEY

The man who is ever looking after money is fitting company only for the devils, of whom, indeed, he is already one. TC 362, XXX.

[B]ut we all know, from the lessons of our early youth, how the love of money increases and gains strength by its own success. DoT 223, XVIII.

True worship of the one loved shrine prevents all other worship.  The records of his money had been his deity....
        How many of us make Faust's bargain!  The bodily atten-dance of the devil may be mythical; but in the spirit he is always with us.  And how rarely have we the power to break the contract!...If we may believe that a future life is to be fitted to the desires and appetites as they are engen-dered here, what shall we think of the future of a man whose desire has been simply for riches, whose appetite has been for heaps of money?  How miserably is such a poor wretch cheated!...Poor, dull Faustus!  What!  thou hast lost every-thing among the thimble-riggers?  Poor, dull, stupid wretch! Ber 785-6, XLIV.

Money easily come by goes easily, and money badly come by goes badly.  CasR 167, IX,II.

Money is a serious thing; and when gone cannot be had back by a shuffle in the game, or a fortunate blow with the battledore, as may political power, or reputation, or fashion.  One hundred thousand pounds gone, must remain as gone, let the person who claims to have had the honour of advancing it to Mrs. B. or my Lord C.  No lucky dodge can erase such a claim from the things that be.  FrP 459, XLVII.

The advantage of being heir to a good property is so mani-
fest--the advantages over and beyond those which are merely
fiscal--that no man thinks of throwing them away, or expects
another man to do so.    Moneys in possession or in expectation do give a set to the head, and a confidence to the
voice, and an assurance to the man, which will help him much
in his walk in life--if the owner of them will simply use
them and not abuse them.    SmaH 10, II.

What aunt, uncle, or cousin, in the uncontrolled possession
of forty thousand pounds was ever unpopular in the family?
CanY 68, VII,I.

A bundle of bank-notes in Prague may be not little, and yet
represent very little money.    When bank-notes are passed for
twopence and become thick with use, a man may have a great
mass of paper currency in his pocket without being rich.
NB 34, III.

The man who goes into the City to look for money is generally one who does not know where to get money when he wants
it.    LasC 285, XLIII.

I know no more uncomfortable walking than that which falls
to the lot of men who go into the City to look for money,
and who find none....It is not only that they are so vain,
but that they are accompanied by so killing a sense of
shame!    To wait about in dingy rooms, which look on to bare
walls, and are approached through some Hook Court; or to
keep appointments at a low coffee-house to which trystings
the money-lender will not trouble himself to come unless it
pleases him; to be civil, almost suppliant, to a cunning
knave whom the borrower loathes; to be refused thrice, and
then cheated with his eyes open on the fourth attempt; to
submit himself to vulgarity of the foulest kind, and to have
to seem to like it; to be badgered, reviled, and at last
accused of want of honesty by the most fraudulent of
mankind; and at the same time to be clearly conscious of the
ruin that is coming--this is the fate of him who goes into
the City to find money, not knowing where it is to be
found!    LasC 39], XLIII.

There is a satisfaction in turning out of doors a nephew or
niece who is pecuniarily dependent, but when the youthful
relative is richly endowed, the satisfaction is much diminished.    It is the duty of a guardian, no doubt, to look
after the ward; but if this cannot be done, the ward's money
should at least be held with as close a fist as possible.
PF 39, XLII,II.

The last fifty pounds of a thousand always goes quicker than
any of the nineteen other fifties.    SHHOH 116, XII.

Such a condition of character is the natural consequence of
such a positon    [a poor man in the society of rich men].
There is, probably, no man who becomes naturally so hard in

regard to money as he who is bound to live among rich men,
who is not rich himself and who is yet honest.  The weight
of the work of life in these circumstances is so crushing,
requires such continued thought, and makes itself so continually felt, that the mind of the sufferer is never free
from the contamination of sixpences.  Of such a one it is
not fair to judge as of other men with similar incomes.
ED 75, IX.

Is there a nobleman in Great Britain who can say that he
could lose the fortune which he possesses or the fortune
which he expects without an agony that would almost break
his heart?  LA 61, VI.

There are men,--and old men too, who ought to know the
world,--who think that if they can only find the proper
Medea to boil the cauldron for them, they can have their
ruined fortunes so cooked that they shall come out of the
pot fresh and new and unembarrassed.  These great conjurors
are kept boiling though the result of the process is seldom
absolute rejuvenescence.  Way 114-5, XIII,I.

Who among us is there that does not teach himself the same
lesson  [that someone should give us money]?  PrM 44,XLV,II.

When a man is in difficulty about money, even a lie,--even a
lie that is sure to be found out to be a lie,--will serve
his immediate turn better than silence.  There is nothing
that the courts hate so much as contempt;--not even perjury.
PrM 52, XLVI,II.

A generous expenditure may be incurred once even by poor
people, but cannot possibly be maintained over a dozen
years.  AS 242, XXXVI.

As long as ready money can be made to be forthcoming without
any charge for interest, a young man must be very foolish
who will prefer to borrow it at twenty-five per cent.
DuC 132, XVII.

...those hard principles which a possessor of money always
feels it to be his business to inculcate.  AyA 315, XXXIII.

When a friend inquires as to the pecuniary distresses of a
friend he feels himself as a matter of course bound to
relieve him.  AyA 515, LIII.

[F]or he that does not love money must be an idiot.
MF 166, XV,I.

## MONEY LENDING

Men...who make their money by lending it out at recognised
rates of interest,--and who are generally very keen in
looking after their principal,--have no mercy whatsoever for
the Davises  [usurers]  of creation, and very little for

their customers.  To have had dealings with a Davis is condemnation in their eyes.  JC 17, II.

## MOONLIGHT

Who does not know the air of complex multiplicity and the
mysterious interesting grace which the moon always lends to
old gable buildings half surrounded...by fine trees!
BaT 168, XIX.

## MORBIDITY

...that morbid interest which we always take in a matter
which has been nearly fatal to us, but from which we have
escaped.  VOB 525, LXXIII.

## MORNING CALLS

...that vagueness which almost always flavours a morning
visit.  HKHWR 121, XIII.

Who does not know the fashion in which the normal young man
conducts himself when he is making a morning call?  He has
come there because he means to be civil....He would enjoy
the moment if he could.  But it is clearly his conviction
that he is bound to get through a certain amount of altogether uninteresting conversation, and then to get himself
out of the room with as little awkwardness as may be.  Unless there be a pretty girl, and chance favour him with her
special companionship, he does not for a moment suppose that
any social pleasure is to be enjoyed.  That rational amusement can be got out of talking to Mrs. Jones does not enter
into his mind.  And yet Mrs. Jones is probably a fair
specimen of that general society in which every one wishes
to mingle.  Society is to him generally made up of several
parts, each of which is a pain, though the total is deemed
to be desirable.  The pretty girl episode is no doubt an
exception,-- though that also has its pains when matter for
conversation does not come readily, or when conversation,
coming too readily, is rebuked.  The morning call may be
regarded as a period of unmitigated agony.  MF 57-8, V,I.

## MORNING PARTIES

Morning parties, as a rule, are failures.  People never know
how to get away from them gracefully.  A picnic on an island
or a mountain or in a wood may perhaps be permitted.  There
is no master of the mountain bound by courtesy to bid you
stay while in his heart he is longing for your departure.
But in a private house or in private grounds a morning party
is a bore.  One is called on to eat and drink at unnatural
hours.  One is obliged to give up the day which is useful,
and is then left without resource for the evening which is
useless.  One gets home fagged and desoeuvre, and yet at an
hour too early for bed.  There is no comfortable resource
left.  Cards in these genteel days are among the things

tabooed, and a rubber of whist is impracticable.
BaT 403, XLII.

## MOTH...FLAME

When the unfortunate moth in his semi-blindness whisks himself and his wings within the flame of the candle, and finds
himself mutilated and tortured, he even then will not take
the lesson, but returns again and again till he is destroyed....Oh!  my friends, if you will but think of it, how
many of you have been moths, and are now going about un-
gracefully with wings more or less burnt off, and with
bodies sadly scorched!   SmaH 103, XI.

## MOTHERS

But...[she], like many other mothers, was apt to be more
free in converse with her daughter than she was with her
son.  LasC 3, I.

Love on the part of a mother may be as injurious as cruelty,
if the mother be both tyrannical and superstitious.
JC 139,XIX.

I have seen a mother force open the convulsively closed jaws
of her child in order that some agonising torture might be
applied,--which though agonising, would tend to save her
sick infant's life.  She did it though the child shrank from
her as from some torturing fiend.   JC 233, XXX.

## MOTHERS...DAUGHTERS

Mothers know that their daughters will leave them.   Even
widowed mothers, mothers with but one child left...are aware
that they will be left alone, and they can bring themselves
to welcome the sacrifice of themselves with something of
satisfaction.  LasC 202, XXIII.

Happily for most young wives, though the new tie may
surmount the old one, it does not crush it or smother it.
The mother retains a diminished hold, and knowing what
nature has intended, is content.   She, too, with some
subsidiary worship, kneels at the new altar, and all is
well.  JC 337-8, XLVI.

## MOTHERS...SONS

[B]ut she was angry, as other mothers are angry, when their
foolish, calf-like boys will go and marry without any incomes on which to support a wife...with the venom with which
mothers will sometimes speak of the girls to whom their sons
are attached....Mothers are so angry when other girls, not
their own, will get offers; so doubly angry when their own
sons make them.  Ber 742-3; 747, XLII.

I suppose there is no pleasure a mother can have more

attractive than giving away money to an only son.
FrP 415, XLIII.

Mothers always so think    [that no struggle is too great to
engage their sons]    of girls engaged to their sons, and so
think especially when the girls are penniless and the sons
are well-to-do in the world.    But such belief, though it is
natural, is sometimes wrong.    Bel 333, XXV.

## MOTIVES

The motives by which men are actuated in their conduct are
not only various, but mixed.    Ber 623, XXXIV.

## MOURNING

...And when it    [note containing news of death]    was
received,    there came over the faces of them all that
lugubrious look, which is, as a matter of course, assumed by
decorous people when tidings come of the death of any one
who has been known to them, even in the most distant way....
Will any one dare call this hypocrisy?    If it be so called,
who in the world is not a hypocrite?    Where is the man or
woman who has not a special face for sorrow before company?
The man or woman who has no such face, would at once be
accused of heartless impropriety.    Cl 35, V.

People must eat and drink even when the grim monarch is in
the house; and it is a relief when they first dare to do so
with some attention to the comforts which are ordinarily so
important to them.    For themselves alone women seldom care
to exercise much trouble in this direction; but the presence
of a man at once excuses and renders necessary the ceremony
of a dinner.    Bel 110, IX.

We all know how silent on such matters    [money]    are the
voices of all in the bereft household, from the hour of
death till that other hour in which the body is consigned to
its kindred dust.    Women make mourning, and men creep about
listlessly, but during those few sad days there may be no
talk about money.    MM 199, XV.

Those who depart must have earned such    [broken-hearted
sorrow]    before it can be really felt.    They who are left
may be overwhelmed by the death--even of their most cruel
tormentors.    Way 338, LXXXVI,II.

[B]ut it is understood in the world that women mourn longer
than men.    DuC 217, XXVIII.

## MURDER

To have known a murdered man is something, but to have been
intimate with a murderer is certainly much more.    PR 84,L,II.

## MUTUALITY

[T]hat homely and somewhat vulgar Scotch proverb, "you scratch my back, and I'll scratch yours," was certainly unknown to them, but nevertheless they fully recognized the wise principle of mutual accommodation which that proverb teaches.  LaV 166, XIII.


# N


## NAMES

It must be owned that we have but a slip-slop way of christening our public buildings.  When a man tells us that he called on a friend at the Horse Guards, or looked in at the Navy Pay, or dropped a ticket at the Woods and Forests, we put up with the accustomed sounds, though they are in themselves, perhaps, indefensible.  TC 1, I.

If one wishes to look out in the world for royal nomenclature, to find children who have been christened after kings and queens, or the uncles and aunts of kings and queens, the search should be made in the families of democrats.  None have so servile a deference for the very nail-parings of royalty....It is the distance which they feel to exist between themselves and the throne which makes them covet the crumbs of majesty, the odds and ends and chance splinters of royalty.  DoT 130. X.

When you first call your lady-love by her Christian name, you do not like to have the little liberty made a subject of ridicule--you feel it by far less if the matter be taken up seriously against you as a crime on your part. Ber 570,XXXI.

I wish they would not alter the names of the streets; was it not enough that the 'Swan with Two Necks' should be pulled down?  Str 131, XXIII.

There are men who seem to be so treated [addressed by their Christian names]  in all societies.  PF 43, V,I.

There is so much in a name,--and then an ounce of ridicule is often more potent than a hundredweight of argument.
ED 140, LV,II.

John is a very respectable name;--perhaps there is no name more respectable in the English language.  Sir John, as the head of a family, is certainly as respectable as any name

can be. For an old family coachman it beats all names. Mr.
John Smith would be sure to have a larger balance at his
banker's than Charles Smith or Orlando Smith,--or perhaps
than any other Smith whatever. The Rev. Frederic Walker
would assuredly be a good clergyman at all points, though
perhaps a little dull in his sermons. Yet almost all Johns
have been Jacks, and Jack, in point of respectability, is
the very reverse of John. How it is, or when it is, that
the Jacks become re-Johned, and go back to the original and
excellent name given to them by their godfathers and god-
mothers, nobody ever knows. EE 56-7, IV,I.

A man should not have his Christian name used by every Tom
and Dick without his sanction. AS 7, I.

**NARRATIONS**

Narrations always are  [wrong in all details]. DuC 497,LXII.

There are stories for the telling of which a peculiar atmosphere is required. Kept 19, V.

**NATURE**

Nature is so good to us that we are sometimes disposed to
think we might have dispensed with art. In the bush, where
doctors do come, but come slowly, the broken bones suit
themselves to such tardiness. HHOG 133, X.

**NEEDS**

Men by dint of misery rise above the need of superfluities.
The poor wretch whom you see rolling himself, as it were, at
the corner of the street within his old tattered filthy
coat, trying to extract something more of life and warmth
out of the last glass of gin which he has swallowed, is by
no means discomposed because he has no clean linen for the
morrow. JC 111, XV.

**NEIGHBOURS**

How little do we know how other people live in the houses
close to us! We see the houses looking like our own, and we
see the people come out of them looking like ourselves. But
a Chinaman is not more different from the English John Bull
than is No. 10 from No. 11. Here there are books, paint-
ings, music, wine, a little dilettanti getting-up of subjects of the day, a little dilettanti thinking on great
affairs, perhaps a little dilettanti religion; few domestic
laws, and those easily broken; few domestic duties, and
those easily evaded; breakfast when you will, with dinner
almost as little binding, with much company and acknowledged
aptitude for idle luxury. That is life at No. 10. At No.
11 everything is cased in iron. There shall be equal
plenty, but at No. 11 even plenty is a bondage. Duty rules
everything, and it has come to be acknowledged that duty is

to be hard.  So many hours of needlework, so many hours of
books, so many hours of prayer! That all the household shall
shiver before daylight is a law, the breach of which by any
member  either  augurs  sickness  or  requires  condign
punishment.  To be comfortable is a sin; to laugh is almost
equal to bad language.  Such and so various is life at No.
10 and at No. 11.  AyA 11-2, II.

## NEW BROOMS

New brooms sweep clean; and official new brooms, I think,
sweep cleaner than any other.  Who has not watched at the
commencement of a Ministry some Secretary, some Lord, or
some Commissioner, who intends by fresh Herculean labours to
cleanse the Augean stables just committed to his care?  Who
does not know the gentleman at the Home Office, who means to
reform the police and put an end to malefactors; or the new
Minister  at  the  Board  of  Works,  who  is  to  make London
beautiful as by a magician's stroke,--or above all, the new
First Lord, who is resolved that he will really built [sic]
us a fleet, purge the dockyards, and save us half a million
a year at the same time?  PrM 96, XI,I.

## NEW THOUGHTS

A man is sufficiently condemned if it can only be shown that
either in politics or religion he does not belong to some
new school established within the last score of years.  He
may then regard himself as rubbish and expect to be carted
away....We must laugh at everything that is established.
Let the joke be ever so bad, ever so untrue to the real
principles of joking; nevertheless we must laugh--or else
beware the cart.  We must talk, think, and live up to the
spirit of the times, and write up to it too, if that
cacoethes be upon us, or else we are nought.  New men and
new measures, long credit and few scruples, great success or
wonderful ruin, such are now the tastes of Englishmen who
know how to live.  BaT 108, XIII.

## NEWCOMERS

Some of my readers may have sat at vestries, and will remember how mild, and, for the most part, mute is a new-comer at
their board.  He agrees generally, with abated enthusiasm;
but should he differ, he apologises for the liberty.  But
anon, when the voices of his colleagues have become habitual
in his ears...he throws off his awe and dismay, and elec-
trifies his brotherhood by the vehemence of his declamation
and the violence of his thumping.  FrP 191, XX.

## NEWS

There  is  a  telegraphic  wire  for  such  tidings  [jury
decisions]  which has been very long in use, and which,
though always used, is as yet but very little understood.
How is it that information will spread itself quicker than

men can travel, and make its way like water into all parts of the world? OrF 370, LXXVI,II.

All such tidings [criminal charges]  travel very quickly, conveyed by imperceptible wires, and distributed by inde-fatigable message boys whom Rumour seems to supply for the purpose. LasC 89, XI.

The news of...death had spread all over...and had been received with that feeling of distant awe which is always accompanied by some degree of pleasurable sensation. LasC 641, LXVII.

Now it is very unpleasant to find that your news is untrue, when you have been at great pains to disseminate it. PF 83, IX,I.

If a man be hurt in the hunting-field, it is always said that he's killed. If the kitchen flue be on fire, it always said that the house is burned down.  VOB 75, XII.

## NEWS, BAD

There is nothing like going to the root of the matter at once when one has on hand an unpleasant piece of business. FrP 147, XV.

Who has not felt the evil tidings conveyed by the exag-gerated tenderness of a special kiss?  Cl 268, XXXII.

## NEWSPAPERS

Who has not heard of Mount Olympus,--that high abode of all the powers of type, that favoured seat of the great goddess Pica, that wondrous habitation of gods and devils, from whence, with ceaseless hum of steam and never-ending flow of Castalian ink, issue forth eighty thousand nightly edicts for the governance of a subject nation?...
    'Is this Mount Olympus?' asks the unbelieving stranger. 'Is it from these small, dark, dingy buildings that those infallible laws proceed which cabinets are called upon to obey; by which bishops are to be guided, lords and commons controlled,--judges instructed in law, generals in strategy, admirals in naval tactics, and orange-women in the management of their barrows?' 'Yes, my friend--from these walls.  From here issue the only known infallible bulls for the guidance of British souls and bodies.  This little court is the Vatican of England.  Here reigns a pope, self-nominated, self-consecrated,--ay, and much stranger too, self-believing;--a pope whom, if you cannot obey him, I would advise you to disobey as silently as possible; a pope hitherto afraid of no Luther; a pope who manages his own in-quisiton, who punishes unbelievers as no most skilful in-quisitor of Spain ever dreamt of doing;--one who can ex-communicate thoroughly, fearfully, radically; put you beyond the pale of men's charity; make you odious to your dearest

friends, and turn you into a monster to be pointed at by the finger!'...

Were it not well for us in our ignorance that we confided all things to the Jupiter? Would it not be wise in us to abandon useless talking, idle thinking, and profitless labour? Away with majorities in the House of Commons, with verdicts from judicial bench given after much delay, with doubtful laws, and the fallible attempts of humanity! Does not the Jupiter, coming forth daily with eighty thousand impressions full of unerring decision on every mortal subject, set all matters sufficiently at rest? Is not Tom Towers here, able to guide us and willing?

Yes, indeed,--able and willing to guide all men in all things, so long as he is obeyed as autocratic should be obeyed--with undoubting submission!...

There are those who doubt the Jupiter! They live and breathe the upper air, walking here unscathed, though scorned,--men born of British mothers and nursed on English milk, who scruple not to say that Mount Olympus has its price, that Tom Towers can be bought for gold!

Such is Mount Olympus, the mouthpiece of all the wisdom of this great country. It may probably be said that no place in this 19th century is more worthy of notice. No treasury mandate armed with the signatures of all the government has half the power of one of those broad sheets, which fly forth from hence so abundantly, armed with no signature at all.

Some great man, some mighty peer,--we'll say a noble duke,--retires to rest feared and honoured by all his countrymen,--fearless himself; if not a good man, at any rate a mighty man,--too mighty to care much what men may say about his want of virtue. He rises in the morning degraded, mean, and miserable; an object of men's scorn, anxious only to retire as quickly as may be to some German obscurity, some unseen Italian privacy, or, indeed, anywhere out of sight. What has made this awful change? What has so afflicted him? An article has appeared in the Jupiter; some fifty lines of a narrow column have destroyed all his grace's equanimity, and banished him for ever from the world. No man knows who wrote the bitter words; the clubs talk confusedly of the matter, whispering to each other this and that name; while Tom Towers walks quietly along Pall Mall, with his coat buttoned close against the east wind, as though he were a mortal man, and not a god dispensing thunderbolts from Mount Olympus. War 168-70, XIV.

'The public is defrauded...whenever private considerations are allowed to have weight.' Quite true, thou greatest oracle of the middle of the nineteenth century, thou sententious proclaimer of the purity of the press--the public is defrauded when it is purposely misled. Poor public! how often is it misled! against what a world of fraud has it to contend. War 190, XV.

Now, we all know that if anything is ever done in any way towards improvement in these days, the public press does it.

And we all know, also, of what the public press consists.
TC 540, XLV.

We are not content in looking to our newspapers for all the
information that earth and human intellect can afford; but
we demand from them what we might demand if a daily sheet
could come to us from the world of spirits.  The result, of
course, is this--that the papers do pretend that they have
come daily from the world of spirits; but the oracles are
very doubtful, as were those of old.  SmaH 435, XLIII.

The editor of a Christian Examiner, if, as is probable, he
have, of his own, very strong and one-sided religious convictions, will think that those who differ from him are in a
perilous way, and so thinking, will feel himself bound to
tell them so.  The man who advocates one line of railway
instead of another, or one prime minister as being superior
to all others, does not regard his opponents as being
fatally wrong--wrong for this world and for the next--and he
can restrain himself.  But how is a newspaper writer to
restrain himself when his opponent is incurring everlasting
punishment, or, worse still, carrying away others to a
similar doom, in that they read, and perhaps even purchase,
that which the lost one has written?  In this way the contents of religious newspapers are apt to be personal; and
heavy, biting, scorching attacks, become the natural vehicle
of Christian Examiners.  MM 320-1, XXIV.

After all, what, in such matters  [morals], is an editor to
do?  Is it not his business to sell his paper?  And if the
editor of a Christian Examiner cannot trust the clergyman he
has sat under, whom can he trust?  Some risk an editor is
obliged to run, or he will never sell his paper.
MM 323, XXIV.

It had all that religious unction which is so necessary for
Christian Examiners, and with it that spice of devilry, so
delicious to humanity that without it even Christian
Examiners cannot be made to sell themselves.  MM 324, XXIV.

These are days, in which, should your wife's grandfather
have ever been insolvent, some newspaper, in its catering
for the public, will think it proper to recall the fact.
IHP 172, XVIII,I.

Who does not know that vices which may be treated with
tenderness, almost with complaisance, while they are kept in
the background, become monstrous, prodigious, awe-inspiring
when they are made public?  A gentleman shall casually let
slip some profane word, and even some friendly parson
standing by will think but little of it; but let the profane
word, through some unfortunate accident, finds [sic] its
way into the newspapers, and the gentleman will be held to
have disgraced himself almost for ever.  JC 220, XXX.

Such is the advice  ['Never notice what may be written about

you in a newspaper'] which a man always gives to his
friend. But when the case comes to himself he finds it
sometimes almost impossible to follow it. 'What's the use?
Who cares what the "Broughton Gazette" says? let it pass,
and it will be forgotten in three days. If you stir the
mud yourself, it will hang about you for months. It is
just what they want you to do...It is very disagreeable to
be worried like a rat by a dog; but why should you go into
the kennel and unnecessarily put yourself in the way of it?'
DrW 129, I, Part V.

There is no duty which a man owes to himself more clearly
than that of throwing into the waste-paper basket, un-
searched and even unopened, all newspapers sent to him without a previously-declared purpose. The sender has either
written something himself which he wishes to force you to
read, or else he has been desirous of wounding you by some
ill-natured criticism upon yourself. DrW 151, II, Part V.

## NEWSPAPER EDITORS

Editors of newspapers are self-willed, arrogant, and stiff-
necked, a race of men who believe much in themselves and
little in anything else, with no feelings of reverence or
respect for matters which are august enough to other men;--
but an injunction from a Court of Chancery is a power which
even an editor respects. PR 234, XXVII,I.

The more potent is a man, the less accustomed to endure injustice, and the more his power to inflict it,--the greater
is the sting and the greater the astonishment when he
himself is made to suffer. Newspaper editors sport daily
with the names of men of whom they do not hesitate to publish almost the severest words that can be uttered;--but let
an editor be himself attacked, even without his name, and he
thinks that the thunderbolts of heaven should fall upon the
offender. PR 236, XXVII,I.

## NOBLESSE OBLIGE

Noblesse oblige. High position will demand, and will often
exact, high work. But that rule holds as good with a Buon-
aparte as with a Bourbon, with a Cromwell as with a Stewart;
and succeeds as often and fails as often with the low born
as with the high. And good blood too will have its effect,
--physical for the most part,--and will produce bottom,
lasting courage, that capacity of carrying on through the
mud. SHHOH 196-7, XX.

## NONFEASANCE

Not to do that which justice demands is so much easier to
the conscience than to commit a deed which is palpably
fraudulent! CoH 263, XXIII.

## NOSES

...that decent look of military decorum which, since the
days of Caesar and the duke, has been always held to
accompany a hook-nose.  Ber 565, XXXI.

How many little noses there are on young women's faces which
of themselves cannot be said to be things of beauty, or joys
for ever, although they do very well in their places!   There
is the softness and colour of youth, and perhaps a dash of
fun, and the eyes above are bright, and the lips below
alluring.   In the midst of such sweet charms, what does it
matter that the nose be puggish,--or even a nose of putty,
such as you think you might improve in the original material
by a squeeze of your thumb and forefinger?  VOB 8, I.

But who has ever seen a nose to be eloquent and expressive,
which did not so spread   [a little at the base]?
DuC 219, XXVIII.

His nose was aqualine, not hooky like a bird's beak, but
with that bend which seems to give to the human face the
clearest indication of individual will.  DrW 9, I, Part I.

## NOVELS

It is indeed a matter of thankfulness that neither the historian nor the novelist hears all that is said by their
heroes or heroines, or how would three volumes or twenty
suffice!   In the present case so little of this sort have I
overheard, that I live in hopes of finishing my work within
300 pages, and of completing that pleasant task--a novel in
one volume.  War 78, VI.

In former times great objects were attained by great work.
When evils were to be reformed, reformers set about their
heavy task with grave decorum and laborious argument....We
get on now with a lighter step, and quicker:   ridicule is
found to be more convincing than argument, imaginary agonies
touch more than true sorrows, and monthly novels convince,
when learned quartos fail to do so.  If the world is to be
set right, the work will be done by shilling numbers.
     Of all such reformers Mr. Sentiment is the most
powerful.   It is incredible the number of evil practices he
has put down:   it is to be feared he will soon lack subjects, and that when he has made the working classes comfortable, and got bitter beer put into proper-sized pint
bottles, there will be nothing further for him left to do.
Mr. Sentiment is certainly a very powerful man, and perhaps
not the less so that his good poor people are so very good;
his hard rich people so very hard; and the genuinely honest
so very honest....Perhaps, however, Mr. Sentiment's great
attraction is in his second-rate characters.  If his heroes
and heroines walk upon stilts, as heroes and heroines, I
fear, ever must, their attendant satellites are as natural
as though one met them in the street:   they walk and talk

like men and women, and live among our friends a rattling,
lively life; yes, live, and will live till the names of
their calling shall be forgotten in their own, and Buckett
and Mrs. Gamp will be the only words left to us to signify a
detective police officer or a monthly nurse.  War 191-2, XV.

What story was ever written without a demon?  What novel,
what history, what work of any sort, what world, would be
perfect without existing principles both of good and evil?
War 192, XV.

It is ordained that all novels should have a male and a
female angel, and a male and a female devil.  BaT 244, XXV.

Far be it from us to follow him thither  [to the bedroom].
There are some things which no novelist, no historian,
should attempt; some few scenes in life's drama which even
no poet should dare to paint.  BaT 303, XXXII.

The end of a novel, like the end of a children's dinner-
party, must be made up of sweetmeats and sugar-plums.
BaT 504, LIII.

[W]ere it not for the fashion of the thing, this last short
chapter might be spared.  It shall at any rate be very
short.
    Were it not that I eschew the fashion of double names
for a book, thinking that no amount of ingenuity in this
respect will make a bad book pass muster, whereas a good
book will turn out as such though no such ingenuity be displayed, I might have called this 'A Tale of the Famine Year
in Ireland.'  CasR 282, XV,III.  See also WRITING OF NOVELS.

## NOVELTY

A few always fall off as time goes on.  Aristides becomes
too just, and the mind of man is greedy of novelty.
PrM 222, LXIII,II.

## NURSING

How is it that poor men's wives, who have no cold fowl and
port wine on which to be coshered up, nurse children without
difficulty, whereas the wives of rich men, who eat and drink
everything that is good, cannot do so, we will for the
present leave to the doctors and mothers to settle between
them.  BaT 212, XXIII.

# O

## OBEDIENCE

Don't let any wife think that she will satisfy her husband
by perfect obedience.  Overmuch virtue in one's neighbours
is never satisfactory to us sinners....
      A woman may see to her husband's dinners and her own
toilet, and yet have too much time for thinking.
Ber 605,XXXIII.

Obedience in this world depends as frequently on the
weakness of him who is governed as on the strength of him
who governs.  That man who was going to the left is ordered
by you with some voice of command to go to the right.  When
he hesitates you put more command in your voice, more
command into your eyes--and then he obeys. RacR 17, II.

## OCCASIONS

...that sort of parade by which most of us deem it necessary
to grace our important doings.  We have housewarmings, chris-
tenings, and gala days; we keep, if not our own birthdays,
those of our children; we are apt to fuss ourselves if
called upon to change our residences, and have, almost all
of us, our little state occasions.  BaT 502, LII.

## OCCUPATIONS

A man may be a stockbroker though he never sells any stock;
as he may be a barrister though he has no practice at the
bar.  LasC 329, XXXVII.

## OCTOBER

Perhaps in our climate, October would of all months be the
most delightful if something of its charms were not de-
tracted from by the feeling that with it will depart the
last relics of the delights of summer.  The leaves are still
there with their gorgeous coloring, but they are going.  The
last rose still lingers on the bush, but it is the last.
The woodland walks are still pleasant to the feet, but
caution is heard on every side as to the coming winter.
DuC 381, XLVII.

## OPENNESS

That she kept back something is probable; but how many are
there who can afford to tell everything?  Cl 115, XIV.

Dear old Jones, who tells his friends at the club of every
pound that he loses or wins at the races, who boasts of

Mary's favours and mourns over Lucy's coldness almost in
public, who issues bulletins on the state of his purse, his
stomach, his stable, and his debts, could not with any
amount of care keep from us the fact that his father was an
attorney's clerk, and made his first money by discounting
small bills. Everybody knows it, and Jones, who likes popularity, grieves at the unfortunate publicity. But Jones is
relieved from a burden which would have broken his poor
shoulders. PrM 3, I,I.

Indeed, how can any man open his heart to one whom he
dislikes? PrM 226, XXIV,I.

## OPINIONS

But with all of us, in the opinion which we form of those
around us, we take unconsciously the opinion of others. A
woman is handsome because the world says so. Music is
charming to us because it charms others. We drink our wines
with other men's palates, and look at our pictures with
other men's eyes. LasC 485, LII.

But in such matters [wondering how someone has reached a
high office] we are, all of us, too apt to form confident
opinions on apparent causes which are near the surface, but
which, as guides to character, are fallacious. RalH 6, I.

In forming our opinion as to others we are daily brought
into difficulty by doubting how much we should allow to
their convictions, and how far we are justified in con-
demning those who do not accede to our own. JC 164, XXII.

## OPPOSITION

How many of us are like the bull, turning away conquered by
opposition which should be as nothing to us, and breaking
our feet, and worse still, our hearts, against the rocks of
adamant. SmaH 210, XXI.

## OPPRESSION

Dogs have turned against their masters, and even Neapolitans
against their rulers, when oppression has been too severe.
BaT 23, III.

## ORDER

It is astonishing how quickly in this world of ours chaos
will settle itself into decent and graceful order, when it
is properly looked in the face, and handled with a steady
hand which is not sparing of the broom. CasR 48, III,III.

P

## PAIN

If a man decide with a fixed decision that his tooth should
come out, or his leg be cut off, let the tooth come out or
the leg be cut off on the earliest possible opportunity.   It
is the flinching from such pain that is so grievously
painful.  CasR 181, IX,I.

## PARASITES

We all know that very distich concerning the great fleas and
the little fleas which tells us that no animal is too humble
to have its parasite.  DuC 287, XXXVI.

## PARDON

A child asks pardon from his mother because he is scolded.
He wishes to avert her wrath in order that he may escape
punishment.   So also may a servant of his master, or an
inferior of his superior.  But when one equal asks pardon of
another, it is because he acknowledges and regrets the
injury he has done.   Such acknowledgment, such regret will
seldom be produced by a stern face and a harsh voice.
Ber 357, XX.

Kings are bound to pardon if they allow themselves to be
personally concerned as to punishment.  MF 266, XXVI,II.

## PARENTS...CHILDREN

Such victims   [of parental cruelty concerning love]   never
do complain.  Cl 349, XLI.

Are we to believe that the very soul of the offspring is to
be at the disposition of the parents?  LT 375, XVI.

And then the hold of a child upon the father is so much
stronger than that of the father on the child!  Our eyes are
set in our face, and are always turned forward.  The glances
that we cast back are but occasional.  SHHOH 165, XVI.

There is nothing, perhaps, in the way of exhortation and
scolding which the ordinary daughter,--or son,--dislikes so
much as to be told of her, or his, 'parent.'   'My dear
fellow, your father will be annoyed,' is taken in good part.
'What will mamma say?'  is seldom received amiss.  But when
young people have their 'parents' thrown at them, they feel
themselves to be aggrieved, and become at once antagonistic.
LA 372-3, XXXV.

A parent is often bound to disregard the immediate comfort of a child.  PrM 76, IX,I.

They say that perfect love casteth out fear.  If it be so the love of children to their parents is seldom altogether perfect,--and perhaps had better not be quite perfect.
DuC 482, LXI.

## PARENTS...DAUGHTERS

In such cases  [prevailing with the girl in asking for her hand rather than with her father]  it is so often the daughter who prevails with her own parents after she has surrendered her own heart.  JC 124, XVII.

## PARLIAMENT

We may say, perhaps, that the highest duty imposed upon us as a nation is the management of India; and we may also say that in a great national assembly personal squabbling among its members is the least dignified work in which it can employ itself.   But the prospect of an explanation,--or otherwise of a fight,--between two leading politicians will fill the House; and any allusion to our Eastern Empire will certainly empty it.   PR 322, XXXVI,I.

## PARLIAMENT, MEMBERS

To be or not to be a member of the British Parliament is a question of very considerable moment in a man's mind.  Much is often said of the great penalties which the ambitious pay for enjoying this honour; of the tremendous expenses of elections; of the long, tedious hours of unpaid labour:  of the weary days passes in the House; but, nevertheless, the prize is one very well worth the price paid for it--well worth any price that can be paid for it short of wading through dirt and dishonour....
    To some men, born silver-spooned, a seat in Parliament comes as a matter of course....
    But to men aspiring to be members, or to those who having been once fortunate have again to fight the battle without assurance of success, the coming election must be a a matter of dread concern.  Oh, how delightful to hear that the long-talked-of rival has declined the contest, and that the course is clear!  or to find by a short canvass that one's majority is safe, and the pleasures of crowing over an unlucky, friendless foe quite secured!  DoT 199-200,XVII.

There is something very pleasant in the close, bosom friend-ship, and bitter, uncompromising animosity, of these human gods....If it were so arranged that the same persons were always friends,...the thing would not be nearly so inter-esting.   But in this Olympus partners are changed, the divine bosom, now rabid with hatred against some opposing deity, suddenly becomes replete with love towards its late enemy, and exciting changes occur which give to the whole

thing all the keen interest of a sensational novel.    No
doubt this is greatly lessened for those who come too near
the scene of action.    Members of Parliament, and the friends
of Members of Parliament, are apt to teach themselves that
it means nothing; that Lord This does not hate Mr. That, or
think him a traitor to his country, or wish to crucify him;
and that Sir John of the Treasury is not much in earnest
when he speaks of his noble friend at the 'Foreign Office'
as a god to whom no other god was ever comparable in
honesty, discretion, patriotism, and genius.    But the
outside Briton who takes a delight in politics,--and this
description should include ninety-nine educated Englishmen
out of every hundred,--should not be desirous of peeping
behind the scenes.    No beholder at any theatre should do
so.    It is good to believe in these friendships and these
enmities, and very pleasant to watch their changes.
CanY 9-10, XLII,II.

It is something to have sat in the House of Commons, though
it has been but for one session!    There is on the left-hand
side of our great national hall.--on the left-hand side as
one enters it, and opposite to the doors leading to the Law
Courts,--a pair of gilded lamps, with a door between them,
near to which a privileged old dame sells her apples and her
oranges solely, as I presume, for the accommodation of the
Members of the House and of the great policeman who guards
the pass.    Between those lamps is the entrance to the House
of Commons, and none but Members may go that way!    It is the
only gate before which I have ever stood filled with envy,--
sorrowing to think that my steps might never pass under it.
There are many portals forbidden to me, as there are many
forbidden to all men; and forbidden fruit, they say, is
sweet; but my lips have watered after no other fruit but
that which grows so high, within the sweep of that great
policeman's truncheon....
    I have told myself, in anger and in grief, that to die
and not to have won that right of way, though but for a
session,--not to have passed by the narrow entrance through
those lamps,--is to die and not to have done that which it
most becomes an Englishman to have achieved....It is the
highest and most legitimate pride of an Englishman to have
the letters M.P. written after his name.    No selection from
the alphabet, no doctorship, no fellowship, be it of ever so
learned or royal a society, no knightship,--not though it be
of the Garter,--confers so fair an honour....[T]his country
is governed from between the walls of that House....[F]rom
thence flow the waters of the world's progress,--the fullest
fountain of advancing civilization.    CanY 43-5, XLV,II.

A gosling from such a flock    [midddle class family]    does
become something of a real swan by getting into Parliament.
PF 17, II,I.

There is nothing to prevent the work of a Chancery barrister
being done by a member of Parliament.    Indeed, the most successful barristers are members of Parliament.    PF 42, V,I.

A member of Parliament is not now all that he was once, but still there is a prestige in the letters affixed to his name which makes him loom larger in the eyes of the world than other men.  Get into Parliament...and the Poeples's Banners all round will be glad of your assistance, as will also companies limited and unlimited to a very marvellous extent. PF 261-2, XXVIII,I.

A man destined to sit conspicuously on our Treasury Bench, or on the seat opposite to it, should ask the gods for a thick skin as a first gift.  The need of this in our national assembly is greater than elsewhere, because the differences between the men opposed to each other are smaller....[W]hen opponents are almost in accord, as is always the case with our parliamentary gladiators, they are ever striving to give maddening little wounds through the joints of the harness.  What is there with us to create the divergence necessary for debate but the pride of personal skill in the encounter?  Who desires among us to put down the Queen, or to repudiate the National Debt, or to destroy religious worship, or even to disturb the ranks of society? When some small measure of reform has thoroughly recommended itself to the country,--so that all men know that the country will have it,--then the question arises whether its details shall be arranged by the political party which calls itself Liberal,--or by that which is termed Conservative. The men are so near to each other in all their convictions and theories of life that nothing is left to them but personal competition for the doing of the thing that is to be done.  It is the same in religion.  The apostle of Christianity and the infidel can meet without a chance of a quarrel; but it is never safe to bring together two men who differ about a saint or a surplice.  PR 296, XXXIII,I.

## PARLIAMENTARY ATTACK

To attack is so easy, when a complete refutation barely suffices to save the Minister attacked,--does not suffice to save him from future dim memories of something having been wrong,--and bring down no disgrace whatsoever on the promoter of the false charge.  The promoter of the false charge simply expresses his gratification at finding that he had been misled by erroneous information.  It is not customary for him to express gratification at the fact, that out of all the mud which he has thrown, some will probably stick!  PF 288, XXXI,I.

## PARLIAMENTARY BILLS

The effects which clauses will produce, the dangers which may be expected from this or that change, the manner in which this or that proposition will come out in the washing, do not strike even Cabinet Ministers at a glance.  A little study in a man's own cabinent, after the reading perhaps of a few leading articles, and perhaps a short conversation with an astute friend or two, will enable a statesman to be

strong at a given time for, or even, if necessary, against a measure, who has listened in silence, and has perhaps given his personal assent, to the original suggestion.
PrM 295, LXXI,II.

## PARLIAMENTARY CANVASSING

Parliamentary canvassing is not a pleasant occupation. Perhaps nothing more disagreeable, more squalid, more revolting to the senses, more opposed to personal dignity, can be conceived. The same words have to be repeated over and over again in the cottages, hovels, and lodgings of poor men and women who only understand that the time has come round in which they are to be flattered instead of being the flatterers. 'I think I am right in supposing that your husband's principles are Conservative, Mrs. Bubbs.' 'I don't know nothing about it. You'd better call again and see Bubbs hissel.' 'Certainly I will do so. I shouldn't at all like to leave the borough without seeing Mr. Bubbs. I hope we shall have your influence, Mrs. Bubbs.' 'I don't know nothing about it. My folk at hom allays vote buff; and I think Bubbs ought to go buff too. Only mind this; Bubbs don't never come home to his dinner. You must come arter six, and I hope he's to have some'at for his trouble. He won't have my word to vote unless he have some'at.' Such is the conversation in which the candidate takes a part, while his cortege at the door is criticising his very imperfect mode of securing Mrs. Bubbs' good wishes. Then he goes on to the next house, and the same thing with some variation is endured again. Some guide, philosopher, and friend, who accompanies him, and who is the chief of the cortege, has calculated on his behalf that he ought to make twenty such visitations an hour, and to call on two hundred constituents in the course of the day. As he is always falling behind in his number, he is always being driven on by his philosopher, till he comes to hate the poor creatures to whom he is forced to address himself, with a most cordial hatred.

It is a nuisance to which no man should subject himself in any weather. But when it rains there is superadded a squalor and an ill-humour to all the party which makes it almost impossible for them not to quarrel before the day is over. To talk politics to Mrs. Bubbs under any circumstance is bad, but to do so with the conviction that the moisture is penetrating from your greatcoat through your shirt to your bones, and that while so employed you are breathing the steam from those seven other wet men at the door, is abominable. To have to go through this is enough to take away all the pride which a man might otherwise take from becoming a member of Parliament. But to go through it and then not to become a member is base indeed! To go through it and to feel that you are probably paying at the rate of a hundred pounds a day for the privilege is most disheartening.
DuC 443-4, LV.

## PARLIAMENTARY DEBATE

It is not very often that so strong a fury rages between
party and party at the commencement of the session that a
division is taken upon the Address.  It is customary for the
leader of the opposition on such occasions to express his
opinion in the most courteous language, that his right
honourable friend, sitting opposite to him on the Treasury
bench, has been, is, and will be wrong in everything that he
thinks, says, or does in public life; but that...the Address
to the Queen...shall be allowed to pass unquestioned.  Then
the leader of the House thanks his adversary for his consideration, explains to all men how happy the country ought to
be that the Government has not fallen into the disgracefully
incapable hands of his right honourable friend opposite; and
after that the Address is carried amidst universal serenity.
PF 48, VI,I.

But a speaker who can certainly be made amenable to authority for vilipending in debate the heart of any specified
opponent, may with safety attribute all manner of ill to the
agglomerated hearts of a party.  PR 323, XXXVI,I.

## PARLIAMENTARY INFLUENCE

The favour was of a kind that had prevailed from time out of
mind in England, between the most respectable of the great
land magnates, and young rising liberal politicians.  Burke,
Fox, and Canning had all been placed in Parliament by
similar influence.  PF 292, XXXI,I.

## PARLIAMENTARY MANAGEMENT

There have been various rocks on which men have shattered
their barks in their attempts to sail successfully into the
harbours of parliamentary management.  There is the great
Senator who declares to himself that personally he will have
neither friend nor foe....He knows that he can be just, he
teaches himself to be eloquent, and he strives to be wise.
But he will not bend;--and at last, in some great solitude,
though closely surrounded by those whose love he had
neglected to acquire,--he breaks his heart.
     Then there is he who seeing the misfortune of that
great one, tells himself that patriotism, judgment, industry, and eloquence will not suffice for him unless he
himself can be loved....So he smiles and learns the necessary wiles....It is well with him for a time;--but he has
closed the door of his Elysium too rigidly.  Those without
gradually become stronger than his friends within, and so he
falls.
     But may not the door be occasionally opened to an out-
sider, so that the exterior force be diminshed?  We know how
great is the pressure of water; and how the peril of an
overwhelming weight of it may be removed by opening the way
for a small current.  There comes therefore the Statesman
who acknowledges to himself that he will be pregnable.

That, as a Statesman, he should have enemies is a matter of course.  Against moderate enemies he will hold his own.  But when there comes one immoderately forcible, violently inimical, then to that man he will open his bosom.  He will tempt into his camp with an offer of high command any foe that may be worth his purchase.  This too has answered well; but there is a Nemesis.  The loyalty of officers so procured must be open to suspicion.  The man who has said bitter things against you will never sit at your feet in contented submission, nor will your friend of old standing long endure to be superseded by such converts.  DuC 163-5, XXI.

The management of a party is a very great work in itself; and when to that is added the management of the House of Commons, a man has enough upon his hands even though he neglects altogether the ordinary pursuits of a Statesman.  DuC 166, XXI.

In these great matters parliamentary management goes for so much!  If a man be really clever and handy at his trade, if he can work hard and knows what he is about, if he can give and take and be not thin-skinned or sore-bored, if he can ask pardon for a peccadillo and seem to be sorry with a good grace, if above all things he be able to surround himself with the prestige of success, then so much will be forgiven him!  DuC 559, LXXI.

## PARLIAMENTARY PROCEDURE

Rights and rules, which are bonds of iron to a little man, are packthread to a giant.  PR 317, XXXV, I.

## PARLIAMENTARY SPEECH

There are many rocks which a young speaker in Parliament should avoid, but no rock which requires such careful avoiding as the rock of eloquence.  Whatever may be his faults, let him at least avoid eloquence.  He should not be inaccurate, which, however, is not much; he should not be long-winded, which is a good deal; he should not be ill-tempered, which is more; but none of these faults are so damnable as eloquence.  CanY 11, XLII, II.

For such a work [to speak in Parliament]  a man should have all his senses about him,--his full courage, perfect confidence, something almost approaching to contempt for listening opponents, and nothing of fear in regard to listening friends.  He should be as a cock in his own farmyard, master of all the circumstances around him.  PF 184, XX, I.

It may be imagined,--probably still is imagined by a great many,--that no such pledge as this  [that it would be 'fixed' that one may speak]  could be given, that the right to speak depends simply on the Speaker's eye, and that energy at the moment in attracting attention would alone be of account to an eager orator.  That some preliminary assistance would be given to the travelling of the Speaker's eye, in so important a debate, he knew very well. PR 286,XXXII,I.

## PARLIAMENTARY SUCCESS

There is no merit in a public man like success....When a man has nailed fortune to his chariot-wheels he is apt to travel about in rather a proud fashion....And then a discreet, commonplace, zealous member of the Lower House does not like to be jeered at, when he does his duty by his constituents and asks a few questions.  An all-successful minister who cannot keep his triumph to himself, but must needs drive about in a proud fashion, laughing at commonplace zealous members--laughing even occasionally at members who are by no means commonplace, which is outrageous!--may it not be as well to ostracise him for a while?  FrP 75, VIII.

## PARSIMONY

I have said that she spent much money in dress, and some people will perhaps think that the two points of character are not compatible.   Such poeple knew nothing of a true spirit of parsimony.  It is from the backs and bellies of other people that savings are made with the greatest constancy and the most satisfactory results.

The parsimony of a mistress of a household is best displayed on matters eatable;--on matters eatable and drinkable; for there is a fine scope for domestic savings in tea, beer, and milk....The miser who starves himself and dies without an ounce of flesh on his bones, while his skinny head lies on a bag of gold, is after all, respectable. There has been a grand passion in his life, and that grandest work of man, self-denial.  You cannot altogether despise one who has clothed himself with rags and fed himself with bone-scrapings, while broadcloth and ortolans were within his easy reach.   But there are women, wives and mothers of families, who would give the bone-scrapings to their husbands and the bones to their servants, while they hide the ortolans for themselves; and would dress children in rags, while they cram chests, drawers, and boxes with silks and satins for their own backs.  Such a woman one can thoroughly despise, and even hate.  OrF 64-5, VII,I.

## PARTIES, GARDEN

For, though of all parties a garden party is the nicest, everybody is always anxious to get out of the garden as quick as may be.  PF 236, LXIII,II.

## PARTINGS

Last days are wretched days; and so are last moments wretched moments.  It is not the fact that the parting is coming which makes these days and moments so wretched, but the feeling that something special is expected from them, which something they always fail to produce.  Spasmodic periods of pleasure, of affection, or even of study, seldom fail of disappointment when premeditated. When last days are coming, they should be allowed to come and to glide away without special notice or mention. And as for last moments, there should be none such. Let them ever be ended, even before their presence has been acknowledged. SmaH 139, XV.

## PARTISANSHIP

I know a man--an excellent fellow, who being himself a strong politician, constantly expresses a belief that all politicians opposed to him are thieves, child-murderers, parricides, lovers of incest, demons upon the earth. He is a strong partisan....He says that he believes all evil of his opponents....LasC 90, XI.

## PATRIOTISM

[F]ew, perhaps, do [know the meaning of patriotism] beyond a feeling that they would like to lick the Russians, or to get the better of the Americans in a matter of fisheries or frontiers. DuC 165, XXI.

## PEACE OFFERINGS

It is much less difficult for the sufferer to be generous than for the oppressor. War 69, VI.

## PEDIGREE

It [a pedigree] is one of those possessions which to have is sufficient. A man having it need not boast of what he has, or show it off before the world. But on that account he values it the more. DoT 367, XXX.

## PEOPLE, OLD

...hung upon him with that wondrous affection which old people with warm hearts feel for those whom they have selected as their favourites. Bel 100, VIII.

Old reminiscences remain very firm with old people.
EE 54, III,I.

## PEOPLE, POOR

[B]ut it should be remembered that among the poor, especially when they live in clusters, such misfortunes cannot be hidden as they may be amidst the decent belongings of more wealthy people. LasC 102, XII.

## PEOPLE, YOUNG

Who can say why it is that those encounters, which are so ardently desired by both sides, are so rarely able to get themselves commenced till the enemies have been long in sight of each other?...Go into any public dancing-room of Vienna, where the girls from the shops and the young men from their desks congregate to waltz and make love, and you shall observe that from ten to twelve they will dance as vigorously as at a later hour, but that they will hardly talk to each other till the mellowness of the small morning hours has come upon them.  NB 81, VII.

## PERSECUTION

For a true spirit of persecution one should always go to a woman, and the milder, the sweeter, the more loving, the more womanly the woman, the stronger will be that spirit within her.  Strong love for the thing loved necessitates strong hatred for the thing hated, and thence comes the spirit of persecution.  They in England who are now keenest against the Jews, who would again take from them rights they have lately won, are certainly those who think most of the faith of a Christian.  The most deadly enemies of the Roman Catholics are they who love best their religion as Protestants.  When we look to individuals we always find it so, though it hardly suits us to admit as much when we discuss these subjects broadly.  RacR 322-3, XXV.

## PERSERVERANCE

But it requires much personal strength,--that standing alone against the well-armed batteries of one's friends.
PF 215, LXII,II.

## PERSUASION

In Ireland it is said of any man who is more than ordinarily persuasive, that he can 'talk the devil out of the liver wing of a turkey!'  Ber 384, XXI.

## PERVERSITY

They who do not understand that a man may be brought to hope for that which of all things is the most grievous to him, have not observed with sufficient closeness the perversity of the human mind.  HKHWR 364, XXXVIII.

## PESSIMISM

It may always be observed that when hunting-men speak seriously of their sport, they speak despondingly.  Everything is going wrong.  Perhaps the same thing may be remarked in other pursuits.  Farmers are generally on the verge of ruin.  Trade is always bad.  The Church is in danger.  The House of Lords isn't worth a dozen years' purchase.  The throne totters.  DuC 496, LXII.

## PHILISTINES

Alas, alas, it is very hard to break asunder the bonds of

the latter-day Philistines.  When a Samson does now and then
pull a temple down about their ears, is he not sure to be
engulfed in the ruin with them?    There is no horse-leech
that sticks so fast as your latter-day Philistine.
FrP 86-7, IX.

## PHILOSOPHY

But such philosophy  [live for the pleasure of the moment]
will too frequently be insufficient for the stoutest hearts.
MSF 270, XXXIX,II.

## PHOTOGRAPHS

That bringing out and giving of photographs, with the demand
for counter photographs, is the most absurd practice of the
day.    'I don't think I look very nice, do I?'    'Oh yes;--
very nice; but a little too old; and certainly you haven't
got those spots all over your forehead.' These are the remarks which on such occasions are the most common.    It may
be said that to give a photograph or to take a photograph
without the utterance of some words which would be felt by a
bystander to be absurd, is almost an impossibility.
PF 173, LVII,II.

## PICNICS

A picnic undertaken from Jerusalem must in some respects be
unlike any picnic elsewhere.  Ladies cannot be carried to it
in carriages, because at Jerusalem there are no carriages;
nor can the provisions be conveyed even in carts, for at
Jerusalem there are no carts....Here, in England, one would
hardly inaugurate a picnic to Kensal Green or the Highgate
Cemetery, nor select the tombs of our departed great ones as
a shelter under which to draw one's corks.  Ber 142-3, IX.

A picnic should be held among green things.  Green turf is
absolutely an essential.    There should be trees,  broken
ground, small paths, thickets, and hidden recesses.    There
should, if possible, be rocks, old timbers, moss, and
brambles.  There should certainly be hills and dales,--on a
small scale, and, above all, there should be running water.
There should be no expanse.  Jones should not be able to see
all Greene's movements, nor should Augusta always have her
eye upon her sister Jane.  CanY 76, VIII.

[F]or ladies, though they like good things at picnics, and,
indeed, at other times, almost as well as men like them,
very seldom prepare dainties for themselves alone.  Men are
wiser and more thoughtful, and are careful to have the good
things, even if they are to be enjoyed without companionship.  HKHWR 147, XVI.

## PINCHBECK

[F]or how seldom is it that the hearts and souls of the

young are able to withstand pinchbeck and gilding?
CasR 147, VIII,II.

## PITY

If you, my reader, ever chanced to slip into the gutter on a
wet day, did you not find that the sympathy of the by-
standers was by far the severest part of your misfortune?
Did you not declare to yourself that all might yet be well,
if the people would only walk on and not look at you? And
yet you cannot blame those who stood and pitied you; or,
perhaps, essayed to rub you down, and assist you in the recovery of your bedaubed hat. You, yourself, if you see a
man fall, cannot walk by as though nothing uncommon had
happened to him. SmaH 312, XXX.

## PLEASURES

There is hardly a pleasure in life equal to that of laying
out money with a conviction that it will come back again.
The conviction, alas, is so often ill-founded,--but the
pleasure is the same. RalH 372, XLIX.

## POACHING

There is no doubt a certain pleasure in poaching which does
not belong to the licit following of game; but a man can't
poach if the right of shooting be accorded to him.
VOB 243, XXXV.

## POISE

[W]hen such is the case with a man   [not being master of
himself], the fact always betrays him. Ber 607, XXXIII.

## POLICEMEN

Now a London policeman in a political row is, I believe, the
most forbearing of men....Trip up a policeman in such a
scramble, and he will take it in good spirit; but mention
the words 'Habeas Corpus,' and he'll lock you up if he can.
As a rule, his instincts are right; for the man who talks
about 'Habeas Corpus' in a political crowd will generally do
more harm than can be effected by the tripping up of any
constable. But these instincts may be the means of individual injustice. PF 235, XXV,I.

When does any policeman ever believe anything?  VOB 98, XV.

It may be doubted whether, to the normal policeman's mind,
any man is ever altogether absolved of any crime with which
that man's name has been once connected. VOB 384, LIII.

## POLITICAL BOLDNESS

Cromwell was bold when he closed the Long Parliament.

Shaftesbury was bold when he formed the plot for which Lord Russell and others suffered. Walpole was bold when, in his lust for power, he discarded one political friend after another. And Peel was bold when he resolved to repeal the Corn Laws. PR 48, V,I.

## POLITICAL ENMITY

We who are conversant with our own methods of politics, see nothing odd in this [advising the Queen to send for the opposition], because we are used to it; but surely in the eyes of strangers our practice must be very singular....The leaders of our two great parties are to each other exactly as are the two champions of the ring who knock each other about for the belt and for five hundred pounds a side once in every two years. How they fly at each other, striking as though each blow should carry death if it were but possible! And yet there is no one whom the Birmingham Bantam respects so highly as he does Bill Burns the Brighton Bully, or with whom he has so much delight in discussing the merits of a pot of half-and-half. PF 82, IX,I.

## POLITICAL HONESTY

[W]hat woman ever understood the necessity or recognized the advantages of political honesty? FrP 13, II.

## POLITICAL PRESSURE

It is the essential nature of a political party in this country to avoid, as long as it can be avoided, the consideration of any question which involves a great change. There is a consciousness on the minds of leading politicians that the pressure from behind, forcing upon them great measures, drives them almost quicker than they can go, so that it becomes a necessity with them to resist rather than to aid the pressure which will certainly be at last effective by its own strength. The best carriage horses are those which can most steadily hold back against the coach as it trundles down the hill. PR 34-5, IV,I.

## POLITICAL SPEECHES

Who makes the speeches, absolutely puts together the words, which are uttered when the Address is moved and seconded? It can hardly be that lessons are prepared and sent to the noble lords and honourable gentlemen to be learned by heart like a schoolboy's task. And yet, from their construction, style, and general tone,--from the platitudes which they contain as well as from the general safety and good sense of the remarks,--from absence of any attempt to improve a great occasion by the fire of oratory, one cannot but be convinced that a very absolute control is exercised. The gorgeously apparelled speakers, who seem to have great latitude allowed them in the matter of clothing, have certainly very little in the matter of language. And then it always seems that either of the four might have made the speech of any of the others.  PR 73-4, VIII,I.

## POLITICIANS

But how many men in his walk of life can be trusted?  And those who can--at how terribly high a price do they rate their own fidelity!  How often must a minister be forced to confess to himself that he cannot afford to employ good faith!   TC 88, V.

...support the prime minister and merit all manner of legal generalships without any self-unbinding.  Alas!  such comfort as this can only belong to the young among politicians! Ber 286, XVI.

When a man gets into his head an idea that the public voice calls for him, it is astonishing how great becomes his trust in the wisdom of the public.  Vox populi, vox Dei.  'Has it not been so always?'  he says to himself, as he gets up and as he goes to bed.  FrP 76, VIII.

They are men of whom in the lump it may be surmised that they take up this or that side in politics...simply because on this side or on that there is an opening.  That gradually they do grow into some shape of conviction from the moulds in which they are made to live, must be believed of them; but these convictions are convictions as to divisions, convictions as to patronage, convictions as to success, convictions as to Parliamentary management; but not convictions as to the political needs of the people.  RalH 303-4, XL,II.

...old-world politicians,--we meet them every day, and they are generally pleasant people,--who enjoy the politics of the side to which they belong without any special belief in them.  If pressed hard they will almost own that their so-called convictions are prejudices.  But not for worlds would they be rid of them....They feel among themselves that everything that is being done is bad,--even though that everything is done by their own party.  It was bad to interfere with Charles, bad to endure Cromwell, bad to banish James, bad to put up with William.  The House of Hanover was bad.  All interference with prerogative has been bad.  The Reform bill was very bad.  Encroachment on the estates of the bishops was bad.  Emancipation of Roman Catholics was the worst of all.  Abolition of corn-laws, church-rates, and oaths and tests were all bad.  The meddling with the Universities has been grievous.  The treatment of the Irish Church has been Satanic.  The overhauling of schools is most injurious to English education.  Education bills and Irish land bills were all bad.  Every step taken has been bad. And yet to them old England is of all countries in the world the best to live in, and is not at all the less comfortable because of the changes that have been made.  These people are ready to grumble at every boon conferred on them, and yet to enjoy every boon.  They know too their privileges,

and, after a fashion, understand their position. It is
picturesque, and it pleases them. To have been always in
the right and yet always on the losing side; always being
ruined, always under persecution from a wild spirit of
republican-demagogism,--and yet never to lose anything, not
even position or public esteem, is pleasant enough. A huge,
living, daily increasing grievance that does one no pal-
pable harm, is the happiest possession that a man can have.
There is a large body of such men in England, and, personally, they are the very salt of the nation. He who said
that all Conservatives are stupid did not know them. Stupid
Conservatives there may be,--and there certainly are very
stupid Radicals. The well-educated, widely-read Conservative, who is well assured that all good things are gradually being brought to an end by the voice of the people, is
generally the pleasantest man to be met. ED 33-4, IV,I.

But what exertion will not a politician make with the view
of getting the point of his lance within the joints of his
enemies' harness? ED 67, VII,I.

A drunkard or a gambler may be weaned from his ways, but not
a politician. PR 118, XIII,I.

...that busy, magpie air which is worn only by those who
have high hopes of good things to come speedily.
PR 283, XXXII,I.

## POLITICS

The use of a little borough of his own, however, is a con-
venience to a great peer. PF 251, XXVII,I.

The highest legal offices in the country are not to be attained by any amount of professional excellence, unless the
candidate shall have added to such excellence the power of
supporting a Ministry and a party in the House of Commons.
...[B]ut...there are various ways in which a lame dog may be
helped over a stile,--if only the lame dog be popular among
dogs. RalH 3, I.

How often has the same thing    ["I should throw up the
contest in the middle of it,--even if I were winning,--if I
suspected that money was being spent improperly"]   been said
by a candidate, and what candidate ever has thrown up the
sponge when he was winning? RalH 149, XX.

Let a man be of what side he may in politics,--unless he be
much more of a partisan than a patriot,--he will think it
well that there should be some equity of division in the
bestowal of crumbs of comfort. Can even any old Whig wish
that every Lord Lieutenant of a county should be an old
Whig? Can it be good for the administration of the law than
none but Liberal lawyers should become Attorney-Generals,
and from thence Chief Justices or Lords of Appeal? Should
no Conservative Peer ever represent the majesty of England

in India, in Canada, or at St. Petersburgh?    PR 2, I,I.

The political feelings of the country are, as a rule, so
well marked that it is easy, as to almost every question, to
separate the sheep from the goats.    PR 69, VIII,I.

It was a simple avowal that...men were to be regarded, and
not measures.    No doubt such is the case, and ever has been
the case, with the majority of active politicians.    The
double pleasure of pulling down an opponent, and of raising
oneself, is the charm of a politician's life....Men and not
measures are, no doubt, the very life of politics.    But then
it is not the fashion to say so in public places.
PR 275-6, XXXI,I.

It is right, according to our constitution, that the Government should be entrusted to the hands of those whom the constituencies of the country have most trusted.    And, on
behalf of the country, it behoves the men in whom the
country has placed its trust to do battle in season and out
of season,--to carry on war internecine,--till the demands
of the country are obeyed.    PR 349, XXXIX,I.

When a man, perhaps through a long political life, has bound
himself to a certain code of opinions, how can he change
that code at a moment?    And when at the same moment,
together with the change, he secures power, patronage, and
pay, how shall the public voice absolve him?    But then again
men, who have by the work of their lives grown into a certain position in the country...cannot free themselves altogether from the responsibility of managing them when a
period comes such as that now reached [a coalition].
PrM 66, VIII,I.

Does not all the world know that when in autumn the
Bismarcks of the world, or they who are bigger than
Bismarcks, meet at this or that delicious haunt of salu-
brity, the affairs of the world are then settled in little
conclaves, with greater ease, rapidity, and certainty than
in large parliaments or the dull chambers of public offices?
Emperor meets Emperor, and King meets King, and as they wander among rural glades in fraternal intimacy, wars are
arranged, and swelling territories are enjoyed in
anticipation.    PrM 188, XX,I.

Such blunderings and quarrellings have been a matter of
course since politics have been politics, and since religion
has been religion.    When men combine to do nothing, how
should there be disagreement?    When men combine to do much,
how should there not be disagreement?    Thirty men can sit
still, each as like the other as peas.    But put your thirty
men up to run a race, and they will soon assume different
forms.    And in doing nothing, you can hardly do amiss.    Let
the doers of nothing have something of action forced upon
them, and they too, will blunder and quarrel.

The wonder is that there should ever be in a reforming party enough of consentaneous action to carry any reform. DuC 162, XXI.

This reassertion of the progress of the tide, this recovery from the partial ebb which checks the violence of every flow, is common enough in politics. DuC 167, XXI.

But the strength of the minority consisted, not in the fact that the majority against them was small, but that it was decreasing.  How quickly does the snowball grow into hugeness as it is rolled on,--but when the change comes in the weather how quickly does it melt, and before it is gone become a thing ugly, weak, and formless!  Where is the individual who does not assert to himself that he would be more loyal to a falling than to a rising friend?  Such is perhaps the nature of each one of us.  But when any large number of men act together, the falling friend is apt to be deserted.  DuC 167-8, XXII.

When any body of statesmen make public asservations by one or various voices, that there is no discord among them, not a dissentient voice on any subject, people are apt to suppose that they cannot hang together much longer.  It is the man who has no peace at home that declares abroad that his wife is an angel.  He who lives on comfortable terms with the partner of his troubles can afford to acknowledge the ordinary rubs of life.  DuC 558, LXXI.

A state of things...must be very common in political life. The hatreds which sound so real when you read the mere words, which look so true when you see their scornful attitudes, on which for the time you are inclined to pin your faith so implicitly, amount to nothing.  The Right Honourable A. has to do business with the Honourable B., and can best carry it on by loud expressions and strong arguments such as will be palatable to readers of newspapers; but they do not hate each other as the readers of the papers have them, and are ready enough to come to terms, if coming to terms is required.  Each of them respects the other, though each of them is very careful to hide his respect. Land 169-70, XLII,III.

## POOR RATES

The country was, and for the matter still is, divided, for purposes of poor-law rating, into electoral districts.  In ordinary times a man, or at any rate a lady, may live and die in his or her own house without much noticing the limits or peculiarities of each district.  In one the rate may be one and a penny in the pound, in another only a shilling. But the difference is not large enough to create inquiry. It is divided between the landlord and the tenant, and neither perhaps thinks much about it.  But when the demand made rises to seventeen or eighteen shillings in the pound --as was the case in some districts in those days,--when out of every pound of rent that he paid the tenant claimed to deduct nine shillings for poor rates, that is, half the amount levied--then a landlord becomes anxious enough as to the peculiarities of his own electoral division.

In the case of Protestant clergymen, the whole rate had to be paid by the incumbent. A gentleman whose half-yearly rent-charge amounted to perhaps two hundred pounds might have nine tenths of that sum deducted from him for poor rates. I have known a case in which the proportion has been higher than this.

And then the tenants in such districts began to decline to pay any rent at all--in very many cases could pay no rent at all. They too, depended on the potatoes which were gone; they, too, had been subject to those dreadful demands for poor rates; and thus a landlord whose property was in any way embarassed had but a bad time of it. CasR 130-2, VII,I.

## POSITION

She was afflicted by the weight of her own position, as we suppose the Queen to be, when we say that her Majesty's altitude is too high to admit of friendships. MM 115, IX. It is no doubt a fact that with the very best of girls a man is placed in a very good light by being heir to a peerage and a large property. EE 50, III,I.

It can not really be that all those who swarm in the world below the bar of gentlehood are less blessed, or intended to be less blessed, than the few who float in the higher air. ...Does any one believe that the Countess has a greater share of happiness than the grocer's wife, or is less subject to the miseries which flesh inherits? But such matters cannot be changed by the will. EE 93-4, V,I.

People are taken and must be taken in the position they frame for themselves. Kept 3, I.

## POSTMEN

There is a general understanding that the wooden-legged men in country parishes should be employed at postmen, owing to the great steadiness of demeanour which a wooden leg is generally found to produce. It may be that such men are slower in their operations than would be biped postmen; but as all private employers of labour demand labourers with two legs, it is well that the lame and the halt should find a refuge in the less exacting service of the government. HKHWR 166-7, XVIII.

## POST OFFICE

[The] letter...[was] conveyed with that lightning rapidity for which the British Post-office has ever been remarkable --and especially that portion of it which has reference to the sister island. CasR 148, VIII,III.

Dukes and Ministers, Barons and Princes, are terms familiar
to the frequenters of the Foreign Office.    Ambassadors,
Secretaries, and diplomatic noblemen generally, are necessarily common in the mouths of all the officials.    But at
the Post Office such titles still...[carry] with them something of awe.    MF 147, XIV,II.

## POST SCRIPTS

They say that the pith of a lady's letter is in the post-
script.    OrF 41, V,I.

## POTHEEN

It was...considered no revenue officer would notice potheen
if he met it as a guest.    People are rather more careful now
on the matter.    MB 156, VII,I.

## POT-HOUSE

There is no sign, perhaps, which gives to a house of this
class so disreputable an appearance as red curtains hung
across the window; and yet there is no other colour for pot-
house curtains that has any popularity.    The one fact probably explains the other.    A drinking-room with a blue or a
brown curtain would offer no attraction to the thirsty navvy
who likes to have his thirst indulged without criticism.
VOB 278, XIL.

## POVERTY

Oh, deliver us from the poverty of those who, with small
means, affect a show of wealth!    There    is no whitening
equal to that of sepulchres whited as they are whited!
SmaH 454, XLV.

None but they who have themselves been poor gentry--gentry
so poor as not to know how to raise a shilling--can understand the peculiar bitterness of the trials which such
poverty produces.    The poverty of the normal poor does not
approach it; or, rather, the pangs arising from such poverty
are altogether of a different sort.    To be hungry and have
no food, to be cold and have no fuel, to be threatened with
distraint for one's few chairs and tables, and with the loss
of the roof over one's head--all these miseries, which, if
they do not positively reach, are so frequently near to
reaching the normal poor, are, no doubt, the severest of the
trials to which humanity is subjected....By hook or crook,
the poor gentleman or poor lady...does not often come to the
last extremity of the workhouse....But there are pangs to
which, at the time, starvation itself would seem to be preferable.    The angry eyes of unpaid tradesmen, savage with an
anger which one knows to be justifiable; the taunt of the
poor servant who wants her wages; the gradual relinquishment
of habits which the soft nurture of earlier, kinder years
had made second nature; the wan cheeks of the wife whose

malady demands wine; the rags of the husband whose outward
occupations demand decency; the neglected children, who are
learning not to be the children of gentlefolk; and, worse
than all, the alms and doles of half-generous friends, the
waning pride, the pride that will not wane, the growing
doubt whether it be not better to bow the head, and acknowledge to all the world that nothing of the pride of
station is left--that the hand is open to receive and ready
to touch the cap, that the fall from the upper to the lower
level has been accomplished--these are the pangs of poverty
which drive the Crawleys of the world to the frequent entertaining of that idea of the bare bodkin.  LasC 77-8, IX.

It is very pretty to talk of the alluring simplicity of a
clean calico gown, but poverty will shew itself to be
meagre, dowdy, and draggled in a woman's dress, let the
woman be ever so simple, ever so neat, ever so independent,
and ever so high-hearted.  HKHWR 546, LVIII.

## POWER

In such institutions [the Dorcas society]  there is generally need of a strong, stirring, leading mind.  If some one
would not assume power, the power needed would not be
exercised.  RacR 9, I.

Marvellous is the power which can be exercised, almost unconsciously, over a company, or an individual, or even upon
a crowd by one person gifted with good temper, good digestion, good intellects, and good looks.   A woman so
endowed charms not only by the exercise of her own gifts,
but she endows those who are near her with a sudden conviction that it is they whose temper, health, talents, and
appearance is doing so much for society.  RacR 336, XXVI.

## PRAISE

[B]ut praise undeserved, though it may be satire in
disguise, is often very useful.  Cl 293, XXXIV.

## PRAYER

Alas!  how any of us from week to week call ourselves worms
and dust and miserable sinners, describe ourselves as chaff
for the winds, grass for the burning, stubble for the
plough, as dirt and filth fit only to be trodden under foot,
and yet in all our doings before the world cannot bring home
to ourselves to conviction that we require other guidance
than our own!  TC 104, IX.

If it was a prayer!  As far as my own experience goes, such
utterances [grace before a formal dinner]  are seldom
prayers, seldom can be prayers.  And if not prayers, what
then?  To me it is unintelligible that the full tide of
glibbest chatter can be stopped at a moment in the midst of
profuse good living, and the Giver thanked becomingly in

words of heartfelt praise....Clergymen there are--one meets
them now and then--who endeavour to give to the dinner-table
grace some of the solemnity of a church ritual, and what is
the effect?   Much the same as though one were to be interrupted for a minute in the midst of one of our church
liturgies to hear a drinking-song....
     Dinner-graces are, probably, the last remaining relic
of certain daily services[1] which the Church in olden days
enjoined:   nones, complines, and vespers were others.   Of
the nones and complines we have happily got quit; and it
might be well if we could get rid of the dinner-graces also.
Let any man ask himself whether, on his own part, they are
acts of prayer and thanksgiving--and if not that, what then?

     [1] It is, I know, alleged that graces are said before
dinner, because our Saviour uttered a blessing before his
last supper.   I cannot say that the idea of such analogy is
pleasing to me. DoT 235-6, XIX [The footnote is Trollope's.]

What would a clergyman say on such an occasion  [a death in
the family]  if the object of his solicitude were to decline
the offer, remarking that prayer at that moment did not seem
to be opportune; and that, moreover, he, the person thus
invited, would like, first of all, to know what was to be
the special object of the proposed prayer, if he found that
he could, at the spur of the moment, bring himself at all
into a fitting mood for the task?  Of him who would decline,
without argument, the clergyman would opine that he was
simply a reprobate....Men and women, conscious that they
will be thus judged, submit to the hypocrisy, and go down
upon their knees unprepared, making no effort, doing nothing
while they are there, allowing their consciences to be eased
if they can only feel themselves numbed into some ceremonial
awe by the occasion....[O]f all the works in which man can
engage himself, that of prayer is the most difficult.
Bel 109, IX.

But they who send others to the throne of heaven for direct
advice are apt to think that the asking will not be done
aright unless it be done with their spirit and their bias,--
with the spirit and bias which they feel when they recommend
the operation.   No one has ever thought that direct advice
from the Lord was sufficient authority for the doing of that
of which he himself disapproved.   JC 339-40, XLVI.

But praying is by no means the easiest work to which a man
can set himself.   Kneeling is easy; the repetition of the
well-known word is easy; the putting on of some solemnity of
mind is perhaps not difficult.   But to remember what you are
aking, why you are asking, of whom you are asking; to feel
sure that you want what you do ask, and that this asking, is
the best way to get it;--that on the whole is not easy.
Ber 473, XXVI.

## PREACHING

But the sermon was the thing to try the man.  It often sur-
prises us that very young men can muster courage to preach
for the first time to a strange congregation.  Men who are
as yet but little more than boys, who have but just left,
what indeed we may not call a school, but a seminary intended for their tuition as scholars, whose thoughts have
been mostly of boating, cricketing, and wine parties, ascend
a rostrum high above the heads of the submissive crowd, not
that they may read God's word to those below, but that they
may preach their own word for the edification of their
hearers.  It seems strange to us that they are not stricken
dumb by the new and awful solemnity of their position.  How
am I, just turned twenty-three, who have never yet passed
ten thoughtful days since the power of thought first came to
me, how am I to instruct these greybeards, who with the
weary thinking of so many years have approached so near the
grave?  Can I teach them their duty?  Can I explain to them
that which I so imperfectly understand, that which years of
study may have made so plain to them?  Has my newly acquired
priviliege, as one of God's ministers, imparted to me as yet
any fitness for the wonderful work of a preacher?
It must be supposed that such ideas do occur to young
clergymen, and yet they overcome, apparently with ease, this
difficulty which to us appears to be all but insurmountable.
We have never been subjected in the way of ordination to the
power of a bishop's hands.  It may be that there is in them
something that sustains the spirit and banishes the natural
modesty of youth....
There is a rule in our church which forbids the younger
order of our clergymen to perform a certain portion of the
service.  The absolution must be read by a minister in
priest's orders.  If there be no such minister present, the
congregation can have the benefit of no absolution but that
which each may succeed in administering to himself....But
this forbearance on the part of youth would be much more
appreciated if it were extended likewise to sermons.  The
only danger would be that congregations would be too anxious
to prevent their young clergymen from advancing themselves
in the ranks of the ministry.  Clergymen who could not
preach would be such blessings that they would be bribed to
adhere to their incompetence. BaT 210, 11, XXIII.

A man who has once been induced to preach to another against
a fault will feel himself somewhat constrained by his own
sermons.  JC 88, XII.

## PREJUDICE

A man cannot rid himself of a prejudice because he knows or
believes it to be a prejudice.  MF 26, II,I.

## PRESTIGE

Many men have learned the value of such ascendancy

[prestigious friends], and most men have known the want of
it.  SHHOH 73, VIII.

## PRIDE

It is hardly possible that the proud-hearted should love
those who despise them.  FrP 113, XI.

But it is so hard for us to give up our high hopes, and willingly encounter poverty, ridicule, and discomfort!
FrP 185, XIX.

Pride must bear pain;--but pain is recompensed by pride.
HKHWR 621, LXV.

## PRIME MINISTERS

It is the special business of Prime Ministers to be civil in
detail, though roughness, and perhaps almost rudeness in the
gross, becomes not unfrequently a necessity of their
position.    To a proposed incoming subordinate a Prime
Minister is, of course, very civil, and to a retreating
subordinate he is generally more so,--unless the retreat be
made under unfavourable circumstances.    And to give good
things is always pleasant, unless there be a suspicion that
the good thing will be thought to be not good enough.
PR 336, LXXVII,II.

But a Prime Minister cannot escape till he has succeeded in
finding a successor; and though the successor be found and
consents to make an attempt, the old unfortunate cannot be
allowed to go free when that attempt is shown to be a
failure.    He has not absolutely given up the keys of his
boxes, and no one will take them from him.    Even a sovereign can abdicate; but the Prime Minister of a constitutional government is in bonds.  PrM 45-6, VI,I.

Unless there be some special effort of lawmaking before the
country, some reform bill to be passed, some attempt at
education to be made, some fetters to be forged or to be re-
laxed, a Prime Minister is not driven hard by the work of
his portfolio,--as are his colleagues.    But many men were in
want of many things, and contrived by many means to make
their wants known to the Prime Minister.    A dean would fain
be a bishop, or a judge a chief justice, or a commissioner a
chairman, or a secretary a commissioner.    Knights would fain
be baronets, baronets barons, and barons earls.    In one
guise or another the wants of gentlemen were made known, and
there was work to be done.    A ribbon cannot be given away
without breaking the hearts of, perhaps, three gentlemen and
of their wives and daughters.  PrM 166-7, XVIII,I.

If one were asked in these days what gift should a Prime
Minister ask first from the fairies, one would name the
power of attracting personal friends.    Eloquence, if it be
too easy, may become almost a curse.    Patriotism is

suspected, and sometimes sinks almost to pedantry. A Jove-born intellect is hardly wanted, and clashes with the infer-iorities. Industry is exacting. Honesty is unpractical. Truth is easily offended. Dignity will not bend. But the man who can be all things to all men, who has ever a kind word to speak, a pleasant joke to crack, who can forgive all sins, who is ever prepared for friend or foe but never very bitter to the latter, who forgets not men's names, and is always ready with little words,--he is the man who will be supported at a crisis....It is for him that men will struggle, and talk, and, if needs be, fight, as though the very existence of the country depended on his political security....[B]ut still the violent deposition of a Prime Minister is always a memorable occasion. PrM 314-5,LXIII,II.

## PRINCIPLES

And yet it is so hard to be true to high principles in little things. The heroism of the Roman, who, for his country's sake, leapt his horse into a bottomless gulf, was as nothing to that of a woman who can keep her temper through poverty, and be cheerful in adversity. TC 558,XLVII.

[B]ut there are circumstances in which a man cannot stick to his ship,--cannot stick, at least, to this special Govern-ment ship. PF 264, LXVI,II.

But it is so hard to bring one's general principles to bear on one's own conduct or in one's own family. ED 273, XXX,I.

There are men who will stick to their sport though Apollyon himself should carry the horn. Who cares whether the lady who fills a theatre be or be not a moral young woman, or whether the bandmaster who keeps such excellent time in a ball has or has not paid his debts? DuC 394, XLIX.

## PRIVACY

A walk in a wood is perhaps almost as good as a comfortable seat in a drawing-room, and is, perhaps, less liable to intrusion. AyA 542, LVI.

## PROCESSIONS

A procession, let it be who it will that proceeds, has in it, of its own nature, something of order. PF 231, XXV,I.

## PROCRASTINATION

We have all some of that cowardice which induces us to post-pone an inevitably evil day. DoT 466, XXXIX.

A strong-minded man goes direct from the hall door to his chamber without encountering the temptation of the drawing-room fire. FrP 5, I.

If it be ordained that a man shall drown, had he not better drown and have done with it?   FrP 322, XXXIII.

The attack and the defence should thus be made suddenly, at [the] ...first meeting.   It is better to pull the string at once when you are in the shower-bath, and not stand shivering, thinking, of the inevitable shock which you can only postpone for a few minutes.   CanY 153, XV,I.

It is, moreover, felt by us all that the time which may fairly be taken in the performance of any task depends, not on the amount of work, but on the performance of it when done.   A man is not expected to write a cheque for a couple of thousand pounds as readily as he would one for five,-- unless he be a man to whom a couple of thousand pounds is a mere nothing.   ED 246-7, LXVII,II.

Who has not felt, as he stood by a stream into which he knew that it was his fate to plunge, the folly of delaying the shock?   AS 515, LXXIV.

**PROFIT**

[P]rofit, like power, comes from the people, and not from the court.   Str 25, IV.

**PROGRESS**

Come, my friend, and discourse with me.   Let us know what are thy ideas of the inestimable benefits which science has conferred on us in these, our latter days.   How dost thou, among others, appreciate railways and the power of steam, telegraphs, telegrams, and our new expresses?   But indif- ferently, you say.   'Time was I've zeed vifteen pair o' 'osses go out of this 'ere yard in vour-and-twenty hour; and now ther be'ant vifteen, no, not ten, in vour-and-twenty days!   There was the duik--not this 'un; he be'ant no gude; but this 'un's vather--why, when he'd come down the road, the cattle did be a-going, vour days an eend.   Here'd be the tooter and the young gen'lemen, and the governess and the young leddies, and then the servants--they'd be al'ays the grandest folk of all--and then the duik and the doochess-- Lord love 'ee, zur; the money did fly in them days!   But now--'and the feeling of scorn and contempt which the lame ostler was enabled by his native talent to throw into that word, 'now,' was quite as eloquent against the power of steam as anything that has been spoken at dinners, or written in pamphlets by the keenest admirers of latter-day lights.
        'Why, luke at this 'ere town,' continued he of the sieve, 'the grass be a-growing in the very streets;--that can't be no gude.   Why, luke -ee here, zur; I do be a- standing at this 'ere gateway, just this way, hour arter hour, and my heyes is hopen, mostly;--I zees who's a-coming and who's a-going.   Nobody's a-coming and nobody's a-going; that can't be no gude.   Luke at that there homnibus; why,

darn me--' and now, in his eloquence at this peculiar point,
my friend became more loud and powerful than ever--'why darn
me, if maister harns enough with that there bus to put hiron
on them there osses' feet, I'll--be--blowed!' And as he
uttered this hypothetical denunciation on himself he spoke
very slowly, bringing out every word as it were separately,
and lowering himself at his knees at every sound, moving at
the same time his right hand up and down. When he had
finished, he fixed his eyes upon the ground, pointing downwards, as if there was to be the site of his doom if the
curse that he had called down upon himself should ever come
to pass: and then, waiting no further converse, he hobbled
away, melancholy, to his deserted stables.
        Oh, my friend! my poor lame friend! it will avail
nothing to tell thee of Liverpool and Manchester; of the
glories of Glasgow, with her flourishing banks; of London,
with its third million of inhabitants; of the great things
which commerce is doing for this nation of thine! What is
commerce to thee, unless it be a commerce in posting on that
worn-out, all but useless great western turnpike-road?
There is nothing left for thee but to be carted away as
rubbish--for thee and for many of us in these now prosperous
days; oh, my melancholy, care-ridden friend! DoT 182-4, XV.

## PROMISES

There is a proverb with reference to the killing of cats,
and those who know anything either of high or low government places, will be well aware that a promise may be made
without positive words, and that an expectant may be put
into the highest state of encouragement, though the great
man on whose breath he hangs may have done no more than
whisper that 'Mr. So-and-so is certainly a rising man.'
BaT 4, I.

## PROMOTIONS

As long as promotions cometh from any human source, whether
north or south, east or west, will not such a claim as this
[fourteen children] hold good, in spite of all our examination tests, detur digniori's and optimist tendencies? It
is fervently to be hoped that it may. Till we can become
divine we must be content to be human, lest in our hurry for
a change we sink to something lower. BaT 419, XLII.

Men lapped in Elysium, steeped to the neck in bliss, must
expect to see their friends fall off from them. Human
nature cannot stand it. If I want to get anything from my
old friend Jones, I like to see him shoved up into a high
place. But if Jones, even in his high place, can do nothing
for me, then his exaltation above my head is an insult and
an injury. Who ever believes his own dear intimate companion to be fit for the highest promotion? FrP 191, XX.

## PROPERTY

Men, when they are acquiring property, think much of such things [grounds surounding a house], but they who live where their ancestors have lived for years, do not feel the misfortune. BaT 206, XXII.

[S]uch a property...does not in England belong altogether to the owner of it.  Those who live upon it, and are closely concerned in it with reference to all they have in the world, have a part property in it.  They make it what it is, and will not make it what it should be, unless in their hearts they are proud of it. RalH 215-6, XXVIII.

That was an injustice...[that an Irish tenant should pay rent to a Protestant landlord]; as is all property in accordance with teaching of some political doctors who are not burdened with any. Land 48, III,I.

## PROPHECY

But it is given to some men to originate such tidings, and the performance of the prophecy is often brought about by the authority of the prophet. FrP 289, XXIX.

## PROPOSALS

Men we believe seldom make such resolves  [to propose].... [B]ut gentlemen generally propose without any absolutely defined determination as to their doing so. BaT 470,XLVIII.

We are inclined to think that these matters are not always discussed by mortal lovers in the poetically passionate phraseology which is generally thought to be appropriate for their description.  A man cannot well describe that which he has never seen nor heard; but the absolute words and acts of one such scene did once come to the author's knowledge.  The couple were by no means plebeian, or below the proper standard of high bearing and high breeding; they were a handsome pair, living among educated people, sufficiently given to mental pursuits, and in every way what a pair of polite lovers ought to be.  The all-important conversation passed in this wise.  The site of the passionate scene was the seashore, on which they were walking, in autumn.
     Gentleman. 'Well, Miss ____, the long and the short of it is this:  here I am; you can take me or leave me.'
     Lady--scratching a gutter on the sand with her parasol, so as to allow a little salt water to run out of one hole into another.  'Of course, I know that's all nonsense.'
     Gentleman.  'Nonsense!  By Jove, it isn't nonsense at all:  come, Jane; here I am:  come, at any rate you can say something.'
     Lady.  'Yes, I suppose I can say something.'
     Gentleman.  'Well, which is it to be; take me or leave me?'
     Lady--very slowly, and with a voice perhaps hardly

articulate, carrying on, at the same time, her engineering works on a wider scale. 'Well, I don't exactly want to leave you.'

And so the matter was settled; settled with much propriety and satisfaction; and both the lady and gentleman would have thought, had they ever thought about the matter at all, that this, the sweetest moment of their lives, had been graced by all the poetry by which such moments ought to be hallowed. DoT 87-8, VII.

Gentlemen who make offers by letter must have a weary time of it, waiting for the return of post. Ber 748, XLII.

Now I here profess my belief, that nine of such offers are commenced with an intimation that the lover is going away. There is a dash of melancholy in such tidings well suited to the occasion. If there be any spark of love on the other side it will be elicited by the idea of a separation. And then, also, it is so frequently the actual fact. This making of an offer is in itself a hard piece of business, --a job to be postponed from day to day. It is so postponed, and thus that dash of melancholy, and that idea of separation are brought in at the important moment with so much appropriate truth. OrF 303, XXX,I.

Shall we be man and wife? Few men, I fancy, dare to put it all at once in so abrupt a way, and yet I do not know that the English language affords any better terms for the question. SmaH 75, VIII.

It is the way of men to carry on such affairs [of love] without any complete arrangement of their own plans or even wishes. RacR 138, XI.

With most ladies, when a gentleman has been on his knees before one of them in the morning, with outspoken protestations of love, with clearly defined proffers of marriage, with a minute inventory of the offerer's worldly wealth,-- down even to the 'mahogany-furnitured' bed-chambers....and when all these overtures have been peremptorily declined,-- a gentleman in such a case, I say, would generally feel some awkwardness in sitting down to tea with the lady at the close of such a performance. CanY 403-4, XXXIX,I.

But there are perhaps few men who make such offers in direct terms without having already said and done that which make such offers simply necessary as the final closing of an accepted bargain. LasC 38, V.

But, as there are men who will allow themselves all imaginable latitude in their treatment of woman, believing that the world will condone any amount of fault of that nature, so are there other men, and a class of men which on the whole is the more numerous of the two, who are tremblingly alive to the danger of censure on this head [being explicit about offering marriage where it has been understood] --and to the danger of censure not only from others but from them-selves also.  LasC 51, VII.

When a lady is frank enough to declare tht her heart is not her own to give, a man can hardly wish to make further prayer for the gift.  HKHWR 158, XVII.

There was once a family of three ancient maiden ladies, much respected and loved in the town in which they lived.  Their manners of life were well known among their friends, and excited no surprise; but a stranger to the locality once asked of the elder why Miss Matilda, the younger, always went first out of the room?  'Matilda once had an offer of marriage,' said the dear simple old lady, who had never been so graced, and who felt that such an episode in life was quite sufficient to bestow brevet rank.  HKHWR 675, LXXII.

In these days men never expect to be refused.  It has gone forth among young men as a doctrine worthy of perfect faith, that young ladies are all wanting to get married,--looking out for lovers with an absorbing anxiety, and that few can dare to refuse any man who is justified in proposing to them.  RalH 207, XXVII.

The offer of herself by a woman to a man is, to us all, a thing so distasteful that we at once declare that the woman must be abominable....But the man to whom the offer is made hardly sees the thing in the same light.  He is disposed to believe that, in his peculiar case, there are circumstances by which the woman is, if not justified, at least excused. ED 321, XXXV,I.

It is inexpressibly difficult for a man to refuse the tender of a woman's love.  We may almost say that a man should do so as a matter of course,--that the thing so offered becomes absolutely valueless by the offer,...and that the fairest beauty and most alluring charms of feminine grace should lose their attraction when thus tendered openly in the market.  No doubt such is our theory as to love and love-making.  But the action to be taken by us in matters as to which the plainest theory prevails for the guidance of our practice, depends so frequently on accompanying circum-stances and correlative issues, that the theory, as often as not, falls to the ground.  ED 126-7, LIII,II.

## PROPRIETY

Is it not a pity that people who are bright and clever should so often be exceedingly improper?  and that those who are never improper should so often be dull and heavy? BaT 317, XXXIII.

## PROSPERITY

Prosperity is always becoming more prosperous. VOB 201,XXIX.

## PROTESTANTS...CATHOLICS

In Ireland stanch Protestantism consists too much in a hatred of Papistry--in that rather than in a hatred of those errors against which we Protestants are supposed to protest. Hence the cross--which should, I presume, be the emblem of salvation to us all--creates a feeling of dismay and often of disgust instead of love and reverence; and the very name of a saint savours in Irish Protestant ears of idolatry, although Irish Protestants on every Sunday profess to believe in a communion of such.    These are the feelings rather than the opinions of the most Protestant of Irish Protestants, and it is intelligible that they should have been produced by the close vicinity of Roman Catholic worship in the minds of men who are energetic and excitable, but not always discreet or argumentative. CasR 185-6, X,I.

I do not wish it to be understood that this sort of feeling hatred always prevailed in Irish parishes between the priest and the parson even before the days of the famine.    I myself have met a priest at a parson's table, and have known more than one parish in which the Protestant and Roman Catholic clergymen lived together on amicable terms.    But such a feeling as that above represented was common, and was by no means held as proof that the parties themselves were quarrelsome or malicious.    It was a part of their religious convictions, and who dares to interfere with the religious convictions of a clergyman? CasR 189-90, X,I.

And indeed there did often exist in England at this time a misapprehension as to Irish wants, which led to some misuses of the funds which England so liberally sent.    It came at that time to be the duty of a certain public officer to inquire into a charge made against a seemingly respectable man in the far west of Ireland, purporting that he had appropriated to his own use a sum of twelve pounds sent to him for the relief of the poor of his parish.    It had been sent by three English maiden ladies to the relieving officer of the parish of Kilcoutymorrow, and had come to his hands, he then filling that position.    He, so the charge said,--and unfortunately said so with only too much truth,--had put the twelve pounds into his own private pocket.    The officer's duty in the matter took him to the chairman of the Relief Committee, a stanch old Roman Catholic gentleman nearly eighty years of age, with a hoary head and white beard,... one who above all things was true to the old religion.
   Then the officer of the government told his story to the old Irish gentleman--with many words, for there were all manner of small collateral proofs, to all of which the old Irish gentleman listened with a courtesy and patience which were admirable.    And when the officer of the government had done, the old Irish gentleman thus replied:    'My neighbour Hobbs,'--such was the culprit's name--'has undoubtedly done this thing.    He has certainly spent upon his own uses the generous offering made to our poor parish by those nobleminded ladies, the three Miss Walkers.    But he has

acted with perfect honesty in the matter.'
    'What!' said the government officer, 'robbing the
poor, and at such a time as this!'
    'No robbery at all, dear sir,' said the good old Irish
gentleman, with the blandest of all possible smiles; 'the
excellent Miss Walkers sent their money for the Protestant
poor of the parish of Kilcoutymorrow, and Mr. Hobbs is the
only Protestant within it.' And from the twinkle in the old
man's eye, it was clear to see that his triumph consisted in
this,--that not only he had but one Protestant in the
parish, but that the Protestant should have learned so
little from his religion.
    But this is an episode. And nowadays no episodes are
allowed....For as some English, such as the three Miss
Walkers, feared on the one hand that the Babylonish woman so
rampant in Ireland might swallow up their money for
Babylonish purposes; so, on the other hand, did others dread
that the too stanch Protestantism of the church militant in
that country might expend the funds collected for the undoubted bodily wants in administering to the supposed wants
of the soul. No such faults did, in truth, at that time
prevail. The indomitable force of the famine had absolutely
knocked down all that; but there had been things done in
Ireland, before the famine came upon them, which gave
reasonable suspicion for such fears. CasR 151-4, VIII,III.

## PROTOCOL

If Providence would only send...a Peer for every dinner-
party, the thing would go more easily; but what woman will
tell me, off-hand, which should go out of a room first; a
C.B., an Admiral of the Blue, the dean of Barchester, or the
Dean of Arches? Who is to know who was everybody's father?
How am I to remember that young Thompson's progenitor was
made a baronet and not a knight when he was Lord Mayor?
LasC 212, XXIV.

## PROVERBS

There is an old saying, which the unenlightened credit, and
which declares that that which is sauce for the goose is
sauce also for the gander. Nothing put into a proverb since
the days of Solomon was ever more untrue. That which is
sauce for the goose is not sauce for the gander, and
especially is not so in official life. TC 549, XLVI.

Is it not a good thing that grapes should become sour which
hang out of reach? Is he not wise who can regard all grapes
as sour which are manifestly too high for his hand? Those
grapes of the Treasury bench, for which gods and giants
fight, suffering so much when they are forced to abstain
from eating, and so much more when they do eat--those grapes
are very sour to me. I am sure that they are indigestible,
and that those who eat them undergo all the ills which the
Revalenta Arabica is prepared to cure. FrP 240, XXV.

...that most unjust of all proverbs, which declares that there is never smoke without fire.  HKHWR 303, XXXII.

With great care and cunning workmanship one may almost make a silk purse out of a sow's ear, but not quite.   IHP 13,I,I.

## PRUDENCE

There are men, and excellent men too, from whose minds the cares of life never banish themselves, who never seem to remember that provision is made for the young ravens.  They toil and spin always, thinking sternly of the worst and rarely hoping for the best.  They are ever making provision for rainy days, as though there were to be no more sunshine. So anxious are they for their children that they take no pleasure in them, and their fear is constant that the earth will cease to produce her fruits.  OrF 409, LXXX,II.

A man in such cases  [helping a former sweetheart]  should do what he is asked to do, and do no more.  Cl 39, V.

There are moments in one's life in which not to be impru- dent, not to be utterly, childishly forgetful of all wordly wisdom, would be to be brutal, inhuman, and devilish. VOB 142, XX.

## PUBLICITY

In such matters as this  [examining all parts of one's life]..., there is often a special cruelty in the exposure of matters which are for the most part happily kept in the background.   A man on some occasion inadvertently takes a little more wine than is good for him.   It is an accident most uncommon with him, and nobody thinks much about it. But chance brings the case to the notice of the police courts, and the victim is published to the world as a drunk- ard in the columns of all the newspapers.  Some young girl fancies herself in love, and the man is unworthy.   The feeling passes away, and none but herself, and perhaps her mother, are the wiser.   But if by some chance, some treachery, a letter should get printed and read, the poor girl's punishment is so severe that she is driven to wish herself in the grave.  JC 292-3, XL.

## PUNISHMENT

...Poena, that just but Rhadamanthine goddess, whom we moderns ordinarily call Punishment, or Nemesis when we wish to speak of her goddess-ship, very seldom fails to catch a wicked man though she have sometimes a lame foot of her own, and though the wicked man may possibly get a start of her. FrP 453, XLVII.

...that partiality for the corporal chastisement of an enemy which is certainly not uncommon to the feminine mind. VOB 349, XLVIII.

...[W]hen a child soils her best frock, we put her in a
corner with a scolding; but when she tells a fib we quell
her little soul within her by a terrible quiescence. To be
eloquently indignant without a word is within the compass of
the thoughtfully stolid. MF 33, III,I.

## PURSUIT

For the flight of the quarry ever adds eagerness to the pursuit of the huntsman. DoT 348, XXIX.

## PYRAMIDS

Oh, those pyramid guides! foul, false, cowardly, bullying
thieves! A man who goes to Cairo must see the Pyramids.
Convention, and the laws of society as arranged on that
point, of course require it. But let no man, and, above
all, no woman, assume that the excursion will be in any way
pleasurable. I have promised that I will not describe such
a visit, but I must enter a loud, a screeching protest
against the Arab brutes--the sheiks being the very worst of
the brutes--who have these monuments in their hands. Their
numbers, the filthiness of their dress--Or one might almost
say no dress--their stench, their obscene indecency, their
clattering noise, their rapacity, exercised without a
moment's intercession; their abuse, as in this wise: 'Very
bad English-man; dam bad; dam, dam, dam! Him want to take
all him money to the grave; but no,no,no! Devil hab him,
and money too!' This, be it remembered, from a ferocious,
almost blackened Arab, with his face within an inch of your
own. And then their flattery, as in this wise: 'Good
English-man--very good!,--and then a tawny hand pats your
face, and your back, and the calves of your leg--'Him gib
poor Arab one shilling for himself--yes, yes, yes! and then
Arab no let him tumble down and break all him legs--yes,
yes; break all him legs.' And then the patting goes on
again. These things, I say, put together, make a visit to
the Pyramids no delightful recreation. My advice to my
countrymen who are so unfortunate as to visit them is this:
Let the ladies remain below--not that they ever will do so,
if the gentlemen who are with them ascend--and let the men
go armed with stout sticks, and mercilessly belabour any
Arab who attempts either to bully or to wheedle.
    Let every Englishman remember this also, that the
ascent is not difficult, though so much noise is made about
the difficulty as naturally to make a man think that it is
so! And let this also be remembered, that nothing is to be
gained by entering the pyramid except dirt, noise, stench,
vermin, abuse, and want of air. Nothing is to be seen there
--nothing to be heard. A man may sprain his ankle, and
certainly will knock his head. He will encounter no other
delights but these.
    But he certainly will come out a wiser man than he went
in. He will then be wise enough to know how wretched a
place is the interior of a pyramid--an amount of wisdom with
which no teaching of mine will imbue him. Ber 673-4,XXXVIII.

Q

## QUAKERS

...that touch of hypocrisy which seems to permeate the now antiquated speeches of Quakers.  MF 168, XV,I.

## QUALITY

'Mother,' said a fastidious child to his parent, 'the bread is gritty and the butter tastes of turnips.'    'Turnips indeed,--and gritty!'  said the mother.  'Is it not a great thing to have bread and butter at all?' I own that my sympathies are with the child.  Bread and butter is a great thing; but I would have it of the best if that be possible. OrF 216, LXI,II.

A gentleman once, on ordering a mackerel for dinner, was told that a fresh mackerel would come to a shilling.  He could have a stale mackerel for sixpence.  'Then bring me a stale mackerel,' said the gentleman.  ED 240, LXVI,II.

## QUARRELS

[B]ut there are affairs in life which will ride over family quarrels and trample them out, unless they be [deep]  and of [long]  standing.  RacR 147, XII.

I wonder whether anyone will read these pages who has never known anything of the bitterness of a family quarrel?  If so, I shall have a reader very fortunate, or else very cold-blooded.  It would be wrong to say that love produces quarrels; but love does produce those intimate relations of which quarrelling is too often one of the consequences--one of the consequences which frequently seem to be so natural, and sometimes seem to be unavoidable.  One brother rebukes the other--and what brothers ever lived together between whom there is no such rebuking?--then some warm word is misunderstood and hotter words follow and there is a quarrel. The husband tyrannizes, knowing that it is his duty to direct, and the wife disobeys, or only partially obeys, thinking that a little independence will become her--and so there is a quarrel.  The father, anxious only for his son's good, looks into that son's future with other eyes than those of his son himself--and so there is a quarrel.  They come very easily, these quarrels, and the quittance from them is sometimes terribly difficult.  Much of thought is necessary before the angry man can remember that he too in part may have been wrong; and any attempt at such thinking is almost beyond the power of him who is carefully nursing

his wrath, lest it cool!   But the nursing of such quarrelling   kills   all   happiness....His   anger   poisons   every
pleasure of his life.   He is sullen at his meals, and cannot understand his book as he turns its pages.   His work,
let it be what it may, is ill done.   He is full of his quar-
rel--nursing it.   He is telling himself how much he has
loved that wicked one, how many have been his sacrifices for
that wicked one, and that now that wicked one is repaying
him simply with wickedness!   And yet the wicked one is at
that very moment dearer to him than ever.   If that wicked
one could only be forgiven how sweet would the world be
again!   And yet he nurses his wrath.   LasC 444, XLIX.


R


## RADICALS

I must beg my reader to understand that a radical is not
necessarily a revolutionist or even a republican.   He does
not, by reason of his social or political radicalism, desire
the ruin of thrones, the degradation of nobles, the spoil-
ation of the rich, or even the downfall of the bench of
bishops....It is in this that he is a radical; that he
desires, expects, works for, and believes in, the gradual
progress of the people.   No doctrine of equality is his.
Liberty he must have, and such position, high or low, for
himself and others, as each man's individual merits will
achieve for him.   The doctrine of outward equality he
eschews as a barrier to all ambition, and to all improvement.   The idea is as mean as the thing is impracticable.
But within,--is it in his soul or in his heart?--within his
breast there is a manhood that will own no inferiority to
the manhood of another.   He retires to a corner that an earl
with his suite may pass proudly through the doorway, and he
grudges the earl nothing of his pride.   It is the earl's
right.   But he also has his right; and neither queen, nor
earl, nor people shall invade it.   That is the creed of a
radical.   RacR 331, XXVI.

All the world over, boots   [bootmakers]   do affect radical
sentiments.   RalH 148, XX.

For a man with sound views of domestic power and marital
rights always choose a Radical!   LA 483, XLV.

The radicalism of a Marquis is apt to be tainted by special
considerations in regard to his own family.   MF 9, I,I.

## RANK, SOCIAL

In the first place there was a dreadful line to be drawn.
Who were to dispose themselves within the ha-ha, and who
without?    To this the unthinking will give an off-hand
answer, as they will to every ponderous question.    Oh, the
bishop and such like within the ha-ha; and Farmer Greenacre
and such like without.    True, my unthinking friend; but who
shall define such likes?    It is in such definitions that the
whole difficulty of society consists.    To seat a bishop on
an arm chair on a lawn and place Farmer Greenacre at the end
of a long table in the paddock is easy enough; but where
will you put Mrs. Lookaloft, whose husband, though a tenant
on the estate, hunts in a red coat, whose daughters go to a
fashionable seminary in Barchester, who calls her farmhouse
Rosebank, and who has a pianoforte in her drawing-room?    The
Misses Lookaloft, as they call themselves, won't sit contented among the bumpkins.    Mrs. Lookaloft won't squeeze her
fine clothes on a bench and talk familiarly about cream to
good Mrs. Greenacre.    And yet Mrs. Lookaloft is no fit companion and never has been the associate of the Thornes and
the Grantleys.    And if Mrs. Lookaloft be admitted within the
sanctum of fashionable life; if she be allowed with her
three daughters to leap the ha-ha, why not the wives and
daughters of other families also?    Mrs. Greenacre is at
present well contented with the paddock, but she might cease
to be if she saw Mrs. Lookaloft on the lawn.    BaT 336, XXXV.

But a man who has once walked in the world as a gentleman
knows not what it is to change his position, and place himself lower down in the social rank.    Much less can he know
what it is so to put down the woman whom he loves.    There
are a thousand things, mean and trifling in themselves,
which a man despises when he thinks of them in his philosophy, but to dispense with which puts his philosophy to so
stern a proof....Who can see his children hungry, and not
take bread if it be offered?    Who can see his wife lying in
sharpest want, and not seek a remedy if there be a remedy
within reach?    FrP 138-9, XIV.

Masses of men will almost feel that a certain amount of injustice ought to be inflicted on their betters, so as to
make things even and will persuade themselves that a
criminal should be declared to be innocent, because the
crime committed has had a tendency to oppress the rich and
pull down the mighty from their seats.    Some few years
since, the basest calumnies that were ever published in this
country, uttered by one of the basest men that ever disgraced the country, levelled, for the most part, at men of
whose characters and services the country was proud, were
received with a certain amount of sympathy by men not themselves dishonest, because they who were thus slandered had
received so many good things from Fortune, that a few evil
things were thought to be due to them.    Way 128, LXIV,II.

There are positions exalted beyond the reach of benevolence,

because benevolence would seem to be self-seeking.
DuC 142, XVIII.

## RASHNESS

When you have done the rashest thing in the world it is very
pleasant to be told that no man of spirit could have acted
otherwise.   PR 102, XII,I.

[T]wo attributes...may serve to make any man famous.   They
were recklessness of life and devotion to an idea.   If Fortune do not help, recklessness of life amidst...dangers...
will soon bring a man to his end, so that there will be no
question of fame.   But we see men occasionally who seem to
find it impossible to encounter death.   Land 245-6, XV,I.

## RATS

Rats always leave a falling house.   MB 187, VI,II.

## READING

Men and women say that they will read, and think so,--those,
I mean, who have acquired no habit of reading,--believing
the work to be, of all works, the easiest.   It may be work,
they think, but of all works it must be the easiest of
achievement.   Given the absolute faculty of reading, the
task of going through the pages of a book must be, of all
tasks, the most certainly within the grasp of the man or
woman who attempts!   Alas, no;--if the habit be not there,
of all tasks it is the most difficult.   If a man have not
acquired the habit of reading till he be old, he shall
sooner in his old age learn to make shoes than learn the
adequate use of a book.   And worse again;--under such circumstances the making of shoes shall be more pleasant to him
than the reading of a book.   Let those who are not old,--who
are still young, ponder this well.   Cl 379-80, XLV.

## REALITY

But, in truth, the artists have been so much in the habit of
painting for us our friends' faces without any of those
flaws and blotches with which work and high living are apt
to disfigure us, that we turn in disgust from a portrait in
which the roughness and pimples are made apparent.
Bel 246-7, XIX.

## REDISTRICTING

In the discussion of any such arrangement how easy is the
picking of holes; how impossible the fabrication of a garment that shall be impervious to such picking!
PF 345, XXXVI,I.

## REFORM

[I]t was known to all men that they advocated Reform as we
all of us advocate doctors.    Some amount of doctoring is
necessary for us....Let us give with an open hand,--but
still with a hand which, though open, shall not bestow too
much.    The coach must be allowed to run down the hill.    Indeed, unless the coach goes on running no journey will be
made.    But let us have the drag on both the hind wheels.
And we must remember that coaches running down hill without
drags are apt to come to serious misfortune.    PF 333,XXXV,I.

The straight-going people of the world, in dealing with
those who go crooked, are almost always unreasonable.
'Because you have been bad,' say they who are not bad to
those who are bad, 'because you have hitherto indulged
yourself with all pleasures within your reach, because you
have never worked steadily or submitted yourself to
restraint, because you have been a drunkard, and a gambler,
and have lived in foul company, therefore now,--now that I
have got a hold of you and can manipulate you in reference
to your repentance and future conduct,--I will require from
you a mode of life that, in its general attractions, shall
be about equal to that of a hermit in the desert.    If you
flinch you are not only a monster of ingratitude towards me,
who am taking all this trouble to save you, but you are also
a poor wretch for whom no possible hope of grace can
remain.' When it is found that a young man is neglecting his
duties, doing nothing, spending his nights in billiard rooms
and worse places, and getting up at two o'clock in the day,
the usual prescription of his friends is that he should lock
himself up in his own dingy room, drink tea, and spend his
hours in reading good books.    It is hardly recognised that a
sudden change from billiards to good books requires a
strength of character which, if possessed, would probably
have kept the young man altogether from falling into bad
habits.    If we left the doors of our prisons open, and
expressed disgust because the prisoners walked out, we
should hardly be less rational.    VOB 367-8, LII.

## REFUSALS

There are men to whom a peal of noes rattling about their
ears never takes the sound of a true denial, and others to
whom the word once pronounced, be it whispered ever so
softly, comes as though it were an unchangeable verdict from
the supreme judgment-seat.    SmaH 427, XLII.

...that answer, which of all answers is the most grievous to
the true-hearted lover.    'She felt for him unbounded esteem,
and would always regard him as a friend.'    A short decided
negative, or a doubtful no, or even an indignant repulse,
may be changed....But an assurance of esteem and friendship
means, and only can mean, that the lady regards her lover as
she might do some old uncle or patriarchal family connection, whom, after a fashion, she loves, but who can never be

to her the one creature to be worshipped above all others.
RalH 110-11, XIV.

There are men to whom such a disappointment [being refused]
as this causes enduring physical pain--as though they had
become suddenly affected with some acute and yet lasting
disease.    And there are men, too, who suffer the more because they cannot conceal the pain.    IHP 8-9, I,I.

There is a tone of refusal, which, though the words used may
be manifestly enough words of denial, is in itself indica-
tive of assent.    AyA 97, XI.

Surely such a proposition as this    ["If you'd only stay and
come as one of my friends"]    is the unkindest that any young
lady can make.    But we believe that it is made not unfrequently.    MSF 313, LXIV,III.

## REFUSING

But there is nothing which requires so much experience to
attain as the power of refusing.    IHP 263, XXVII,I.

## REJECTION

There is a sort of disgrace often felt, if never acknowledged, which attaches itself to a man for having put
himself into...this present position, and this generally
prevents him from confessing his defeat in such matters.
The misfortune in question is one which doubtless occurs not
unfrequently to mankind; but as mankind generally bear their
special disappointments in silence, and as the vanity of
women is generally exceeded by their good-nature, the
secret, we believe, in most cases remains a secret.
          Shall I, wasting in despair,
          Die because a woman's fair?
          If she be not fair for me,
          What care I how fair she be?
     This was the upshot of the consideration which Withers,
the poet, gave to the matter, and Withers was doubtless
right.    'Tis thus that rejected lovers should think, thus
that they should demean themselves; but they seldom come to
this philosophy till a few days have passed by, and talking
of their grievance does not assist them in doing so.
TC 149, XIII.

A man, if he be not absolutely rejected, is generally inclined to think that any answer from a lady may be taken as
having in it some glimmer of favour....If a lady bids a
gentleman wait awhile for his answer, he thinks himself
quite justified in letting all the world know that she is
his own.    We all know what a reference to a parent's judgment means.    A lady must be very decisive-very, if she means
to have her "no" taken at its full meaning.    Ber 184, X.

There can, I think, be no doubt that in all such calamities

[being rejected and having it known]   as that...the agony of
the misfortune is much increased by the conviction that the
facts of the case are known to those round about the
sufferer.   A most warm-hearted and intensely-feeling young
gentleman might, no doubt, eat an excellent dinner after
being refused by the girl of his devotions, provided that he
had reason to believe that none of those in whose company he
ate it knew anything of his rejection.   But the same warm-
hearted and intensely-feeling young gnetleman would find it
very difficult to go through the ceremony with any appearance of true appetite or gastronomic enjoyment if he were
aware that all his convives knew all the facts of his little
misfortune.   Generally, we may suppose, a man in such condition goes to his club for his dinner, or seeks consolation
in the shades of some adjacent Richmond or Hampton Court.
There he meditates on his condition in silence, and does ultimately enjoy his little plate of whitebait, his cutlet,
and his moderate pint of sherry.   He probably goes alone to
the theatre, and, in his stall, speculates with a somewhat
bitter sarcasm on the vanity of the world.   Then he returns
home, sad indeed, but with a moderated sadness, and as he
puffs out the smoke of his cigar at the open window--with
perhaps the comfort of a little brandy-and-water at his
elbow--swears to himself that, 'By Jove, he'll have another
try for it.'   Alone, a man may console himself, or among a
crowd of unconscious mortals; but it must be admitted that
the position [of a man among friends is] ...severe.
SmaH 590, LVIII.

Women, when they have loved in vain, often almost wish that
their misfortune should be known.   They love to talk about
their wounds mystically,--telling their own tales under
feigned names, and extracting something of a bitter sweetness out of the sadness of their own romance.   But a man,
when he has been rejected,--rejected with a finality that is
acknowledged by himself,--is unwilling to speak or hear a
word upon the subject, and would willingly wash the episode
out from his heart if it were possible.   Bel 158, XIII.

A young man when he has been rejected by one of the young
ladies of a family has rather a hard time of it till he gets
away.   RalH 288, XXXVIII.

A woman always has a triumph when she rejects a man,--and
more especially when she does so at a certain time of life.
Way 339, XXXVI.

## RELATIVES

Near relatives, when they are on good terms with each other,
are not gracious.   MM 95, VIII.

It is certainly of service to a man to know who were his
grandfathers and who were his grandmothers if he entertain
an ambition to move in the upper circles of society, and
also of service to be able to speak of them as of persons

who were themselves somebodies in their time.  No doubt we
all entertain great respect for those who by their own
energies have raised themselves in the world; and when we
hear that the son of a washerwoman has become Lord
Chancellor or Archbishop of Canterbury we do, theoretically
and abstractedly, feel a higher reverence for such self-made
magnate than for one who has been as it were born into
forensic or ecclesiastical purple.  But not the less must
the offspring of the washerwoman have had very much trouble
on the subject of his birth, unless he has been, when young
as well as when old, a very great man indeed.  After the
goal has been absolutely reached, and the honour and the
titles and the wealth actually won, a man may talk with some
humour, even with some affection, of the maternal tub....But
if a man never mentions his belongings among those with whom
he lives, he becomes mysterious, and almost open to
suspicion.  It begins to be known that nobody knows anything
of such a man, and even friends beome afraid.  It is
certainly convenient to be able to allude, if it be but once
in a year, to some blood relation.  PrM 1-2, I,I.

RELIEF

My readers may probably have dreamt before now that they
have had before them some terribly long walk to accomplish,
some journey of twenty or thirty miles, an amount of labour
frightful to anticipate, and that immediately on starting
they have ingeniously found some accommodating short cut
which has brought them without fatigue to their work's end
in five minutes.  BaT 467, XLVIII.

RELIGION

It would not be becoming were I to travesty a sermon, or
even to repeat the language of it in the pages of a novel.
In endeavoring to depict the characters of the persons of
whom I write, I am to a certain extent forced to speak of
sacred things.  I trust, however, that I shall not be
thought to scoff at the pulpit, though some may imagine that
I do not feel all the reverence that is due to the cloth.  I
may question the infallibility of the teachers, but I hope
that I shall not therefore be accused of doubt as to the
thing to be taught.  BaT 47, VI.

There are but few, very few, to whom it is given to be a
Huss, a Wickliffe, or a Luther; and a man gains but little
by being a false Huss, or a false Luther,--and his neighbours gain less.  DoT 381, XXXII.

When we read of those who have massacred and tortured their
opponents in religion, have boiled alive the unfortunates
who have differed from themselves as to the meaning of an
unintelligible word or two, have vigorously torn the en-
trails out of those who have been pious with a piety different from their own, how shall we dare to say that they
should be punished for their fidelity?...Let us pray for

what we will with earnestness,--though it be for the
destruction of half of a world,--we are sure to think that
our prayers have been heard.  JC 164-5, XXII.

## REMEDIES

In sickness it may irk us because we are not allowed to take
the cool drink that would be grateful; but what man in his
senses would willingly swallow that by which his very life
would be endangered?  OrF 231, LXIII,II.

## RENTS

It is in such language  ["Mrs. O'Neil, your terms for such
rooms as these are much too low"]  that the widows of Scotch
doctors generally speak of their lodgings when they are
paying their weekly bills.  Ber 391, XXII.

If this was ever so in the world's history, it was so in
Ireland at the time of which I am speaking  [1846-7].  The
country, especially in the south and west, had been brought
to a terrible pass;--not as so many said and do say, by the
idolatry of popery, or by the sedition of demagogues, or
even mainly by the idleness of the people....
    The fault had been the lowness of education and
consequent want of principle among the middle classes; and
this fault had been found as strongly marked among the
Protestants as it had been among the Roman Catholics.  Young
men were brought up to do nothing.  Property was regarded as
having no duties attached to it.  Men became rapacious, and
determined to extract the uttermost farthing out of the land
within their power, let the consequences to the people on
that land be what they might.
    We used to hear much of absentees.  It was not the
absence of the absentees that did the damage, but the
presence of those they left behind them on the soil.  The
scourge of Ireland was the existence of a class who looked
to be gentlemen living on their property, but who should
have earned their bread by the work of their brain, or,
failing that, by the sweat of their brow....
    Most Englishmen have heard of profit-rent.  In Ireland
the term is so common that no man cannot have heard of it.
It may, of course, designate a very becoming sort of
income.  A man may, for instance, take a plot of land for
one hundred pounds a year, improve and build on it till it
be fairly worth one thousand pounds a year, and thus enjoy a
profit-rent of nine hundred pounds.  Nothing can be better
or fairer.  But in Ireland the management was very
different.  Men there held tracts of ground, very often at
their full value, paying for them such proportion of rent as
a farmer could afford to pay in England and live.  But the
Irish tenant would by no means consent to be a farmer.  It
was needful to him that he should be a gentleman, and that
his sons should be taught to live and amuse themselves as
the sons of gentlemen--barring any such small trifle as education.  They did live in this way; and to enable them to do

so, they underlet their land in small patches, and at an amount of rent to collect which took the whole labour of their tenants, and the whole produce of the small patch, over and above the quantity of potatoes absolutely neces- sary to keep that tenant's body and soul together.

It is with thorough rejoicing, almost with triumph, that I declare that the idle, genteel class has been cut up root and branch, has been driven forth out of its holding into the wide world, and has been punished with the penalty of extermination. The poor cotter suffered sorely under the famine, and under the pestilence which followed the famine; but he, as a class, has risen from his bed of suffering a better man. He is thriving as a labourer either in his own country or in some newer--for him better--land to which he has emigrated....But the other man has gone, and his place is left happily vacant. CasR 122-5, VII,I.

## REPENTANCE

And...repentance itself, is it not a work of agony and of tears? It is very easy to talk of repentance; but a man has to walk over hot plough shares before he can complete it; to be skinned alive as was St. Bartholomew, to be stuck full of arrows as was St. Sebastian; to lie broiling on a gridiron like St. Lorenzo. BaT 109, XIII.

[A] sheep that was very dark in colour might become white again. If it be not so, what is all this doctrine of re- pentance in which we believe? SHHOH 42, V.

## REPLIES

Let a man be ready with a reply, be it ever so bad a reply, and any attack is parried. VOB 502, LXIX.

## REPROBATES

There are many...[such men] about in the world, [one of those men who, through their long, useless, ill-flavoured lives, always contrive to live well, to eat and drink of the best, to lie softly, and to go about in purple and fine linen,--and yet, never have any money....He was good- tempered, well-mannered, sprightly in conversaiton, and had not a scruple in the world....To lie, to steal,--not out of tills or pockets, because he knew the danger; to cheat--not at the card-table, because he had never come in the way of learning the lesson; to indulge every passion, though the cost to others might be ruin for life; to know no gods but his own bodily senses, and no duty but that which he owed to those gods; to eat all, and produce nothing; to love no one but himself; to have learned nothing but how to sit at table like a gentleman; to care not at all for his country, or even his profession; to have no creed, no party, no friend, no conscience, to be troubled with nothing that touched his heart;--such had been, was and was to be...his life], known well to be so at clubs, in drawing-rooms, and by the trades-

men who supply them.  Men give them dinners and women smile
upon them.  The best of coats and boots are supplied to
them.  They never lack cigars nor champagne.  They have
horses to ride, and servants to wait upon them more obse-
quious than the servants of other people.  And men will lend
them money too,--well knowing that there is no chance of re-
payment.  Now and then one hears a horrid tale of some young
girl who surrenders herself to such a one, absolutely for
love!  Upon the whole...[these men]  are popular.  It is
hard to follow such a man quite to the end and to ascertain
whether or no he does go out softly at last, like the snuff
of a candle,--just with a little stink.  VOB 228-9, XXXIII.

## REPULSES

Generals who are beaten out of the field are not quick to
talk of their own repulses.  LasC 429, XLVII.

When a man is reduced to that consolation,  [saying "he
can't eat me"]  as many a man often is, he may be nearly
sure that he will be eaten.  VOB 189, XXVII.

## REPUTATION

When the perfume of the rose grows stale, the flower is at
once thrown aside, and carried off as foul refuse.
TC 532, XLIV.

Fortune favours the brave; and the world certainly gives the
most credit to those who are able to give an unlimited
credit to themselves.  Ber 633, XXXV.

## RESERVE

Reserve is beautiful in a maiden if it be rightly timed.
Sometimes one would fain have more of it.  But when the
heart is full, and when it may speak out; when time, and
circumstances, and the world permit--then we should say that
honesty is better than reserve.  Ber 755, XLII.

## RESIGNATION

There are times in one's life in which the absence of all
savour seems to be sufficient for life in this world.
AS 407, LIX.

## RESPECT

In Egypt the donkeys of a man are respected, ay, and even
his donkey-boys, when he shows himself able and willing to
knock down all those around him.
     A great man there, a native, killed his cook one
morning in a rage; and a dragoman, learned in languages,
thus told the story to an Englishman:--'De sahib, him vera
respecble man.  Him kill him cook, Solyman, this morning.
Oh, de sahib particklar respecble!'  After all, it may be

questioned whether this be not a truer criterion of respectability than that other one of keeping a gig. Ber 672-3, XXXVIII.

It is well that some respect should be maintained from the low in station towards those who are high, even when no respect has been deserved. Cl 377, XLIV.

A man will almost always respect him whom those around him respect, and will generally look up to one who is evidently above himself in his own daily avocation. PF 227, LXIII,II.

...respect in the minds of those around him which is itself a great element of love. MSF 231, LVIII,III.

## RESPONSIBILITY

[Remaining on watch]   is the lot of those who take upon themselves the management of men, without any power to ensure obedience to their orders. LaV 124, IX.

We are all of us responsible for our friends, fathers-in-law for their sons-in-law, brothers for their sisters, husbands for their wives, parents for their children, and children for their parents. We cannot wipe off from us, as with a wet cloth, the stains left by the fault of those who are near to us. The ink-spot will cling. TC 552, XLVI.

A man owes it to his country, to his friends, even to his acquaintance, that he shall not be known to be going about wanting a dinner, with never a coin in his pocket. It is very well for a man to boast that he is lord of himself, and that having no ties he may do as he pleases with that possession. But it is a possession of which, unfortunately, he cannot rid himself when he finds that there is nothing advantageous to be done with it. Doubtless there is a way of riddance. There is the bare bodkin. Or a man may fall overboard between Holyhead and Kingston in the dark, and may do it in such a cunning fashion that his friends shall think that it was an accident. But against these modes of rid-dance there is a canon set, which some men still fear to disobey. PR 9, I,I.

...that absence of responsibility which must be as a fresh perfumed bath to a minister just freed from the trammels of office. PrM 1, XLI,II.

## RESOLUTIONS

Yes, contemptible enough, as humanity so often is. Who amongst us have not made such resolves--some resolve of self-devotion, at the sound of the preacher's voice--and forgotten it before our foot was well over the threshold? It is so natural, that wish to do a great thing; so hard, that daily task of bathing in Jordan. Ber 117, VII.

But the majority of men, as I take it, make no such resolution  [to become a success], and very many men resolve
that they will be unsuccessful.  SmaH 458, XLV.

## RESTORATION

How long will it be before some second La Vendee shall
successfully, but bloodlessly, struggle for another re-
establishment of the monarchy?  Surely before the expiration
of half a century since the return of Louis, France will con-
gratulate herself on another restoration.*
      *Five-and-twenty years have again passed away since
this tale was completed, and restoration has not yet been
effected, though the self-congratulations of the royalists
were the other day all but uttered.  France must again wait
till the legitimate heir of the old family shall be willing
to reign as a constitutional sovereign.  LaV 397, XXXIV.

## RETICENCE

That which we call reticence is more frequently an inability
than an unwillingness to express itself.  The man is silent,
not because he would not have the words spoken, but because
he does not know the fitting words with which to speak.  His
dignity and his so-called manliness are always near to him,
and are guarded, so that he should not melt into open ruth.
Kept 68, XVIII.

...the difficulty of reticence when the heart is full.
MSF 61, V,I.

## RETIREMENT

It is hardly too much to say, that no old officers who have
lacked the means to distinguish themselves, retire from
either of our military services, free from...bitter disappointment and sour feelings of neglected worth....A clergyman, or a doctor, or a lawyer, feels himself no whit disgraced if he reaches the end of his worldly labours without
special note or honour.  But to a soldier or a sailor, such
indifference to his merit is wormwood.  It is the bane of
the professions.  Nine men out of ten who go into it must
live discontented, and die disappointed.  TC 35-6, IV.

Such moments occur in lives of most of us,--moments in which
the real work of life is brought to an end,--and they cannot but be sad.   It is very well to talk of ease and
dignity; but ease of spirit comes from action only, and the
world's dignity is given to those who do the world's work.
Let no man put his neck from out the collar till in truth he
can no longer draw the weight attached to it.
RacR 360, XXVIII.

No man should abdicate,--unless, indeed, he does so for his
soul's advantage.  As to happiness in this life it is hardly
compatible with that diminished respect which ever attends

the relinquishing of labour.    Otium cum dignitate is a dream.    There is no such positon at any rate for the man who has once worked.    He may have the ease or he may have the dignity; but he can hardly combine the two.    RacR 384, XXX.

## REVENGE

...not meditated revenge; but that revenge which springs up without any meditation, and is often therefore the most bitter.    MSF 185, XIV,I.

## RICHES

How hard it is for a rich man not to lean upon his riches! harder, indeed, than for a camel to go through the eye of a needle.    FrP 79, VIII.

To be rich is not to have one or ten thousand a year, but to be able to get out of that one or ten thousand all that every pound, and every shilling, and every penny will give you.    Cl 110, XIV.

## RIDDLES

Riddles may be read very accurately by those who will give sufficient attention and ample time to the reading of them. They who will devote twelve hours a day to the unravelling of acrostics, may discover nearly all the enigmas of a weekly newspaper with a separate editor for such difficulties.    MF 53, V,I.

## RIDING

To ride with fair women over turf, through a forest--with a woman who may perhaps some day be wooed--can be a matter of indifference only to a very lethargic man.    HHOG 46, III.

## RIGHT...WRONG

Wise people, when they are in wrong, always put themselves right by finding fault with the people against whom they have sinned....A man in the right relies easily on his rectitude, and therefore goes about unarmed.    His very strength is his weakness.    A man in the wrong knows that he must look to his weapons; his very weakness is his strength.    The one is never prepared for combat, the other is always ready.    Therefore it is that in this world the man that is in the wrong almost invariably conquers the man that is in the right, and invariably despises him.
    A man must be an idiot or an angel, who after the age of forty shall attempt to be just to his neighbors.
BaT 357, XXXVII.

The laws of meum and tuum are sufficiently clear if a man will open his eyes to look at them.    CasR 90, V,II.

A man always can do right, even though he has done wrong before. But that previous wrong adds so much difficulty to the path--a difficulty which increases in tremendous ratio, till a man at last is choked in his struggling, and is drowned beneath the waters. FrP 120, XII.

The scandal, or loud reproach due to evil doings, may be silenced by subsequent conduct. The merited punishment may not come visibly. But nothing happening after could make it right that a young lady should come home from hunting in a postchaise alone with a young unmarried man. AS 269-70,XL.

## RISK

I remember to have dined at a house, the whole glory and fortune of which depended on the safety of a glass goblet. We all know the story. If the luck of Edenhall should be shattered, the doom of the family would be sealed. Nevertheless I was bidden to drink out of the fatal glass, as were all guests in that house. It would not have contented the chivalrous mind of the master to protect his doom by lock and key and padded chest. SmaH 2, I.

## ROADS, FRENCH

Whatever may be said or thought here in England of the late imperial rule in France, it must at any rate be admitted that good roads were made under the Empire. GLOG 1, I.

## ROBBERY

There were two cares which sat near his heart: first, that no one should rob him; and secondly, that he should rob no one. It will often be the case that the first will look after itself, whereas the second will require careful watching. Land 6, I,I.

## ROGUES

Alas, alas! how is it that in these days such men become rogues? How is it that we see in such frightful instances the impotency of educated men to withstand the allurements of wealth?...The rich rogue, or the rogue that would rich, is always a laborious man. He allows himself but little recreation, for dishonest labour admits of no cessation....
    Every great man, who gains a great end by dishonest means, does more to deteriorate his country and lower the standard of his countrymen than legions of vulgar thieves, or nameless unaspiring rogues. Who has injured us so much in this way as he whose name still stands highest among modern politicians? Who has given so great a blow to political honesty, has done so much to banish from men's minds the idea of a life-ruling principle, as Sir Robert Peel?...
    He has taught us a great lesson, that a man who has before him a mighty object may dispense with those old-

fashioned rules of truth to his neighbours and honesty to
his own principles, which should guide us in ordinary life.
...How prone we are, each of us, to look on our own object
as great, how ready to make excuses for receiving such a
lesson for our guide; how willing to think that we may be
allowed to use this dispensing power ourselves--this
experience teaches us in very plain language....

That Sir Robert Peel should be a worshipper of expediency might be a matter of small moment to any but his
biographer, were it not that we are prone to copy the
example of those whose names are ever in our mouths. It has
now become the doctrine of a large class of politicians that
political honesty is unnecessary, slow, subversive of a
man's interests, and incompatible with quick onward movement. Such a doctrine in politics is to be deplored; but
alas! who can confine it to politics? It creeps with
gradual, but still with sure and quick motion, into all the
doings of our daily life. How shall the man who has taught
himself that he may be false in the House of Commons, how
shall he be true in the Treasury chambers? or if false
there, how true on the Exchange? and if false there, how
shall he longer have any truth within him? TC 354-7, XXIX.

It is hard for any tame domestic animal to know through what
fire and water a poor fox is driven as it is hunted from
hole to hole and covert to covert. It is a wonderful fact,
but no less a fact, that no men work so hard and work for so
little pay as scoundrels who strive to live without any work
at all, and to feed on the sweat of other men's brows.
CasR 209-10, XI,III.

There is a sackcloth harsher to the skin than that of the
penal settlement, and ashes more bitter in the crunching
than convict rations. It would be sad indeed if we thought
that those rascals who escape the law escape also the just
reward of their rascality. May it not rather be believed
that the whole life of the professional rascal is one long
wretched punishment, to which, if he could but know it, the
rations and comparative innocence of Bermuda would be so
preferable?...Have I not said truly that he is hunted like a
fox, driven from covert to covert with his poor empty
craving belly? prowling about through the wet night, he returns with his prey, and finds that he is shut out from his
lair; his bloodshot eye is ever over his shoulder, and his
advanced foot is ever ready for a start; he stinks in the
nostrils of the hounds of the law, and is held by all men to
be vermin.

One would say that the rascal if he but knew the truth,
would look forward to Spike Island and the Bermudas with
impatience and raptures. The cold, hungry, friendless,
solitary doom of unconvicted rascaldom has ever seemed to me
to be the most wretched phase of human existence,--that
phase of living in which the liver can trust no one, and be
trusted by none; in which the heart is ever quailing at the
policeman's hat, and the eye ever shrinking from the policeman's gaze. The convict does trust his gaoler, at any rate

his master gaoler, and in so doing is not all wretched. It
is Bill Sikes before conviction that I have ever pitied.
Any man can endure to be hanged; but how can any man have
taken that Bill Sikes' walk and have lived through it?
CasR 257-9, XIV,III.

[W]e are all apt to be too hard in forming an opinion upon
the rogues of the world.  FrP 430, XLIV.

There are some things that no rogue can do.  He can understand what it is to condemn roguery, to avoid it, to dislike
it, to disbelieve in it;--but he cannot understand what it
is to hate it.  SHHOH 54, VI.

[He] waltzed well.  All such men  [rogues]  do.  It is a
part of their stock-in-trade.  SHHOH 55, VI.

It is very nice to walk about one's own borough and be voted
unanimously worthy of confidence, and be a great man; but if
you are a scoundrel, and not used to being a scoundrel,
black care is apt to sit very close behind you as you go
caracolling along the streets.  ED 323, XXXV,I.

## ROMANCE

It is the hardship of men that when called upon by women for
romance, they are bound to be romantic, whether the opportunity serves them or does not.  A man must produce romance,
or at least submit to it, when duly summoned, even though he
should have a sore throat or a headache.  He is a brute if
he decline such an encounter--and feels that, should he
decline persistently, he will ever after be treated as a
brute.  LasC 473, LI.

## ROOMS

Large rooms when full of people and full of light look well,
because they are large, and are full, and are light.  Small
rooms are those which require costly fittings and rich
furniture.  BaT 81, X.

Most of us know when we enter a drawing-room whether it is a
pretty room or no; but how few of us know how to make a
drawing-room pretty!  There has come up in London in these
latter days a form of room so monstrously ugly that I will
venture to say that no other people on earth but Londoners
would put up with it.  Londoners, as a rule, take their
houses as they can get them, looking only to situation,
size, and price.  What Grecian, what Roman, what Turk, what
Italian would endure, or would have endured, to use a room
with a monstrous cantle in the form of a parallelogram cut
sheerly out of one corner of it?  This is the shape of room
we have now adopted,--or rather which the builders have a-
dopted for us,--in order to throw the whole first floor into
one apartment which may be presumed to have noble dimensions,--with such drawback from it as the necessities of the

staircase may require.   A sharp unadorned corner projects
itself into these would-be noble dimensions, and as ugly a
form of chamber is produced as any upon which the eye can
look....There is to be found no such abomination of shape in
the buildings of our ancestors,--not even in the days of
George the Second.  CanY 9-10, II,I.

RUIN

A horse will gallop for some scores of yards, after his back
has been broken, before he knows of his great ruin.
PF 130, LIII,II.

RUIN, SELF-IMPOSED

We know not what may be the nature of that eternal punishment to which those will be doomed who shall be judged to
have been evil at last; but methinks that no more terrible
torment can be devised than memory of self-imposed ruin....
'You have had your cake, and eaten it--eaten it greedily.
Is not that sufficient for you?  Would you eat your cake
twice?   Would you have a succession of cakes?   No, my
friend; there is no succession of these cakes for those who
eat them greedily.  Your propostion is not a fair one, and
we who have the whip hand of you will not listen to it.  Be
good enough to vanish.  Permit yourself to be swept quietly
into the dung-hill.  All that there was about you of value
has departed from you; and allow me to say that you are now
--rubbish.'  And then the ruthless besom comes with irresis-
tible rush, and the rubbish is swept into the pit, there to
be hidden for ever from the sight.  And the pity of it is
this--that a man, if he will only restrain his greed, may
eat his cake and yet have it; aye, and in so doing will have
twice more the flavour of the cake than he who with gorman-
dising maw will devour his dainty all at once.  Cakes in
this world will grow by being fed on, if only the feeder be
not too insatiate.  FrP 265, XXVII.

RUMOUR

[B]ut we all know that Rumour, when she takes to such topics
[being jilted], exaggerates the truth, and sets down much in
malice.  SmaH 162, XVII.

[A]nd rumour, though she flies so fast and so far, is
often slow in reaching those ears which would be most interested in her tidings.  PF 22, XL,II.

When such rumours [of a crime]  are spread abroad, they are
always believed.   There is an exictement and a pleasure in
believing them.  Reasonable hesitation at such a moment is
dull and phlegmatic.  If the accused one be near enough to
ourselves to make the accusation a matter of personal pain,
of course we disbelieve.  But, if the distance be beyond
this, we are almost ready to think that anything may be true
of anybody.  Way 103, LXII,II.

## S

### SACRIFICES

The little sacrifices of society are all made by women, as are also the great sacrifices of life. A man who is good for anything is always ready for his duty, and so is a good woman always ready for a sacrifice. SmaH 124, XIII.

And let it be remembered that very many who can devote themselves for great sacrifices, cannot bring themselves to the endurance of little injuries. SmaH 126, XIII.

There is, perhaps, nothing so pleasant as the preparation for self-sacrifice. LasC 545, LVIII.

...that feminine sweetness which has its most frequent foundation in self-denial. PrM 39, V, I.

### SADDLES, TURKISH

...the accursed saddle [Turkish] which had been specially contrived with the view of lacerating the nether Christian man. Ber 96, VI.

### SAILING

Who, indeed, was ever too late at the docks? Who, that ever went there, had not to linger, linger, linger, till every shred of patience was clean worn out?...Why, we have often wondered, are ships designated as A 1, seeing that all ships are of that class? Where is the excellence, seeing that all share it? Of course the Flash of Lightning was A 1. The author has for years been looking out, and has not yet found a ship advertised as A 2, or even as B 1. What is this catalogue of comparative excellence, of which there is but one visible number? TC 537, XLIV.

### SAINTS

The statue of St. John Nepomucene is a single figure, standing in melancholy weeping posture on the balustrade of the bridge, without any of that ponderous strength of wide-spread stone which belongs to the other groups. This St. John is always pictured to us as a thin, melancholy, half-starved saint, who has had all the life washed out of him by his long immersion. There are saints to whom a trusting religious heart can turn, relying on their apparent physical capabilities. St. Mark, for instance, is always a tower of strength, and St. Christopher is very stout, and St. Peter carries with him an ancient manliness which makes one marvel at his cowardice when he denied his Master. St. Lawrence, too, with his gridiron, and St. Bartholomew with his flaying-knife and his own skin hanging over his own arm, look as though they liked their martyrdom, and were proud of it, and could be useful on an occasion. But this St. John of the Bridges has no pride in his appearance, and no strength in his look. He is a mild, meek saint, teaching one rather by his attitude how to bear with the malice of the waters, than offering any protection against their violence. NB 182, XV.

## SATIETY

The palate accustomed to Cayenne pepper can hardly be gratified by simple salt. PrM 221, LXIII,II.

## SATISFACTION

Such a feeling [of triumphant satisfaction]...was natural, and is natural to all men and women who are conscious that they have done well in the adjustment of their own affairs. SmaH 122, XIII.

## SCHEMES

Schemes will often be successful, let them be ever so trans-parent. Little intrigues become necessary, not to conquer unwilling people, but people who are willing enough, who, nevertheless, cannot give way except under the machinations of an intrigue. LasC 311, XXXV.

## SCHISM

We are much too apt to look at schism in our church as an unmitigated evil. Moderate schism, if there may be such a thing, at any rate calls attention to the subject, draws in supporters who would otherwise have been inattentive to the matter, and teaches man to think upon religion. How great an amount of good of this description has followed that movement in the Church of England which commenced with the publication of Froud's Remains! BaT 173, XX.

## SCHOLARSHIPS

In those days, a lad of eighteen who could get a scholarship at Trinity was considered to be nearly safe in his career. I do not know how far this may be altered now. Ber 14, I.

## SCHOOLMASTERS

So may be seen the inspired schoolmaster who has beneath his hand the wretched verses of a dull pupil. For a while he attempts to reduce to reason and prosody the futile efforts of the scholar, but anon he lays aside in disgust the dis-

tasteful task, and, turning his eyes upward to the Muse,
who has ever been faithful, he dashes off a few genial lines
of warm poetry.  The happy juvenile, with his wondering pen,
copies the work, and the parent's heart rejoices over the
prize which his child has won.  Str 125, XXII.

## SCRUPLES

In the ordinary cutting of blocks a very fine razor is not
an appropriate instrument.  LasC 771, LXXXIII.

Perhaps there is no question more difficult to a man's mind
than that of the expediency or inexpediency of scruples in
political life.  Whether would a candidate for office be
more liable to rejection from a leader because he was known
to be scrupulous, or because he was known to be the reverse?
PF 179-80, LVIII,II.

## SECRETS

Secrets such as...[being engaged]  are made to be told; but
those other secrets, those which burn up the heart instead
of watering it as with a dew from heaven, those secrets for
the most part are not made to be told.  Ber 263, XV.

Are not most of our innermost secrets known to all the
world?  Ber 464, XXV.

But then there is nothing more difficult of attainment than
discretion in the preservation of such mysteries.  To keep a
friend's secret well the keeper of it should be firmly
resolved to act upon it in no way,--not even for the advantage of the owner of it.  If it be confided to you as a
secret that your friend is about to make his maiden speech
in the House, you should not even invite your acquaintances
to be in their places,--not if secrecy be the first object.
In all things the knowledge should be to you as though you
had it not.  Great love is hardly capable of such secrecy as
this.  RalH 321, XLIII.

It is literally true that the tongue will itch with a desire
to tell a secret.  Kept 29, VIII.

There are thus so many who can divulge to none those secret
wishes!  And how can such an one have a friend who can
advise him as to what he shall do?  Scarcely can the honest
man have such a friend, because it is so difficult for him
to find a man who will believe in him!  MSF 302, LXIII,III.

## SECRETARY OF STATE

A Secretary of State who has to look after the police and
the magistrates, to answer questions in the House of
Commons, and occasionally to make a telling speech in
defence of his colleagues, and, in addition to this, is
expected to perform the duties of a practical court of

appeal in criminal cases, must have something to do.    To
have to decide whether or no some poor wretch shall be
hanged, when, in spite of the clearest evidence, humani-
tarian petitions by the dozen overwhelm him with claims for
mercy, must be a terrible responsibility.    'No, your
Majesty, I think we won't hang him.    I think we'll send him
to penal servitude for life;--if your Majesty pleases.'
That is so easy, and would be so pleasant....

I remember to have seen a man at Bermuda whose fate was
peculiar.    He was sleek, fat, and apparently comfortable,
mixing pills when I saw him, he himself a convict and administering to the wants of his brother convicts.    He remonstrated with me on the hardness of his position.    'Either I
did do it, or I didn't,' he said.    'It was because they
thought I didn't that they sent me here.    And if I didn't,
what right had they to keep me here at all?'    I passed on in
silence, not daring to argue the matter with the man in the
face of the warder.    But the man was right.    He had murdered
his wife;--so at least the jury had said,--and had been
sentenced to be hanged.    He had taken the poor woman to a
little island, and while she was bathing had drowned her.
Her screams had been heard on the mainland, and the jury had
found the evidence sufficient.    Some newspaper had thought
the reverse, and had mooted the question;--was not the distance too great for such screams to have been heard, or at
any rate, understood?    So the man was again brought to trial
in the Court of the Home Office, and was,--not pardoned, but
sent to grow fat and make pills at Bermuda....

What was a Secretary of State to do in such a case?    No
doubt he believed that the wretch had murdered his wife.    No
doubt the judge believed it.    All the world believed it.
But the newspaper was probably right in saying that the
evidence was hardly conclusive,--probably right because it
produced its desired effect.    If the argument had been successfully used with the jury, the jury would have acquitted
the man.    Then surely the Secretary of State should have
sent him out as though acquitted; and, not daring to hang
him, should have treated him as innocent.    Another trial
was, in truth, demanded.    JC 395-6, LIV.

## SELF

Every man to himself is the centre of the whole world;--the
axle on which it all turns.    All knowledge is but his own
perception of the things around him.    All love, and care for
others, and solicitude for the world's welfare, are but his
own feelings as to the world's wants and the world's merits.
CanY 305-6, XXIX,I.

## SELF-CENTEREDNESS

To the ordinary run of minds it is impossible not to do this
[to go on with their existence without making themselves the
centre of any special outward circle].    A man's own dinner
is to himself so important that he cannot bring himself to
believe that it is a matter utterly indifferent to every one

else. A lady's collection of baby-clothes, in early years, and of house linen and curtain-fringes in later life, is so very interesting to her own eyes, that she cannot believe but what other people will rejoice to behold it. I would not, however, be held as regarding this tendency as evil. It leads to conversation of some sort among people, and perhaps to a kind of sympathy. Mrs Jones will look at Mrs White's linen chest, hoping that Mrs White may be induced to look at hers. One can only pour out of a jug that which is in it. For the most of us, if we do not talk of ourselves, or at any rate of the individual circles of which we are the centres, we can talk of nothing. I cannot hold with those who wish to put down the insignificant chatter of the world. As for myself, I am always happy to look at Mrs Jones's linen, and never omit an opportunity of giving her the details of my own dinners. FrP 98-9, X.

## SELF-DEPRECIATION

...that half-insincere depreciation of self which is common to all of us when we speak of our own attributes, but which we by no means intend that they who hear us shall accept as strictly true, or shall re-echo as their own approved opinions. Bel 140, XI.

## SELF-DISCIPLINE

But who does not know how hard it is for a man in such matters to keep his word to himself? Who has not said to himself at the very moment of his own delinquency, 'Now,--it is now,--at this very instant of time, that I should crush, and quench, and kill the evil spirit within me; it is now that I should abate my greed, or smother my ill-humour, or abandon my hatred...,'and yet has failed? DuC 589, LXXIV.

## SELF-HATRED

We are told to love others as ourselves, and it is hard to do so. But I think that we never hate others, never despise others, as we are sometimes compelled by our own convictions and self-judgment to hate and despise ourselves. Cl 261, XXXI.

## SELFISHNESS

Nothing is so powerful in making a man selfish as misfortune. CasR 222, XI,II.

## SELF-SUFFICIENCY

The higher a man raises his head, the more necessary is it that he should learn to lean only on his own strength, and to walk his path without even the assistance of sympathy. Str 89, XVI.

When the little dog snarls, the big dog does not connect the snarl with himself, simply fancying that the little dog must be uncomfortable.  PR 23, XLIII,II.

## SELLING

If you, sir, have a horse to sell, never appear anxious for the sale....If you, madam, have a daughter to sell, it will be well for you also to remember this.  Or, my young friend, if you have yourself to sell, the same rule holds good.  But it is hard to put an old head on young shoulders. Ber 518, XXVIII.

## SEPTEMBER

...that pleasantest of all months in the year, when the sun is not too hot, and the air is fresh and balmy, and one is still able to linger abroad, loitering either in or out of the shade, when the midges cease to bite, and sun no longer scorches and glares; but the sweet vestiges of summer remain, and everything without doors is pleasant and friendly, and there is the gentle unrecognised regret for the departing year, the unconscious feeling that its glory is going from us, to add the inner charm of a soft melancholy to the outer luxury of the atmosphere.  GLOG 42, IV.

## SERMONS

There is, perhaps, no greater hardship at present inflicted on mankind in civilised and free countries, than the necessity of listening to sermons.  No one but a preaching clergyman has, in these realms, the power of compelling an audience to sit silent, and be tormented....Let a professor of law or physic find his place in a lecture-room and there pour forth jejune words and useless empty phrases and he will pour them forth to empty benches.  Let a barrister attempt to talk without talking well, and he will talk but seldom.  A judge's charge need be listened to perforce by none but the jury, prisoner, and gaoler.  A member of Parliament can be coughed down or counted out.  Town-councillors can be tabooed.  But no one can rid himself of the preaching clergyman.  He is the bore of the age, the old man whom we Sindbads cannot shake off, the nightmare that disturbs our Sunday rest, the incubus that overloads our religion and makes God's service distasteful.  We are not forced to go into church!  No: but we desire more than that.  We desire not to be forced to stay away....
    With what complacency will a young parson deduce false conclusions from misunderstood texts, and then threaten us with all the penalties of Hades if we neglect to comply with the injunctions he has given us?  Yes, my too self-confident juvenile friend, I do believe in those mysteries, which are so common in your mouth.  I do believe in the unadulterated word which you hold there in your hand; but you must pardon me if, in some things, I doubt your interpretation.  The Bible is good, the prayer-book is good....But you must

excuse me, my insufficient young lecturer, if I yawn over
your imperfect sentences, your repeated phrases, your false
pathos, your drawlings and denouncings, your humming and
hawing, you oh-ing and ah-ing, your black gloves and your
white handkerchief....
     And here I must make a protest against the pretence, so
often put forward by the working clergy, that they are over-
burdened by the multitude of sermons to be preached....His
sermon is the pleasant morsel of his life, his delicious
moment of self-exaltation.    'I have preached nine sermons
this week,' said a young friend to me the other day, with
hand languidly raised to his brow, the picture of an over-
burdened martyr.  'Nine this week, seven last week, four the
week before.    I have preached twenty-three sermons this
month.  It is really too much.'  'Too much, indeed,' said I,
shuddering; 'too much for the strength of any one.'    'Yes,'
he answered meekly, 'indeed it is; I am beginning to feel it
painfully.'   'Would,' said I, 'you could feel it--would that
you could be made to feel it.'   But he never guessed that my
heart was wrung for the poor listeners.  BaT 49-50, VI.

It is very easy for a clergyman in his pulpit to preach eloquently upon the vileness of worldly wealth, and the
futility of worldly station; but where will you ever find
one, who, when the time of proof shall come, will give proof
that he himself feels what he preaches?  CasR 300, XV,II.

It is very hard, that necessity of listening to a man who
says nothing.  SmaH 111, XII.

But if...this,   [going to church and listening to sermons]
was right,--then why has the world been made so pleasant?
Why is the fruit of the earth so sweet; and the trees,--why
are they so green; and the mountains so full of glory?  Why
are women so lovely:   and why is it that the activity of
man's mind is the only sure forerunner of man's progress?
In listening thrice a day to outpourings from the clergyman
...there certainly was no activity of mind.  Bel 89, VII.

## SERVANTS

But when things are out of course servants are always out of
course also.  As a rule, nothing will induce a butler to go
into a stable, or persuade a housemaid to put her hand to a
frying-pan.  FrP 426, XLIV.

At such times a certain amount of hypocrisy must always be
practiced in closely domestic circles   [times when one has
been jilted].   At mixed dinner-parties people can talk before Richard and William the same words that they would use
if Richard and William were not there.  People so mixed do
not talk together their inward home thoughts.   But when
close friends are together, a little conscious reticence is
practiced till the door is tiled.  SmaH 324, XXXIII.

If people would only have their doors opened to you by such
assistance as may come most easily and naturally to the
work!   I stood lately for some minutes on a Tuesday afternoon at a gallant portal, and as I waxed impatient a pretty
maiden came and opened it.   She was a pretty maiden, though
her hands and face and apron told tales of the fire-grates.
'Laws, sir' she said, 'the visitors' day is Wednesday; and
if you would come then, there would be the man in livery!'
She took my card with the corner of her apron, and did just
as well as the man in livery; but what would have happened
to her had her little speech been overheard by her mistress?
SmaH 403-4, XL.

Serious footmen are very plentiful, and even coachmen are to
be found who, at a certain rate of extra payment, will be
punctual at prayer time, and will promise to read good
little books; but gardeners, as a class, are a profane
people, who think themselves entitled to claim liberty of
conscience, and who will not submit to the domestic despotism of a serious Sunday.   They live in cottages by themselves, and choose to have an opinion of their own on church
matters....A man must be paid well who will submit to daily
inquiries as to the spiritual welfare of himself, his wife,
and family.  Bel 88, VII.

Servants are wonderful actors, looking often as though they
knew nothing when they know everything--as though they
understood nothing, when they understood all....It is seldom
that servants are not good in such straits as that [family
suicide].  LasC 619, LXIV.

There is something peculiarly pleasing to the democratic ear
in the word lacquey!  Anyone serving a big man, whatever the
service may be, is the big man's lacquey in the People's
Banner.   PF 73, XLVII,II.

And therefore her own identity was not strong to her, as it
is strong to those whose business permits them to look frequently into themselves, or whose occupations are of a
nature to produce such introspection....It is so, reader,
with your gardener, your groom, or your cook, if you will
think of it.   Till you tell them by your pity that they are
the sufferers, they will think that is is you who are most
affected by their ailments.   And the man who loses his daily
wage because he is ill complains of his loss and not of his
ailment.    His own identity is half-hidden from him by the
practical wants of his life.  GLOG 94, IX.

If you do not desire either your friend or your enemy to be
received into your house, you communicate your desire to the
person who has charge of the door.   But the cook!
HKHWR 95, XII.

[I]n that matter of followers, privileges are allowed to
young ladies which are not accorded to maid servants.   A
young lady may do things,--have young men to walk and talk

with them, to dance with them and embrace them, and perhaps
even more than this,--when for half so much a young woman
would be turned into the streets without a character.
HKHWR 673, LXXII.

[M]en and women in their class of life [servants] always
moving towards marriage with great precaution.
HKHWR 930, XCIX.

There are people, in that respect very fortunately circumstanced, whose servants, as a matter of course, know all
their affairs, have an interest in their concerns, sympathise with their demands, feel their wants, and are
absolutely at one with them.  But in such cases the servants
are really known, and are almost as completely a part of the
family as the sons and daughters....Mr. Binns, the butler,
would almost foam at the mouth if it were suggested to him
that the plate at Silvercup Hall was not the undoubted
property of the old squire; and Mrs. Pouncebox could not be
made to believe, by any amount of human evidence, that the
jewels which her lady has worn for the last fifteen years
are not her ladyship's very own.  Binns would fight for the
plate, and so would Pouncebox for the jewels, almost till
they were cut to pieces.  The preservation of these
treasures on behalf of those who paid them their wages, and
fed them, who occasionally scolded them but always succoured
them, would be their point of honour.  No torture would get
the key of the cellar from Binns; no threats extract from
Pouncebox a secret of the toilet.  ED 190, XXI,I.

Servants have a way of announcing a woman as a lady, which
clearly expresses their own opinion that the person in
question is not a lady.  PrM 143, LV,II.

...that animosity...which domestics feel for habitual guests
who omit the ceremony of tipping.  AyA 278, XXIX.

It is true that gentlemen and ladies who have servants do
not usually wish to talk about their private matters before
all the household, even though the private matters may be
known.  MSF 99, VII,I.

## SERVICE

There are certain favours in life which are very charming,--
but very unjust to others, and which we may perhaps lump under the name of priority of service.  Money will hardly buy
it.  When money does buy it, there is no injustice....Rank
will often procure it; most unjustly,--as we, who have no
rank, feel sometimes with great soreness.  Position other
than that of rank, official position or commercial position,
will secure it in certain cases.  A railway train is stopped
at a wrong place for a railway director, or a post-office
manager gets his letter taken after time.  These, too, are
grievances.  But priority of service is perhaps more readily

accorded to feminine beauty, and especially to unprotected
feminine beauty, than to any other form of claim. Whether
or no this is ever felt as a grievance, ladies who are not
beautiful may perhaps be able to say. There flits across
our memory at the present moment some reminiscence of angry
glances at the too speedy attendance given by custom-house
officers to pretty women. But this priority of service is,
we think, if not deserved, at least so natural, as to take
it out of the catalogue of evils of which complaint should
be made. One might complain with as much avail that men
will fall in love with pretty girls instead of with those
who are ugly. RalH 28, IV.

## SERVILITY

Very little of that servility can be enjoyed by persons of
the...[lower]  class when money ceases to be ready in their
hands and pockets, and there is, perhaps, nothing that they
enjoy so keenly as servility. CasR 168, IX,II.

## SHAKING HANDS

...that half-unwilling, unsatisfactory manner which most of
us have experienced when shaking hands with some cold-
blooded, ungenial acquaintance. PrM 129, XIV,I.

## SHIPBOARD ROMANCE

There will arrive on occasions a certain pitch of intimacy
...so close as to forbid such mere shaking of the hands....
Who does not know the sagacious lady who, after sitting at
table with the same gentleman for a month, can say, 'Good-
bye, Mr. Jones,' just as though Mr. Jones had been a
stranger under her notice but for a day. But others gush
out, and when Mr. Jones takes his departure, hardly know how
not to throw themselves into his arms. JC 60, VIII.

## SHYNESS

If anything would make a girl talk to a man, such a ducking
...[during a hunt] would do so. Such sudden events, when
they come in the shape of misfortune, or the reverse, generally have the effect of abolishing shyness for the time.
Let a girl be upset with you in a railway train, and she
will talk like a Rosalind, though before the accident she
was as mute as death. ED 2, XXXIX,II.

## SILENCE

At this moment there came a silence over the House which was
almost audible. They who know the sensation which arises
from the continued hum of many suppressed voices will know
also how plain to the ear is the feeling caused by the dis-
continuance of the sound. Way 312, LXXXIII,II.

## SINS

There are those to whom a father's sins, or a husband's sins, or a brother's sins are no sins at all.  And of such one may say, that though we must of compulsion find their judgment to be in some sort delinquent, that their hearts more than make up for such delinquency.  One knows that they are wrong, but can hardly wish them to be less so.
Ber 593, XXXIII.

There are deeds which will not bear a gloss--sins as to which the perpetrator cannot speak otherwise than as a reptile; circumstances which change a man and put upon him the worthlessness of vermin.  SmaH 273, XXVII.

But then sins committed against oneself are so much more sinful than any other sins.  VOB 106, XVI.

And then, what is the good of withdrawing a wife, if the wife thinks that she ought not to be withdrawn?  There are sins as to which there is no satisfaction in visiting the results with penalties.  The sin is in the mind, or in the heart, and is complete in its enormity, even though there be no result.  IHP 21, XXXV, II.

[B]ut there is no law from God or man entitling a man to escape from misery at the expense of falsehood and sin.
DrW 32, III, Part I.

## SINNERS

For my own part, I believe that the reputed sinners are much more numerous than the sinners.  SmaH 436, XLIII.

...because the sinner was a man, and because it is the way of the world to forgive men.  RalH 352, XLVII.

## SISTERS

A man in talking to another man about women is always supposed to consider those belonging to himself as exempt from the incidents of the conversation.  The dearest friends do not talk to each other about their sisters when they have once left school; and a man in such a position [courting his friend's sister]  has to make fight for his ground as closely as though there had ben no former intimacies.  My friend Smith in such a matter as that, though I have been hail fellow with him for the last ten years, has very little advantage over Jones, who was introduced to the house for the first time last week.  OrF 395-6, XXXIX, I.

[S]isters in such circumstances  [bringing lovers together] will sometimes be very treacherous to their friends.
PF 261, LXVI, II.

### SISTERS...BROTHERS

To sisters who have nothing of their own--not even some special god for their own individual worship--generous, affectionate, unmarried brothers, with sufficient incomes, are gods upon earth.  LasC 124, XV.

### SITTING...STANDING

It is generally considered an offensive thing for a gentleman to keep his seat while another is kept standing before him, and we presume the same law holds with regard to ladies.  It is often so felt; but we are inclined to say that it never produces half the discomfort or half the feeling of implied inferiority that is shown by a great man who desires his visitor to be seated while he himself speaks from his legs.  Such a solecism in good breeding, when construed into English means this:  'The accepted rules of courtesy in the world require that I should offer you a seat; if I did not do so you would bring a charge against me in the world of being arrogant and ill-mannered; I will obey the world; but, nevertheless, I will not put myself on an equality with you.  Sit, therefore, at my bidding, and I'll stand and talk at you.  BaT 243, XXVI.

[H]e understood very well how great is the advantage of a standing orator over a sitting recipient of his oratory. PF 158, LV,II.

### SLEEP

Macbeth and Sancho have been equally eloquent in the praise of sleep.  'Sleep that knits up the ravelled sleave of care!'  But sleep will knit up effectually no broken stitches unless it be enjoyed in bed.  'Blessings on him who invented sleep,' said Sancho.  But the great inventor was he who discovered mattresses and sheets and blankets. JC 264, XXXVI.

### SMILES

Very many women smile as they answer the words which are spoken to them, and most who do so flatter by their smile. The thing is so common that no one thinks of it....But she has thereby made her little contribution to society.  She will make the same contribution a hundred times in the same evening.  No one knows that she has flattered anybody; she does not know it herself; and the world calls her an agreeable woman.  SmaH 432-3, XLIII.

Ah!  how I hate the smile of a woman who smiles by rote! SmaH 563, LV.

She smiled as some women smile when you offer them a third glass of champagne.  ED 333, LXXVI,II.

[B]ut she smiled as some women smile at everybody who has any intercourse with them.  AS 83, XII.

## SOCIETY

[B]ut there are houses to which people go without any reason.  PF 200, XXII,I.

It is to be hoped that no readers of these pages will be so un-English as to be unable to appreciate the difference between county society and town society,--the society, that is, of a provincial town, or so ignorant as not to know also that there may be persons so privileged, that although they live distinctly within a provincial town, there is accorded to them, as though by brevet rank, all the merit of living in the county....It is very rarely, indeed, that money alone will bestow this acknowledged rank....Good blood, especially if it be blood good in Devonshire, is rarely rejected. Clergymen are allowed within the pale,--though by no means as certainly as used to be the case....And, as has been said, special merit may prevail.  HKHWR 58-9, VII.

## SOCIETY, COST OF

Let nobody dream that he can be somebody without having to pay for that honour;--unless, indeed, he be a clergyman. When you go to a concert at Buckingham Palace you pay nothing, it is true, for your ticket; and a Cabinet Minister dining with you does not eat or drink more than your old friend Jones the attorney. But in some insidious unforessen manner,--in a way that can only be understood after much experience,--these luxuries of fashion do make a heavy pull on a modest income.  ED 293, XXXII,I.

## SOFTNESS

In social life we hardly stop to consider how much of that daring spirit which gives mastery comes from hardness of heart rather than from high purpose, or true courage.  The man who succumbs to his wife, the mother who succumbs to her daughter, the master who succumbs to his servant, is as often brought to servility by a continual aversion to the giving of pain, by a softness which causes the fretfulness of others to be an agony to himself,--as by any actual fear which the firmness of the imperious one may have produced. There is an inner softness, a thinness of the mind's skin, an incapability of seeing or even thinking of the troubles of others with equanimity, which produces a feeling akin to fear; but which is compatible not only with courage, but with absolute firmness of purpose, when the demand for firmness arises so strongly as to assert itself.
Way 441-2, XLVII,I.

## SOLDIER OF FORTUNE

[A] soldier of fortune, which, generally, I believe, means a
soldier without a fortune.  Ber 8, I.

## SOLITUDE

It is hard to conceive that the old, whose thoughts have
been all thought out, should ever love to live alone.  Solitude is surely for the young, who have time before them for
the execution of schemes, and who can, therefore, take
delight in thinking.  LasC 448, XLIX.

## SONS

The hopes and aspirations of his eldest son are as the
breath of his nostrils to an Englishman who has been born to
land and fortune.  CasR 23, I,III.

But it is not easy to expel a son.  Human fledglings cannot
be driven out of the nest like young birds.  An Honourable
John turned adrift into absolute poverty will make himself
heard of in the world--if in no other way, by his ugliness
as he starves.  A thorough-going ne'er-do-well in the upper
classes has eminent advantages on his side in the battle
which he fights against respectability.  He can't be sent to
Australia against his will.  He can't be sent to the poor-
house without the knowledge of all the world.  He can't be
kept out of tradesmen's shops; nor, without terrible scandal, can he be kept away from the paternal properties.
SmaH 159-60, XVII.

## SPEAKING

It is so easy to speak when one has little or nothing to
say; but often so difficult when there is much that must be
said:  and the same paradox is equally true of writing.
CasR 129, VIII,III.

When a man knows that he can speak with ease and energy, and
that he will be listened to with attentive ears, it is all
but impossible that he should fail to be enthusiastic, even
though his cause be a bad one.  OrF 325, LXXII,II.

There are a class of men...to whom a power of easy
expression by means of spoken words comes naturally.
English country gentlemen, highly educated as they are,
undaunted as they usually are, self-confident as they in
truth are at the botton, are clearly not in this section.
...The fact, for it is a fact, that some of the greatest
orators whom the world has known have been found in this
class, does not in any degree affect the truth of my proposition.  The best grapes in the world are perhaps grown in
England, though England is not a land of grapes.  And for
the same reason....The power of vocal expression which seems
naturally to belong to an American is to an ordinary

Englishman very marvellous; but in America the talking man
is but little esteemed. "Very wonderful power of delivery,
--that of Mr. So-and-So," says the Englishman, speaking of
an American.
    'Guess we don't think much of that kind of thing here,'
says the Yankee. 'Theres 'a deal too much of that coin in
circulation.'...
    The men who speak thus easily and with natural fluency,
are also they who learn languages easily. They are men who
observe rather than think, who remember rather than create,
who may not have great mental powers, but are ever ready
with what they have, whose best word is at their command at
a moment, and is then serviceable though perhaps incapable
of more enduring service. RacR 319-20, XXIV.

The first necessity for good speaking is a large audience.
PF 162, XVIII,I.

[B]ut this sort of feeling [faltering voice], though it be
real, is at the command of orators on certain occasions, and
does them yeoman's service. PF 232, XXV,I.

When a speaker is in possession of the floor, he is in possession even though he be somewhat dilatory in looking to
his references, and whispering to his neighbour. And, when
that speaker is a chairman, of course some additional latitude must be allowed to him. Way 343-4, XXXVII,I.

## SPECTACLES

There are spectacles which are so much more spectacles than
other spectacles, that they make the beholder feel that
there is before him a pair of spectacles carrying a face,
rather than a face carrying a pair of spectacles.
IHP 161, XVII,I.

## SPECULATION

If a man intends to make a fortune in the share-market he
will never do it by being bold one day and timid the next.
...No man, it is true, can calculate accurately what may be
the upshot of a single venture; but a sharp fellow may calculate with a fair average of exactness what will be the
aggregate upshot of many ventures. All mercantile fortunes
have been made by the knowledge and understanding of this
rule. If a man speculates but once and again, now and then,
as it were, he must of course be a loser. He will be
playing a game which he does not understand, and playing it
against men who do understand it. Men who so play always
lose. But he who speculates daily puts himself exactly in
the reversed position. He plays a game which experience
teaches him to play well, and he plays generally against men
who have no such advantage. Of course he wins. TC 361,XXIX.

And this, perhaps, is one of the greatest penalties to which
men who embark in such trade [speculation]   are doomed,

that they can never shake off the remembrance of their calculations;    they   can   never   drop   the   shop;   they   have   no
leisure,  no  ease;  they  can  never  throw  themselves  with  loose
limbs  and  vacant  mind  at  large  upon  the  world's  green  sward,
and  call  children  to  come  and  play  with  them.    TC 362, XXIX.

### SPEECH

...that  peculiar  power  which  enables  a  man  to  have  the  last
word  in  every  encounter,--a  power  which  we  are  apt  to  call
repartee,  which  is  in  truth  the  readiness  which  comes  from
continual   practice.    You  shall  meet  two  men  of  whom  you
shall  know  the  one  to  be  endowed  with  the  brilliancy  of  true
genius,  and  the  other  to  be  possessed  of  but  moderate  parts,
and  shall  find  the  former  never  able  to  hold  his  own  against
the   latter.    In  a  debate,  the  man  of  moderate  parts  will
seem  to  be  greater  than  the  man  of  genius.    But  this  skill
of  tongue,  this  glibness  of  speech  is  hardly  an  affair  of
intellect  at  all.    It  is,--as  is  style  to  the  writer,--not
the  wares  which  he  has  to  take  to  market,  but  the  vehicle  in
which  they  may  be  carried.    Of  what  avail  to  you  is  it  to
have  filled  granaries  with  corn  if  you  cannot  get  your  corn
to  the  consumer?   DuC 201, XXVI.

### SPEECHES

...that  special  oratory  to  which  the  epithet  flowery  may  be
most  appropriately  applied.    It  has  all  the  finished  polish
of  England,  joined  to  the  fervid  imagination  of  Ireland....
It  comes  without  the  slightest  effort,  and  it  goes  without
producing  any  great  effect.    It  is  sweet  at  the  moment.    It
pleases  many,  and  can  offend  none.    But  it  is  hardly  afterwards  much  remembered,  and  is  efficacious  only  in  smoothing
somewhat  the  rough  ways  of  this  harsh  world.    But  I  have
observed  that  in  what  I  have  read  of  British  debates,  those
who  have  been  eloquent  after  this  fashion  are  generally  firm
to  some  purpose  of  self-interest.    FiP 218-9, X.

### SPENDTHRIFTS

We  see  and  hear  of  such  men...,and  are  apt  to  think  that
they  enjoy  all  that  the  world  can  give,  and  that  they  enjoy
that  all  without  payment  either  in  care  or  labour;  but  I
doubt   that,   with   even   the   most   callous   of   them,   their
periods  of  wretchedness  must  be  frequent,  and  that  wretchedness  very  intense.    Salmon  and  lamb  in  February,  and  green
pease  and  new  potatoes  in  March,  can  hardly  make  a  man
happy,  even  though  nobody  pays  for  them....Let  not  anyone
covet  the  lot  of  a  spendthrift,  even  though  the  days  of  his
early  pease  and  champagne  seem  to  be  unnumbered;  for  that
lame  Nemesis  will  surely  be  up  before  the  game  has  been  all
played  out.    FrP 359; 361, XXXVII.

### SPOILING

...[A]nd  girls  are  always  happier  in  spoiling  some  man  than in being spoiled by men.  CanY 45, V,I.

A gentleman's favourite in a country village...is very apt to be spoiled by the kindness that is shown him.  VOB 33, V.

## SPRING

[T]he spring was giving way to the early summer almost before the spring had itself arrived.  It is so, I think, in these latter years.  The sharpness of March prolongs itself almost through April; and then, while we are still hoping for the spring, there falls upon us suddenly a bright, dangerous, delicious gleam of summer.  Cl 192-3, XXIII.

## SQUANDERING

There can be nothing more bitter to a man than such a sur- render [to lose his patrimony].  What, compared to this, can be the loss of wealth to one who has himself made it, and brought it together, but has never actually seen it with his bodily eyes?  Such wealth has come by one chance, and goes by another:  the loss of it is part of the game which the man is playing; and if he cannot lose as well as win, he is a poor, weak, cowardly creature.  Such men, as a rule, do know how to bear a mind fairly equal to adversity.  But to have squandered the acres which have descended from gener- ation to generation; to be the member of one's family that has ruined that family; to have swallowed up in one's own maw all that should have graced one's children, and one's grandchildren!  It seems to me that the misfortunes of this world can hardly go beyond that!  FrP 260, XXVII.

## STANDING

It is singular how strong a propensity some men have to get upon their legs this way [to speak].  CasR 76, IV,II.

...both standing on the rug, as two men always do stand when they first get into a room together.  CasR 129, VII,III.

## STARVATION

In those days there was a form of face which came upon the sufferers when their state of misery was far advanced, and which was a sure sign that their last stage of misery was nearly run.  The mouth would fall and seem to hang, the lips at the two ends of the mouth would be dragged down, and the lower parts of the cheeks would fall as though they had been dragged and pulled.  There were no signs of acute agony when this phasis of countenance was to be seen, none of the horrid symptoms of gnawing hunger by which one generally supposes that famine is accompanied.  The look is one of apathy, desolation, and death.  When custom had made these signs easily legible, the poor doomed wretch was known with certainty.  'It's no use in life meddling with him; he's gone,' said a lady to me in the far west of the south of

Ireland, while the poor boy, whose doom was thus spoken, stood by listening. Her delicacy did not equal her energy in doing good,--for she did much good; but in truth it was difficult to be delicate when the hands were so full. And then she pointed out to me the signs on the lad's face, and I found that her reading was correct. CasR 72-3, IV,III.

## STATESMEN

It is easy for a peer to be a statesman, if the trouble of the life be not too much for him. PF 89, X,I.

## STOCKJOBBER

If any spirit ever walks it must be that of the stockjobber, for how can such a one rest in its grave without knowing what shares are doing? TC 470, XXXVIII.

## STOICISM

Is not modern stoicism, built though it be on Christianity, as great an outrage on human nature as was the stoicism of the ancients? The philosophy of Zeno was built on true laws, but on true laws misunderstood, and therefore misapplied. It is the same with our stoics here, who would teach us that wealth and worldly comfort and happiness on earth are not worth the search. Alas, for a doctrine which can find no believing pupils and no true teachers. BaT 181, XX.

## STUDIES

How many men have declared to themselves the same thing [to study in spite of sorrow], but have failed when the trial came! Who can command the temper and the mind? At ten I will strike the lyre and begin my poem. But at ten the poetic spirit is under a dark cloud--because the water for the tea had not boiled when it was brought in at nine. And so the lyre remains unstricken. OrF 363, XXXVI,I.

## STRENGTH

But the slender, half-knit man, whose arms are without muscles and whose back is without pith, will strive in vain to lift the weight which the brawny vigour of another tosses from the ground almost without an effort. It is with the mind and the spirit as with the body; only this, that the muscles of the body can be measured, but not so those of the spirit. CasR 24, I,III.

## STRUGGLING

The swimmer when first he finds himself in the water, conscious of his skill and confident in his strength, can make his way through the water with the full command of all his powers. But when he begins to feel that the shore is

receding from him, that his strength is going, that the
footing for which he pants is still far beneath his feet,--
that there is peril where before he had contemplated no
danger,--then he begins to beat the water with strokes rapid
but impotent, and to waste in anxious gaspings the breath on
which his very life must depend. Way 423, XCV,II.

## STYLES

[F]or how otherwise is it that the forms of new caps and remodelled shapes for women's waists find their way down into
agricultural parts, and that the rural eye learns to appreciate grace and beauty?  There are those who think that remodelled waists and new caps had better be kept to the
towns; but such people if they would follow out their own
argument, would wish to see ploughboys painted with ruddle
and milkmaids covered with skins. FrP 149, XVI.

## STYLES, WEDDING

We must have the spaces round our altars greatly widened if
this passion for bevies of attendant nymphs be allowed to go
on increasing--and if crinolines increase also.  If every
bride is to have twelve maidens, and each maiden to stand on
no less than a twelve-yard circle, what modest temple will
ever suffice for a sacrifice to Hymen?  TC 180, XVI.

## SUBMISSION

So, when two dogs have fought and one has conquered, the
conquered dog will always show an unconscious submission to
the conqueror. LasC 180, XXI.

## SUCCESS

[A]nd the top rung of the ladder is always more easily
attained when a man has already ascended a step or two.
FrP 453, XLVII.

Success does beget pride, as failure begets shame.
FrP 468, XLVIII.

After all, success in this world is everything; it is at any
rate the only thing the pleasure of which will endure.
PF 203, LX,II.

[T]he world...[is] a closed oyster to be again opened....
[T]his oyster becomes harder and harder in the opening as
the man who has to open it becomes older.  It is an oyster
that will close to again with a snap, after you have got
your knife well into it, if you withdraw your point but for
a moment.  PR 10, I,I.

It is success that creates success, and decay that produces
decay.  DrW 150, II, Part V.

## SUFFERING

There are periods in the lives of some of us--I trust but of
few--when, with the silent inner voice of suffering, we call
on the mountains to fall and crush us, and on the earth to
gape open and take us in. When, with an agony of intensity,
we wish that our mothers had been barren. In those moments
the poorest and most desolate are objects to us of envy, for
their sufferings can be as nothing to our own.
OrF 49, XLV,II.

But the suffering spirit cannot descend from its dignity of
reticence. It has a nobility of its own, made sacred by
many tears, by the flowing of streams of blood from unseen
wounds, which cannot descend from its dais to receive pity
and kindness. A consciousness of undeserved woe produces a
grandeur of its own, with which the high-souled sufferer
will not easily part. LasC 462, L.

## SUICIDE

In such cases as this it is for the jury to say whether the
unfortunate one who has found his life too hard for endurance, and has rushed away to see whether he could not find
an improved condition of things elsewhere, has or has not
been mad at the moment. Surviving friends are of course
anxious for a verdict of insanity, as in that case no further punishment is exacted. The body can be buried like any
other body, and it can always be said afterwards that the
poor man was mad. Perhaps it would be well that all
suicides should be said to have been mad, for certainly the
jurymen are not generally guided in their verdicts by any
accurately ascertained facts. If the poor wretch has, up to
his last days, been apparently living a decent life; if he
be not hated, or has not in his last moments made himself
specially obnoxious to the world at large, then he is
declared to have been mad. Who would be heavy on a poor
clergyman who has been at last driven by horrid doubts to
rid himself of a difficulty from which he saw no escape in
any other way? Who would not give the benefit of the doubt
to the poor woman whose lover and lord had deserted her?
Who would remit to unhallowed earth the body of the once
beneficent philospher who has simply thought that he might
as well go now, finding himslef powerless to do further good
upon earth? Such, and such like, have of course been
temporarily insane, though no touch even of strangeness may
have marked their conduct up to their last known dealings
with their fellow-mortals. But let a Melmotte be found
dead, with a bottle of prussic acid by his side--a man who
has become horrid to the world because of his late
iniquities, a man who has so well pretended to be rich that
he has been able to buy and to sell properties without
paying for them, a wretch who has made himself odious by his
ruin to friends who had taken him up as a pillar strength in
regard to wealth, a brute who had got into the House of
Commons by false pretences, and had disgraced the House by

being drunk there,--and, of course, he will not be saved by a verdict of insanity from the cross roads, or whatever scornful grave may be allowed to those who have killed themselves with their wits about them. Way 356-7, LXXVIII,II.

## SUMMER

There is no time of the year equal in beauty to the first week in summer; and no colour which nature gives, not even the gorgeous hues of autumn, which can equal the verdure produced by the first warm suns of May. FrP 350, XXXVI.

## SUNDAY SCHOOLS

[C]atechisms and collects are quite as hard work to the young mind as book-keeping is to the elderly; and...quite as little feeling of worship enters into the one task as the other. BaT 53, VII.

## SURGEONS

But a surgeon, to be of use, should be ruthless in one sense. He should have the power of cutting and cauterizing, of phlebotomy and bone-handling without effect on his own nerves. CasR 85, V,II.

## SURPRISE

Very many men now-a-days...adopt or affect to adopt the nil admirari doctrine; but nevertheless, to judge from their appearance, they are just as subject to sudden emotions as their grandfathers and grandmothers were before them. BaT 484,L.

## SURVIVAL

With a little courage and hardihood we can survive very great catastrophes, and go through them even without broken bones. PR 134, XVI,I.

## SUSPICIONS

Men when they are worried by fears and teased by adverse circumstances become suspicious of those on whom suspicion should never rest. LasC 517, LVI.

## SWEARING

I do not know that a woman is very much the worse because her husband may forget himself on an occasion and 'rap out an oath at her,' as he would call it when making the best of his own sin....I have known ladies who would think little or nothing about it,--who would go no farther than the mildest protest,--'Do remember where you are!' or, 'My dear John!'--if no stranger were present. But then a wife should be initiated into it by degrees; and there are different tones of

bad language, of which by far the most general is the good-
humoured tone.  We all of us know men who never damn their
servants, or any inferiors, or strangers, or women,--who in
fact keep it all for their bosom friends; and if a little
does sometimes flow over in the freedom of domestic life,
the wife is apt to remember that she is the bosomest of her
husband's friends, and so to pardon the transgression.
PrM 35-6, XLIV,II.

Will one have to expiate the anathemas which are well kept
within the barrier of the teeth, or only those which have
achieved some amount of utterance?  AyA 270, XXIX.

## SWINDLERS

No one wishes to dine with a swindler. No one likes even to
have dined with a swindler,--especially to have dined with
him at a time when his swindling was known or suspected.
Way 76, LVIII,II.

## SYMPATHY

If we are to sympathize only with the good, or worse still,
only with the graceful, how little will there be in our
character that is better than terrestial?  CasR 166, IX,II.

Young men of the present day, when got up for the eyes of
the world, look and talk as though they could never tell
their mothers anything,--as though they were harder than
flint, and as little in want of a woman's counsel and a
woman's help as a colonel of horse on the morning of a
battle.  But the rigid virility of his outward accoutre-
ments does in no way alter the man of flesh and blood who
wears them; the young hero, so stern to the eye, is, I
believe, as often tempted by stress of sentiment to lay bare
the sorrow of his heart as is his sister.  OrF 370,XXXVII,I.

Sympathy may, no doubt, be conveyed by letter; but there are
things on which it is almost impossible for any writer to
express himself with adequate feeling; and there are things,
too, which can be spoken, but which cannot be written.
CanY 230, XLIII,II.

It is not, I think, surprising that a man when he wants
sympathy in such a calamity [losing a sweetheart]...should
seek it from a woman.  Women sympathise most effectually
with men, as men do with women.  But it is, perhaps, a
little odd that a man when he wants consolation because his
heart has been broken, always likes to receive it from a
pretty woman.  One would be disposed to think that at such a
moment he would be profoundly indifferent to such a matter,
that no delight could come to him from female beauty, and
that all he would want would be the softness of a simply
sympathetic soul.  But he generally wants a soft hand as
well, and an eye that can be bright behind the mutual tear,

and lips that shall be young and fresh as they express their
concern for his sorrow.   PF 144, LIV,II.

Sympathy, like electricity, will run so quick that no man
may stop it.   VOB 497, LXIX.

<br>

T

## TACT

It is very hard to tune oneself aright to a disappointed
man.  Ber 31, II.

## TEACHING

I may question the infallibility of the teachers, but I hope
that I shall not therefore be accused of doubt as to the
thing to be taught. BaT 47, VI.

We all know that story of the priest, who, by his question
in the confessional, taught the ostler to grease the horses'
teeth.   'I never did yet,' said the ostler,'but I'll have a
try at it.'  SmaH 431, XLIII.

## TEARS

And is it not known to all men--certainly it is to all
women--how dangerous are such tears  [those of sympathy]?
Ber 305, XVII.

## TEDIUM

To all of us a single treasure counts for much more when the
outward circumstances of our life are dull, unvaried, and
melancholy, than it does when our days are full of pleasure,
or excitement, or even of business.  HKHWR 495, LIII.

In ordinary life events are so unfrequent, and when they do
arrive they give such a flavour of salt to hours which are
generally tedious, that sudden misfortunes come as godsends,
--almost even when they happen to ourselves.  Even a funeral
gives a tasteful break to the monotony of our usual occupations, and small-pox in the next street is a gratifying
excitement.  MF 95, IX,II.

## TEETH

...teeth...perfect in form and whiteness,--a characteristic
which, though it may be a valued item in a general catalogue

of personal attraction, does not generally recommend a man
to the unconscious judgment of his acquaintance.
PrM 4-5, I,I.

Who does not know that look of ubiquitous ivory produced by
teeth which are too perfect in a face which is otherwise
poor?  DuC 219, XXVIII.

## TELEGRAPH

...something of that awe had been felt with which such
missives [telegraph messages]  were always accompanied in
their earliest days.  Bel 251, XX.

It may be well doubted whether upon the whole the tele-
graph has not added more to the annoyances than to the comforts of life, and whether the gentlemen who spent all the
public money without authority ought not to have been punished with special severity in that they had injured
humanity, rather than pardoned because of the good they had
produced.  Who is benefited by telegrams?  The newspapers
are robbed of all their old interest, and the very soul of
intrigue is destroyed.  Way 471, L,I.

## TEMPER

There is nothing so prejudicial to a cause as temper.  This
man is declared to be unfit for any positon of note, because
he always shows temper.  Anything can be done with another
man,--he can be made to fit almost any hole,--because he has
his temper under command.  It may, indeed, be assumed that a
man who loses his temper while he is speaking is
endeavouring to speak the truth such as he believes it to
be, and again it may be assumed that a man who speaks
constantly without losing his temper is not always entitled
to the same implicit faith.  Whether or not this be a reason
the more for preferring the calm and tranquil man may be
doubted; but the calm and tranquil man is preferred for
public services.  We want practical results rather than
truth.  A clear head is worth more than an honest heart.  In
a matter of horseflesh of what use is it to have all manner
of good gifts if your horse won't go whither you want him,
and refuses to stop when you bid him?  PR 76, IX,I.

## TEMPTATIONS

Let him [the devil]  but have a fair hearing, and he seldom
does  [plead in vain]....To listen is to be lost.  'Lead us
not into temptation, but deliver us from evil!'  Let that
petition come forth from a man's heart, a true and earnest
prayer, and he will be so led that he shall not hear the
charmer, let him charm ever so wisely.  TC 103-4, IX.

[T]emptations will affect even those who appear to be least
subject to them.  The town horse, used to gaudy trappings,
no doubt despises the work of his country brother; yet, now

and again, there comes upon him a sudden desire to plough.
PrM 68-9, VIII,I.

## THANKS

One never likes to be thanked over much for doing anything.
It creates a feeling that one has given more than was
expedient.  AS 237, XXXV.

## THEORY...PRACTICE

People are so much more worldly in practice than they are in
theory, so much keener after their own gratification in
detail than they are in the abstract, that the narrative of
many an adventure would shock us, though the same adventure
would not shock us in the action.  One girl tells another
how she has changed her mind in love; and the friend
sympathises with the friend, and perhaps applauds.  had the
story been told in print, the friend who had listened with
equanimity would have read of such vacillation with indignation....This man, in his confidences, asserts broadly that
he does not mean to be thrown over, and that man has a
project for throwing over somebody else; and the intention
of each is that scruples are not to stand in the way of his
success.  The 'Ruat coelum, fiat justitia,' was said, no
doubt, from an outside balcony to a crowd, and the speaker
knew that he was talking buncombe.  LasC 528, LVI.

## THINKING

When a man's heart is warmly concerned in any matter, it is
almost useless for him to endeavour to think of it.  Instead
of thinking, he gives play to his feelings, and feeds his
passion by indulging it.  DoT 178, XIV.

One forms half the conclusions of one's life without any
distinct knowledge that the premises have even passed
through one's mind.  FrP 335, XXXV.

To a man not accustomed to thinking there is nothing in the
world so difficult as to think.  After some loose fashion we
turn over things in our mind and ultimately reach some decision, guided probably by our feelings at the last moment
rather than by any process of ratiocination;--and then we
think that we have thought.  But to follow out one argument
to an end, and then to found on the base so reached the
commencement of another, is not common to us.
Way 406, XCIII,II.

But, as is so usual with the world at large, she had thought
altogether of the past, and not of the future.  The past was
a valley of dreams, which could easily be surveyed, whereas
the future was high mountain which it would require much
labour to climb.  When we think that we will make our calculations as to the future, it is so easy to revel in our memories instead.  OML 37-8, IV.

**THOUGHTS**

...[F]or thought is an exertion which requires a combination of ideas and results in the deducing of conclusions from premises.  CasR 179-80, IX,I.

[G]etting of the thoughts to work rightly is, by-the-by, as I take it, the hardest work which a man is called upon to do.  Not that the subject to be thought about need in itself be difficult....But let any man take any subject fully within his own mind's scope, and strive to think about it steadily, with some attempt at calculation as to results. The chances are his mind will fly off, will-he-nill-he, to some utterly different matter.  When he wishes to debate within himself that question of his wife's temper, he will find himself considering whether he may not judiciously give away half a dozen pairs of those old boots; or when it behoves him to decide whether it shall be manure and a green crop, or a fallow seson and then grass seeds, he cannot keep himself from inward inquiry as to the meaning of that peculiar smile on Mrs. Walker's face when he shook hands with her last night.
      Lord Brougham and Professor Faraday can, no doubt, command their thoughts.    If many men could do so, there would be many Lord Broughams and many Professor Faradays. CasR 246-7, XII,I.

It takes some time before a man can do this  [remodel his thoughts].  He has to struggle with himself in a very uncomfortable way, making efforts which are often unsuccessful. It is sometimes easier to lift a couple of hundredweights than to raise a few thoughts in one's mind which at other moments will come galloping in without a whistle. SmaH 178, XVIII.

On such subjects  [the ballot]  men think long, and be sure that they have thought in earnest, before they are justified in saying that their opinions are the results of their own thoughts.   PF 243, XXVI,I.

...how much thought must be given to a germ of truth before it can be made to produce fruit for the multitude.   And then, in speaking, grand words come so easily, while thoughts,--even little thoughts,--flow so slowly! Ral 123, XVI.

[B]ut how often does it come to pass that we are unable to drive our thoughts into that channel in which we wish them to flow?  MF 310, XXX,II.

[A]ll...thoughts had been filled with...[the problem], which is a matter of much greater moment to a man than the loss of his time.  MSF 214, XVI,I.

## THOUGHTS, MORNING

Who does not know that sudden thoughtfulness at waking, that first matutinal retrospection, into things as they have been and are to be; and the lowness of heart, the blankness of hope which follows the first remembrance of some folly lately done, some word ill-spoken, some money missepent,--or perhaps a cigar too much, or a glass of brandy and soda-water which he should have left untasted? And when things have gone well, how the waker comforts himself among the bedclothes as he claims for himself to be whole all over, teres atque rotundus,--so to have managed his little affairs that he has to fear no harm, and to blush inwardly at no error!  Way 337, XXXVI, I.

## THREATS

Threatened folks live long.  TC 350, XXIX.

When a man has been long consuming red pepper, it takes much red pepper to stimulate his palate....There may be those who think that a wife goes too far in threatening a husband with a commission of lunacy, and frightening him with a prospect of various fatal diseases; but the dose must be adapted to the constitution, and the palate that is accustomed to large quantities of red pepper must have quantities larger than usual whenever some special culinary effect is to be achieved.  RacR 348-9, XXVII.

## TIES

After all, such ties as these [son-in-law] avail more than any predilection, more than any effort of judgement in the choice of the objects of our affections.  We associate with those with whom the tenor of life has thrown us, and from habit we learn to love those with whom we are brought to associate.  TC 183, XVI.

## TIME

He [Time] is sure, but slow; Ruin works fast enough un-aided, where once he puts his foot.  MB 6-7, I, I.

However even when a man is waiting by the road side in winter for a coach, time will at last pass away.
MB 59, II, III.

Nothing ever goes so quick as a Hansom cab when a man starts for a dinner-party a little too early;--nothing so slow when he starts too late.  Way 371, XXXIX, I.

## TITLES

The love of titles is common to all men, and a vicar or fellow is as pleased at becoming Mr. Archdeacon or Mr. Provost, as a lieutenant at getting his captaincy, or a city

tallow-chandler in becoming Sir John on the occasion of a
Queen's visit to a new bridge. War 236, XIX.

What may a man not do, and do with eclat, if he be heir to a
peer and have plenty of money in his pocket?
HKHWR 815, LXXXVII.

While rank, wealth, and money are held to be good things by
all around us, let them be acknowledged as such.    It is
natural that a mother should be as proud when her daughter
marries an Earl's heir as when her son becomes Senior
Wrangler; and when we meet a lady...who purposely abstains
from mentioning the name of her titled daughter, we shall be
disposed to judge harshly of the secret workings of that
lady's thoughts on the subject.    We prefer the exhibition,
which we feel to be natural.  HKHWR 863-4, XCII.

But it is much to be a wife; and more to be a peeress.
ED 74, VIII,I.

And yet who would say that an old lady and her daughters
could be poor with three thousand pounds a year to spend?
It may be taken almost as a rule by the unennobled ones of
this country, that the sudden possession of a title would at
once raise the price of every article consumed twenty per
cent.    Mutton that before cost ninepence would cost ten-
pence a pound, and the mouths to be fed would demand more
meat.    The chest of tea would run out quicker.    The
labourer's work, which for the farmer is ten hours a day,
for the squire nine, is for the peer only eight.    Miss
Jones, when she becomes Lady de Jongh, does not pay less
than threepence apiece for each 'my lady' with which her ear
is tickled.    Even the baronet when he becomes a lord has to
curtail his purchases, because of increased price, unless he
be very wide awake to the affairs of the world.
ED 79-80, IX,I.

Perhaps if there is one thing in England more difficult than
another to be understood by men born and bred out of
England, it is the system under which titles and property
descend together, or in various lines....They who are
brought up among it, learn it as children do a language, but
strangers who begin the study in advanced life, seldom make
themselves perfect in it.  Way 220-1, XXIII,I.

But Dukes and Duchesses must sit upon chairs,--or at any
rate upon sofas,--as well as their poorer brethren, and
probably have the same regard for their comfort.
DuC 567, LXXII.

A lord is like a new hat.  The one on the arm the other on
the head are no evidences of mental superiority.  But yet
they are taken, and not incorrectly taken, as signs of
merit.  MF 76, VII,I.

## TOAST

A supply of buttered toast fully to gratify the wants of three or four men just home from hunting has never yet been created by the resources of any establishment.   But the greater marvel is that the buttered toast has never the slightest effect on the dinner which is to follow in an hour or two.   AyA 472, XLIX.

## TORIES

A high Tory, with a great Whig interest to back him, is never a popular person in England.   No one can trust him, though there may be those who are willing to place him, untrusted, in high positions.   DoT 5, I.   See also CONSERVATIVES.

## TOWN...COUNTRY

A moated grange in the country is bad enough for the life of any Mariana, but a moated grange in town is much worse. MM 5, I.

In granges, and such rural retreats, people expect solitude. ...For me, if I am to live in a moated grange, let it be in the country.   Moated granges in the midst of populous towns are very terrible.   MM 162-3, XIII.

## TRADE

[F]or though there is in the West of Ireland a very general complaint of the stagnation of trade, trade itself is never so stagnant as are the tradesmen, when work is to be done; and it is useless for a poor wight to think of getting his coat or his boots, till such time as absolute want shall have driven the artisan to look for the price of his job-- unless some private and underhand influence be used. Kel 442, XXXIV.

[A]nd a man who gets himself to be made a baronet cleanses himself from the stains of trade, even though he have traded in leather.   MM 2-3, I.

Wonderful are the ways of trade!   If one can only get the tip of one's little finger into the right pie, what noble morsels, what rich esculents, will stick to it as it is extracted!   Way 89, X,I.

## TRAIN STATIONS

I don't know anything so tedious as waiting at a second-class station for a train.   There is the ladies' waiting-room, into which gentlemen may not go, and the gentlemen's waiting-room, in which the porters generally smoke, and the refreshment room, with its dirty counter covered with dirtier cakes.   And there is the platform, which you walk up

and down till you are tired.  You go to the ticket-window
half a dozen times for your ticket, having been warned by
the company's bills that you must be prepared to start at
least ten minutes before the train is due.  But the man
inside knows better, and does not open the little hole to
which you have to stoop your head till two minutes before
the time named for your departure.  Then there are five fat
farmers, three old women, and a butcher at the aperture, and
not finding yourself equal to struggling among them for a
place, you make up your mind to be left behind.  At last,
however, you do get your ticket just as the train comes up;
but hearing that exciting sound, you nervously cram your
change into your pocket without counting it, and afterwards
feel quite convinced that you have lost a shilling in the
transaction.  Ber 503-4, XXVII.

I know of no hours more terrible than those so passed  [at a
railroad station]....A man walks up and down the platform,
and in that way obtains something of the advantage of exercise; but a woman finds herself bound to sit still within
the dreary dullness of the waiting-room.  There are,
perhaps, people who under such circumstances can read, but
they are few in number.  The mind altogether declines to be
active, whereas the body is seized by a spirit of rest-
lessness to which delay and tranquility are loathsome.  The
advertisements on the walls are examined, the map of some
new Eden is studied--some Eden in which an irregular pond
and a church are surrounded by a multiplicity of regular
villas and shrubs--till the student feels that no consideration of health or economy would induce him to live
there.  Then the porters come in and out, till each porter
has made himself odious to the sight.  Everything is
hideous, dirty, and disagreeable; and the mind wanders away,
to consider why station-masters do not more frequently
commit suicide.  Bel 81, VII.

## TRAVEL BY SHIP

There is no peculiar life more thoroughly apart from life in
general, more unlike our usual life, more completely a life
of itself, governed by its own rules and having its own
roughnesses and amenities, than life on board ship.  What
tender friendship it produces, and what bitter enmities!
How completely the society has formed itself into separate
sets after the three or four first days!  How thoroughly it
is acknowledged that this is the aristocratic set, and that
the plebian!... And the women have to acknowledge all their
weaknesses, and to exercise all their strength....They
assume indifference, but are hard at work with their usual
weapons.  The men can do very well by themselves.  For them
there is drinking, smoking, cards, and various games; but
the potency of female spells soon works upon them, and all
who are worth anything are more or less in love by the end
of the first week.  Of course it must all come to an end
when the port is reached....No work is required from any
one.  The lawyer does not go to his court, nor the merchant

to his desk.    Pater-familias receives no bills; mater-
familias orders no dinners.   The daughter has no household
linen to disturb her.    The son is never recalled to his
books.   There is no parliament, no municipality, no vestry.
There are neither rates nor taxes nor rents to be paid.   The
goverment is the softest despotism under which subjects were
ever allowed to do almost just as they please.   That the
captain has a power is known, but hardly felt.   He smiles on
all...and makes one fancy that there must be something wrong
with men on shore because first-class nations cannot be
governed like first-class ships.   JC 37, V.

At sea you have always to look for your musicians among the
second-class passengers....On board ship there are many
sources of joy of which the land knows nothing.   You may
flirt and dance at sixty; and if you are awkward in the turn
of a valse, you may put it down to the motion of the ship.
You need wear no gloves, and may drink your soda-and-brandy
without being ashamed of it.   JC 42, V.

## TRAVELLERS

All my readers will probably at different times have made
part of a tabled'hote assemblage, and most of them,
especially those who have travelled with small parties, will
know how essential it is to one's comfort to get near to
pleasant neighbours.   The young man's idea of a pleasant
neighbour is of course a pretty girl.   What the young
ladies' idea may be I don't pretend to say.   But it certainly does seem to be happily arranged by Providence that
the musty fusty people, and the nicey spicy people, and the
witty pretty people do severally assemble and get together
as they ought to do.   Ber 99, VI.

But travellers will always observe that the dear new friends
they have made on the journey are not interesting to the
dear old friends whom they meet afterwards.   There may be
some touch of jealousy in this....They suspect, perhaps,
that the new friend was a bagman, or an opera dancer, and
think that the affair need not be made of importance.
HKHWR 374-5, XL.

## TRAVELLING

There is something enticing to an Englishman in the idea of
riding off through the desert with a pistol girt about his
waist, a portmanteau strapped on one horse before him, and
an only attendent seated on another behind him.   There is a
soupcon of danger in the journey just sufficient to give it
excitement; and then it is so un-English, oriental, and in-
convenient; so opposed to the accustomed haste and comfort
of a railway; so out of his hitherto beaten way of life,
that he is delighted to get into the saddle.   But it may be
a question whether he is not generally more delighted to get
out of it; particularly if that saddle be a Turkish one.
Ber 73-4, VI.

At Jerusalem, as elsewhere, these after all are the
traveller's first main questions. When is the table d'hote?
Where is the cathedral? At what hour does the train start
to-morrow morning? It will be some years yet, but not very
many, before the latter question is asked at Jerusalem.
Ber 97, VI.

When a traveller in these railroad days takes leave of
Florence, or Vienna, or Munich, or Lucerne, he does so without much of the bitterness of a farewell. The places are
now comparatively so near that he expects to see them again,
or at any rate, hopes that he may do so. But Jerusalem is
still distant from us no Sabbath-day's journey. A man who,
having seen it once, takes his leave, then sees it probably
for the last time. And a man's heart must be very cold who
can think of Palestine exactly as of any other land.
Ber 202, XI.

Who is it that consumes the large packets of sandwiches with
which parting guests are always laden? I imagine that
stationmasters' dogs are mainly fed upon them.
Ber 496,XXVII.

There is no romance now, gentle readers, in this journey
from Alexandria to Cairo....Men now go by railway, and then
they went by the canal boat. It is very much like English
travelling, with this exception, that men dismount from
their seats, and cross the Nile in a ferry-boat, and that
they pay five shillings for their luncheon instead of
sixpence. This ferry does, perhaps, afford some remote
chance of adventure, as was found the other day, when a carriage was allowed to run down the bank, in which was sitting
a native prince, the heir to the pasha's throne. On that
occasion the adventure was important, and the prince was
drowned. But even this opportunity for incident will soon
disappear; for Mr. Brunel, or Mr. Stephenson, or Mr. Locke,
or some other British engineering celebrity, is building a
railway bridge over the Nile, and then the modern traveller's heart will be contented, for he will be able to
sleep all the way from Alexandria to Cairo....
    I will not trouble my readers by a journey up the Nile;
nor will I even take them up a pyramid. For do not fitting
books for such purposes abound at Mr. Mudie's?
Ber 669-70, XXXVIII.

In these days men go from Cairo to Suez as they do from
London to Birmingham--by railway; in those days--some ten or
twelve years back, that is--they went in wooden boxes, and
were dragged by mules through the desert. Ber 689, XXXIX.

Why passengers for Turin, who reach Susa dusty, tired, and
sleepy, should be detained at that place for an hour and a
half instead of being forwarded to their beds in the great
city, is never made very apparent. All travelling officials
on the continent of Eurpoe are very slow in their manipu-
lation of luggage; but as they are equally correct we will

find the excuse for their tardiness in the latter quality.
HKHWR 359, XXXVII.

When a man has been much abroad, and has passed his time
there under unusual circumstances, his doings will necessarily become subjects of conversation to his companions.
To have travelled in France, Germany, or in Italy, is not
uncommon; nor is it uncommon to have lived a year or years
in Florence or in Rome.   It is not uncommon now to have
travelled all through the United States.   The Rocky
Mountains or Peru are hardly uncommon, so much has the taste
for travelling increased.  DrW 57-8, VI, Part II.

## TREASURY BENCH

For why, indeed, should any gentleman sit on the Treasury
bench if he be not able, when so questioned, to give very
satisfactory replies?   Giving satisfactory replies to ill-
natured questions is, one may say, the constitutional work
of such gentlemen, who have generally well learned how to do
so, and earned their present places by asking the selfsame
questions themselves, when seated as younger men in other
parts of the House.  TC 333, XXVII.

## TRIALS

The importance of such an affair increases like a snowball
as it is rolled on.   Many people talk much, and then very
many people talk very much more.   The under-sheriffs of the
City, praiseworthy gentlemen not hitherto widely known to
fame, became suddenly conspicuous and popular, as being the
dispensers of admissions to seats in the court.
PR 153, LVII,II.

The task of seeing an important trial at the Old Bailey is
by no means a pleasant business, unless you be what the
denizens of the Court would call 'one of the swells,' --so
as to enjoy the privilege of being a benchfellow with the
judge on the seat of judgment.   And even in that case the
pleasure is not unalloyed.  You have, indeed, the gratification of seeing the man whom all the world has been talking
about for the last nine days, face to face, and of being
seen in a position which causes you to be acknowledged as a
man of mark; but the intolerable stenches of the Court and
it horrid heat come up to you there, no doubt, as powerfully
as they fall on those below.  And then the tedium of a prolonged trial, in which the points of interest are apt to be
few and far between, grows upon you till you begin to feel
that though the Prime Minister who is out should murder the
Prime Minister who is in, and all the members of the two
Cabinets were to be called in evidence, you would not attend
the trial, though the seat of honour next to the judge were
accorded to you....And it will probably strike you that the
length of the trial is proportioned not to the complicity
but to the importance, or rather to the public interest, of
the case,--so that the trial which has been suggested of a

disappointed and bloody-minded ex-Prime Minister would certainly take at least a fortnight, even though the Speaker of the House of Commons and the Lord Chancellor had seen the blow struck, whereas a collier may knock his wife's brains out in the dark and be sent to the gallows with a trial that shall not last three hours.  And yet the collier has to be hung,--if found guilty,--and no one thinks that his life is improperly endangered by reckless haste.  Whether lives may not be improperly saved by more lengthened process is another question.

But...the task becomes very tiresome when the spectator has to enter the Court as an ordinary mortal.  There are two modes open to him, either of which is subject to grievous penalties....[H]e may get introduced to that overworked and greatly perplexed official, the under-sheriff, who...will probably find a seat for him if he persevere to the end. But the seat when obtained must be kept in possession from morning to evening, and the fight must be renewed from day to day.  And the benches are hard, and the space is narrow, and you feel that the under-sheriff would prod you with his sword if you ventured to sneeze, or to put to your lips the flask which you have in your pocket.  And then, when all the benchfellows go out to lunch at half-past one, and you are left to eat your dry sandwich without room for your elbows, a feeling of unsatisfied ambition will pervade you.

But you may be altogether independent, and, as a matter of right, walk into an open English court of law as one of the British public.  You will have to stand of course,--and to commence standing very early in the morning if you intend to succeed in witnessing any portion of the performance. And when you have made once good your entrance as one of the British public, you are apt to be a good deal knocked about, not only by your public brethren, but also by those who have to keep the avenues free for witnesses, and who will regard you from first to last as a disagreeable excrescence on the officialities of the work on hand.  Upon the whole it may be better for you, perhaps, to stay at home and read the record of the affair as given in the next day's Times.  Impartial reporters, judicious readers, and able editors between them will preserve for you all the kernel, and will save you from the necessity of having to deal with the shell.
PR 84-7, LXI,II.

## TRIUMPHS

[H]er triumphs were mainly of that quiet nature which one sometimes sees to be achieved with so little effort by beautiful women.  Ber 603, XXXIII.

Who does not know that interval of triumph which warm a man's heart when he has delivered his blow, and the return blow has not been yet received?  The blow has been so well struck that it must be successful, nay, may probably be death-dealing.  MM 324, XXIV.

Her first feeling was one of triumph,--as it must be in such a position to any woman who has already acknowledged to herself that she loves the man who then asks her to be his wife. Bel 125, X.

## TROUBLES

We are all apt to think when our days are dark that there is no darkness so dark as our own. Ber 599, XXXIII.

When a man finds himself compelled to wade through miles of mud, in which he sinks at every step up to his knees, he becomes forgetful of the blacking of his boots. Whether or no his very skin will hold out, is then his thought.
Ber 813, XLVI.

[B]ut let one's sorrow be what it may, there is always a better and a worse way of meeting it. Let what trouble may fall on a man's shoulders, a man may always bear it manfully. And are not troubles when so borne half cured? It is the flinching from pain which makes pain so painful.
CasR 180. IX,I.

It is the first plunge into the cold water that gives the shock. We may almost say that every human misery will cease to be miserable if it be duly faced; and something is done towards conquering our miseries, when we face them in any degree, even if not with due courage. CAsR 218, XI,II.

A self-imposed trouble will not allow itself to be banished. If a man lose a thousand pounds by a friend's fault, or by a turn in the wheel of fortune, he can, if he be a man, put his grief down and trample it under foot; he can exorcise the spirit of his grievance, and bid the evil one depart from out of his house. But such exorcism is not to be used when the sorrow has come from a man's own folly and sin;--especially not if it has come from his own selfishness. Such are the cases which make men drink; which drive them on to the avoidance of all thought; which create gamblers and reckless prodigals; which are the promoters of suicide. SmaH 279-80, XXVIII.

It is well to be rid of them [troubles] at any time, or at all times, if only they can be banished without danger. But when a man has over-used his liver till it will not act for him any longer, it is not well for him to resolve that he will forget the weakness of his organ just as he sits down to dinner. CanY 57, XLVI,II.

[B]ut let the horseman be ever so rich, or the horseman's daughter, and the stud be ever so good, it is seldom they can ride fast enough to shake off their cares.
SHHOH 242, XXIV.

It is always so with us. The heart when it is burdened, though it may have ample strength to bear the burden, loses

its buoyancy and doubts its own power.  It is like the
springs of a carriage which are pressed flat by the super-
incumbent weight.  But, because the springs are good, the
weight is carried safely, and they are the better afterwards
for their required purposes because of the trial to which
they have been subjected.  HKHWR 496, LIII.

We all have felt how on occasions our own hopes and fears,
nay, almost our own individuality, become absorbed in and
obliterated by the more pressing cares and louder voices or
those around us.  HKHWR 594-5, LXIII.

These and such like are the troubles that sit heavy on a
man's heart.  If search for bread, and meat, and raiment, be
set aside, then, beyond that, our happiness or misery here
depends chiefly on success or failure in small things.
Though a man when he turns into bed may be sure that he has
unlimited thousands at his command, though all society be
open to him, though he know himself to be esteemed handsome,
clever, and fashionable, even though his digestion be good,
and he have no doctor to deny him tobacco, champagne, or
made dishes, still, if he be conscious of failure there
where he has striven to succeed, even though it be in the
humbling of an already humble adversary, he will stretch,
and roll, and pine,--a wretched being.  How happy is he who
can get his fretting done for him by deputy!  VOB 427, LX.

In the midst of calamities caused by the loss of fortune, it
is the knowledge of what the world will say that breaks us
down;--not regret for those enjoyments which wealth can
give, and which had been long anticipated.
RalH 261, XXXIV,II.

We all probably know how some trouble will come upon us and
for a period seem to quell all that is joyous in our life,
and that then by quick degrees the weight of the trouble
will grow less, till the natural spring and vivacity of the
mind will recover itself, and make little or nothing of that
which a few hours ago was felt to be so grievous a burden.
JC 178, XXIV.

It may be said that nothing in the world is charming unless
it be achieved at some trouble.  If it rained ' '64
Leoville',--which I regard as the most divine of nectars,--I
feel sure that I should never raise it to my lips....A
lovely bonnet, is it not more lovely because the destined
wearer knows that there is some wickedness in achieving
it?...
        Perhaps the only pleasure left to the very rich is that
of thinking of the deprivations of the poor.  AyA 40, V.

There are such  "whips and scorns" in the world to which a
man shall be so subject as to have the whole tenor of his
life changed by them.  The hero bears them heroically,
making no complaints to those around him.  The common man

shrinks, and squeals, and cringes, so that he is known to those around him as one specially persecuted. MSF 222,XVI,I.

Who does not know the sort of sensation which falls upon a man when he feels that even the elements have turned against him, how he buttons up his coat and bids the clouds open themselves upon his devoted bosom?

 Blow, winds, and crack your cheeks!  Rage, blow,
 You cataracts and hurricanes!
 It is thus that a man is apt to address the soft rains of heaven when he is becoming wet through in such a frame of mind.  MSF 37, XXIV,II.

## TRUST

[A]nd what person who is not trustful ever remains trust-worthy?  Who can be fit for confidence who cannot himself confide?  Ber 141, IX.

But then it is so easy to trust oneself, and so easy also to distrust others.  RacR 120, IX.

## TRUTH

In these days we are becoming very strict about truth with our children; terribly strict occasionally, when we consider the natural weakness of the moral courage at the ages of ten, twelve, and fourteen.  But I do not know that we are at all increasing the measure of strictness with which we, grown-up people, regulate our own truth and falsehood. Heaven forbid that I should be thought to advocate falsehood in children; but an untruth is more pardonable in them than in their parents.  FrP 151-2, XVI.

On few matters of moment to a man's own heart can he speak out plainly the whole truth that is in him. OrF 397,XXXIX,I.

I believe that schoolmasters often tell fibs to schoolboys, although it would be so easy for them to tell the truth. But how difficult it is for the schoolboy always to tell the truth to his master!  OrF 142, LIV,II.

One hears stories that told to oneself, the hearer, are manifestly false; and one hears stories as to the truth or falsehood of which one is in doubt; and stories again which seem to be partly true and partly untrue.  But one also hears that of the truth of which no doubt seems to be possible. Cl 63, VIII.

...and it [a hypocritical sermon]  did, probably, more good than harm,--unless, indeed, we should take into our calcula-tion, in giving our award on this subject, the permanent utility of all truth, and the permanent injury of all falsehood.  Cl 378, XLV.

But in such discussions  [blackmail]   one man hardly expects truth from another.  PrM 108, LI,II.

Men have not seen, as yet, how much more lovely it is to tell frankly all that has been done, to give openly such evidence as a man may have to police magistrates and justices of the peace, than to keep anything wrapped within his own bosom.  The charm of such outspoken truth does not reconcile itself at once to the untrained mind; but the fact of the loveliness does gradually creep in, and the hideous ugliness of the other venture.  Land 272, XLVIII,III.

# U

## USE

O reader!   should it chance that thou art a clergyman, imagine what it would be to thee, wert thou asked what is the exact use of the Church of England; and that, too, by some stubborn catechist whom thou wert bound to answer; or, if a lady, happy in husband and family, say, what would be thy feelings if demanded to define the exact use of matrimony?  Use!   Is it not all in all to thee?  TC 541,XLV.

## USHERS

And who can say where the usher ends and the schoolmaster begins?  He, perhaps, may properly be called an usher, who is hired by a private schoolmaster to assist himself in his private occupation, whereas Henry Clavering had been seleted by a public body out of a hundred candidates, with much real or pretended reference to certificates of qualification.  He was certainly not an usher, as he was paid three hundred a year for his work,--which is quite beyond the mark of ushers.  Cl 7, II.

# V

## VAGABONDS

The vagabondism of the colonies is proverbial.  Vagabonds are taken in almost everywhere throughout the bush; but the welcome given to them varies.  Sometimes they are made to

work before they are fed, to their infinite disgust.
HHOG 79, VI.

Men, such as he, wander away from one colony into the next,
passing from one station to another, or sleeping on the
ground, till they become as desolate and savage as solitary
animals. And at last they die in the bush, creeping, we may
suppose, into hidden nooks as the beasts do when the hour of
death comes on them. HHOG 148, XI.

## VALUE

The fruit that falls easily from the tree, though it is ever
the best, is never valued by the gardener. Let him have
well-nigh broken his neck in gathering it, unripe and crude,
from the small topmost boughs of the branching tree, and the
pippin will be esteemed by him as invaluable. Bel 134, XI.

I fear that it is so with everything that we value,--with
our horses, our houses, our wines, and, above all, with our
women. Where is the man who has heart and soul big enough
to love a woman with increased force of passion because she
has at once recognized in him all that she has herself
desired? Bel 379, XXIX.

## VANITY

Men remember these things  [condescending and patronizing
others]  of themselves quite as quickly as others remember
them.  Str 124, XXII.

Yes; to the vain all will be vanity; and to the poor of
heart all will be poor. SmaH 562, LV.

But it is to the vain and foolish that the punishments fall;
--and to them they fall so thickly and constantly that the
thinker is driven to think that vanity and folly are of all
sins those which may be the least forgiven. SmaH 599, LIX.

But there are men who have the most lively gratification in
calling lords and marquises their friends, though they know
that nobody believes a word of what they say....It is a
gentle insanity which prevails in the outer courts of every
aristocracy; and as it brings with itself considerable
annoyance and but a lukewarm pleasure, it should not be
treated with too keen a severity. SmaH 600, LIX.

...that soreness which affects us all when we are made to
understand that we are considered to have failed there,
where we have most thought that we excelled.
HKHWR 448, XLVIII.

Who does not know how such sounds  [a mournful flute player]
may serve to enhance the bitterness of remorse, to add a
sorrow to the present thoughts, and to rob the future of its
hopes?

There come upon us all as we grow up in years, hours in which it is impossible to keep down the conviction that everything is vanity, that the life past has been vain from folly, and that the life to come must be vain from impotence. It is the presence of thoughts such as these that needs the assurance of a heaven to save the thinker from madness or from suicide. It is when the feeling of this pervading vanity is strongest on him, that he who doubts of heaven most regrets his incapacity for belief. If there be nothing better than this on to the grave,--and nothing worse beyond the grave, why should I bear such fardels?
RalH 392, LI.

## VENGEANCE

Those who offend us are generally punished for the offence they give; but we so frequently miss the satisfaction of knowing that we are avenged! It is arranged, apparently, that the injurer shall be punished, but that the person injured shall not gratify his desire for vengeance.
SmaH 504, L.

There is nothing more difficult for a man than the redressing of injuries done to a woman who is very near to him and very dear to him....What man ever forgave an insult to his wife or an injury to his sister, because he had taught himself that to forgive trespass is a religious duty? Without an argument, without a moment's thought, the man declares to himself that such trespasses as those are not included in the general order. But what is he to do? Thirty years since his course was easy, and unless the sinner were a clergyman, he could in some sort satisfy his craving for revenge by taking a pistol in his hand, and having a shot at the offender. That method was doubtless barbarous and unreasonable, but it was satisfactory and sufficed. But what can he do now? A thoughtful, prudent, painstaking man...feels that it is not given to him to attack another with his fists, to fly at his enemy's throat, and carry out his purpose after the manner of dogs....In many, perhaps in most of such cases, he may, if he please, have recourse to the laws. But any aid that the law can give him is altogether distasteful to him. The name of her that is so dear to him should be kept quiet as the grave under such misfortune, not blazoned through ten thousand columns for the amusement of all the crowd. There is nothing left for him but to spurn the man,--not with his foot but with his thoughts; and the bitter consciousness that to such spurning the sinner will be indifferent. The old way was barbarous certianly, and unreasonable,--but there was a satisfaction in it that has been often wanting since the use of pistols went out of fashion among us.
Cl 235, XXVIII.

There is no duty more certain or fixed in the world than that which calls upon a brother to defend his sister from ill-usage; but, at the same time, in the way we live now, no

duty is more difficult, and we may say generally more in-
distinct....We are not allowed to fight duels, and that
banging about of another man with a stick is alwyas disagreeable and seldom successful....There is a feeling, too,
when a girl has been jilted,--thrown over, perhaps, is the
proper term,--after the gentleman has had the fun of making
love to her for an entire season, and has perhaps even been
allowed the privileges as her promised husband, that the
less said the better....Though this one has been false, as
were perhaps two or three before, still the road to success
is open....The injured one probably desires that she may be
left to fight her own little battles alone.  Way 183,LXX,II.

As a dog, when another dog has got him well by the ear,
thinks not at all of his own wounds, but only how he may
catch his enemy by the lip....DrW 151, II, Part V.

### VICTORY

[V]ictory generally makes men generous.  DoT 402, XXXIV.

### VIEWPOINT

It is astonishing how much difference the point of view
makes in the aspect of all that we look at!  BaT 223, XXIV.

### VILLAINY

There are few of us who have not allowed our thoughts to
work on this or that villainy, arranging the method of its
performance, though the performance itself is far enough
from our purpose.  The amusement is not without its danger.
RalH 87, XI.  See also ROGUES.

### VIRTUES

...troubles will sometimes come from rigid virtue when rigid
virtue is not accompanied by sound sense, and especially
when it knows little or nothing of the softness of mercy.
LT 199, I.

...to be unselfish, generous, trusting, and pure.  These may
be regarded as feminine virtues, and may be said to be sometimes tarnished by faults which are equally feminine.  Un-
selfishness may become want of character; generosity essentially unjust; confidence may be weak, and purity insipid.
MSF 123, X,I.

### VIRTUE, MOCK

After all, mock virtue imposes on but few people.  The man
of the world is personally known for such; as also are known
the cruel, the griping, the avaricious, the unjust.  That
which enables the avaricious and the unjust to pass scathe-
less through the world is not the ignorance of the world as
to their sins, but the indifference of the world whether
they be sinful or no.  Ber 528, XXIX.

# W

## WAITERS

There are two distinct classes of waiters, and as far as I have been able to perceive, the special status of the waiter in question cannot be decided by observation of the class of waiter to which he belongs.  In such a town as Barchester you may find the old waiter with the dirty towel in the head inn, or in the second-class inn, and so you may the dapper waiter.  Or you may find both in each, and not know which is senior waiter and which junior waiter.  But for service I always prefer the old waiter with the dirty towel, and I find it more easy to satisfy him in the matter of sixpences when my relations with the inn come to an end.
LasC 373, XLII.

## WAITING

How are you to bid a starving man to wait when you put him down at a well-covered board?  Bel 413, XXXI.

## WAITING-ROOMS

[A]nd in no respect can the different ranks of different public offices be more plainly seen than in the presence or absence of such little items of accommodation as this [waiting-room].  TC 328, XXVII.  See also TRAIN STATIONS.

## WALKING

Now in such a situation [being alone a village], to take a walk is all the brightest man can do, and the dullest always does the same.  There is a kind of gratification in seeing what one has never seen before, be it ever so little worth seeing, particularly if the chances be, that it will never be seen again; and in going where one has never been before, and whither one will never return.  MB 1-2, I,I.

Alas! how few women can walk! how many are wilfully averse to attempting any such motion!  They scuffle, they trip, they trot, they amble, they waddle, they crawl, they drag themselves on painfully, as though the flounces and furbelows around them were a burden too heavy for easy, graceful motion; but, except in Spain they rarely walk.
Ber 139, IX.

The man who has laboured from his youth upwards can endure with his arms.  It is he who has had leisure to shoot, to play cricket, to climb up mountains, and to handle a racket, that can walk.  JC 82, XI.

**WASTE**

No man can have a string of hunters idle through the winter without feeling himself to be guilty of an unpardonable waste of property.  A customer at an eating-house will sometimes be seen to devour the last fragments of what has been brought to him, because he does not like to abandon that for which he must pay.  So it is with the man who hunts.  It is not perhaps that he wants to hunt.  There are other employments in life which would at the moment be more to his taste.  It is his conscience which prompts him,--the feeling that he cannot forgive himself for intolerable extravagance if he does not use the articles with which he has provided himself.  You can neglect your billiard-table, your books, or even your wine-cellar,--because they eat nothing.  But your horses soon eat their heads off their own shoulders if you pass weeks without getting on their backs.  MF 63,VI,II.

**WATER, RUNNING**

The Rhine was running by with that delicious sound of rapidly moving waters, that fresh refreshing gurgle of the river, which is so delicious to the ear at all times.  If you be talking, it wraps up your speech, keeping it for yourselves, making it difficult neither to her who listens nor to him who speaks.  If you would sleep, it is of all lullabies the sweetest.  If you are alone and would think, it aids all your thoughts.  If you are alone, and, alas! would not think,--if thinking be too painful,--it will dispel your sorrow, and give the comfort which music alone can give.  CanY 49, V,I.

**WEALTH**

They    [the attractions of wealth and the privations of poverty]    do not become so manifest to those to whom the wealth falls,--at any rate, not in early life,--as to the opposite party.  AyA 10, I.

**WEATHER**

[B]ut snow and winds and rain affect young married people less, I think, than they do other folk.  RacR 391, XXX.

[A] foul, rainy, muddy, sloppy morning, without a glimmer of sun, with that thick pervading, melancholy atmosphere which forces for the time upon imaginative men a conviction that nothing is worth anything.  RalH 223, XXIX.

**WEDDINGS**

But in these days, in which splendid things were done on so very splendid a scale, a young lady cannot herself lay out her friends' gifts so as to be properly seen by her friends. Some well-skilled, well-paid hand is needed even for that, and hence comes this public information on affairs which

should surely be private.   In our grandmothers' time the
happy bride's happy mother herself compounded the cake;--or
at any rate the trusted housekeeper.   But we all know that
terrible tower of silver which now stands niddle-noddling
with its appendages of flags and spears on the modern
wedding breakfast-table.   It will come to pass with some of
us soon that we must deny ourselves the pleasures of having
young friends, because their marriage presents are so
costly.   DuC 630, LXXIX.

## WEDDING BREAKFASTS

Then came the breakfast, that dullest, saddest, hour of all.
To feed heavily about twelve in the morning is always a
nuisance,--a nuisance so abominable that it should be
avoided under any other circumstances than a wedding in
your own family.   But that wedding-breakfast, when it does
come, is the worst of all feeding.   The smart dresses and
bare shoulders seen there by daylight, the handing people in
and out among the seats, the very nature of the food, made
up of chicken and sweets and flummery, the profusion of
champagne, not sometimes of the very best on such an
occasion;--and then the speeches!   They fall generally to
the lot of some middle-aged gentlemen, who seem always to
have been selected for their incapacity!   But there is a
worse trouble yet remaining,--in the unnatural repletion
which the sight even of so much food produces, and the fact
that your dinner for that day is destroyed utterly and for
ever.   MSF 238-9, LIX,III.

## WEDGE

We have all heard of the little end of the wedge, and we
have most of us an idea that the little end is the
difficulty.   DoT 378, XXXI.

## WEEPING

Women weep, and men too, not from grief, but from emotion.
DuC 608, LXXVII.

## WHIGS

Now among all the ranks of Englishmen and Englishwomen...no
one is so hostile to lowly born pretenders to high station
as the pure Whig.   BaT 324, XXXIII.   See LIBERALS.

## WHISKY

But whisky punch does leave behind a savour of its intrinsic
virtues, delightful no doubt to those who have imbibed its
grosser elements, but not equally acceptable to others who
may have been less fortunate.   CasR 196, X,I.

## WHISPERS

...in a whisper, such as seems to come naturally to every
one, when speaking by the bed-side of those who are in great
danger, but which is generally much more painfully audible
to a sick man than the natural voice.  LaV 378, XXXII.

## WHIST

Was Napoleon more triumphant, did a brighter glow of self-
satisfied inward power cross his features, when at Ulm he
succeeded in separating poor Mack from all his friends?
      Play on, ladies.  Let us not begrudge you your amuse-
ments.  We do not hold with pious Mr. O'Callaghan, that the
interchange of a few sixpences is a grievous sin.  At other
hours ye are still soft, charitable, and tender-hearted;
tender-hearted as English old ladies are, and should be.
But, dear ladies, would it not be well to remember the
amenities of life--even at the whist table?  Ber 411, XXII.

## WHITEHALL OFFICIALS

Whence...[came] the notions as to the way in which officials
at Whitehall pass their time  [sitting in a big room down at
Whitehall, and reading a newspaper with...feet up on a
chair]  I cannot say....The British world at large is slow
to believe that the great British housekeeper keeps no more
cats than what kill mice.  PF 227, LXIII,II.

## WIDOWS

We hear a good deal of jolly widows; and the slanderous
raillery of the world tells much of conjugal disturbances as
a cure for which women will look forward to a state of
widowhood with not unwilling eyes.  The raillery of the
world is very slanderous.  In our daily jests we attribute
to each other vices of which neither we, nor our neighbours,
nor our friends, nor even our enemies are ever guilty.  It
is our favourite parlance to talk of the family troubles of
Mrs. Green on our right, and to tell how Mrs. Young on our
left is strongly suspected of having raised her hand to her
lord and master.  What right have we to make these charges?
What have we seen in our own personal walks through life to
make us believe that women are devils?  There may possibly
have been a Xantippe here and there, but Imogenes are to be
found under every bush.  DoT 288, XXIV.

[I]t is astonishing how soon we get used even to a widow's
cap!  Ber 57, IV.

When a recently bereaved widow attempts to enjoy her freedom
without money, then it behoves the world to speak aloud;--
and the world does its duty.  CanY 73, VII,I.

What business had any widow to want a husband?  It is so
easy for wives to speak and think after that fashion when

they are satisfied with their own ventures.  Cl 238, XXVIII.

There will, of course, be some to say that a young widow should not be happy and comfortable,--that she should be weeping her lost lord, and subject to the desolation of bereavement.  But as the world goes now, young widows are not miserable; and there is, perhaps, a growing tendency in society to claim from them year by year still less of any misery that may be avoidable....A woman may thoroughly respect her husband, and mourn him truly, honestly, with her whole heart, and yet enjoy thoroughly the good things which he has left behind for her use.  ED 193-4, XXI,I.

## WIGS

No doubt an effort was made to hide the wiggishness of his wigs, but what effect in that direction was ever made successfully?  Cl 20, III.

## WILES

My brother, when you see these tricks played upon other men, the gall rises black within your breast, and you loudly condemn wiles which are so womanly, but which are so un-worthy of women.  But how do you feel when they are played upon yourself?  The gall is not so black, the condemnation less loud; your own merit seems to excuse the preference which is shown you; your heart first forgives and then applauds.  Is it not so, my brother, with you?
Ber 701-2, XXXIX.

## WINDOWS

No,...not even an oriel, beautiful as is an oriel window. It has not about it so perfect a feeling of quiet English homey comfort.  Let oriel windows grace a college, or the half public mansions of a potent peer; but for the sitting room of quiet country ladies, of ordinary homely folk, nothing can equal the square mullioned windows of the Tudor architects.  BaT 204, XXII.

We all know the beautiful old Tudor window, with its stout stone mullions and its stone transoms, crossing from side to side at a point much nearer to the top than the bottom.  Of all windows ever invented it is the sweetest.  SmaH 5, I.

Who does not know such windows  [strong deep mullions, longer than deep], and has not declared to himself often how sad a thing it is that sanitary or scientific calculations should have banished the like of them from our houses?
SHHOH 23-4, III.

## WINE

Whatever women may say about wild-fowl, men never profess an indifference to good wine, although there is a theory about

the world, quite as incorrect as it is general, that they
have given up drinking it.  Cl 67-8, VIII.

When a man pays 110s. a dozen for his champagne, and then
gives it to guests like Lord Mongrober who are not even
expected to return the favour, then that man ought to be
allowed to talk about his wine without fear of rebuke.  One
doesn't have an agreement to that effect written down on
parchment and sealed; but it is as well understood and ought
to be as faithfully kept as any legal contract.  PrM 89,X,I.

## WINTER

The comic almanacs give us dreadful pictures of January and
February; but, in truth, the months which should be made to
look gloomy in England are March and April.  Let no man
boast himself that he has got through the perils of winter
till at least the seventh of May.  DoT 564, XLVII.

## WINTER LIGHT

There is a special winter's light, which is very clear
though devoid of all brilliancy,--through which every object
strikes upon the eye with well-marked lines, and under which
almost all forms of nature seem graceful to the sight if not
actually beautiful.  But there is a certain melancholy which
ever accompanies it.  It is the light of the afternoon, and
gives token of the speedy coming of the early twilight.  It
tells of the shortness of the day, and contains even in its
clearness a promise of the gloom of night.  It is absolute
light, but it seems to contain the darkness which is to
follow it.  I do not know that it is ever to be ssen and
felt so plainly as on the wide moorland, where the eye
stretches away over miles, and sees at the world's end the
faint low lines of distant clouds settling themselves upon
the horizon.  CanY 324, XXXI,I.

## WISDOM

And in this way they got through their work, not perhaps
with the sagacity of Solomon, but as I have said, with an
average amount of wisdom, as will always be the case when
men set about their tasks with true hearts and honest minds.
CasR 81, IV,II.

No mortal man can be seriously wise at all hours.  FrP 52,VI.

## WIT

Wit is the outward mental casing of the man, and has no more
to do with the inner mind of thoughts and feelings than have
the rich brocaded garments of the priest at the altar with
the asceticism of the anchorite below them, whose skin is
tormented with sackcloth, and whose body is half flayed with
rods.  Nay, will not such a one often rejoice more than any
other in the rich show of his outer apparel?  Will it not be

food for his pride to feel that he groans inwardly, while he
shines outwardly?  So it is with the mental efforts which
men make.  Those which they show forth daily to the world
are often the opposites of the inner workings of the spirit.
BaT 182, XX.

## WITNESSES

Who can tell when the caes may come on....Attorneys' clerks
have been round diligently to all witnesses...warning you
that the important hour is at hand--that on no account may
you be absent, so much as ten minutes walk from the court.
...It is evident that you cannot leave the filthy town with
its running gutters--the filthy inn with its steamy stinking
atmosphere, and bed-room porter drinkers for good and all...
but that you must, willy nilly, in spite of rain, crowd, and
offensive smell stay....Into court therefore return, unfortunate witness, other shelter have you none--and now being
a man of strong nerves, except when put into a chair to be
stared at by judge--bar--grand jury--little jury--attorney--
galleries, &c.,&c., you can push your way into a seat, and
listen with attention to the quiddities of the legally
erudite Mr. Allenwinde, as on behalf of his cliend he ingeniously attempts, nay, as he himself afterwards boasts to
the jury, succeeds in making that disconcerted young gentleman in the witness chair commit perjury.  MB 227-9, VI,III.

A rival lawyer could find a protection on the bench when his
powers of endurance were tried too far; but a witness in a
court of law has no protection.  He comes there unfeed, without hope of guerdon, to give such assistance to the State in
repressing crime and assisting justice as his knowledge in
this particular case may enable him to afford; and justice,
in order to ascertain whether his testimony be true, finds
it necessary to subject him to torture.  One would
naturally imagine that an undisturbed thread of clear
evidence  would be best obtained from a man whose position
was made easy and whose mind was not harassed; but this is
not the fact:  to turn a witness to good account, he must be
badgered this way and that till he is nearly mad; he must be
made a laughing-stock for the court; his very truths must be
turned into falsehoods, so that he may be falsely shamed; he
must be accused of all manner of villany, threatened with
all manner of punishment; he must be made to feel that he
has no friend near him, that the world is all against him;
he must be confounded till he forget his right hand from his
left, till his mind be turned into chaos, and his heart into
water; and then let him give evidence.  What will fall from
his lips when in this wretched collapse must be of special
value, for the best talents of practised forensic heroes are
daily used to bring it about; and no member of the Humane
Society interferes to protect the wretch.  Some sorts of
torture are, as it were, tacitly allowed even among humane
people.  Eels are skined alive, and witnesses are sacrificed, and no one's blood curdles at the sight, no soft
heart is sickened at the cruelty.  TC 480, XL.

[U]nless they were suborned or false they were there doing a
painful duty to the public, for which they were to receive
no pay from which they were to obtain no benefit.  Of whom
else in that court could so much be said?  The judge there
had his ermine and his canopy, his large salary and his seat
of honour.  And the lawyers had their wigs, and their own
loud voices, and their places of precedence.  The attorneys
had their seats and their big tables, and the somewhat
familiar respect of the tipstaves.  The jury, though not
much to be envied, were addressed with respect and flattery,
had their honourable seats, and were invariably at least
called gentlemen.  But why should there be no seat of honour
for the witnesses?  To stand in a box, to be bawled after by
the police, to be scowled at and scolded by the judge, to be
browbeaten and accused falsely by the barristers, and then
to be condemned as perjurers by the jury,--that is the fate
of the one person who during the whole trial is perhaps
entitled to the greatest respect, and is certainly entitled
to the most public gratitude.  Let the witness have a big
armchair, and a canopy over him, and a man behind him with a
red cloak to do him honour and keep the flies off; let him
be gently invited to come forward from some inner room where
he can sit before a fire.  Then he will be able to speak
out, making himself heard without scolding, and will perhaps
be able to make a fair fight with the cocks who can crow so
loudly on their own dunghills.  OrF 360, LXXV,II.

[B]ut the little men in authority are always stern on such
points, and witnesses are usually treated as persons who are
not entitled to have any views as to their own personal comfort or welfare.  Lawyers, who are paid for their presence,
may plead other engagements, and their pleas will be considered; and if a witness be a lord, it may perhaps be thought
very hard that he should be dragged away from his amusements.  But the ordinary commonplace witness must simply
listen and obey--at his peril.  VOB 469, LXVI.

It is always hard to make an honest witness understand that
it may be the duty of others to believe him to be a liar.
JC 370, L.

## WIVES, MOULDED

The idea of a wife thus moulded to fit a man's own grooves,
and educated to suit matrimonial purposes according to the
exact views of the future husband was by no means original.
...On the whole I think that the ordinary plan is the
better, and even the safer.  Dance with a girl three times,
and if you like the light of her eye and the tone of voice
with which she, breathless, answers your little questions
about horseflesh and music--about affairs masculine and
feminine,--then take the leap in the dark.  There is danger,
no doubt; but the moulded wife is, I think, more dangerous.
OrF 328-9, XXXIII,I.

That hobby of moulding a young lady is perhaps of all

hobbies the most expensive to which a young gentleman can apply himself.  OrF 223, LXII,II.

## WIVES, WRONGED

Let the female married victim ever make the most of such positive wrongs as Providence may vouchsafe to her.
OrF 208, XXI,I.

## WOMEN

A woman can rarely be really offended at the expression of love, unless it be from some one unfitted to match with her, either in rank or age.  Kel 503-4, XXXIX.

Girls below twenty and old ladies above sixty will do her justice; for in the female heart the soft springs of sweet romance reopen after many years, and again gush out with waters pure as in earlier days, and greatly refresh the path that leads downwards to the grave.  But I fear that the majority of those between these two eras will not approve.
...I fear that unmarried ladies of thirty-five will declare that there can be no probability of so absurd a project being carried through; that young women on their knees before their lovers are sure to get kisses, and that they would not put themselves in such a position did they not expect it.  War 130, XI.

As a general rule, it is highly desirable that ladies should keep their temper; a woman when she storms always makes herself ugly, and usually ridiculous, also....There is nothing so odious to man as a virago....A low voice 'is an excellent thing in women.'
    Such may be laid down as a very general rule; and few women should allow themselves to deviate from it, and then only on rare occasions.  But if there be a time when a woman may let her hair to the winds, when she may loose her arms, and scream out trumpet-tongued to the ears of men, it is when nature calls out within her not for her own wants, but for the wants of those whom her womb has borne, whom her breasts have suckled, for those who look to her for their daily bread as naturally as man looks to his Creator.
BaT 227-8, XXV.

[B]ut as I and others have so often said before, 'Women grow on the sunny side of the wall.'  DoT 83, VI.

Ladies have little ways of talking to each other, with nods and becks and wreathed smiles, which are quite beyond the reach of men.  Ber 353, XX.

But pretty women can say almost as much as is necessary on such occasions  [meeting a former lover]  without opening their lips.  Ber 607, XXXIII.

[W]omen always give more than they claim.  Ber 775, XLIII.

In such periods of misfortune [high poor rates], a woman has always some friend.  Let her be who she may, some pair of broad shoulders is forthcoming on which may be laid so much of the burden as is by herself unbearable.  It is the great privilege of womanhood, that which compensates them for the want of those other privileges which belong exlusively to manhood--sitting in Parliament, for instance, preaching sermons, and going on "Change."  CasR 132, VII,I.

There is a story current, that in the west of England the grandeur of middle-aged maiden ladies is measured by the length of the tail of their cats.  CasR 177, IX,II.

Women love a bold front, and a voice that will never own its master to have been beaten in the world's fight.
CasR 241, XII,II.

The obedience of women to men--to those men to whom they are legally bound--is, I think, the most remarkable trait in human nature.  Nothing equals it but the instinctive loyalty of a dog.  CasR 204, X,III.

An English lady of the right sort will do all things but one for a sick neighbour;  but for no neighbour will she wittingly admit contagious sickness within the precincts of her own nursery.  FrP 332-3, XXXIV.

Women for the most part are prone to love-making--as nature has intended that they should be; but there are women from whom all such follies seem to be as distant as skittles and beer are distant from the dignity of the Lord Chancellor.
OrF 19, II,I.

Many of the sweetest, kindest, best of women are weak in this way [agreeing to make someone happy].  It is not every woman that can bring herself to say hard, useful, wise words in opposition to the follies of those they love best.   A woman to be useful and wise no doubt should have such power.  For myself I am not to sure that I like useful and wise women.  OrF 352, XXV,I.

Why is it that commercial honesty has so seldom charms for women?  A woman who would give away the last shawl from her back will insist in smuggling her gloves through the Custom-house!  Who can make a widow understand that she should not communicate with her boy in the colonies under the dishonest cover of a newspaper?  Is not the passion for cheap purchases altogether a female mania?  And yet every cheap purchase--every purchase made at a rate so cheap as to deny the vendor his fair profit, is, in truth, a dishonesty--a dishonesty to which the purchaser is indirectly a party. Would that women could be taught to hate bargains!  How much less useless trash would there be in our houses, and how much fewer tremendous sacrifices in our shops!  Str 80, XIV.

There are women, very many women, who could bear this
[losing two chances at a husband], if with sadness, still
without bitterness.  Str 115, XXI.

It is so natural to women to be so  [nursing an afflicted
person], that I think even Regan would have nursed Lear, had
Lear's body become impotent instead of his mind.
Str 117, XXI.

There are women who cannot grow alone as standard trees;--
for whom the support and warmth of some wall, some paling,
some post, is absolutely necessary....A woman in want of a
wall against which to nail herself will swear conjugal
obedience sometimes to her cook, sometimes to her grand-
child, sometimes to her lawyer.  Any standing corner, post,
or stump strong enough to bear her weight will suffice; but
to some standing corner, post, or stump, she will find her
way and attach herself, and there she will be married.
RacR 3, I.

What should a woman do with her life?...Fall in love, marry
the man, have two children, and live happy ever afterwards.
I maintain that answer has as much wisdom in it as any other
that can be given;--or perhaps more.
     A woman's life is important to her,--as that of a man
to him,--not chiefly in regard to that which she shall do
with it.  The chief thing for her to look to is the manner
in which that something shall be done.  It is of moment to a
young man when entering life to decide whether he shall make
hats or shoes; but not of half the moment that will be that
other decision, whether he shall make good shoes or bad.
And so with a woman;--if she shall have recognized the
necessity of truth and honesty for the purposes of her life,
I do not know that she need ask herself many questions as to
what she will do with it.  CanY 110, XI,I.

There are women, high in rank, but poor in pocket, so gifted
with the particular grace of aristocracy, that they show by
every word spoken, by every turn of the head, by every step
taken, that they are among the high ones of the earth, and
that money has nothing to do with it.  MM 73-4, VI.

There are women who can fight such battles  [against other
women]  when they have not an inch of ground on which to
stand.  MM 105, VIII.

It is, I think certainly the fact that women are less
pervious to ideas of honesty than men are.  They are less
shocked by dishonesty when they find it, and are less clear
in their intellect as to that which constitutes honesty.
Where is the woman who thinks it wrong to smuggle?  What
lady's conscience ever pricked her in that she omitted the
armorial bearings on her silver forks from her tax papers?
What wife ever ceased to respect her husband because he
dealt dishonestly in business?  Whereas, let him not go to
church, let him drink too much wine, let him go astray in

his conversation, and her wrath arises against these faults. But this lack of feminine accuracy in the matter of honesty tends rather to charity in their judgement or others, than to deeds of fraud on the part of women themselves. MM 125-6, X.

With many women I doubt whether there by any more effectual way of touching their hearts than ill-using them and then confessing it. If you wish to get the sweetest fragrance from the herb at your feet, tread on it and bruise it. MM 131, X.

There are women who seem to have an absolute pleasure in fixing themselves for business by the bedside of a sick man. They generally commence their operations by laying aside all fictitious feminine charms, and arraying themselves with a rigid, unconventional, unenticing propriety.  Though they are still gentle--perhaps more gentle than ever in their movements--there is a decision in all they do very unlike their usual mode of action.  The sick man, who is not so sick but what he can ponder on the matter, feels himself to be like a baby, whom he has seen the nurse to take from its cradle, pat on the back, feed, and then return to its little couch, all without undue violence or tyranny, but still with a certain consciousness of omnipotence as far as that child was concerned.  The vitality of the man is gone from him, and he, in his prostrate condition, debarred by all the features of his condition from spontaneous exertion, feels himself to be more a woman than the woman herself.  She, if she be such a one as our Miss Mackenzie, arranges her bottles with precision; knows exactly how to place her chair, her lamp, her teapot; settles her cap usefully on her head, and prepares for the night's work certainly with satisfaction.  And such are the best women of the world. MM 182-3, XIV.

It has been said of women that they have an insane desire for matrimony.  I believe that the desire, even if it be as general as is here described, is no insanity.  MM 397, XXX.

But we all know what such commands    [to leave and marry another] mean.  Cl 226, XXVII.

...that point on which no woman can endure a caution    [that one loves another woman].  Cl 240, XXVIII.

A woman, when she doubts whether she loves or not, is inclined five parts out of six towards the man of whom she is thinking.  When a woman doubts she is lost, the cynics say.  I simply assert, being no cynic, that when a woman doubts she is won.  Cl 277, XXXIII.  See also DOUBT.

[B]ut what woman, within her own breast, accuses the man she loves?  Cl 307, XXXVI.

...one of those women who have always believed that their

own sex is in every respect inferior to the other.
Bel 90, VII.

The...[pious ladies] of this world allow themselves little
spiteful pleasures of this kind, repenting of them, no
doubt, in those frequent moments in which they talk to their
friends of their own terrible vilenesses. Bel 100, VIII.

A woman, when she is jealous, is apt to attribute to the
other woman with whom her jealousy is concerned, both weakness and timidity, and to the man both audacity and
strength.    A woman who has herself taken perhaps twelve
months in the winning, will think that another woman is to
be won in five minutes. LasC 340, XXXVIII.

We know how quickly women arrive at an understanding of the
feelings of those with whom they live. PF 248, XXVII,I.

But there are women...who think that the acerbities of
religion are intended altogether for their own sex.    That
men ought to be grateful to them who will deny?  Such women
seem to think that Heaven will pardon that hardness of heart
which it has created in man, and which the affairs of the
world seem almost to require; but that it will extend no
such forgiveness to the feminine creation.    It may be
necessary that a man should be stiff-necked, self-willed,
eager on the world, perhaps even covetous and given to
worldly lusts.    But for a woman, it behoves her to crush
herself, so that she may be at all points submissive, self-
denying, and much-suffering.    She should be used to thorns
in the flesh, and to thorns in the spirit too.    Whatever may
be the thing she wants, that thing she should not have.    And
if it be so that, in her feminine weakness, she be not able
to deny herself, there should be those around her to do the
denial for her.    Let her crush herself as it becomes a poor
female to do, or let there be some other female to crush her
if she lack the strength, the purity, and the religious fervour which such self-crushing requires. LT 204, I.

...that look of command...which women, who judge of men by
their feelings rather than their thoughts, always love to
see.   GLOG 56, V.

It is thus, in general, that women regard the feelings,
desires, and aspirations of other women.    You will hardly
ever meet an elderly lady who will not speak of her juniors
as living in a state of breathless anxiety to catch
husbands.    And the elder lady will speak of the younger as
though any kind of choice in such catching was quite dis-
regarded.    The man must be a gentleman,--or, at least,
gentlemanlike,--and there must be bread.    Let these things
be given, and what girl won't jump into what man's arms?
Female reader, is it not thus that the elders of your sex
speak of the younger?  HKHWR 319-20, XXXIV.

In such matters  [where a man pursues a woman]   a woman is always angry with the woman,--who has probably been quite passive, and rarely with the man, who is ever the real transgressor.  HKHWR 672, LXXII.

...that conviction so common to woman and the cause of so much delight to men,--that ill-usage and suffering are intended for woman.  SHHOH 109, XI.

The appreciation of a woman in such matters  [hearing a loved one speak to another woman]  is as fine as the nose of a hound, and is all but unintelligible to a man.
RalH 284, XXXVIII.

Women like to feel that the young men belonging to them are doing something in the world, so that a reflected glory may be theirs....Brothers do not always care much for a brother's success, but a sister is generally sympathetic.
ED 29-30, IV,I.

And it is not the case that false pretexts against public demands are always held to be justifiable by the female mind?  What lady will ever scruple to avoid her taxes?  What woman ever understood her duty to the State!
ED 361-2, LXXIX,II.

Women in such matters  [seduction]  are always hard against women, and especially hard against those whom they believe to belong to a class below their own.  EE 159, IX,I.

There are women, who in regard to such troubles...[a pregnant unmarried girl]  always think that the woman should be punished as the sinner and that the man should be assisted to escape....It is as though a certain line were drawn to include all women,--a line, but, alas, little more than a line,--by overstepping which, or rather by being known to have overstepped it, a woman ceases to be a woman in the estimation of her own sex.  That the existence of this feeling has strong effect in saving women from passing the line, none of us can doubt.  That its general tendency may be good rather than evil, is possible.  But the hardness necessary to preserve the rule, hardness which must be exclusively feminine but which is seldom wanting, is a marvellous feature in the female character.
EE 116-7,VII,II.

Why is it that when men and women congregate, though the men may beat the women in numbers by ten to one, and though they certainly speak the louder, the concrete sound that meets the ears of any outside listener is always a sound of women's voices?  PR 139, XVI,I.

In these days men regard the form and outward lines of a woman's face and figure more than either the colour or the expression, and women fit themselves to men's eyes.  With padding and false hair without limit a figure may be con-

structed of almost any dimensions.  The sculptors who
construct them, male and female, hairdressers and milliners,
are very skilful, and figures are constructed of noble
dimensions, sometimes with voluptuous expansion, sometimes
with classic reticence, sometimes with dishevelled negli-
gence which becomes very dishevelled indeed when long out of
the sculptor's hands.  Colours indeed are added, but not the
colours which we used to love.  The taste for flesh and
blood has for the day given place to an appetite for horsehair and pearl powder.  Way 240-1, XXVI,I.

Where is the woman who does not wish to charm, and is not
proud to think that she has succeeded with those whom she
most likes?  IHP 9, XXXIII,II.

The married woman who has not some pet lares of her own is
but a poor woman.  IHP 256, LIX,II.

In all our colonies the women are beautiful; and in the
large towns a society is soon created, of which the fastidious traveller has very little ground to complain; but in
the small distant bush-towns, as they are called, the
rougher elements must predominate.  JC 102, XIV.

Married ladies seldom estimate even the girls they like best
at their full value....The speciality of the attraction is
of course absent to the women, and unless she has considered
the matter so far as to be able to clothe her thoughts in
male vestments, as some women do, she cannot understand the
longing that is felt for so small a treasure.
AyA 340-1, XXXVI.

A man when he is conscious of the presence of a mere woman,
to whom he feels that no worship is due, may for his own
purpose be able to tell a lie to her, and make her believe
that he acknowledges a divinity in her presence.  But, when
he feels the goddess, he cannot carry himself before her as
though she were a mere woman, and, as such, inferior to himself in her attributes.  AyA 528-9, LIV.

...--but yet a woman, with a woman's propensity to follow
her feelings rather than either facts or reason.
CoH 180, XVI.

But there is, I think, an involuntary tendency among women
to make more than necessary use of assistance when the
person tendering it has made himself really welcome.
MF 225, XXI,I.

There are women who have a special gift of hiding their dis-
likings from the objects of them, when occasion requires.
They can smile and be soft, with bitter enmity in their
hearts, to suit the circumstances of the moment.  And as
they do so, their faces will overcome their hearts, and
their enmity will give way to their smiles.  They will
become almost friendly because they look friendly.  They

will cease to hate because hatred is no longer convenient.
MF 203-4, XX,II.

There are women whose grace is so remarkable as to demand
the attention of all.   But then it is known of them, and
momentarily seen, that their grace is peculiar.   They have
studied their graces, and the result is there only too
evident.  MSF 124, X,I.

There are ladies...who like to ride across the country with
a young man before them, or perhaps following; and never
think much of their fifty years.  MSF 81, XXVII,II.

...the greatest lesson we may say which a man or a woman can
learn.   And though she taught it immoderately, fancying, as
a woman, that another woman should sacrifice everything to a
man, still she taught it with truth.  OML 39, IV.

[O]f all her gifts  [a feminine weakness]  is the most
valuable to an English woman, till she makes the mistake of
bartering it away for women's rights.  We can imagine, however, that the stanchest women's-right lady should cry for
her lost lover.  Land 17-8, XVIII,II.

Whatever may be the position in which a woman may find herself, whatever battle she may have to carry on, she has
first to protect herself from unseemly attitudes.
Land 195, XLIII,III.

## WOMEN, OLD

Ladies--especially discreet old ladies...--are bound to
entertain pacific theories, and to condemn all manner of
violence....But, nevertheless, deeds of prowess are still
dear to the female heart, and a woman, be she ever so old
and discreet, understands and appreciates the summary
justice which may be done by means of a thrashing.
SmaH 523, LII.

But let an old lady be ever so strict towards her own sex,
she likes a little wickedness in a young man,--if only he
does not carry it to the extent of marrying the wrong sort
of young woman.  EE 51, III,I.

## WOMEN, RELIGIOUS

How great may be the misery inflicted by an energetic, unmarried, healthy woman in that condition  [very religious]
--a woman with no husband, or children, or duties, to dis-
tract her from her work--I pray that my readers may never
know.  SmaH 161, XVII.

## WOMEN, UNMARRIED

There is a distressing habitual humility in many unmarried
ladies of an uncertain age, which at the first blush tells

the tale against them which they are so painfully anxious to leave untold.   In order to maintain their places but yet a little longer in that delicious world of love, sighs, and dancing partners, from which it must be so hard for a maiden, with all her youthful tastes about her, to tear herself for ever away, they smile and say pretty things, put up with the caprices of married women, and play second fiddle, though the doing so in no whit assists them in their task. Nay, the doing so does but stamp them the more plainly with that name from which they would so fain escape.   Their plea is for mercy--'Have pity on me, have pity on me; put up with me but for one other short twelve months; and then, if then I shall still have failed, I will be content to vanish from the world for ever.'   When did such plea for pity from one woman ever find real entrance into the heart of another? TC 292-3, XXV.

Unmarried ladies of a certain age, whatever may be their own feelings in regard to matrimony on their own behalf, seem always impressd with a conviction that other ladies in the same condition would certainly marry if they got an opportunity.  Ber 578-9, XXXII.

## WOMEN, YOUNG

[B]ut then it is allowed to young ladies to be hypocrites when the subject under discussion is the character of a young gentleman.   FrP 105, XI.

There is nothing among the wonders of womanhood more wonderful than this, that the young mind and young heart--hearts and minds young as youth can make them, and in their natures as gay,--can assume the gravity and discretion of threescore years and maintain it successfully before all comers.   And this is done, not as a lesson that has been taught, but as the result of an instinct implanted from the birth.   Let us remember the mirth of our sisters in our homes, and their altered demeanours when those homes were opened to strangers; and remember also that this change had come from the inward working of their own feminine natures! OrF 184, XIX,I.

We have all seen those efforts  [graceful motions], and it may be that many of us have liked them when they have been made on our own behalf.   VOB 9, I.

Young ladies,--some young ladies,--can be very ferocious. Land 114-5, VII,I.

## WORDS

We generally use three times the number of words which are necessary for the purpose which we have in hand. CasR 234, XII,II.

An angry man will often cling to his anger because his anger has been spoken; he will do evil because he has threatened evil, and is ashamed to be better than his words.
CasR 20, I,III.

Oh, those delicious private words the need for which comes so often during those short halcyon days of one's lifetime!
Cl 362, XLIII.

There are certain words usually confined to the vocabularies of men, which women such as Lady Aylmer delight to use on special occasions, when strong circumstances demand strong language.  Bel 222, XVII.

[B]ut a man when he wishes to use burning words should use them while the words are on fire.  OML 93, IX.

## WORDS, SPOKEN

But words spoken cannot be recalled, and many a man and many a woman who has spoken a word at once regretted, are far too proud to express that regret....There is so much in a turn of the eye and in the tone given to a word when such things [forbiding someone's company to a wife]  have to be said,--so much more of importance than in the words themselves.
HKHWR 7-8, I.

[A]nd, let what apology there may be made, a word uttered cannot be retracted.  PrM 177, XIX,I.

A written letter remains, and may be taken as evidence of so much more than it means.  But a word sometimes may be spoken which, if it be well spoken,--the assurance of its truth be given by the tone and by the eye of the speaker,--shall do so much more than by any letter, and shall yet only remain with the hearer as the remembrance of the scent of a flower remains!  AS 550, LXXIX.

There are moments in which stupid people say clever things, obtuse people say sharp things, and good-natured people say ill-natured things.  DuC 248, XXXI.

## WORDS, WRITTEN

The word that is written is a thing capable of permanent life, and lives frequently to the confusion of its parent. A man should make his confession always by word of mouth if it be possible.  Cl 353, XLII.

Words when once written remain, or may remain, in testimony for ever.  DuC 405, LI.

## WORK

There is no harder life than this  [the life of an idle man with a moderate income].  Here and there we may find a man who has so trained himself that day after day he can devote his mind without compulsion to healthy pursuits, who can induce himself to work, though work be not required from him for any ostensible object, who can save himself from the curse of misusing his time, though he has for it no defined and necessary use; but such men are few.  PR 183, XXI,I.

The popular newspaper, the popular member of Parliament, and the popular novelist,--the name of Charles Dickens will of course present itself to the reader who remembers the Circumlocution office,--have had it impressed on their several minds,--and have endeavoured to impress the same idea on the minds of the public generally,--that the normal Government clerk is quite indifferent to his work.  No greater mistake was ever made, or one showing less observation of human nature.  It is the nature of a man to appreciate his own work.  The felon who is made simply to move shot, perishes because he knows his work is without aim.  The fault lies on the other side.  The policeman is ambitious of arresting everybody.  The lawyer would rather make your will for you gratis than let you make your own. The General can believe in nothing but in well-trained troops.  JC 346, XLVII.

## WORSHIP

We have read how private and peculiar forms of worship have been carried on from age to age in families, which to the outer world have apparently adhered to the services of some ordinary church.  BaT 197, XXII.

## WOUNDS

But wounds cannot be cured as easily as they may be inflicted.  FrP 402, XLI.

To have a festering wound and to be able to show the wound to no surgeon, is wretchedness indeed!  PrM 5, XLI,II.

## WRINKLES

[B]ut as there are wrinkles which seem to come from the decay of those muscles which should uphold the skin, so are there others which seem to denote that the owner has simply got rid of the watery weaknesses of juvenility.  AS 50,VIII.

## WRITING

[B]ut it is not always easy to use simple, plain language-- by no means so easy as to mount on stilts, and to march along with sesquipedalian words, which pathos, spasms, and notes of interjection.  FrP 379, XXXIX.

It is all very well for a man to write when he himself is the sole judge of what shall be written, but it is a terrible thing to have to draw up any document for the approval

of others. One's choicest words are torn away, one's
figures speech are maltreated, one's stops are misunderstood, one's very syntax is put to confusion; and then, at
last, whole paragraphs are cashiered as unnecessary. First
comes the torture and then the execution. 'Come, Wilkins,
you have the pen of a ready writer; prepare for us this document.' In such words is the victim addressed by his
colleagues. Unhappy Wilkins! he little drams of the misery
before him as he proudly applies himself to work.

But it is beautiful to hear and see, when two scribes
have been appointed, how at first they praise each other's
words, as did Trissotin and Vadius; how gradually each
objects to this comma or to that epithet; how from moment
to moment their courage will arise, till at last every word
that the other has written is foul nonsense and flat blas-
phemy--till Vadius at last will defy his friend in prose and
verse, in Greek and Latin. Str 126-7, XXII.

I am not going to describe the...Swiss tour. It would not
be fair to my readers. 'Six Weeks in the Bernese Oberland,
by a party of three,' would have but very small chance of
success in the literary world at present, and I should consider myself to be dishonest if I attempted to palm off such
matter on the public in the pages of a novel. It is true
that I have just returned from Switzerland, and should find
such a course of writing very convenient. But I dismiss the
temptation, strong as it is. Retro age, Satanas. No living
man or woman any longer wants to be told anything of the
Grimsell or of the Gemmi. Ludgate Hill is now-a-days more
interesting than the Jungfrau. CanY 43-4, V,I.

## WRITING CONCLUSIONS

These leave-takings in novels are as disagreeable as they
are in real life; not so sad, indeed, for they want the
reality of sadness; but quite as perplexing, and generally
less satisfactory. What novelist, what Fielding, what
Scott, what George Sand, or Sue, or Dumas, can impart an
interest to the last chapter of his fictitious history?
Promises of two children and superhuman happiness are of no
avail, nor assurance of extreme respectability carried to an
age far esceeding that usually allotted to mortals. The
sorrows of our heroes and heroines, they are your delight,
oh public! their sorrows or their sins, or their absurdities; not their virtues, good sense, and consequent rewards. When we begin to tint our final pages with <u>couleur
de rose</u>, as in accordance with fixed rule we must do, we
altogether extinguish our own powers of pleasing. When we
become dull we offend your intellect; and we must become
dull or we should offend your taste. A late writer, wishing
to sustain his interest to the last page, hung his hero at
the end of the third volume. The consequence was, that no
one would read his novel. And who can apportion out and
dovetail his incidents, dialogues, characters, and descriptive morsels, so as to fit them all exactly into 439 pages,
without either compressing them unnaturally, or extending

them artificially at the end of his labour?  Do I not myself
know that I am at this moment in want of a dozen pages, and
that I am sick with cudgelling my brains to find them?  And
then when everything is done, the kindest-hearted critic of
them all invariably twits us with the incompetency and
lameness of our conclusion.  We have either become idle and
neglected it, or tedious and over-laboured it.  It is
insipid or unnatural, over-strained or imbecile.  It means
nothing, or attempts too much.  The last scene of all, as
all last scenes we fear must be,
     Is second childishness, and mere oblivion,
     Sans teeth, sans eyes, sans taste, sans everything.
     I can only say that if some critic, who thoroughly
knows his work, and has laboured on it till experience has
made him perfect, will write the last fifty pages of a novel
in the way they should be written, I, for one, will in
future do my best to copy the example.  Guided by my own
lights only, I confess that I despair of success.
BaT 490, LI.

The web of our story has now been woven, the piece is finished, and it is only necessary that the loose threads
should be collected, so that there may be no unravelling.
In such chronicles as this, something no doubt might be left
to the imagination without serious injury to the story; but
the reader, I think, feels a deficiency when, through tedium
or coldness, the writer omits to give all the information
which he possesses.  JC 465, LXIV.

In this last chapter of our short story I will venture to
run rapidly over a few months so as to explain how the
affairs...arranged themselves up to the end of the current
year.  I cannot pretend that the reader shall know, as he
ought to be made to know, the future fate and fortunes of
our personages.  They must be left still struggling.  But
then is not such always in truth the case, even when the
happy marriage has been celebrated?--even when, in the
course of two rapid years, two normal children make their
appearance to gladden the hearts of their parents?
DrW 263, XII.

## WRITING INTRODUCTIONS

Dramatists, when they write their plays, have a delightful
privilege of prefixing a list of their personages;--and the
dramatists of old used to tell us who was in love with whom,
and what were the blood relationships of all the persons.
In such a narrative as this, any proceeding of that kind
would be unusual,--and therefore the poor narrator has been
driven to expend his first four chapters in the mere task of
introducing his characters.  He regrets the length of these
introductions, and will now begin at once the action of his
story.  ED 36, IV,I.

## WRITING NOVELS

And here, perhaps, it may be allowed to the novelist to
explain his views on a very important point in the art of
telling tales.  He ventures to reporbate that system which
goes so far to violate all proper confidence between the
author and his readers, by maintaining nearly to the end of
the third volume a mystery as to the fate of their favourite
personage.  Nay, more, and worse than this, is too frequently done.  Have not often the profoundest efforts of
genius been used to baffle the aspirations of the reader, to
raise false hopes and false fears, and to give rise to ex-
pectations which are never to be realised?  Are not promises
all but made of delightful horrors, in lieu of which the
writer produces nothing but more commonplace realities in
his final chapter?  And is there not a species of deceit
in this to which the honesty of the present age should lend
no countenance?
    And what can be the worth of that solicitude which a
peep into the third volume can utterly dissipate?  What the
value of those literary charms which are absolutely destroyed by their enjoyment?  When we have once learnt what
was that picture before which was hung Mrs. Ratcliffe's
solemn curtain, we feel no further interest about either the
frame or the veil.  They are to us, merely a receptacle for
old bones, an inappropriate coffin, which we would wish to
have decently buried out of our sight.
    And then, how grievous a thing it is to have the
pleasure of your novel destroyed by the ill-considered triumph of a previous reader.  'Oh, you needn't be alarmed for
Augusta, of course she accepts Gustavus in the end.'  'How
very ill-natured you are, Susan,' says Kitty, with tears in
her eyes; 'I don't care a bit about it now.'  Dear Kitty, if
you will read my book, you may defy the ill-nature of your
sister.  There shall be no secret that she can tell you.
Nay, take the last chapter if you please--learn from its
pages all the results of our troubled story, and the story
shall have lost none of its interest, if indeed there be any
interest to lose.
    Our doctrine is, that the author and the reader should
move along together in full confidence with each other.  Let
the personages of the dramas undergo ever so complete a
comedy of errors among themselves, but let the spectator
never mistake the Syracusan for the Ephesian; otherwise he
is one of the dupes, and the part of a dupe is never
dignified.  BaT 132-3, XV.

I quite feel that an apology is due for beginning a novel
with two long dull chapters full of description.  I am
perfectly aware of danger of such a course;...but twist it
as I will I cannot do otherwise.  I find that I cannot make
poor Mr. Gresham hem and haw and turn himself uneasily in
his arm-chair in a natural manner till I have said why he is
uneasy.  I cannot bring in my doctor speaking his mind
freely among the bigwigs till I have explained that it is in
accordance with his usual character to do so.  This is in-

artistic on my part, and shows want of imagination as well
as want of skill. Whether or not I can atone for these
faults by straightforward, simple, plain storytelling--that,
indeed, is very doubtful. DoT 17-8, II.

There is a mode of novel-writing which used to be much in
vogue, but which has now gone out of fashion. It is, nevertheless, one which is very expressive when in good hands,
and which enables the author to tell his story, or some
portion of his story, with more natural trust than any
other, I mean that of familiar letters. I trust I shall be
excused if I attempt it as regards this one chapter; though,
it may be, that I shall break down and fall into commonplace
narrative, even before the one chapter be completed.
DoT 447-8, XXXVIII.

It has been suggested that the modern English writers of
fiction should among them keep a barrister, in order that
they may be set right on such legal points as will arise
in their little narratives, and thus avoid that exposure of
their own ignorance of the laws, which now, alas! they too
often make. The idea is worthy of consideration, and I can
only say, that if such an arrangement can be made, and if a
counsellor adequately skilful can be found to accept the
office, I shall be happy to subscribe my quota; it would be
but a modest tribute towards the cost. DoT 536, XLV.

I abhor a mystery. I would fain, were it possible, have my
tale run through from its little prologue to the customary
marriage in its last chapter, with all the smoothness inci-
dental to ordinary life. I have no ambition to surprise my
reader. Castles with unknown passages are not compatible
with my homely muse. I would as lief have to do with a
giant in my book--a real giant, such as Goliath--as with a
murdering monk with a scowling eye. The age for such delights is, I think, gone. We may say historically of Mrs.
Radcliffe's time that there were mysterious sorrows in those
days. They are now as much out of date as are the giants.
    I would wish that a serene gratification might flow
from my pages, unsullied by a single start. Now I am aware
that there is that in the last chapter which appears to
offend against the spirit of calm recital which I profess.
People will begin to think that they are to be kept in the
dark as to who is who; that it is intended that their
interest in the novel shall depend partly on a guess. I
would wish to have no guessing, and therefore I at once
proceed to tell all about it. Ber 231-2, XIII.

[I]n these days the unities are not much considered, and a
hiatus which would formerly have been regarded as a fault
utterly fatal is now no more than a slight impropriety.
Ber 279, XVI.

But to me Barset has been a real county, and its city a real
city, and the spires and towers have been before my eyes,
and the voices of the people are known to my ears, and the

pavement of the city ways are familiar to my footsteps.
LasC 782, LXXXIV.

The poor fictionist very frequently finds himself to have
been wrong in his description of things in general, and is
told so, roughly by the critics, and tenderly by the friends
of his bosom.   He is moved to tell of things of which he
omits to learn the nature before he tells of them--as should
be done by a strictly honest fictionist.   He catches salmon
in October; or shoots his partridges in March.   His dahlias
bloom in June, and his birds sing in the autumn.   He opens
the opera-houses before Easter, and makes Parliament sit on
a Wednesday evening.   And then those terrible meshes of the
Law!   How is a fictionist, in these excited days, to create
the needed biting interest without legal difficulties; and
how again is he to steer his little bark clear of so many
rocks,--when the rocks and the shoals have been purposely
arranged to make the taking of a pilot on board a necessity?
...But from whom is any assistance to come in the august
matter of a Cabinet assembly?   There can be no such assistance.   No man can tell aught but they who will tell
nothing.   But then, again, there is this safety, that let
the story be ever so mistold,--let the fiction be ever so
far removed from the truth, no critic short of a Cabinet
Minister himself can convict the narrator of error.
PF 267-8, XXIX,I.

I would that it were possible so to tell a story that a
reader should beforehand know every detail of it up to a
certain point, or be so circumstanced that he might be
supposed to know.   In telling the little novelettes of our
life, we commence our narrations with the presumption that
these details are borne in mind, and though they be all forgotten, the stories come out intelligible at last.   'You remember Mary Walker.   Oh yes, you do;--that pretty girl, but
such a queer temper!   And how she was engaged to marry Harry
Jones, and said she wouldn't at the church-door, till her
father threatened her with bread and water; and how they
have been living ever since as happy as two turtle-doves
down in Devonshire, till that scoundrel, Lieutenant Smith,
went to Bideford! Smith has been found dead at the bottom of
a sawpit.   Nobody's sorry for him.   She's in a madhouse at
Exeter; and Jones has disappeared, and couldn't have had
more than thirty shillings in his pocket.' This is quite as
much as anybody ought to want to know previous to the
unravelling of the tragedy of the Jones's.   But such stories
as those I have to tell cannot be written after that
fashion.   We novelists are constantly twitted with being
long; and to the gentlemen who condescend to review us, and
who take up our volumes with a view to business rather than
pleasure, we must be infinite in length and tedium.   But the
story must be made intelligible from the beginning, or the
real novel readers will not like it.   The plan of jumping at
once into the middle has been often tried, and sometimes
seductively enough for a chapter or two; but the writer

still has to hark back, and to begin again from the be-
ginning--not always very comfortably after the abnormal
brightness of his few opening pages; and the reader who is
then involved in some ancient family history, or long local
explanation, feels himself to have been defrauded. It is as
though one were asked to eat boiled mutton after woodcocks,
caviare, or maccaroni cheese. I hold that it is better to
have the boiled mutton first, if boiled mutton there must
be.

The story which I have to tell is something in its
nature akin to that of poor Mrs. Jones, who was happy enough
down in Devonshire till that wicked Lieutenant Smith came
and persecuted her; not quite so tragic, perhaps, as it is
stained neither by murder nor madness. But before I can
hope to interest the readers in the perplexed details of the
life of a not unworthy lady, I must do more than remind them
that they do know, or might have known, or should have
known, the antecedents of my personages....A hundred and
twenty little incidents must be dribbled into the reader's
intelligence, many of them, let me hope, in such manner that
he shall himself be insensible to the process. But unless I
make each one of them understood and appreciated by my in-
genious, open-hearted, rapid reader--by my reader who will
always have his fingers impatiently ready to turn the page--
he will, I know, begin to masticate the real kernel of my
story with infinite prejudices against Mary Lovelace.
IHP 1-2, I,I.

Perhaps the method of rushing at once 'in midea res' is, of
all the ways of beginning a story, or a separate branch of a
story, the least objectionable. The reader is made to think
that the gold lies so near the surface that he will be
required to take very little trouble in digging for it.
And the writer is enabled,--at any rate for a time, and till
his neck has become, as it were, warm to the collar,--to
throw off from him the difficulties and dangers, the tedium
and prolixity, of description. This rushing 'in media res'
has doubtless the charm of ease. 'Certainly, when I threw
her from the garret window to the stony pavement below, I
did not anticipate that she would fall so far without injury
to life or limb.' When a story has been begun after this
fashion, without any prelude, without description of the
garret or of the pavement, or of the lady thrown, or of the
speaker, a great amount of trouble seems to have been saved.
The mind of the reader fills up the blanks,--if erroneously,
still satisfactorily. He knows, at least, that the heroine
has encountered a terrible danger, and has escaped from it
with almost incredible good fortune; that the demon of the
piece is a bold demon, not ashamed to speak of his own
iniquity, and that the heroine and the demon are so far
united that they have been in a garret together. But there
is the drawback on the system,--that it is almost impossible
to avoid the necessity of doing, sooner or later, that which
would naturally be done at first. It answers, perhaps, for
half-a-dozen chapters;--and to carry the reader pleasantly
for half-a-dozen chapters is a great matter!--but after that

a certain nebulous darkness gradually seems to envelope the
characters and the incidents.   'Is all this going on in the
country, or is it in town,--or perhaps in the Colonies?   How
old was she?   Was she tall?   Is she fair?   Is she heroine-
like in her form and gait?   And, after all, how high was the
garret window?'   I have always found that the details would
insist on being told at last, and that by rushing 'in media
res' I was simply presenting the cart before the horse.   But
as readers like the cart the best, I will do it once again,
--trying it only for a branch of my story,--and will
endeavour to let as little as possible of the horse be seen
afterwards....
      I am aware that, in the word of beauty, and perhaps,
also, in the word young, a little bit of the horse is
appearing; and I am already sure that I shall have to show
his head and neck, even if not his very tail.
DuC 69-70, IX.

A novelist or two of a morning might perhaps aid me in my
general pursuit, but would, I think, interfere with the
actual daily tally of pages.   AyA 32, IV.

And now, O kind-hearted reader, I feel myself constrained,
in the telling of this little story, to depart altogether
from those principles of story-telling to which you probably
have become accustomed, and to put the horse of my romance
before the cart.   There is a mystery...which, according to
all laws recognised in such matters, ought not to be
elucidated till, let us say, the last chapter but two, so
that your interest should be maintained almost to the end,--
so near the end that there should be left only space for
those little arrangements which are necessary for the well-
being, or perhaps for the evil-being, of our personages.   It
is my purpose to disclose the mystery at once, and to ask
you to look for your interest,--should you choose to go on
with my chronicle,--simply in the conduct of my persons,
during this disclosure, to others....It may be said that
when I shall have once told the mystery there will no longer
be any room for interest in the tale to you.   That there are
many such readers of novels I know....What would the 'Black
Dwarf' be if every one knew from the beginning that he was a
rich man and a baronet?--or 'The Pirate', if all the truth
about Norna of the Fitfulhead had been told in the first
chapter?   Therefore, put the book down if the revelation of
some future secret be necessary for your enjoyment.   Our
mystery is going to be revealed in the next paragraph,--in
the next half-dozen words.   DrW 27-8, III,I.   See also
HEROES; HEROINES; IRISH NOVELS.

## WRITING PERSONAL DESCRIPTIONS

It is to be regretted that no mental method of dageurreotype
or photography has yet been discovered, by which the characters of men can be reduced to writing and put into grammatical language with an unerring precision of truthful description.   How often does the novelist feel, ay, and the

historian also and the biographer, that he has conceived
within his mind and accurately depicted on the tablet of his
brain the full character and personage of a man, and that
nevertheless, when he flies to pen and ink to perpetuate the
protrait, his words forsake, elude, disappoint, and play the
deuce with him, till at the end of a dozen pages the man
described has no more resemblance to the man conceived than
the sign board at the corner of the street has to the Duke
of Cambridge?

And yet such mechanical descriptive skill would hardly
give more satisfaction to the reader than the skill of the
photographer does to the anxious mother desirous to possess
an absolute duplicate of her beloved child.  The likeness is
indeed true; but it is a dull, dead, unfeeling, inaus-
picious likeness.   The face is indeed there, and those
looking at it will know at once whose image it is; but the
owner of the face will not be proud of the resemblance.

There is no royal road to learning; no short cut to the
acquirement of any valuable art.   Let photographers and
daguerreotypers do what they will, and improve as they may
with further skill on that which skill has already done,
they will never achieve a portrait of the human face divine.
Let biographers, novelists, and the rest of us groan as we
may under the burdens which we so often feel too heavy for
our shoulders; we must either bear them up like men, or own
ourselves too weak for the work we have undertaken.   There
is no way of writing well and also of writing easily.
BaT 171-2, XX.

[F]or let an author describe as he will, he cannot by such
course paint the characters of his personages on the minds
of his readers.  It is by gradual, earnest efforts that this
must be done--if it be done.  Ten, nay, twenty pages of the
finest descriptive writing that ever fell from the pen of a
novelist will not do it.  CasR 18, II,I.

There is nothing more difficult in the writing of a story
than to describe adequately the person of a hero or a heroine, so as to place before the mind of the reader any clear
picture of him or her who is described.  A courtship is
harder still--so hard that we may say generally that it is
impossible.   Southey's Lodore is supposed to have been
effective; but let any one with the words in his memory
stand beside the waterfall and say whether it is such as the
words have painted it.  It rushes and it foams, as described
by the poet, much more violently than does the real water;
and so does everything described, unless in the hands of a
wonderful master.   But I have clear images on my brain of
the characters of the persons introduced.  I know with fair
accuracy what was intended by the character as given of
Amelia Booth, of Clarissa, of Di Vernon, and of Maggie
Tulliver.  But as their persons have not been drawn with the
pencil for me by the artists who themselves created them, I
have no conception how they looked.  Of Thackery's Beatrix I
have a vivid idea, because she was drawn for him by an
artist under his own eye.  OML 24, III.

## Y

## YIELDING

It is so hard to throw off a tyrant; so much easier to yield, when we have been in the habit of yielding. DoT 458, XXXVIII.

But a man, or a nation, when yielding must still resist even in yielding.  RacR 358, XXVII.

It is very well to tell a man that he should yield, but there is nothing so wretched to a man as yielding.  Young people and women have to yield,--but for such a man as this, to yield is in itself a misery.  DuC 397, L.

## Z

## ZEAL, RELIGIOUS

...that zeal which is so dear to the youthful mind but which so often seems to be weak and flabby to their elders. DrW 7-8, I, Part I.

# Index to Digressions
# on People and Places

# Bibliographical Notes

Cockshut, A.O.J. <u>Anthony Trollope</u>. New York: New York University Press, 1968. Comments on the authorial obtrusions.

Hardwick, Michael. <u>A Guide to Anthony Trollope</u>. New York: Charles Scribner's Sons, 1974. Contains comments on the digressions.

Hennessy, James Pope. <u>Anthony Trollope</u>. Boston: Little Brown and Company, 1971. A good illustrated biography.

Pollard, Arthur. <u>Anthony Trollope</u>. London: Routledge & Kegan Paul, 1978. Good discussions of the novels.

Roberts, Ruth ap. <u>The Moral Trollope</u>. Athens, Ohio: University of Ohio Press, 1971. Contains comments regarding Trollope's discussions and authorial distance.

Sadleir, Michael. <u>Trollope: a Commentary</u>. London: Constable, 1927. The most widely accepted biography.

Trollope, Anthony. <u>An Autobiography</u>. London: Oxford University Press, 1953. The World's Classics # 239. Essential to any study of Trollope.

## About the Compiler

MARY L. DANIELS is a former Instructor in English at Seminole Community College in Sanford, Florida. She wrote the music for the play *Muse of Fire* which won the 1972 Florida Theatre Conference Contest and authored several journal articles. Her most recent work is a remedial program for writers and speakers of Black English.